Medieval Monstrosity

This volume examines various manifestations and understandings of the concept of monstrosity in medieval Europe around 500–1500 CE through a collection of contextual chapters and primary sources.

The main chapters focus on a specific theme, a type of monster or representation of monstrosity, and consist of a contextual essay synthesizing recent scholarship on that theme, excerpts from primary sources and a bibliography of additional primary and secondary sources on the topics addressed in the chapter. In addition to building upon the wealth of scholarship on monsters and monstrosity produced in recent decades, the book engages with the current fascination with monsters in popular culture, especially in movies, television, and video games. The book presents a survey of medieval monstrosity for a non-specialist audience and provides a theoretical framework for interpreting the monstrous.

This book is ideal for undergraduate students working on the theme of monstrosity, as well as being useful for undergraduate courses that cover the supernatural and manifestations of the monstrous covered in the book. With materials drawn from a wide range of medieval sources, it will also appeal to courses in English, French, Art History, and Medieval Studies.

Dr. Charity Urbanski is Teaching Professor at the University of Washington, Seattle, Washington, specializing in twelfth-century England and France. Her research interests include historiography, gender, power, and monstrosity. She is the author of *Writing History for the King: Henry II and the Politics of Vernacular Historiography*.

Medieval Monstrosity

Imagining the Monstrous in Medieval Europe

Charity Urbanski

LONDON AND NEW YORK

Designed cover image: Barcelona, Catalonia, Spain. Casa Amatller
(Puig i Cadafalch; 1898–1900) 43, Passeig de Gracia. Facade. St George
and dragon. *PjrTravel/Alamy Stock Photo*

First published 2024
by Routledge
4 Park Square, Milton Park, Abingdon, Oxon OX14 4RN

and by Routledge
605 Third Avenue, New York, NY 10158

Routledge is an imprint of the Taylor & Francis Group, an informa business

© 2024 Charity Urbanski

British Library Cataloguing-in-Publication Data
A catalogue record for this book is available from the British Library

ISBN: 978-0-367-19743-8 (hbk)
ISBN: 978-0-367-19742-1 (pbk)
ISBN: 978-0-429-24300-4 (ebk)

DOI: 10.4324/9780429243004

Typeset in Times New Roman
by Apex CoVantage, LLC

Every effort has been made to contact copyright-holders. Please advise
the publisher of any errors or omissions, and these will be corrected in
subsequent editions.

For my mother, Laura Swick, and my aunt, Nancy Adkins

Contents

Acknowledgments

This book has taken far longer to write than I initially envisioned. It was interrupted by a pandemic and then by a brain injury, and I still find it somewhat miraculous that it has been completed at all. The fact that it is now in front of you is due to the assistance and support of my family, friends, colleagues, department, and publisher. I would especially like to thank my husband, Mike Carver, for his patience with the writing process and his care and support during the months after my injury. I would also like to thank my friend and colleague, Purnima Dhavan, for her advice on using technology to overcome my limited ability to read or type during my recovery. And I cannot thank my editor, Laura Pilsworth, enough for her patience and guidance in seeing this book through to completion.

I owe a special debt to the three undergraduate students who served as my assistants on this project. Alexandru Luncasu-Rolea and Alexander Clark were both invaluable in helping me compile bibliographies of primary and secondary sources in the early stages of the project. And I owe an enormous thanks to Claire Jacobs who meticulously transcribed most of the primary sources contained in this volume at a time when I was physically unable to do so. It is largely due to her committed assistance, carried out over more than a year, that I was finally able to bring this project to fruition.

I would also like to thank my colleagues Robert Stacey, Lynn Thomas, and Tyler Lange for reading drafts of some of the chapters and offering me their feedback. Their thoughtful advice has greatly improved the work, and any remaining flaws are entirely my own.

I would also like to express my gratitude to Glennys Young, the Chair of the Department of History, University of Washington, for her support throughout this process. She was a source of optimism and guidance during a very challenging period. Much of the research for this book was enabled by the generosity of the Hanauer family, especially funding from the Joff Hanauer Endowed Faculty Fellowship, which I held from 2015 to 2018, and Hanauer Faculty Research Funds, as well as a Keller Grant.

Finally, I would especially like to acknowledge Dr. Amanda Hopkins, who died in July 2022. She was principally a medievalist, with interests in the romance genre – notably the Breton lay in Old French, Middle English, and Old Norse – but she also published in the fields of comparative literature and disability studies. From 2002 until 2022, Amanda was a teaching fellow at the University of Warwick, working across the Department of French and the Department of English and Comparative Literary Studies. The Editorial Board of the Liverpool Online Series and the author of this volume hereby acknowledge Amanda's contribution to the fields of textual editing and translation.

The Liverpool Online Series was founded in 1999 in the Department of French (now part of the Department of Languages, Cultures and Film) at the University of Liverpool, UK. It was one of the pioneers of Open Access publishing, its remit being to make freely available unedited or otherwise unobtainable material or material which for scholarly reasons required an up-to-date edition. Volumes in the series are single texts or anthologies and cover a range of areas throughout French and Francophone studies from the medieval period to the twentieth century. All volumes in the Liverpool Online Series remain available on an Open Access basis at:

www.liverpool.ac.uk/languages-cultures-and-film/research/research-activities/liverpool-online-series/

Introduction

This book grew out of an undergraduate seminar on monstrosity in medieval Europe that I began teaching at the University of Washington in 2011. These seminars are designed to introduce students to historical research methodologies and theoretical frameworks and are generally organized around themes. I chose monsters for two reasons. The first was simply that I have always been fascinated by monsters, but they did not fit neatly into any of my existing lecture courses. A seminar focused on medieval monsters offered the perfect forum for exploring the topic. The second reason was more explicitly pedagogical. Monsters have massive popular appeal, and many of my students are already interested in them, at least superficially. They have grown up in a culture that features monsters in its movies, television shows, and video games, and the appeal of these creatures is already established. I wanted to cater to that preexisting interest in the hope that my students would be more engaged in the research process and more enthusiastic about their projects if I organized a seminar around a topic that truly appealed to them.

Most importantly, I envisioned the seminar as a means of getting my students to engage with monsters on a critical level, to examine them as cultural constructions that do meaningful work and tell us about the anxieties, fears, prejudices, and preoccupations of the people who created, believed in, or told stories about them. Medieval Europeans were just as fascinated by monsters as we are now. Medieval sources are positively littered with monsters: they populate the margins of medieval manuscripts and architecture, they tempt and torment the saints, they serve as formidable adversaries for heroes to vanquish, and they reinforce morality by embodying vice and sin, but they do much more than that. Ideas about monstrosity were fundamental to ancient and medieval debates about the nature of humanity, and the rhetoric of monstrosity was widely used to dehumanize certain groups in medieval Europe and authorize violence against them. My intention in this seminar was to draw students in with an appealing topic and then teach them something about medieval philosophy, theology, and the intellectual framework for the historical persecution of certain groups. Finally, I wanted my students to think about how the rhetoric of monstrosity is still used to demonize various groups today.

This book seeks to extend the work begun in my seminar to other classrooms by making primary source materials available to other instructors and their students. Because this book is intended as an introduction for undergraduates, and

DOI: 10.4324/9780429243004-1

not a comprehensive treatment of medieval European monsters and ideas about monstrosity, many of the monsters that roamed the medieval imagination will not be found in the pages that follow. The absence of any particular monster is not intended as a rejection or a slight; it is solely the result of the book reflecting my own areas of expertise and research interests. There are a multitude of worthy monsters that I regrettably do not have the space or necessary expertise to include. As a historian who specializes in twelfth-century France and England, I have focused on the monsters with whom I am most familiar – those of northern Europe in the High Middle Ages. I occasionally stray from the English and French kingdoms into Scandinavia, which had close ties with both England and France, to draw parallels or highlight cultural differences in the appearance and habits of some monsters, such as dragons and revenants. In a similar fashion, I sometimes reach further back into the past or come closer to the present to demonstrate how certain ideas about monsters developed over time, and I have included a chapter on ancient, medieval, and modern monster theory to contextualize medieval European ideas about monstrosity and offer students useful tools with which to examine them.

I have attempted to split this book broadly into two halves. The first half addresses monster theory, the opposition between monsters and humans, and some of the peoples who were historically portrayed as monstrous in medieval Europe: Jews, Muslims, and women. The second half deals with entirely fictional monsters: revenants, werewolves, and dragons. The rationale for this is simply to maintain what I believe is an important distinction between the real people who were designated as monstrous, and for whom this had real consequences, and the monsters that existed only in the imaginations of medieval Europeans.

Finally, I need to define two terms that are central to this book: monsters and the rhetoric of monstrosity. Broadly speaking, monsters are physically deviant creatures that defy the laws of nature. This physical deviance can take a whole range of forms – monsters can be hybrids, they can be excessively large or small, have too many appendages or heads, they can be deficient in limbs or features, they can shape-shift, or they can simply be deformed versions of otherwise recognizable creatures. Whatever the case, monsters do not fit neatly into our established categories and interpretive frameworks – their very existence calls into question our understanding of nature and its laws and forces us to reconsider our own place in the world. Monsters are creatures that should not exist. This general rule applies to all monsters, but monsters are also culturally and historically specific. Every culture makes its own unique monsters, breathing its particular anxieties and fears into them, and what is considered monstrous in one culture may not be considered monstrous at all in another. For a monster to be a monster, a culture must perceive that it is one. Even within a single culture, monsters and their meanings change over time. Old monsters evolve and new monsters are created that reflect shifts in cultural attitudes, and some monsters simply disappear when they cease to serve any cultural purpose. Some of the medieval European monsters that appear in this book have recognizable modern descendants (the modern walking dead, werewolves, and dragons that appear in books, television, and movies), but even when a familiar monster reappears across time, its meaning shifts according to the cultural and historical context of each particular incarnation. As we will see, the werewolves and walking dead of the High Middle Ages were quite distinct from their modern counterparts and reflect very different cultural concerns.

We often think of monsters as being completely imaginary and terrifying creatures, like vampires and zombies, but this definition leaves out many of the creatures and people that were considered monstrous in medieval Europe. From antiquity until well into the twentieth century, any creature or person whose physical appearance deviated from the norm was by definition a "monster" (*teras* in Greek or *monstrum* in Latin). Qualities like hybridity, excess, deficiency, and deformity were all considered features of monstrosity in antiquity, and by the medieval Europeans who inherited most of their ideas about monstrosity from the ancient Greeks and Romans. Creatures displaying such monstrous qualities were not always just terrifying, they could inspire awe or wonder as well, and they were not always imaginary either. Imaginary hybrid animals like griffins or dragons and animal-human hybrids like centaurs certainly qualified as monsters, but so did real human beings and animals with features we would now describe as birth defects, such as extra digits or missing limbs, as well as those with rarer physical anomalies like conjoined twins. In this sense, ancient and medieval monsters really existed, and the fact that some humans were considered monstrous on the basis of their physical appearance had profoundly negative consequences. Humans and animals born with birth defects were routinely referred to as "monstrous births" from antiquity until into the twentieth century, and the term *teras* is still used in medicine to describe any fetus with abnormal features. Monstrous births were generally interpreted as omens or signs of divine displeasure in ancient and medieval Europe, and one normal course of action was to kill them. I want to be clear from the outset that while I will be using the term monster as it was historically applied to various groups of people (especially malformed fetuses and infants, Jews, Muslims, and women), this does not mean that I view them as anything less than fully human. Quite the opposite is true. Examining what it meant for real people to be deemed monstrous and to have their very humanity questioned is a central task of this book and central to the task of studying monsters more generally.

This brings us to the rhetoric of monstrosity, or the language that was used to portray a person or group of people as monstrous. Not every monster was physically deviant; entire groups of people were categorized as monstrous based on their actual behavior or the behavior ascribed to them. The rhetoric of monstrosity goes beyond merely calling someone a monster; it encompasses language covering a whole range of behaviors that were associated with monstrosity. Just as hybridity, excess, deficiency, and deformity served as physical markers of monstrosity and could be marshaled to depict a person or group as monstrous, certain behaviors or customs were also associated with monstrosity. For the ancient Greeks and Romans, anyone who exhibited a lack of "civilization" and thus a lack of humanity was considered monstrous. The classical list of uncivilized or monstrous behaviors was long and included practices like eating uncooked foods, wearing skins or rough clothing, speaking an unintelligible language, failing to engage in agriculture or live in towns, and engaging in behaviors deemed taboo, especially incest and

cannibalism. These behaviors were associated with many of the so-called monstrous races discussed in Chapter 1 and comprised part of their monstrosity, along
with their physical characteristics. Medieval European Christians inherited these
ideas about monstrous behavior from the ancient Greeks and Romans, but differed from their pagan predecessors by adding idolatry and a whole range of sexual
practices to this list. Since some of the strictest taboos in medieval Europe were
Christian prohibitions against idolatry, heresy, cannibalism, incest, and other sexual behaviors that Christians considered deviant (such as sodomy, orgies, adultery,
and bestiality), these behaviors tended to be the ones most frequently invoked to
brand other groups as monstrous.

The idea of monstrosity served as a useful vehicle for defining what it meant
to be human in ancient and medieval Europe, just as it does today. As a construct,
monstrosity can be placed in opposition to humanity and monsters can embody
anything a society considers unnatural, bestial, or subhuman. Monstrous behaviors serve a similar purpose; by definition, engaging in monstrous behavior makes
one monstrous and imputing such behaviors to a person or group is a particularly
effective way to strip them of their humanity and justify violence against them.
Accusations of monstrous behavior were a standard means of dehumanizing entire
groups of people in medieval Europe, and such accusations were most notoriously
leveled against Europe's Jews. In the high and late Middle Ages, Christians routinely accused Jews of engaging in a range of monstrous behaviors, including des-
ecrating the Host, kidnapping Christian children to torture and murder in mockery
of the Crucifixion, and even eating Christian children. These inflammatory charges
were the basis for the prosecution and execution of both individual Jews and entire
Jewish communities, and the repetition of these charges in case after case across
Europe eventually led to a widespread acceptance among European Christians that
their Jewish neighbors actually engaged in such monstrous behavior. Unsurpris-
ingly, these beliefs were accompanied by outbreaks of anti-Jewish violence in the
High and Late Middle Ages, as well as the expulsion of Jewish communities from
every kingdom in western Europe beginning in the twelfth century.

While Christians frequently lodged allegations of monstrous behavior against
their Jewish neighbors, similar charges were often used against Muslims and even
against other Christians, especially those the Church deemed heretical. The medieval Church used allegations of monstrous behavior to defame popular Christian
sects that were critical of the Church, like the Cathars and Waldensians, and these
charges proved so potent and so flexible that they were sometimes wielded by
secular powers against the clergy. Philip IV of France, for example, used monstrous
allegations of sodomy, idolatry, and heresy to defame Pope Boniface VIII and to
destroy one of the most powerful Christian groups in medieval Europe, the Knights
Templar. What all of these groups, both Christian and non-Christian, had in common was the fact that the rhetoric of monstrosity was deployed against them and
used to portray them as dangerous and deviant threats to society, threats that had
to be neutralized.

In the following chapters, I present both fictional monsters and real groups of
people who were portrayed as monstrous in medieval Europe. The essays I provide

at the beginning of each chapter are intended as introductions to each topic and are supplemented by primary sources presented in English translation and suggestions for further secondary reading. My goal is not to present an exhaustive analysis of any of the topics covered in this book, but to offer undergraduates some insights drawn from my own work and the work of other scholars that can serve as a starting point for their own research. I hope that both teachers and students will find the monsters that stalk these pages as endlessly fascinating, perplexing, and rewarding as I do.

1 Monster Theory and the Monstrous Races

When I first started teaching a seminar on monsters, my students were excited and a little confused. They assumed that historians dealt with politics, economics, institutions, and societies, but monsters seemed to belong to some other realm, some other discipline. One of the most frequent questions my students asked me was why historians should study monsters. Sure, monsters are fascinating, but what can historians actually learn from them? The short answer is that studying monsters allows us to examine a culture's anxieties and fears, to explore how specific societies defined what it meant to be human, and to reveal how powerful groups and individuals attempted to dehumanize and demonize other groups by employing the rhetoric of monstrosity against them. The study of monsters is not restricted to fascinating but fictional creatures, it is also the study of those who have been defined as "other" by the dominant culture and relegated to the fringes of society. To study monsters is also to study those who are regarded as less than human, dangerous to humans, or the very antithesis of human.

Monster scholarship has experienced a boom over the past 30 years or so, but the truth is that historians assiduously avoided studying monsters for a very long time. Like some of my students, historians assumed that monsters had little to offer beyond their novelty. For historians of medieval Europe, in particular, this required ignoring the fact that we encounter monsters practically everywhere in both the imaginative and physical remains of the Middle Ages. Monsters appear in a wide variety of medieval literary genres, they decorate the margins of manuscripts and sometimes appear as features in them, they are depicted endlessly in medieval art and architecture, and they frequently appear in the most historical of medieval sources – the chronicles themselves. This scholarly approach to monsters, which amounted to regarding them as unimportant and mostly embarrassing, began to change in 1936, when J.R.R. Tolkien gave a lecture on *Beowulf* entitled "The Monsters and the Critics." In his lecture, Tolkien took to task the literary scholars and historians of his own day for pointedly ignoring or lamenting the monsters in the poem. It can be difficult to imagine now, but for well over a century, both literary scholars and historians had been dissecting a poem that recounts the great warrior Beowulf's three battles with monsters (his youthful triumphs over the fearsome Grendel and Grendel's slightly less terrifying mother and his final, fatal encounter with a fire-breathing dragon), while treating those very same monsters

DOI: 10.4324/9780429243004-2

as extraneous, irrelevant, undignified, and embarrassing. Tolkien, a philologist and professor of Anglo-Saxon at Oxford, berated his fellow academics for failing to recognize the loftiness of the poem's contents and the central role that the monsters play in Beowulf's heroism. He also took aim at historians for soullessly mining the poem for verifiable historical details, such as Hygelac's raid on Frisia in 516 CE and then discarding the rest of the poem as virtually useless. Tolkien criticized the critics of his own time for expecting *Beowulf* to be something other than what it is, for belittling or dismissing it as a result, and above all for wishing it were free of monsters.

Tolkien may have been a bit too harsh on his fellow academics, but his lecture (later published as an essay) ushered in a new era in *Beowulf* scholarship and spurred a new focus on the monsters among *Beowulf* scholars. Historians, however, were a bit slower to catch on. It was not until the 1990s that historians began to seriously engage with the monsters that populated the medieval imagination, and studies began to appear that were devoted to these marginalized and maligned creatures. The impetus for this interest came from scholarship produced in the fields of English and Art History. Works such as John Block Friedman's *The Monstrous Races in Medieval Art and Thought* (1981), Michael Camille's *Image on the Edge: The Margins of Medieval Art* (1992), and Andy Orchard's *Pride and Prodigies: Studies in the Monsters of the Beowulf Manuscript* (1995) focused on medieval depictions of the monstrous and gave the topic serious scholarly attention. One of the first studies authored by a medieval historian was Jean-Claude Schmitt's *Ghosts in the Middle Ages*, which appeared in 1994. While Schmitt's examination of medieval religious culture was mostly concerned with exploring how the living and the dead related to each other, his work also treated beliefs about ghosts and the walking corpses known as revenants. With Schmitt's work, medieval Europe's monsters were finally receiving serious attention from respected cultural historians.

Modern monster theory largely relies upon Sigmund Freud's work on the *unheimlich* (the uncanny, eerie, or weird), which he described as the dread we feel when something reminds us of repressed material from our childhoods. It also draws upon Julia Kristeva's work on the abject, the parts of ourselves that have been rejected and concealed and are neither self nor other, and abjection, which refers to the sense of horror we feel when the boundary between the self and the other is threatened. In a more general sense, abjection also refers to the casting out of anything or anyone that cannot be classified within a taxonomic system, and the abjection of others is a means of reinforcing boundaries that are threatened. Drawing upon these concepts, modern monster theory posits that monstrosity is a cultural construction that encompasses all of the taboo or forbidden aspects of humanity, all of the features of ourselves that we wish to repress. One of the most influential works in modern monster theory is Jeffrey Jerome Cohen's 1996 essay "Monster Culture (Seven Theses)" in which he lays out a theoretical framework for monster scholarship. These seven theses have profoundly influenced subsequent scholarship, so it is worth going over them briefly here.

Cohen's first thesis is that the monster's body is a cultural body. Every monster is the product of a specific historical time and place, and the monster's body functions as a vessel containing the fears, anxieties, fantasies, and desires of the particular culture and historical moment that produced it. Even monsters that superficially appear to be very similar, such as eastern and western dragons, have very different functions and meanings upon closer inspection that reflect the different cultures that produced them.

The second thesis is that the monster always escapes. No matter how many times a given monster is vanquished, it somehow manages to return later, reincarnated. And when the monster returns, we find that its meaning has changed and that every reincarnation has its own historical and cultural context, a time and a place that it embodies. Cohen uses the example of the vampire to demonstrate this evolution, beginning with Bram Stoker's Dracula as a hyper-sexualized embodiment of fear and repressed sexual desire produced in 1897 in the historical context of Victorian England and ending with the homosexual subtext and use of blood as a leitmotif in Francis Ford Coppola's movie *Bram Stoker's Dracula* that was produced in 1992 at the height of the AIDS crisis. The monsters may look similar and even act in similar ways, but their meaning has shifted as the culture that created them has changed. Every new appearance of the monster requires a new investigation into the historical and cultural circumstances of that avatar's production.

Cohen's third thesis is that the monster is the harbinger of category crises. Monsters are often hybrids that dwell on boundaries, both geographical and taxonomic. They are often creatures that combine physical characteristics of different species, and they tend to live in liminal spaces at the edges of the inhabited world, like mountains, oceans, forests, or wastelands (as is the case with the Monstrous Races examined later in the chapter). By resisting easy classification and defying the laws of science, monsters pose a danger to our modes of organizing knowledge and understanding the world. They challenge our very conception of boundaries and normality.

In his fourth thesis, Cohen explains that the monster dwells at the gates of difference. Monsters are by definition others; they embody alterity. Monstrosity does not just consist of physical difference or hybridity, it also encompasses differences of culture, politics, economics, gender norms, and sexuality. Monsters do monstrous things, things that the dominant culture deems uncivilized, like eating exotic foods (especially engaging in cannibalism), wearing animal skins as clothing, not living in cities or houses, not engaging in agriculture, doing anything to excess (having monstrous appetites), and violating sexual or gender norms. Medieval European monsters often embodied racial difference as well. Most notably, medieval European images of demons depicted them with black skin that echoed that of Ethiopians and other Africans. Medieval European Christians explicitly associated blackness with sinfulness and attributed the dark skin of Africans partly to their climate but largely to their presumed sinfulness. All of these monstrous characteristics could be recombined and applied to whole groups of people in order to designate them as monstrous. The formula was even used to vilify European nations, as Gerald of Wales does in his *Topographia Hibernia* when he describes the Irish as a filthy and vicious race whose barbaric customs and disgusting gender norms run completely counter to those of the "civilized" English who were trying to conquer them; for instance, he alleges that Irish women ride their horses astride and urinate standing up. However, it was especially used to demonize religious outsiders such as Jews and Muslims, as we will see in Chapter 2, who European Christians routinely portrayed as not only having monstrous religious beliefs and barbaric customs, but also were depicted with dark skin, exaggerated and monstrous features, and a proclivity for engaging in sexual perversions. The result of these attacks, whether on the Irish, Ethiopians, Jews, Muslims, or any other group, was to dehumanize the group in question and to authorize their mistreatment, conquest, subjugation, or even annihilation.

Cohen's fifth thesis is that the monster polices the border of the possible. By virtue of their position just beyond the edges of civilized space and their uncivilized behavior, monsters enforce cultural norms. They enforce prohibitions and prevent people from wandering too far afield, whether geographically or behaviorally, for fear that they will either encounter terrifying monsters or become monsters themselves. As Cohen points out, these monsters of prohibition are frequently employed to reinforce the cultural norms of hierarchical and patriarchal societies by enforcing sexual and gender taboos and policing group purity. Concerned with maintaining the existing gender and racial hierarchy, medieval Europeans constructed monsters of prohibition that expressed both their misogyny and their fears of miscegenation and often cast women, non-Christians, and non-Europeans as monsters. In the High and Late Middle Ages, for instance, clerical authors regularly presented women as dangerous sources of temptation who could potentially imperil male salvation as part of their effort to enforce clerical celibacy. This clerical anti-feminist polemic was intended to make celibacy appear preferable to marriage, but it fueled the growth of misogyny in society at large.

As for fears of miscegenation, these tended to focus on mixing between Christians and Jews in medieval Europe. In the High and Late Middle Ages, the Church prohibited Christians from even socializing with their Jewish neighbors, as well as from intermarrying with them and required Jews to wear distinctive clothing so Christians could recognize and avoid them. Secular authorities drove Jews into specific neighborhoods to physically segregate them from Christians, and both religious and secular leaders accused Jews of actively working to undermine Christian society and of engaging in monstrous acts like kidnapping, torturing, murdering, and eating Christian children. By the end of the fifteenth century, all of the kingdoms of western Europe had expelled their Jewish populations and forced any remaining Jews to convert to Christianity. Both women who posed a challenge to the drive for clerical celibacy and Jews who threatened the medieval racial and religious hierarchy were transformed into monsters that had to be avoided, contained, exiled, or destroyed.

In his sixth thesis, Cohen explains that fear of the monster is really a kind of desire. Monsters are linked to behaviors that are forbidden, and this makes them at once repulsive to us and incredibly appealing. We fear the monster, but in some sense, we want to be the monster too. We envy the monster's freedom, and we play out our escapist fantasies through its actions, safe in the knowledge that the monster will inevitably be conquered and contained, and that order will ultimately be restored. We are able to vicariously transgress taboos through the monster.

In his seventh and final thesis, Cohen reminds us that monsters are our children. They are our creations, and as such they carry cultural knowledge, knowledge about how their creators perceived the world and attempted to categorize and make sense of it. When we study monsters, we uncover historically situated cultural assumptions about the nature of humanity, race, gender, sexuality, and other expressions of difference. Just as monsters bring us knowledge about the people of the past, they also force us to reevaluate our own cultural assumptions and recognize them as historical, constructed, and contingent.

Modern monster theory provides us with the tools to investigate monsters as cultural creations that do meaningful work, but the study of monsters is transhistorical and transregional. In order to understand the monsters produced by medieval Europeans, we also need to examine how they defined the monstrous, and how they theorized the functions of the monster. Medieval Europeans derived their views about monstrosity from their cultural ancestors, the ancient Greeks and Romans, but interpreted monstrosity within a Christian framework. For them, monsters carried philosophical and theological meaning. Monsters were representatives of alterity that helped medieval Europeans define their own identities and explore the dialectics of good and evil, civilized and barbaric, self and other, but they were also regarded as portents, as manifestations of God's ineffable power and part of a divine plan.

Medieval European ideas about monsters were largely derived from the ancient Greeks and Romans. The Greek word *teras* refers to omens, portents, or physical abnormalities. The term teratology is used to describe the study of such physical abnormalities, as well as the study of monsters more generally, and the term *teras* is still used in medicine today to describe a fetus displaying abnormal features. The English word monster, on the other hand, comes to us from the Romans. The Latin word *monstrum* refers to both supernatural events and beings and derives from *monstrare* (to show) and *monere* (to warn). For the ancient Greeks and Romans, as well as their medieval European cultural descendants, monsters were both warnings and demonstrations of divine might. They were also creatures that excited mixed emotions, eliciting both wonder and terror, awe and repulsion. In the religious context of ancient Greece and Rome, monsters were generally interpreted as being signs of divine displeasure and were often the result of divine punishment. The Minotaur is a good example of a monster produced as a result of divine wrath. In this case, the god Poseidon punished Minos for failing to sacrifice a bull to him by causing Minos' wife Pasiphaë to fall in love with the bull and mate with it. The half-man, half-bull Minotaur that Pasiphaë bore after her sexual encounter with the bull was the direct result of this divine punishment. On a more prosaic level, common human and animal birth defects were also regarded as monstrous and therefore as ominous signs that the gods were displeased and punishing humanity with unnatural occurrences.

The Greeks and Romans also viewed monsters as representing primeval chaos, disorder, destruction, the barbaric, and the uncivilized. Hesiod's *Theogony* (eighth century BCE) describes the cosmos as originating out of the empty void of Chaos and being populated with the monsters produced by the coupling of Gaia (Earth) and Ouranos (Sky). According to this Greek creation myth, the earliest beings were monsters like the Titans and Cyclopes that represented disorder and cruelty. The arrival of the gods brought order into this chaotic universe, beginning with Zeus, the son of the Titan Cronos, who managed to escape being eaten by his father. Zeus' triumph over both his father Cronos and the monster Typhoeus, who represented the disordered and savage forces of nature, marked the beginning of civilization and rationality. Zeus, however, did not defeat all of the monsters. The Greek heroes who came later made their names by battling the monstrous creatures that had been produced at the beginning of the cosmos, as well as their monstrous progeny. Like Zeus, these heroes represent the forces of civilization and rationality defeating chaos, savagery, and nature.

The Romans adopted these Greek monsters, along with the rest of the Greek religion, without changing much. If anything, the Romans displayed even more fascination with monsters than the Greeks. While the Greeks tended to relegate monsters to the chronological and geographical fringes of the world, the Romans were also obsessed with monsters closer to home. Romans displayed a heightened interest in anything strange or unusual, including deformed animals and humans that they regarded as monstrosities, as well as exotic and largely fictional animal and human hybrids. Sadly, both real Roman children and animals born with physical abnormalities were likely to be killed due to the fear of divine wrath that their deformities engendered or be put on display in a monster-market like the one Plutarch describes in section 10 of *De Curiositate*.

European Christians inherited many of these ideas about monsters from the Greeks and Romans, but fitted them within a Christian framework and imbued them with Christian meaning. One of the most important ancient texts for transmitting these classical ideas into medieval Europe was Pliny the Elder's *Natural History* which was first published in 77 CE and circulated throughout western Europe in the Middle Ages. Pliny drew upon even older Greek and Roman authorities to compile this encyclopedic work, covering all of the natural world, and includes information on the monstrous races believed to inhabit the fringes of the world in Book VII. Pliny prefaces his discussion of these fabulous beings by addressing any potential skepticism about their existence. He points out that there are many things that would have been unbelievable before they were discovered and reminds his reader that he is relying on the authority of Greek scholars who were revered for their industriousness and reliability.

Pliny details a wide variety of humans whose departure from physical or cultural norms made them "monstrous" (in the sense of both wonderous and repulsive) to the Greeks and Romans. I want to pause a moment to address the term "monstrous races" as it is applied to these peoples. Pliny does not consistently use the word *monstra* to describe these peoples. He also uses terms like prodigious, incredible, marvelous, and miraculous. However, the term "monstrous" predominated among the medieval European authors who followed Pliny; it became the most common term to describe these peoples and was then imported into modern scholarship. As for the use of the word "race," the Latin terms Pliny uses most frequently are *humani* (humans) and *homini* (men), but he also uses *gens* (a race or tribe of people sharing descent from a common ancestor), and this is where we derive our modern English terminology for the "monstrous races" from. There has been a great deal of debate about whether modern historians should continue using the term "monstrous races" since it now carries so much cultural baggage accrued during the centuries separating us from these ancient authors. Some scholars have suggested using a term like "wonderous tribes" to emphasize the humanity and dignity of these peoples and align with our own modern values. While these arguments are well-intentioned, replacing the term is also problematic. The term monstrous races does imply that these races were viewed in some ways as threatening or less than human, and that is precisely why I believe it is important to retain it instead of using something more neutral. We could certainly use tribe or people instead of race since they also convey the meaning of the original Latin but lack modern associations with nineteenth-century pseudo-science, but this would obscure an important part of the historical processes by which certain peoples were racialized in the modern era. The term monstrous is more even more difficult to replace. All of the other English terms (wonderous, marvelous, fantastic, incredible, portentous) that are available fail to convey the repulsion, terror, awe, and wonder of the Latin *monstra*. All of these meanings are necessary to understand the reasons for which and the processes by which certain peoples were defined as others by the Greeks, the Romans, and medieval European Christians, and this othering is essential to understanding the processes of dehumanization and racialization that came later.

Whether we call them monstrous races or wonderous tribes, Pliny leaves no doubt that he is describing different groups of human beings whose physical forms and/or customs deviated from Roman norms, and, in that sense, they were monstrous to Pliny. The first tribes Pliny describes are a good example of this. Pliny recounts that there are tribes in Scythia who engage in cannibalism and compares them to the Cyclopes and Laestrygones who also ate human flesh, as well as to the Celts, who until recently practiced human sacrifice. Both cannibalism and human sacrifice violated Roman norms of behavior and qualified as monstrous. Indeed, these practices violate modern norms as well, and we consider them monstrous. This discussion of cannibalism and human sacrifice is the only instance in which Pliny actually uses the term monstrous [*gentes huius monstri*] in chapter 2 of Book VII. Cannibalism and human sacrifice were considered so egregious that Pliny marked them out by using the term *monstra* rather than some more neutral term.

Some of the other races Pliny describes are monstrous not in their behavior, but in their physical appearance or certain physical qualities, such as the one-eyed Arimaspi, the Psylli whose bodies produce a poison that can kill snakes, the androgynous Machlyes, the one-footed Monocoli, the people who have eyes in their shoulders (later known as *Blemmyae*), and the Astomi who are covered in hair and have no mouths. Others are marvels due to their excessive height like some Indian tribes, or their shortness like the Pygmies, for their ability to withstand walking over charred logs like the Hirpi, or for their unusual reproductive habits. While they do not necessarily engage in monstrous behavior, they all violate physical norms in one way or another, and the fact that they violate western taxonomies qualifies them as monstrous. Pliny, however, refers to them in fairly neutral terms, describing them as marvels and as evidence of nature's endless variety.

Some of the peoples Pliny describes, such as the dog-headed people later called Cynocephali, are not only physically monstrous, in the sense that they are literally human–animal hybrids, they are culturally monstrous as well. Pliny says that these dog-headed people wear only animal skins, bark instead of speaking, live solely by hunting and fishing, and use their nails as weapons when hunting. Here, Pliny is implicitly making a comparison between Roman cultural norms, what he considers "civilized" behavior, and the "uncivilized" or "barbaric" behavior of the Cynocephali. Although the Cynocephali are not engaging in cannibalism or human sacrifice, their attire, speech, and lack of agriculture and man-made weapons mark them as barbaric in comparison with the Romans. And this comparison is not restricted to the Cynocephali; many of the monstrous races were believed to lack qualities the Greco-Romans considered hallmarks of civilization, such as living in houses, wearing clothing, engaging in agriculture, eating or avoiding certain foods, and observing certain taboos.

The Cynocephali also raise an interesting and important question: why were they considered dog-headed people rather than dogs with human bodies? Pliny assumes that they are human and so did the Greek authors Hesiod, Herodotus, Ctesias, and Aelian who also described them. This is most likely because they were thought to possess human reason – the one trait above all others that the ancient Greeks and Romans believed separated men from beasts. At least since Aristotle's time (fourth century BCE), humanity was defined above all by the possession of reason, the ability to conceive plans, and execute them with forethought. Reason defined man and was believed to be exclusive to humanity. Although none of the authors explicitly give a reason for considering these dog-headed creatures men, the key seems to be their rationality. Without this, the Greeks and Romans would have considered them beasts and not men.

For Pliny, and for the ancient Greek authorities he drew upon, the monstrous races were embodiments of alterity who inhabited the fringes of the known world. Not only did they deviate culturally and/or physically from ancient Greeks and Romans, they were located in the extreme north of Europe, the Eurasian Steppe, the far east, the Indian subcontinent, or Africa as well. The ancient authorities all agreed that these races were human, but they were humans who inhabited the geographical fringes of the world and who transgressed physical or cultural boundaries. They existed in a space that was geographically, taxonomically, and culturally liminal, and they were marked as others due to their appearance and/or behavior. For Greek and Roman authors alike, the monstrous races were as useful as they were marvelous. They not only illustrated nature's genius and ingenuity, they reinforced Greco-Roman notions of civilized behavior by exhibiting uncivilized behavior, and they reinforced Greco-Roman definitions of humanity by displaying rationality in spite of all their physical and cultural differences as well.

Just after his description of the monstrous races, Pliny turns to discussing individual examples of marvels. Here, he includes multiple births, women who give

birth to a prodigious number of children, hermaphrodites or Androgyni who possess both sexes, as well as monstrous births, or situations in which women were
believed to have given birth to animals like elephants and snakes (today we would
recognize these as severely deformed fetuses). There are two very interesting things
going on here. The first is the inclusion of hermaphrodites, people we would now
call intersex, and the fact that they call into question binary assumptions about sex
by having both male and female sexual organs. The second is how Pliny describes
all of these unusual births as portents. He notes that the birth of two sets of twins
to the same woman portended a food shortage, that hermaphrodites were once considered portents but are now regarded as entertainments, and that the Marsic War
was preceded by Alcippe giving birth to an elephant. The belief that unusual births
were omens or warnings was already ancient by the time Pliny was writing, and it
survived well into the early modern period. Just as importantly, Pliny also reveals
that these births were regarded as curiosities and mentions a hippo-centaur born in
Egypt that was preserved in honey and brought to Rome for Claudius Caesar. His
comments emphasize both the wonder and the terror that such births provoked in
antiquity.

The monstrous races made their way into medieval European culture partly due
to the popularity of Pliny's *Natural History*, but it was their appearance in Saint
Augustine of Hippo's *City of God* that proved decisive. Augustine was so influential, and the *City of God* such a foundational Christian text that it ensured stories
about the monstrous races would continue to circulate in medieval Europe. Augustine wrote the *City of God* in the wake of the Visigothic sack of Rome in 410 CE.
In it, Augustine refutes pagan arguments that the sack of Rome had been due to
the adoption of Christianity and the abandonment of traditional Roman religion
and argues instead that God had intended for Rome (the Earthly City) to aid in the
spread of Christianity. In doing so, Augustine articulates a providential theory of
history in which the Christian God works His will through the unfolding of human
history. Augustine's conception of providential history went on to dominate western European understandings of history for more than 1,000 years. Augustine takes
a detour into the monstrous races in Book XVI while discussing the progress of the
City of God and the Earthly City from the time of Noah to the time of Abraham.
Augustine introduces the monstrous races by addressing the question of whether
these peoples descended from Noah's sons, since Christians believed that the rest
of humanity had been destroyed in the Flood, and only Noah, his sons, and their
families had been saved. The central question for Augustine is whether these races
are human.

Unlike Pliny, Augustine consistently uses the term monstrous races of men
(*monstrosa hominum genera*) to describe all of these peoples, and most medieval
authors followed him in using this designation. He also notes that people in his day
not only read about these races, they also encountered images of them in places like
the esplanade in the Carthage harbor where they were depicted in mosaics. Augustine displays a good deal of skepticism about the monstrous races, remarking that
we are not obliged to believe everything we hear about them and that some of the
peoples described by ancient Greek and Roman authors must surely be beasts. Still,

he thinks it worthwhile to devote several paragraphs to them rather than dismissing them out of hand. Interestingly, he thinks the Cynocephali, or dog-headed men, are beasts rather than men due to their barking since speech was viewed as an aspect of human reason. Despite his consistent use of the term monstrous to describe these peoples, Augustine views them, if they exist, as evidence of God's omnipotence and omniscience rather than deformities. He argues that only God can see the whole of creation, and that only He is aware of the similarity and diversity that make up the beauty of creation. If God has created anything that appears deformed to us, it is only because we lack His understanding of the whole of creation and cannot see how the pieces fit together.

Like Pliny, Augustine moves on to comparing these races of men to cases of individuals closer to home who physically deviate from the norm. He uses the examples of monstrous births (*genere humano quaedam monstra*) – people born with extra or missing digits, misshapen hands and feet, hermaphrodites, and conjoined twins to make his point that just as individual humans can differ substantially from one another and from the norm in appearance, so can whole peoples. While Augustine describes these individuals as monstrous, he does so in the sense that their appearance differs from the norm. He consistently asserts that, if they exist and are men, then they are fully human and the creations of a God who is a perfect workman and who knows the purpose of His creation better than we do. Augustine begins his inquiry with the assertion that anyone who is born a man, which he helpfully defines as a rational, mortal animal, is a descendant of Adam, and he ends it with a return to this question of humanity. He concludes that either these so-called monstrous races are entirely made up or they exist but they are not human or they are human and are therefore descendants of Adam. The question of their humanity is vital to Augustine because if these monstrous races are human, then they are eligible for salvation. Augustine's work was so influential that when Christian missionaries from western Europe ventured east into Mongolia during the thirteenth century, some of them, like John of Plano Carpini, expected to meet these tribes and hoped to convert them to Christianity. Some of the peoples the missionaries encountered, like the Tartars, were familiar enough with western belief in these marvelous races ("wonders of the East" as they were sometimes called) that they teased the missionaries with stories about them.

Augustine may have remained skeptical about the existence of the monstrous races, but by including them in the *City of God*, he incorporated them into a Christian framework, affirmed their theoretical humanity, and ensured that other Christian authors would discuss them and treat their existence as at least possible. The second most influential Christian author to discuss them was Isidore of Seville (d. 636 CE), who included them in his massive compendium of classical knowledge called the *Etymologies*. Isidore's work largely summarizes the works of classical authors, and it enjoyed a wide circulation and enormous influence in the Middle Ages. Isidore discusses the monstrous races in Book XI in a chapter on portents. Isidore begins by explaining that Varro (a Roman scholar who lived in the first century BCE) defines portents as beings that are contrary to nature. Isidore corrects this and says that portents are not contrary to nature, but contrary to what is known nature, pointing out that all beings are created by God, who the pagans sometimes called nature, and therefore portents are exactly as God intended them to be. Like Pliny, Isidore is interested in discerning the meaning of these unusual beings, but like Augustine, he is also fitting them into a distinctively Christian framework. Isidore takes the Greco-Roman idea of the portent and incorporates it into the providential theory of history that Augustine developed in the *City of God*; portents retain their pagan function of foreshadowing or warning humanity, but now they are messages sent by the Christian God.

Isidore also take us on a helpful excursus through the various names given to these portents. He says that some portents (*portentum*) are called signs (*ostentum*) or prodigies (*prodigium*), and that these predict the future, but others are called omens (*monstrum*) and they warn humanity by indicating what might happen. He also notes that omens derive their name from *monitus*, meaning admonition, reinforcing the sense that they are more ominous and negative than the more neutral signs and prodigies. Isidore consistently uses the term *monstra* when discussing negative portents or omens and notes that these "monsters" die as soon as they are born. He also points out that there is a difference between portents in general, which he defines as beings who are transformed in appearance, like a human child who has the appearance of a serpent, and "unnatural beings" (*portentuosus*) who have only slight deviations from the norm, like a person with six fingers. Having pointed out this fine distinction between portents and unnatural beings, Isidore goes on to refer to the races he describes as monstrous (*genere humano quaedam monstra sunt gentium*).

Isidore's description of what constitutes a portent agrees in many respects with the qualities modern scholars use to define monstrosity. Isidore says that portents can be people who are excessively large or small, people who have a misshapen body part or extra or missing body parts, people who have some features of an animal or the full appearance of an animal, people who have features in unusual places (like eyes in the chest), people who age prematurely, or individuals who have both male and female sexual organs. He then explains that just as individual people can have monstrous qualities (he uses the term *monstra*), so can whole races. Isidore's discussion of the monstrous races largely follows Pliny and contains many of the same associations, but he does add some new faces, including giants, peoples from the Far East who lack noses, and the horse-hooved Hippopodes. Like Augustine, he displays some skepticism about the existence of at least some of the monstrous races. In Isidore's case, he does this by using language like "they claim," "they tell of," or "there are said to be" in describing certain peoples, indicating that he may not completely believe in the veracity of some of the material he is summarizing.

Isidore's main departure from both Pliny and Augustine is that he includes legendary monsters from Greco-Roman myths among his portents. In this section, his main concern is disputing the existence of creatures like Gorgons, Sirens, Scylla, Cerberus, Hydra, and the Chimera and explaining that these are all imaginary monsters concocted by men to explain certain phenomena. Isidore claims that some of these portents are based on misunderstandings of actual creatures. For example, he explains the Gorgons as three sisters whose beauty was so intense that it stunned the beholder as if they had been turned to stone. In other cases, such as Cerberus, he asserts that the creature is entirely fictional and was created only as a signifier – in this case, signifying the three ages in which "death devours a human being." Isidore displays only mild skepticism about the existence of the monstrous races, but he is determined to demystify monsters from Greco-Roman myth. This is a testament to the fact that the monstrous races were really believed to exist, or at least to possibly exist, and were not regarded as merely the stuff of myth or legend. This belief is due partly to the fact that the existence of the monstrous races was attested to by a whole range of respected Greek and Roman pagan authors who included them in their works on history and natural history, but for Christian authors like Isidore, it is also due to the fact that one of the most revered fathers of the Christian Church, Augustine of Hippo, had admitted their possible existence.

Finally, Isidore turns to metamorphoses as an aspect of monstrosity, especially the transformation of men into beasts. Although Isidore disputes the existence of mythical creatures, he reverts to displaying only mild skepticism regarding cases of metamorphoses like Circe changing Ulysses' companions into pigs and the Arcadians changing into wolves. Isidore explains some of these transformations as instances of sorcery, effected by means of magical charms or poisonous herbs, but he also asserts that many creatures are naturally transformed into different species when they decay, indicating that he finds instances of metamorphoses more believable than the existence of mythical creatures like centaurs or Gorgons. What is interesting here is the implicit association between the monstrous races and cases of complete transformation from man into animal. Many of the monstrous races are human–animal hybrids, men with certain animal features, and the werewolves we will encounter in a later chapter are humans with the ability to entirely transform themselves into wolves. In all of these cases, these creatures transgress the boundary between human and animal. By exhibiting the physical appearance, some characteristics, and/or the behavior of beasts, they call definitions of humanity into question.

Augustine's *City of God* and Isidore of Seville's *Etymologies* were two of the most influential works of the early Middle Ages. They were endlessly copied and circulated throughout Europe. Along with Pliny's *Natural History*, they ensured that stories about the monstrous races were transmitted to later generations and spawned an entire medieval corpus of works on the monstrous races. These included works like the *Book of Monsters* (*Liber monstrorum*) compiled by an anonymous English author in the late-seventh or early-eighth century who made copious use of Isidore's *Etymologies*. The work contains many of the Plinian Races, along with creatures from Greco-Roman myth. While the author is dismissive about the existence of some of the more fabulous races he describes, calling them fables and lies, the work still contributed to debates about and belief in the monstrous races. Another anonymous English author produced a Latin text known as *De rebus in Oriente mirabilibus* in the ninth or tenth century, which draws in part from the *Book of Monsters*. This work was translated into Old English around the year 1000 as *The Wonders of the East*. The Old English version survives in three manuscripts, all of which are illustrated with images of the races and creatures described in it; one of them, the Nowell Codex (British Library, Cotton Vitellius A. xv), also contains the only surviving version of the poem *Beowulf.*

The Wonders of the East presents some of the same monstrous races we have already seen, but three interesting changes have taken place. The first is that these monstrous races are now associated with monsters like dragons. The author notes that there are men without heads who have their eyes and mouths in their chest living on an island south of the Brixontes, but says that it is difficult to reach this place due to the abundance of enormous dragons that live there. The linkage between the monstrous races and fabulous creatures like dragons tends to make the monstrous races themselves even more alien and exotic.

The second change is that some of the monstrous races are now specifically described as female. There are women who have beards down to their breasts who hunt wild beasts and raise tigers and leopards in place of dogs. These women transgress gender norms in both their physical ability to grow beards and their behavior as they hunt and raise wild animals. In both cases, they are taking on male roles and this makes them monstrous to the Anglo-Saxon author. He also describes incredibly tall women who are as white as marble and have boar's tusks, hair down to their heels, ox-tails on their loins, and camel's feet. The author says that these women were killed by Alexander the Great because their bodies were so disgusting that he could not capture them alive. These women are monstrous in the sense that their appearance combines human and animal elements, but they are portrayed as more offensive than similarly hybrid men. So repulsive in fact, that they are killed due to their appearance. The monstrosity of women will be treated more fully in Chapter 3, but it is worth noting here that just as hermaphrodites were regarded as monstrous, women who had masculine attributes or hybrid characteristics were seen as monstrous as well, and they seem to have inspired particular disgust.

The final change is that many of these races are explicitly fearful of humans or threatening to humans. For example, the three-colored people who inhabit Ciconia are described as fleeing and sweating blood if they see anyone in their lands, and this is despite the fact that they are 20 feet tall. The Homodubii, humans with the lower bodies of donkeys, also flee if they see anyone. On the other hand, the Hostes, who are black, devour any person they catch, as do the Donestre, a race of soothsayers who use lies to beguile and capture their victims before eating their bodies and weeping over their heads. The presentation of these races emphasizes the distrust between them and other humans, which makes them even more alien. In fact, the author often indicates that these races are "thought to be men." By implicitly questioning their humanity, he reinforces their otherness.

All of these changes subtly shifted the perception of the monstrous races. Peoples that Pliny had described in fairly neutral terms became progressively more monstrous, more alien, and more threatening during the Middle Ages. This was partly due to a shift in the language as terms like wonderous, marvelous, or incredible that were used to describe them were increasingly replaced by the term monstrous, but it was also due to the way they were portrayed. In Pliny's work, these peoples are evidence of nature's diversity. In Augustine's, they are potential descendants of Adam who may be eligible for salvation. In Isidore's, they are portents who communicate God's will in some way, even if we are not always able to discern their meaning. By the year 1000, the monstrous races were still considered human, but just barely. They represented the limits of what constituted humanity, and they were increasingly threatening to or afraid of humans.

In the High Middle Ages, the monstrous races made their way into a variety of media and genres. They appeared in romance literature like the *Deeds of the Romans* (*Gesta Romanorum*) and the *Roman d'Alexandre*, they were featured in collections of homilies, they were represented on maps, and they were illustrated and explicated in bestiaries (Fitzwilliam Museum MS 254, Cambridge University Library MS Kk. 4.25, Westminster Abbey Library MS 22, and Oxford Bodley Library MS Douce 88, II). They were so ingrained in the medieval imagination that they became part of the stock of characters that peered out of the margins of manuscripts and adorned the walls of churches. The monstrous races were appreciated as sources of entertainment, as strange and exotic peoples who inhabited strange and exotic lands. However, they were still believed to be sources of divine instruction as well, and they provided moralists with a rich source of material that was used to illustrate both virtues and vices, but most often vices. Sources from this period, like Thomas of Cantimpré's thirteenth-century work, *Of Monstrous Men* (*De monstruosis hominibus*, Book III of *De natura rerum*), tend to focus on the exoticism and difference of the peoples who inhabit the East, the ugliness of their appearance, the barbarity of their customs, and their lack of morality, all while insisting that they are divine signs and attempting to discern their meaning.

The monstrous races were a distant source of fascination for most western Europeans, at once marvelous and disgusting, a perplexing part of God's creation and a challenge to western ideas of humanity. In some senses, they were the equivalent of extraterrestrial aliens today – practically everyone knew about them, even though their existence was uncertain, they differed from western Europeans in profound and disturbing ways that challenged European conceptions of humanity and their place in the universe, and few people had ever claimed to encounter them or expected to do so. That began to change in the thirteenth century when western European merchants, diplomats, and missionaries started traveling in larger numbers and going further into the Middle East, Asia, India, and Africa than most of their predecessors had. The texts these travelers produced provide evidence that stories about the monstrous races affected their expectations about the kinds of people they would encounter, as well as the way they viewed the peoples they actually encountered. Two Franciscan friars, John of Plano Carpini and William of Rubruck, went on diplomatic missions to the Mongols in the thirteenth century and attempted to convert them to Christianity. While William was skeptical about the existence of the Plinian races, his predecessor John clearly expected to encounter some of the monstrous races rumored to inhabit the east and seems to have been disappointed when he did not. In both John of Plano Carpini's *History of the Mongols* (1245–47) and *The Journey of William of Rubruck* (1253–55), many of the attitudes about the monstrous races get shifted onto the Mongols, who are called Tartars in the texts. The authors describe the unusual appearance of the Mongols, their clothing, their tents, their marriage practices, their food, and especially their idolatrous religious practices and their cruelty in warfare in terms that recall descriptions of the monstrous races. John even asserts that the Mongols are cannibals, although he never witnessed this practice. These accounts of the Mongols focus on their alleged barbarity, ferocity, and danger and encourage western Europeans to conquer them.

Other accounts disputed the existence of some of the monstrous races while confirming the existence of others. The thirteenth-century *Travels of Marco Polo*, also known as *The Book of the Marvels of the World*, whose original title draws upon the wonders of the east tradition, is one example of this. Marco Polo narrated his experiences to the romance author, Rustichello Da Pisa, who actually wrote the work while the two were imprisoned together in Genoa in 1298; however, I will refer to the author as Marco Polo for the sake of clarity. Polo's work reveals western assumptions about the exoticism of the east and the peoples who inhabit it, along with skepticism about their accuracy. Polo goes to great lengths to explain that the dried bodies of pigmies brought from India are fakes, and that they are really the preserved bodies of small monkeys that have been foisted upon unsuspecting traders who then sell them all over the world. In this case, Polo not only reveals his own familiarity with the western belief in pigmies (one of the Plinian monstrous races), but also indicates that the Indians themselves are aware of this belief and exploit it for profit. Most notably, Polo explains the phenomenon away in a manner that is almost scientific, describing the entire process of manufacturing fake pigmies and explaining why the Indians make them.

After thoroughly debunking mummified pigmies, Polo turns to describing other places and peoples, including the Cynocephali, whose existence he accepts. He says that the inhabitants of the island of Angaman have heads, eyes, and teeth that resemble dogs. Polo adds some details to his description of the Cynocephali that are new. First, he says that they only resemble dogs, not that they are dog-headed, but he also says that they kill and eat strangers, that they are idolators, and he calls them a cruel, brutish, and savage race. The relatively peaceful Cynocephali whom Pliny described as hunting and fishing have been transformed into frighteningly savage cannibals who eat any foreigner they can lay their hands on. Just as importantly, they are now described as idolators. Idolatry was associated with barbarity by medieval Christians who used the word as a term of abuse, an insult that they hurled at non-Christians (and some heretical Christians) to discredit them and portray them as monstrous. Idolatry, and its frequent companions heresy and sorcery, were considered such monstrous behaviors by the High Middle Ages that they were on par with cannibalism. As we will see in Chapter 2, many of the same attributes were projected onto Jews and Muslims in efforts to dehumanize them as well.

This brings us to our final primary source on the monstrous races in this chapter, *The Travels of Sir John Mandeville*, which purports to be an accurate account of the exotic travels of a fourteenth-century English knight from St. Albans. Like *The Travels of Marco Polo*, it was enormously popular, but its authorship is now disputed. In this case, there may never have been a Sir John Mandeville at all and the work is based on a variety of previous accounts, although there may be some parts that relate genuine first-hand knowledge. Whoever the author was and whatever the sources of his information, his main interest is marvels, and the farther east the account gets, the more it relies on earlier stories about the monstrous races. Most of the peoples the author describes are monstrous races derived from Pliny, but their description has subtly shifted in ways that makes them appear more bestial. More of them are described as being like beasts, lacking speech, or lacking the wit to build themselves houses. The author describes the giants as hideous, the Blemmyae as cursed, and the Amyktyren (people with plate-like lower lips) as foul-looking. And he describes a group of people who are difficult to distinguish from animals at all, men who are covered in skin and feathers and walk on all fours like beasts and who leap from tree to tree like squirrels or apes. Finally, the Cynocephali make another appearance. This time they are described as having dogs' heads but possessing human reason, save for the fact that they worship an ox. The charge of idolatry is less pointed here than in *The Travels of Marco Polo*, but it has stuck to the Cynocephali. They are also described as being great warriors who fight with a spear and large shield, who go naked except for a small loin-cloth, and eat the enemies they take in battle. Far from being peaceful hunters, they are now warriors who barely use clothing and cannibals who eat their enemies.

Works like *The Travels of Marco Polo* and *The Travels of Sir John Mandeville* proved to be just as popular, if not more popular, than the earlier accounts of the monstrous races. They were even used as reference works by explorers like Christopher Columbus and continued to influence the expectations of western Europeans who ventured east, and those who ventured west thinking they would get to the east, in the late medieval and early modern periods. While men like Columbus failed to find any of these monstrous races inhabiting the New World, attitudes toward the monstrous races informed the way in which western Europeans viewed and treated the peoples they found in the Americas, as well as the way they viewed and treated the peoples of Africa, India, and Asia. The long-held view that these peoples were barbaric and barely human helped to authorize violence against them in the form of conquest and enslavement. It also fed directly into western European attempts to civilize indigenous peoples across the globe and convert them to Christianity. Even when western Europeans encountered civilizations that they considered almost equal to their own, as they did in China, the influence of the monstrous races shaped their view of them as being radically different, inscrutable, and exotic. Without the legacy of the monstrous races, western European encounters with other cultures in the early modern period might have gone quite differently.

While many of the monstrous races are fantastical and fictional, there are several that actually existed. The Ethiopians, Scythians, Celts, Gymnosophists, and Pygmies are just a few. In the last few decades, a great deal of effort has gone into determining which historical peoples authors like Pliny were describing, in order to demonstrate that these ancient authorities were not just inventing things but misunderstanding and therefore misrepresenting people, or animals, who really existed. It is important to recognize that there were some historical peoples who inspired the creation of the monstrous races, that not all of them were fantasy, but we must also remember that belief in the monstrous races *as they were described* was widespread during Greco-Roman antiquity and that it continued unabated through the European Middle Ages. For the most part, Greeks, Romans, and medieval Europeans accepted that these peoples existed and that they appeared and behaved in the ways described by ancient and respected authorities. Even the sceptics admitted that some of these peoples might exist, as we saw with Augustine and the anonymous author of the *Book of Monsters*. The important point is that belief in the monstrous races endured and that even sceptics contributed to this endurance by discussing them at all.

An equally important point is that these peoples, whether real or imagined, were believed to exist far from Greeks, Romans, and medieval Europeans; they did not come into contact with the monstrous races, even though these races loomed large in their cultural imaginations. Since many of these races were fictional, or at the very least far from Europe, it meant that being described as monstrous was not nearly as problematic for them as it was for peoples like Jews and Muslims who either lived in western Europe during the Middle Ages or had close contact with Europeans. For the most part, the monstrous races served as proof of nature's or God's ingenuity and as a useful construct that helped Greeks, Romans, and medieval Europeans think about what it meant to be human, what it meant to be civilized, and define themselves against an imagined other.

PRIMARY SOURCES

Pliny the Elder, *Natural History*, trans. H. Rackham, Loeb Classical Library 394 (Harvard University Press, 1952), vol. II, VII.i–iv, pp. 511–31.

I. And about the human race as a whole we have in large part spoken in our account of the various nations. Nor shall we now deal with manners and customs, which are beyond counting and almost as numerous as the groups of mankind; yet there are some that I think ought not to be omitted, and especially those of the people living more remote from the sea; some things among which I doubt not will appear portentous and incredible to many. For who ever believed in the Ethiopians before actually seeing them? or what is not deemed miraculous when first it comes into knowledge? how many things are judged impossible before they actually occur? Indeed the power and majesty of the nature of the universe at every turn lacks credence if one's mind embraces parts of it only and not the whole. Not to mention peacocks, or the spotted skins of tigers and panthers and the colourings of so many animals, a small matter to tell of but one of measureless extent if pondered on is the number of national languages and dialects and varieties of speech, so numerous that a foreigner scarcely counts as a human being for someone of another race! Again though our physiognomy contains ten features or only a few more, to think that among all the thousands of human beings there exist no two countenances that are not distinct – a thing that no art could supply by counterfeit in so small a number of specimens! Nevertheless in most instances of these I shall not myself pledge my own faith, and shall preferably ascribe the facts to the authorities who will be quoted for all doubtful points: only do not let us be too proud to follow the Greeks, because of their far greater industry or older devotion to study.

II. We have pointed out that some Scythian tribes, and in fact a good many, feed on human bodies – a statement that perhaps may seem incredible if we do not reflect that races of this portentous character [*gentes huius monstri*] have existed in the central region of the world, named Cyclopes and Laestrygones, and that quite recently the tribes of the parts beyond the Alps habitually practised human sacrifice, which is not far removed from eating human flesh. But also a tribe is reported next to these, towards the North, not far from the actual quarter whence the North Wind rises and the cave that bears its name, the place called the Earth's Doorbolt the Arimaspi whom we have spoken of already, people remarkable for having one eye in the centre of the forehead. Many authorities, the most distinguished being Herodotus and Aristeas of Proconnesus, write that these people wage continual war around their mines with the griffins, a kind of wild beast with wings, as commonly reported, that digs gold out of mines, which the creatures guard and the Arimaspi try to take from them, both with remarkable covetousness.

But beyond the other Scythian cannibals, in a certain large valley of the Imavus Mountain, there is a region called Abarimon where are some people dwelling in forests who have their feet turned backward behind their legs, who run extremely fast and range abroad over the country with the wild animals. It is stated by Baeton, Alexander the Great's route-surveyor on his journeys, that these men are unable to breathe in another climate, and that consequently none of them could be brought to the neighbouring kings or had ever been brought to Alexander.

According to Isogonus of Nicaea the former cannibal tribes whom we stated to exist to the north, ten days' journey beyond the river Borysthenes, drink out of human skulls and use the scalps with the hair on as napkins hung round their necks. The same authority states that certain people in Albania are born with keen grey eyes and are bald from childhood, and that they see better by night than in the daytime. He also says that the Sauromatae, thirteen days' journey beyond the Borysthenes, always take food once every two days.

Crates of Pergamum states that there was a race of men round Parium on the Hellespont, whom he calls Ophiogenes, whose custom it was to cure snakebites by touch and draw the poison out of the body by placing their hand on it. Varro says that there are still a few people there whose spittle is a remedy against snakebites. According to the writings of Agatharchides there was also a similar tribe in Africa, the Psylli, named after King Psyllus, whose tomb is in the region of the greater Syrtis. In their bodies there was engendered a poison that was deadly to snakes, and the smell of which they employed for sending snakes to sleep, while they had a custom of exposing their children as soon as they were born to the most savage snakes and of using that species to test the fidelity of their wives, as snakes do not avoid persons born with adulterous blood in them. This tribe itself has been almost exterminated by the Nasamones who now occupy that region, but a tribe of men descended from those who had escaped or had been absent when the fighting took place survives today in a few places. A similar race lingers on in Italy also, the Marsi, said to be descended from the son of Circe and to possess this natural property on that account. However, all men contain a poison available as a protection against snakes: people say that snakes flee from contact with saliva as from the touch of boiling water, and that if it gets inside their throats they actually die; and that this is especially the case with the saliva of a person fasting.

Beyond the Nasamones and adjacent to them Calliphanes records the Machlyes, who are Androgyni and perform the function of either sex alternately. Aristotle adds that their left breast is that of a man and their right breast that of a woman. Isogonus and Nymphodorus report that there are families in the same part of Africa that practise sorcery, whose praises cause meadows to dry up, trees to wither and infants to perish. Isogonus adds that there are people of the same kind among the Triballi and the Illyrians, who also bewitch with a glance and who kill those they stare at for a longer time, especially with a look of anger, and that their evil eye is most felt by adults; and that what is more remarkable is that they have two pupils in each eye. Apollonides also reports women of this kind in Scythia, who are called the Bitiae, and Phylarchus also the Thibii tribe and many others of the same nature in Pontus, whose distinguishing marks he records as being a double pupil in one eye and the likeness of a horse in the other, and he also says that they are incapable of drowning, even when weighed down with clothing. Damon records a tribe not unlike these in Ethiopia, the Pharmaces, whose sweat relieves of diseases bodies touched by it. Also among ourselves Cicero states that the glance of all women who have double pupils is injurious everywhere. In fact when nature implanted in man the wild beasts' habit of devouring human flesh, she also thought fit to implant poisons in the whole of the body, and with some persons in the eyes as well, so that there should be no evil anywhere that was not present in man.

There are a few families in the Faliscan territory, not far from the city of Rome, named the Hirpi, which at the yearly sacrifice to Apollo performed on Mount Soracte walk over a charred pile of logs without being scorched, and who consequently enjoy exemption under a perpetual decree of the senate from military service and all other burdens. Some people are born with parts of the body possessing special remarkable properties, for instance King Pyrrhus in the great toe of his right foot, to touch which was a cure for inflammation of the spleen; it is recorded that at his cremation it proved impossible to burn the toe with the rest of the body, and it was stored in a chest in a temple.

India and parts of Ethiopia especially teem with marvels. The biggest animals grow in India: for instance Indian dogs are bigger than any others. Indeed the trees are said to be so lofty that it is not possible to shoot an arrow over them, and [the richness of the soil, temperate climate and abundance of springs bring it about] that, if one is willing to believe it, squadrons of cavalry are able to shelter beneath a single fig-tree; while it is said that reeds are of such height that sometimes a single section between two knots will make a canoe that will carry three people. It is known that many of the inhabitants are more than five cubits tall, never spit, do not suffer from headache or toothache or pain in the eyes, and very rarely have a pain in any other part of the body – so hardy are they made by the temperate heat of the sun; and that the sages of their race, whom they call Gymnosophists, stay standing from sunrise to sunset, gazing at the sun with eyes unmoving, and continue all day long standing first on one foot and then on the other in the glowing sand. Megasthenes states that on the mountain named Nulus there are people with their feet turned backwards and with eight toes on each foot, while on many of the mountains there is a tribe of human beings with dogs' heads, who wear a covering of wild beasts' skins, whose speech is a bark and who live on the produce of hunting and fowling, for which they use their nails as weapons; he says that they numbered more than 120,000 when he published his work.

Ctesias writes that also among a certain race of India the women bear children only once in their lifetime, and the children begin to turn grey directly after birth; he also describes a tribe of men called the Monocoli who have only one leg, and who move in jumps with surprising speed; the same are called the Umbrella-foot tribe, because in the hotter weather they lie on their backs on the ground and protect themselves with the shadow of their feet; and that they are not far away from the Trogodytae; and again westward from these there are some people without necks, having their eyes in their shoulders. There are also satyrs in the mountains in the east of India (it is called the district of the Catarcludi); this is an extremely swift animal, sometimes going on all fours and sometimes standing upright as they run, like human beings; because of their speed only the old ones or the sick are caught. Tauron gives the name of Choromandae to a forest tribe that has no speech but a horrible scream, hairy bodies, keen grey eyes and the teeth of a dog.

Eudoxus says that in the south of India men have feet eighteen inches long and the women such small feet that they are called Sparrowfeet. Megasthenes tells of a race among the Nomads of India that has only holes in the place of nostrils, like snakes, and bandy-legged; they are called the Sciritae. At the extreme boundary of India to the East, near the source of the Ganges, he puts the Astomi tribe, that has no mouth and a body hairy all over; they dress in cotton-wool and live only on the air they breathe and the scent they inhale through their nostrils; they have no food or drink except the different odours of the roots and flowers and wild apples, which they carry with them on their longer journeys so as not to lack a supply of scent; he says they can easily be killed by a rather stronger odour than usual. Beyond these in the most outlying mountain region we are told of the Three-span men and Pygmies, who do not exceed three spans {i.e. twenty-seven inches} in height; the climate is healthy and always spring-like, as it is protected on the north by a range of mountains; this tribe Homer has also recorded as being beset by cranes. It is reported that in springtime their entire band, mounted on the backs of rams and she-goats and armed with arrows, goes in a body down to the sea and eats the cranes eggs and chickens, and that this outing occupies three months; and that otherwise they could not protect themselves against the flocks of cranes that would grow up; and that their houses are made of mud and feathers and eggshells. Aristotle says that the Pygmies live in caves, but in the rest of his statement about them he agrees with the other authorities. The Indian race of Cyrni according to Isigonus live to 140; and he holds that the same is true of the Long-lived Ethiopians, the Seres and the inhabitants of Mount Athos – in the last case because of their diet of snakes' flesh, which causes their head and clothes to be free from creatures harmful to the body. Onesicritus says that in the parts of India where there are no shadows there are men five cubits and two spans a high, and people live a hundred and thirty years, and do not grow old but die middle-aged. Crates of Pergamum tells of Indians who exceed a hundred years, whom he calls Gymnetae, though many call them Macrobii. Ctesias says that a tribe among them called the Pandae, dwelling in the mountain valleys, live two hundred years, and have white hair in their youth that grows black in old age; whereas others do not exceed forty years, this tribe adjoining the Macrobii, whose women bear children only once. Agatharchides records this as well, and also that they live on locusts, and are very swift-footed. Clitarchus gave them the name of Mandi; and Megasthenes also assigns them three hundred villages, and says that the women bear children at the age of seven and old age comes at forty. Artemidorus says that on the Island of Taprobane the people live very long lives without any loss of bodily activity. Duris says that some Indians have union with wild animals and the offspring is of mixed race and half animal; that among the Calingi, a tribe of the same part of India, women conceive at the age of five and do not live more than eight years, and that in another part men are born with a hairy tail and extremely swift, while others are entirely covered by their ears.

The river Arabis is the frontier between the Indians and the Oritae. These are acquainted with no other food but fish, which they cut to pieces with their nails and roast in the sun and thus make bread out of them, as is recorded by Clitarchus. Crates of Pergamum says that the Trogodytae beyond Ethiopia are swifter than horses; also that there are Ethiopians more than twelve feet in height, and that this race is called the Syrbotae. The tribe of the Ethiopian nomads along the river Astragus towards the north called the Menismini is twenty days' journey from the Ocean; it lives on the milk of the animals that we call dog-headed apes, herds of which it keeps in pastures, killing the males except for the purpose of breeding. In the deserts of Africa ghosts of men suddenly meet the traveller and vanish in a moment.

These and similar varieties of the human race have been made by the ingenuity of Nature as toys for herself and marvels for us. And indeed who could possibly recount the various things she does every day and almost every hour? Let it suffice for the disclosure of her power to have included whole races of mankind among her marvels. From these we turn to a few admitted marvels in the case of the individual human being.

III. The birth of triplets is attested by the case of the Horatii and Curiatii; above that number is considered portentous, except in Egypt, where drinking the water of the Nile causes fecundity. Recently on the day of the obsequies of the deified Augustus a certain woman of the lower orders named Fausta at Ostia was delivered of two male and two female infants, which unquestionably portended the food shortage that followed. We also find the case of a woman in the Peloponnese who four times produced quintuplets, the greater number of each birth surviving. In Egypt also Trogus alleges cases of seven infants born at a single birth.

Persons are also born of both sexes combined – what we call Hermaphrodites, formerly called androgyni and considered as portents, but now as entertainments. Pompey the Great among the decorations of his theatre placed images of celebrated marvels, made with special elaboration for the purpose by the talent of eminent artists; among them we read of Eutychis who at Tralles was carried to her funeral pyre by twenty children and who had given birth 30 times, and Alcippe who gave birth to an elephant – although it is true that the latter case ranks among portents, for one of the first occurrences of the Marsic War was that a maidservant gave birth to a snake, and also monstrous births [*monstra partus*] of various kinds are recorded among the ominous things that happened. Claudius Caesar writes that a hippocentaur was born in Thessaly and died the same day; and in his reign we actually saw one that was brought here for him from Egypt preserved in honey. One case is that of an infant at Saguntum which at once went back into the womb, in the year in which that city was destroyed by Hannibal.

IV. Transformation of females into males is not an idle story. We find in the Annals that in the consulship of Publius Licinius Crassus and Gaius Cassius Longinus a girl at Casinum was changed into a boy, under the observation of the parents, and at the order of the augurs was conveyed away to a desert island. Licinius Mucianus has recorded that he personally saw at Argos a man named Arescon who had been given the name of Arescusa and had actually married a husband, and then had grown a beard and developed masculine attributes and had taken a wife; and that he had also seen a boy with the same record at Smyrna. I myself saw in Africa a person who had turned into a male on the day of marriage to a husband; this was Lucius Constitius, a citizen of Thysdritum . . . [37] [It is said that] at the birth of twins neither the mother nor more than one of the two children usually lives, but that if twins are born that are of different sex it is even more unusual for either to be saved; that females are born more quickly than males, just as they grow older more quickly; and that movement in the womb is more frequent in the case of males, and males are usually carried on the right side, females on the left.

Augustine of Hippo, *The City of God*, trans. and Rev. Marcus Dods (T. & T. Clark, 1884), vol. II, XVI.viii, pp. 116–8.

8. Whether Certain Monstrous Races of Men are Derived from the Stock of Adam or Noah's Sons

It is also asked whether we are to believe that certain monstrous races of men, spoken of in secular history, have sprung from Noah's sons, or rather, I should say, from that one man from whom they themselves descended. For it is reported that some have one eye in the middle of the forehead; some, feet turned backwards from the heel; some, a double sex, the right breast like a man, the left like a woman, and that they alternately beget and bring forth: others are said to have no mouth, and to breathe only through the nostrils; others are but a cubit high, and are therefore called by the Greeks "Pigmies:" they say that in some places the women conceive in their fifth year, and do not live beyond their eighth. So, too, they tell of a race who have two feet but only one leg, and are of marvelous swiftness, though they do not bend the knee: they are called Skiopodes, because in the hot weather they lie down on their backs and shade themselves with their feet. Others are said to have no head, and their eyes in their shoulders; and other human or quasi-human races are depicted in mosaic in the harbour esplanade of Carthage, on the faith of histories of rarities. What shall I say of the Cynocephali, whose dog-like head and barking proclaim them beasts rather than men? But we are not bound to believe all we hear of these monstrosities. But whoever is anywhere born a man, that is, a rational mortal animal, no matter what unusual appearance he presents in colour, movement, sound, nor how peculiar he is in some power, part, or quality of his nature, no Christian can doubt that he springs from that one protoplast. We can distinguish the common human nature from that which is peculiar, and therefore wonderful.

The same account which is given of monstrous births in individual cases can be given of monstrous races. For God, the Creator of all, knows where and when each thing ought to be, or to have been created, because He sees the similarities and diversities which can contribute to the beauty of the whole. But He who cannot see the whole is offended by the deformity of the part, because he is blind to that which balances it, and to which it belongs. We know that men are born with more than four fingers on their hands or toes on their feet: this is a smaller matter; but far from us be the folly of suspecting that the Creator mistook the number of a man's fingers, though we cannot account for the difference. And so in cases where the divergence from the rule is greater. He whose works no man justly finds fault with, knows what He has done. At Hippo-Diarrhytus there is a man whose hands are crescent-shaped, and have only two fingers each, and his feet similarly formed. If there were a race like him, it would be added to the history of the curious and wonderful. Shall we therefore deny that this man is descended from that one man who was first created? As for the Androgyni, or Hermaphrodites, as they are called, though they are rare, yet from time to time there appear persons of sex so doubtful, that it remains uncertain from which sex they take their name; though it is customary to give them a masculine name, as the more worthy. For no one ever called them Her-maphroditesses. Some years ago, quite within my own memory, a man was born in the East, double in his upper, but single in his lower half – having two heads, two chests, four hands, but one body and two feet like an ordinary man; and he lived so long that many had an opportunity of seeing him. But who could enumerate all the human births that have differed widely from ascertained parents? As, therefore, no one will deny that these are all descended from that one man, so all the races which are reported to have diverged in bodily appearance from the usual course which nature generally or almost universally preserves, if they are embraced in that defi-nition of man as rational and mortal animals, unquestionably trace their pedigree to that one first father of all. We are supposing these stories about various races who differ from one another and from us to be true; but possibly they are not: for if we are not aware that apes, and monkeys, and sphinxes are not men, but beasts, those historians would possibly describe them as races of men, and flaunt with impunity their false and vainglorious discoveries. But supposing they are men of whom these marvels are recorded, what if God has seen fit to create some races in this way, that we might not suppose that the monstrous births which appear among ourselves are the failures of that wisdom whereby He fashions the human nature, as we speak of the failure of a less perfect workman?

Accordingly, it ought not to seem absurd to us, that as in individual races there are monstrous births, so in the whole race there are monstrous races. Wherefore, to conclude this question cautiously and guardedly, either these things which have been told of some races have no existence at all; or if they do not exist, they are not human races; or if they are human, they are descended from Adam.

Isidore of Seville, *The Etymologies of Isidore of Seville*, ed. and trans. Stephen A. Barney, W.J. Lewis, J.A. Beach, and Oliver Berghof (Cambridge University Press, 2006), XI.iii–iv, pp. 243–6.

iii. Portents (De portentis)

1. Varro defines portents as beings that seem to have been born contrary to nature – but they are not contrary to nature, because they are created by divine will, since the nature of everything is the will of the Creator. Whence even the pagans address God sometimes as 'Nature' (Natura), sometimes as 'God.'

2. A portent is therefore not created contrary to nature, but contrary to what is known nature. Portents are also called signs, omens, and prodigies, because they are seen to portend and display, indicate and predict future events.

3. The term 'portent' (portentum) is said to be derived from foreshadowing (portendere), that is, from 'showing beforehand' (praeostendere). 'Signs' (ostentum), because they seem to show (ostendere) a future event. Prodigies (prodigium) are so called, because they 'speak hereafter' (porro dicere), that is, they predict the future. But omens (monstrum) derive their name from admonition (monitus), because in giving a sign they indicate (demonstrare) something, or else because they instantly show (monstrare) what may appear; and this is its proper meaning, even though it has frequently been corrupted by the improper use of writers.

4. Some portents seem to have been created as indications of future events, for God sometimes wants to indicate what is to come through some defects in newborns, and also through dreams and oracles, by which he may foreshadow and indicate future calamity for certain peoples or individuals, as is indeed proved by abundant experience.

5. In fact, to Xerxes a fox born of a mare was a portent for the destruction of the empire. A monster to which a woman gave birth, whose upper body parts were human, but dead, while its lower body parts came from diverse animals, yet were alive, signified to Alexander the sudden murder of the king – for the worse parts had outlived the better ones. However, those monsters that are produced as omens do not live long – they die as soon as they are born.

6. There is a difference between a 'portent' (portentum) and 'an unnatural being' (portentuosus). Portents are beings of transformed appearance, as, for instance, is said to have happened when in Umbria a woman gave birth to a serpent. Whence Lucan says (Civil War 1.563): And the child terrified its own mother. But an unnatural being strictly speaking takes the form of a slight mutation, as for instance in the case of someone born with six fingers.

7. Portents, then, or unnatural beings, exist in some cases in the form of a size of the whole body that surpasses common human nature, as in the case of Tityos who, as Homer witnesses, covered nine jugers (i.e. about six acres) when lying prostrate; in other cases in the form of a smallness of the whole body, as in dwarfs (nanus), or those whom the Greeks call pygmies (pygmaeus), because they are a cubit tall. Others are so called due to the size of parts of their bodies, as for instance a misshapen head, or due to superfluous parts of their limbs, as in the case of two-headed and three-headed individuals, or in the case of the cynodontes (i.e. "dog-toothed" people), who have a pair of projecting fangs.

8. Yet others are so called due to missing parts of the body, individuals in whom one corresponding part is deficient compared with the other, as when one hand is compared with the other hand and one foot with the other foot. Others due to a cutting off, as in the case of those born without a hand or without a head, whom the Greeks call steresios (cf. στέρησις, "deprivation"). Others in the form of praenumeria, when only the head or a leg is born.

9. Others, who are transformed in a part of the body, as for instance those who have the features of a lion or of a dog, or the head or body of a bull, as they relate in the case of the Minotaur born of Pasiphae – what the Greeks call ἑτερομορφία. Others become a portent due to a complete transformation into a different creature, as in the story of a woman who gave birth to a calf. Others, who have a change in the position of features without any transformation, such as those with eyes in their chest or forehead, or ears above their temples, or, as Aristotle relates, someone who had his liver on the left side and his spleen on the right.

10. Others, because of a joined begetting, as when in one hand several fingers are found joined at birth and fused together, and in the other hand fewer – and likewise with the feet. Others, with a feature that is premature and untimely, as those who are born with teeth or a beard or white hair. Others, with a complex of several oddities, like the multiformed portent of Alexander's about which I spoke above (see section 5).

11. Others, from a mixing of sexes, like those they call the ἀνδρόγυνοι ("androgynes") and ἑρμαφροδίται. Hermaphrodites are so named because both sexes appear in them, as in Greek Ἑρμῆς signifies the male, Ἀφροδίτη the female. These, having a male right breast and a female left breast, in sexual intercourse sire and bear children in turn.

12. Just as, in individual nations, there are instances of monstrous people, so in the whole of humankind there are certain monstrous races, like the Giants, the Cynocephali (i.e. 'dog-headed people'), the Cyclopes, and others.

13. Giants (Gigantes) are so called according to the etymology of a Greek term; the Greeks suppose that they are γηγενεῖς, that is, "earthborn," because in their fable the parent Earth begot them as like itself, with their immense mass – for γη means "earth" and γένος "offspring." However, those whose parentage is uncertain are also commonly called 'sons of the earth.'

14. But some, inexperienced with Holy Scripture (i.e. Genesis 6:4), falsely suppose that apostate angels lay with the daughters of humans before the Flood, and that from this the Giants were born – that is, excessively large and powerful men – and filled the earth.

15. The Cynocephali are so called because they have dogs' heads, and their barking indeed reveals that they are rather beasts than humans. These originate in India.

16. India also produces the Cyclopes, and they are called Cyclops because they are believed to have a single eye in the middle of their foreheads. These are also called ἀγιοφαγίται, because they eat only the flesh of wild animals.

17. People believe that the Blemmyans in Libya are born as trunks without heads, and having their mouth and eyes in their chest, and that another race is born without necks and having their eyes in their shoulders.

18. Moreover, people write about the monstrous faces of nations in the far East: some with no noses, having completely flat faces and a shapeless countenance; some with a lower lip so protruding that when they are sleeping it protects the whole face from the heat of the sun; some with mouths grown shut, taking in nourishment only through a small opening by means of hollow straws. Some are said to have no tongues, using nods or gestures in place of words.

19. They tell of the Panotians of Scythia, who have such huge ears that they cover all the body – for πάν is the Greek word for "all," and ὦτα means "ears.

20. The Artabatitans of Ethiopia are said to walk on all fours, like cattle; none passes the age of forty.

21. The Satyrs are little people with hooked noses; they have horns on their foreheads, and feet like goats' – the kind of creature that Saint Anthony saw in the wilderness. When questioned by the servant of God, this Satyr is said to have responded (Jerome, Life of Paul the Hermit 8; PL 23.23): "I am one of the mortals that dwell in the desert, whom the pagans, deluded by their fickle error, worship as Fauns and Satyrs."

22. There are also said to be a kind of wild men, whom some call Fauns of the fig.

23. The race of Sciopodes are said to live in Ethiopia; they have only one leg, and are wonderfully speedy. The Greeks call them σκιοπόδες ("shade-footed ones") because when it is hot they lie on their backs on the ground and are shaded by the great size of their feet.

24. The Antipodes in Libya have the soles of their feet twisted behind their legs, and eight toes on each foot.

25. The Hippopodes are in Scythia, and have a human form and horses' hooves.

26. In India there are said to be a race called Μακρόβιοι, who are twelve feet tall. There, too, is a race a cubit tall, whom the Greeks from the term 'cubit' call pygmies (pigmaeus; cf. πυγμή, "cubit"), of whom I have spoken above (section 7). They live in the mountainous regions of India, near the Ocean.

27. They claim also that in the same India is a race of women who conceive when they are five years old and do not live beyond eight.

28. Other fabulous human monstrosities are told of, which do not exist but are concocted to interpret the causes of things – like Geryon, the Spanish king fabled to have three bodies, for there were three brothers of such like minds that there was, so to speak, one soul in their three bodies.

29. And there are the Gorgons, harlots with serpentine locks, who would turn anyone looking at them into stone, and who had only one eye which they would take turns using. But these were three sisters who had a single beauty, as if they had a single eye, who would so stun those beholding them that they were thought to turn them into stone.

30. People imagine three Sirens who were part maidens, part birds, having wings and talons; one of them would make music with her voice, the second with a flute, and the third with a lyre. They would draw sailors, enticed by the song, into shipwreck.

31. In truth, however, they were harlots, who, because they would seduce passers-by into destitution, were imagined as bringing shipwreck upon them. They were said to have had wings and talons because sexual desire both flies and wounds. They are said to have lived among the waves because the waves gave birth to Venus.

32. People tell of Scylla as a woman girded with the heads of dogs, with a great barking, because of the straits of the sea of Sicily, in which sailors, terrified by the whirlpools of waves rushing against each other, suppose that the waves are barking, waves that the chasm with its seething and sucking brings into collision.

33. They also imagine certain monstrosities from among irrational living creatures, like Cerberus, the dog of the nether world that has three heads, signifying through him the three ages in which death devours a human being – that is, infancy, youth, and old age. Some think that he is called Cerberus as if the term were κρεοβόρος ("flesh-eating"), that is, devouring flesh.

34. They talk also of Hydra, a serpent with nine heads, which in Latin is called 'water-snake' (excetra), because when one head was cut off (caedere) three would grow back. But in fact Hydra was a place that gushed out water, devastating a nearby city; if one opening in it were closed, many more would burst out. Seeing this, Hercules dried up the area, and thus closed the opening for the water.

35. Indeed hydra means "water" (cf. ὕδωρ). Ambrose makes mention of this in a comparison of it with heresies, saying (On Faith 1.4): "For heresy, like a certain hydra in the fables, grew from its own wounds, and as often as it would be cut down, it spread; it should be fed to the fire and will perish in a conflagration."

36. They also imagine the Chimaera as a tri-form beast: the face of a lion, the rear of a dragon, and a she-goat in the middle. Certain natural scientists of the Physiologus say that the Chimaera is not an animal but a mountain in Cilicia that nourishes lions and she-goats in some places, emits fire in some places,

and is full of serpents in some places. Because the Physiologus made this the dwelling place of Bellerophon, he is said to have killed the Chimaera.

37. Their appearance gave their name to the Centaurs, that is, a man combined with a horse. Some say that they were horsemen of Thessaly, but because, as they rushed into battle, the horses and men seemed to have one body, they maintained the fiction of the Centaurs.

38. Again, the Minotaur took its name from 'bull' and 'man.' They say in their fables that a beast of this kind was enclosed in the Labyrinth. On this, Ovid (Art of Love 2.24):
    The man half bull, and the bull half man.

39. The Onocentaur is so called because it seems to look half like a human, half like an ass. Likewise the Hippocentaur, which is thought to combine the natures of horse and human in itself.

iv. Metamorphoses (De transformatis)

1. There are accounts of certain monstrous metamorphoses and changes of humans into beasts, as in the case of that most notorious sorceress Circe, who is said to have transformed the companions of Ulysses into beasts, and the case of the Arcadians who, when their lot was drawn, would swim across a certain pond and would there be converted into wolves.

2. That the companions of Diomede were transformed into birds is not a lie from story-telling, but people assert this with historical confirmation. Some people claim that witches (Striga) were transformed from humans. With regard to many types of crimes, the appearance of the miscreants is changed and they wholly metamorphose into wild animals, by means of either magic charms or poisonous herbs.

3. Indeed, many creatures naturally undergo mutation and, when they decay, are transformed into different species – for instance bees, out of the rotted flesh of calves, or beetles from horses, locusts from mules, scorpions from crabs. Thus Ovid (Met. 15.369): If you take its curved arms from a crab on the shore a scorpion will emerge and threaten with its hooked tail.

Wonders of the East (Old English Version), in *Pride and Prodigies: Studies in the Monsters of the Beowulf-Manuscript*, trans. Andy Orchard (University of Toronto Press, 1995), pp. 189–203.

§ 8. In one land people are born who are six feet tall. They have beards to their knees, and hair to their heels. They are called Homodubii, that is 'doubtful ones', and they eat raw fish and live on them.

§11. There are people born there, who are fifteen feet tall and have white bodies and two faces on a single head, feet and knees very red, and long noses and black hair. When they want to give birth, they travel in ships to India, and bring their young into the world there.

§ 12. There is a land called Ciconia in Gallia, where people are born of threefold colour, whose heads have manes like lions' heads, and they are twenty feet tall, and have mouths as big as fans. If they see or perceive anyone in those lands, or if anyone is following them, then they take flight and flee, and sweat blood. They are thought to be men.

§ 13. Beyond the River Brixontes, east from there, there are people born big and tall, who have feet and shanks twelve feet long, flanks with chests seven feet long. They are of a black colour, and are called Hostes. As certainly as they catch a person they devour him.

§ 15. Then there is another island, south of the Brixontes, on which there are born men without heads who have their eyes and mouth in their chests. They are eight feet tall and eight feet wide.

§ 16. Dragons are born there, who are one hundred and fifty feet long, and are as thick as great stone pillars. Because of the abundance of the dragons, no one can travel easily in that land.

§ 17. From this place there is another country on the south side of the ocean, which is reckoned in the lesser measurement known as stadia 323, and in the greater which is called leuuae 255. There are born there Homodubii^ that is 'doubtful ones'. They have a human shape to the navel and below that the shape of a donkey, and they have long legs like birds, and a soft voice. If they see or perceive anyone in those lands, they run far off and flee.

§ 18. Then there is another place with barbarous people, and they have kings under them to the number of 110. They are the worst and most barbarous people, and there are two lakes there, one of the sun and the other of the moon. The suns lake is hot in the day and cold at night, and the moon's lake is hot at night and cold in the day. Their width is in the lesser measurement which is called stadia 200 units and in the greater called leuuae one hundred and thirty-three and a half.

§ 20. Then there is an island in the Red Sea where there is a race of people we call Donestre, who have grown like soothsayers from the head to the navel, and the other part is human. And they know all human speech. When they see someone from a foreign country, they name him and his kinsmen with the names of acquaintances, and with lying words they beguile him and capture him, and after that eat him all up except for the head, and then sit and weep over the head.

§ 21. Going east from there is a place where people are born who are in size fifteen feet tall and ten broad. They have large heads and ears like fans. They spread one ear beneath them at night, and they wrap themselves with the other. Their ears are very light and their bodies are as white as milk. And if they see or perceive anyone in those lands, they take their ears in their hands and go far and flee, so swiftly one might think that they flew.

§ 22. Then there is an island on which people are born whose eyes shine as brightly as if one had lit a great lantern on a dark night.

§ 26. Around those places there are born women, who have beards down to their breasts, and have made clothes out of horses hide. They are called great huntresses, and instead of dogs they breed tigers and leopards, that are the fiercest beasts. And they hunt for all the kinds of wild beasts which are born on the mountain.

§ 27. Then there are other women who have boars tusks and hair down to their heels and ox-tails on their loins. Those women are thirteen feet tall and their bodies are of the whiteness of marble. And they have camels feet and boars teeth. Because of their uncleanness they were killed by Alexander the Great of Macedon. He killed them because he could not capture them alive, because they have offensive and disgusting bodies.

§ 28. By the ocean is a breed of wild animals that is called Catini, and they are very beautiful animals. And there are people there who live on raw meat and honey.

§ 29. On the left-hand side is the kingdom in which there are wild animals called Catini, and there are hospitable people there, kings who have subdued many tyrants. Their boundaries border on the Ocean, and from there, from the left-hand section, there are many kings.

§ 30. This race of people live for many years, and they are generous people. If anyone visits them they give him a woman before they let him go. When Alexander of Macedon visited them, he was amazed at their humanity, and would not kill them or cause them any harm.

§ 32. There is another race of people there of black colour to look at, who are called Ethiopians (sigelwara).

The Travels of Marco Polo, the Venetian, ed. **Thomas Wright** (**George Bell and Sons, 1886**), pp. 368–9 and 377.

It should be known that what is reported respecting the dried bodies of diminutive human creatures, or pigmies, brought from India, is an idle tale, such pretended men being manufactured in this island in the following manner. The country produces a species of monkey, of a tolerable size, and having a countenance resembling that of a man. Those persons who make it their business to catch them, shave off the hair, leaving it only about the chin, and those other parts where it naturally grows on the human body. They then dry and preserve them with camphor and other drugs; and having prepared them in such a mode that they have exactly the appearance of little men, they put them into wooden boxes, and sell them to trading people, who carry them to all parts of the world. But this is merely an imposition, the practice being such as we have described; and neither in India, nor in any other country, however wild (and little known), have pigmies been found of a form so diminutive as these exhibit. Sufficient having been said of this kingdom, which presents nothing else remarkable, we shall now speak of another, named Samara.

Angaman is a very large island, not governed by a king. The inhabitants are idolators, and are a most brutish and savage race, having heads, eyes, and teeth resembling those of the canine species. Their dispositions are cruel, and every person, not being of their own nation, whom they can lay their hands upon, they kill and eat. They have abundance and variety of drugs. Their food is rice and milk, and flesh of every description. They have Indian nuts, apples of paradise, and may other fruits different from those which grow in our country.

**The Travels of Sir John Mandeville: The Version of the Cotton
Manuscript in Modern Spelling**, ed. A.W. Pollard (Macmillan, 1900),
pp. 105, 130, and 133–5.

In Ethiopia all the rivers and all the waters be trouble, and they be somedeal salt for
the great heat that is there. And the folk of the country be lightly drunken and have
but little appetite to meat. And they have commonly the flux of the womb. And
they live not long. In Ethiopia be many diverse folk; and Ethiope is clept Cusis. In
that country be folk that have but one foot, and they go so blyve that it is a marvel.
And the foot is so large, that it shadoweth all the body against the sun, when they
will lie and rest them. In Ethiopia, when the children be young and little, they be
all yellow; and, when that they wax of age, that yellowness turneth to be all black.

And from that isle men go by sea, from isle to isle, unto an isle that is clept
Tracoda, where the folks of that country be as beasts, and unreasonable, and dwell
in caves that they make in the earth; for they have no wit to make them houses.
And when they see any man passing through their countries they hide them in their
caves. And they eat flesh of serpents, and they eat but little. And they speak nought,
but they hiss as serpents do. And they set no price by no avoir ne riches, but only of
a precious stone, that is amongst them, that is of sixty colours. And for the name of
the isle, they clepe it Tracodon. And they love more that stone than anything else;
and yet they know not the virtue thereof, but they covet it and love it only for the
beauty.

After that isle men go by the sea ocean, by many isles, unto an isle that is
clept Nacumera, that is a great isle and good and fair. And it is in compass about,
more than a thousand mile. And all the men and women of that isle have hounds'
heads, and they be clept Cynocephales. And they be full reasonable and of good
understanding, save that they worship an ox for their God. And also every one of
them beareth an ox of gold or of silver in his forehead, in token that they love well
their God. And they go all naked save a little clout, that they cover with their knees
and their members. They be great folk and well-fighting. And they have a great
targe that covereth all the body, and a spear in their hand to fight with. And if they
take any man in battle, anon they eat him.

In one of these isles be folk of great stature, as giants. And they be hideous for
to look upon. And they have but one eye, and that is in the middle of the front. And
they eat nothing but raw flesh and raw fish.

And in another isle toward the south dwell folk of foul stature and of cursed kind
that have no heads. And their eyen be in their shoulders.

And in another isle be folk that have the face all flat, all plain, without nose and
without mouth. But they have two small holes, all round, instead of their eyes, and
their mouth is plat also without lips.

And in another isle be folk of foul fashion and shape that have the lip above the
mouth so great, that when they sleep in the sun they cover all the face with that lip.

And in another isle there be little folks, as dwarfs. And they be two so much as
the pigmies. And they have no mouth; but instead of their mouth they have a little
round hole, and when they shall eat or drink, they take through a pipe or a pen or
such a thing, and suck it in, for they have no tongue; and therefore they speak not,

but they make a manner of hissing as an adder doth, and they make signs one to another as monks do, by the which every of them understandeth other.

And in another isle be folk that have great ears and long, that hang down to their knees.

And in another isle be folk that have horses' feet. And they be strong and mighty, and swift runners; for they take wild beasts with running, and eat them.

And in another isle be folk that go upon their hands and their feet as beasts. And they be all skinned and feathered, and they will leap as lightly into trees, and from tree to tree, as it were squirrels or apes.

And in another isle be folk that be both man and woman, and they have kind of that one and of that other. And they have but one pap on the one side, and on that other none. And they have members of generation of man and woman, and they use both when they list, once that one, and another time that other. And they get children, when they use the member of man; and they bear children, when they use the member of woman.

And in another isle be folk that go always upon their knees full marvellously. And at every pace that they go, it seemeth that they would fall. And they have in every foot eight toes.

Many other diverse folk of diverse natures be there in other isles about, of the which it were too long to tell, and therefore I pass over shortly.

Bibliography

Bartlett, Robert. "Medieval and Modern Concepts of Race and Ethnicity." *Journal of Medieval and Early Modern Studies* 31/1 (2001): 39–56.

Berger, John. *Ways of Seeing*. Penguin Books, 1974.

Bildhauer, Bettina and Robert Mills. "Introduction: Conceptualizing the Monstrous." In *The Monstrous Middle Ages*. Eds. Bettina Bildhauer and Robert Mills. University of Wales Press, 2003.1–27.

Bindman, David and Henry Louis Gates, Eds. *The Image of the Black in Western Art, Volume II: From the Early Christian Era to the 'Age of Discovery'*. Jr. Belknap, 2010.

Bovey, Alixe. *Monsters and Grotesques*. University of Toronto Press, 2002.

Braga, C. "Marvelous India in Medieval European Representations." *Rupkatha Journal on Interdisciplinary Studies in Humanities* 7/2 (2015): 30–41.

Braude, Benjamin. "The Sons of Noah and the Construction of Ethnic and Geographical Identities in the Medieval and Early Modern Periods." *The William and Mary Quarterly* 54/1 (1997): 103–42.

Bynum, Caroline Walker. "Why All the Fuss About the Body? A Medievalist's Perspective." *Critical Inquiry* 22/1 (1995): 1–33.

Bynum, Caroline Walker. *Metamorphosis and Identity*. Zone Books, 2001.

Calkin, Siobhain Bly. "Marking Religion on the Body: Saracens, Categorization, and the *King of Tars*." *Journal of English and Germanic Philology* 104/2 (2005): 219–38.

Camille, Michael. *Image on the Edge: The Margins of Medieval Art*. Harvard University Press, 1992.

Camille, Michael. *The Gargoyles of Notre-Dame: Medievalism and the Monsters of Modernity*. University of Chicago Press, 2008.

Campbell, Mary B. *Witness and the Other World: Exotic European Travel Writing*. Cornell University Press, 1988.

Carroll, Noel. *The Philosophy of Horror; or, Paradoxes of the Heart.* Routledge, 1990.

Clarke, M. "The Lore of the Monstrous Races in the Developing Text of the Irish *Sex Aetates Mundi.*" *Cambrian Medieval Celtic Studies* 63 (2012): 15–49.

Cohen, Jeffrey J. "The Limits of Knowing: Monsters and the Regulation of Medieval Popular Culture." *Medieval Folklore: An Interdisciplinary, International Bi-Annual Journal Dedicated to All Aspects of Folklore in the Middle Ages and XVIth Century* 3 (1994): 1–37.

Cohen, Jeffrey J. "Monster Culture (Seven Theses)." In *Monster Theory: Reading Culture.* University of Minnesota Press, 1996.3–25.

Cohen, Jeffrey J. "The Order of Monsters: Monster Lore and Medieval Narrative Traditions." In *Telling Tales: Medieval Narratives and the Folk Tradition.* Eds. Francesca Canadé-Sautman, Diana Conchado, and Giuseppe Carlo Di Scipio. St. Martin's Press, 1998.37–58.

Cohen, Jeffrey J. *Of Giants: Sex, Monsters and the Middle Ages.* University of Minnesota Press, 1999.

Cohen, Jeffrey J. *Medieval Identity Machines.* University of Minnesota Press, 2003.

Cohen, Jeffrey J. *Hybridity, Identity, and Monstrosity in Medieval Britain: On Difficult Middles.* Palgrave Macmillan, 2006.

Cohen, Jeffrey J. "Race." In *A Handbook of Middle English Studies.* Ed. Marion Turner. Wiley Blackwell, 2013.109–22.

DeVun, Leah. "The Monstrous Races: Mapping the Borders of Sex." In *The Shape of Sex: Nonbinary Gender from Genesis to the Renaissance.* Columbia University Press, 2021.40–69.

Douglas, Mary. *Purity and Danger: An Analysis of the Concepts of Pollution and Taboo.* Routledge & Kegan Paul, 1966.

Duzer, C.V. "Bring on the Monsters and Marvels: Non-Ptolemaic Legends on Manuscript Maps of Ptolemy's Geography." *Viator: Medieval and Renaissance Studies* 45/2 (2014): 303–34.

Felton, D. "Rejecting and Embracing the Monstrous in Ancient Greece and Rome." In *The Ashgate Research Companion to Monsters and the Monstrous.* Eds. Asa Simon Mittman and Peter J. Dendle. Ashgate, 2012.103–31.

Freud, Sigmund. *The Uncanny.* Trans. David McClintock. Penguin, 2003.

Friedman, John B. *The Monstrous Races in Medieval Art and Thought.* Harvard University Press, 1981.

Friedman, John B. "Monsters at the Earth's Imagined Corners: Wonders and Discovery in the Late Middle Ages." In *Monsters, Marvels and Miracles: Imaginary Journeys and Landscapes in the Middle Ages.* Eds. Leif Søndergaard and Rasmus Hansen. University Press of Southern Denmark, 2005.41–64.

Friedman, John B. "Monsters and Monstrous Races." In *Encyclopedia of the Medieval Chronicle.* Eds. Graeme Dunphy and Cristian Bratu. Brill, 2010.

Frilingos, Christopher. *Spectacle of Empire: Monsters, Martyrs, and the Book of Revelation.* University of Pennsylvania Press, 2004.

Goldberg, David. "The Development of the Idea of Race: Classical Paradigms and Medieval Elaborations." *International Journal of the Classical Tradition* 5 (1999): 561–70.

Graham, Elaine L. *Representations of the Post/Human: Monsters, Aliens, and Others in Popular Culture.* Rutgers University Press, 2002.

Grinberg, Ana. "The Lady, the Giant, and the Land: The Monstrous in *Fierabras.*" *eHumanista* 18 (2011): 186–92.

Hahn, Thomas. "The Difference the Middle Ages Makes: Color and Race before the Modern World." *Journal of Medieval and Early Modern Studies* 31/1 (2001): 1–38.

Halpern, G. "The Monstrous Races of India in the Early Stages of Reconnaissance." In *The Routledge Handbook of Identity and the Environment in the Classical and Medieval Worlds*. Eds. Rebecca Futo Kennedy and Molly Jones-Lewis. Taylor and Francis, 2016.413–33.

Hartog, Francois. *Mirror of Herotodus: The Representation of the Other in the Writing of History*. Trans. Janet Lloyd. University of California Press, 1988.

Hassig, Debra. *The Mark of the Beast*. Routledge, 1993.

Hassig, Debra. *Medieval Bestiaries: Text, Image, Ideology*. Cambridge University Press, 1995.

Heng, Geraldine. *The Invention of Race in the European Middle Ages*. Cambridge University Press, 2018.

Houwen, L.A.J.R., Ed. *Animals and the Symbolic in Mediaeval Art and Literature*. Egbert Forsten, 1997.

Jones, T. and David Sprunger. *Marvels, Monsters, and Miracles: Studies in the Medieval and Early Modern Imaginations*. Medieval Institute Publications, 2002.

Kline, Naomi Reed. "The World of the Strange Races." In *Monsters, Marvels and Miracles: Imaginary Journeys and Landscapes in the Middle Ages*. Eds. Leif Søndergaard and Rasmus Hansen. University Press of Southern Denmark, 2005.27–40.

Kristeva, Julia. *Powers of Horror: An Essay on Abjection*. Trans. Leon Roudiez. Columbia University Press, 1982.

Kristeva, Julia. *Strangers to Ourselves*. Trans. Leon Roudiez. Columbia University Press, 1991.

McCartney, E. "Modern Analogues to Ancient Tales of Monstrous Races." *Classical Philology* 36/4 (1941): 390–4.

Mellinkoff, Ruth. "Cain's Monstrous Progeny in *Beowulf*: Part I, Noachic Tradition." *Anglo-Saxon England* 8 (1979): 143–62.

Miller, William Ian. *The Anatomy of Disgust*. Harvard University Press, 1997.

Mittman, Asa Simon. *Maps and Monsters in Medieval England*. Routledge, 2006.

Mittman, Asa Simon. "Are the 'Monstrous Races' Races?" *Postmedieval: A Journal of Medieval Cultural Studies* 6/1 (2015): 36–51.

Münkler, M. "Experiencing Strangeness: Monstrous Peoples on the Edge of the Earth as Depicted on Medieval Mappae Mundi." *The Medieval History Journal* 5/2 (2002): 195–222.

Olsen, K.E. and L.A.J.R. Houwen, Eds. *Monsters and the Monstrous in Medieval Northwest Europe*. Peeters, 2001.

Orchard, Andy. *Pride and Prodigies: Studies in the Monsters of the Beowulf Manuscript*. University of Toronto Press, 1995.

Ramey, Lynn. "Mapping the Monstrous: Humanness in the Age of Discovery." In *Black Legacies: Race and the European Middle Ages*. University Press of Florida, 2014.89–110.

Said, Edward. *Orientalism*. Vintage Books, 1979.

Salisbury, Joyce. *The Beast Within: Animals in the Middle Ages*. Routledge, 1994.

Simek, R. *Heaven and Earth in the Middle Ages: The Physical World before Columbus*. Boydell Press, 1996.

Strickland, Debra Higgs. "Monstrosity and Race in the Late Middle Ages." In *The Ashgate Research Companion to Monsters and the Monstrous*. Eds. Asa Simon Mittman and Peter J. Dendle. Ashgate, 2012.365–86.

Van Duzer, C. "A Northern Refuge of the Monstrous Races: Asia on Waldseemüller's 1516 Carta Marina." *Imago Mundi* 62/2 (2010): 221–31.

Verner, Lisa. *The Epistemology of the Monstrous in the Middle Ages*. Routledge, 2005.

Warner, Marina. *Monsters of Our Own Making: The Peculiar Pleasures of Fear*. University Press of Kentucky, 1998.

Weinstock, Jeffrey Andrew, Ed. *The Monster Theory Reader*. University of Minnesota, 2020.

Williams, David. *Deformed Discourse: The Function of the Monster in Mediaeval Thought and Literature*. McGill-Queen's University Press, 1999.

Wittkower, Rudolf. "Marvels of the East: A Study in the History of Monsters." *Journal of the Warburg and Courtauld Institutes* 5 (1942): 159–97.

Wood, Ian. "Where the Wild Things Are." In *Visions of Community in the Post-Roman World: The West, Byzantium and the Islamic World, 300–1100*. Eds. Walter Pohl, Clemens Gantner, and Richard Payne. Ashgate, 2012.531–42.

2   Non-Christians as Monsters

Jews and Muslims

The monstrous races discussed in Chapter 1 existed largely in the imaginations of medieval Europeans. If these peoples existed at all, they lived far from Europe, and the vast majority of Europeans only encountered them through texts, images, and stories. Even in cases where these peoples actually existed, the fact that medieval Europeans imagined them as monstrous had very little negative effect on them during the Middle Ages due to their lack of proximity to and contact with Europeans. There were two groups closer to home, however, that medieval Europeans also described in terms of radical alterity and monstrosity, and for whom this had profoundly negative consequences. Jews and Muslims were radically different from the majority of medieval Europeans in their religious beliefs, they lived in close proximity to western European Christians, and they were increasingly viewed as being monstrous threats to Christian society in the High and Late Middle Ages. Western European Christians routinely used the rhetoric of monstrosity against them and portrayed them as dangerous threats that had to be contained or eliminated.

Jews had inhabited a whole swath of the Roman Empire, and, as the western Roman Empire faded in the fifth century, some of these Jewish communities found themselves situated in the newly formed Germanic kingdoms of western Europe. Western Europe's Jewish communities tended to be small and were concentrated around the Mediterranean in the Early Middle Ages. While their numbers may have been small, tensions between western European Christians and their Jewish neighbors began early and intensified as the Germanic tribes converted to Catholicism. Although persecuting Jews was not habitual at this point, western European Christians intermittently subjected Jews to forced conversions, expulsions, and other forms of violence in the Early Middle Ages. By the High Middle Ages, Jews had settled all over western Europe, only to find themselves increasingly ostracized by their Christian neighbors, accused of a variety of monstrous crimes, and targeted for violence. Christian persecution of Jews increased dramatically around the time of the First Crusade in 1096 as western European Christians prepared to drive Muslims, whom they characterized as monstrous infidels, from the Holy Land. Christian knights and unruly Christian mobs massacred entire Jewish communities along the Rhine and Danube rivers as they made their way to the Holy Land, in an effort to cleanse Christendom of Jewish infidels, just as they intended to cleanse the Holy Land of Muslim infidels.

DOI: 10.4324/9780429243004-3

Although the papacy and many other Church leaders condemned this anti-Jewish violence, and some of the clergy even attempted to protect the Jews, the Christian tradition of viewing Jews as deicides, or killers of Christ, created an atmosphere in which Jews were regarded as enemies of the Christian community as a whole. The Church's official position was that the Jewish people had incurred a curse for their role in Christ's death (Matthew 27:25), that the Jews had already suffered the destruction of the Temple in 70 CE and a diaspora in fulfillment of that curse, and that all living Jews would be converted and saved when Christ returned (Romans 11:25–27). Christians were enjoined to refrain from violence against Jews but were reminded of the alleged monstrosity of the Jews even as they were told not to harm them. As Abbot Peter the Venerable of Cluny (c. 1092–1156) put it, "God does not want them (Jews) to be killed; he wants them to live, so they might live a life worse than death, like Cain, the fratricide, with the greatest torment and a greater shame." The Christian beliefs that the Jews were collectively guilty of Christ's death, that they were associated with Cain, and that Satan was the father of the Jews (John 8:44) created an environment in which western European Christians viewed Jews as monsters who posed a very real threat to Christian society.

The sense that Jews were a foreign and malignant presence within the body of Christ grew stronger over time, and ever more monstrous behaviors were attributed to Jews. By the twelfth century, stories were circulating that Jews routinely kidnapped Christian children and tortured them in mockery of Christ's crucifixion before murdering them. Some of the alleged Christian victims of these ritual murders, like William of Norwich (d. 1144) and Hugh of Lincoln (d. 1255), were venerated as martyrs. These stories first appeared in England in 1144 and then moved to the Continent, and, within a century, these tabloid stories of ritual murder were further embroidered with accusations that Jews ate the bodies or ashes of the children they had kidnapped, tortured, and murdered. Imputing such monstrous atrocities to the Jewish community authorized further Christian violence against Jews in the form of burnings, executions, and mob violence. In 1215, canon 68 of the Fourth Lateran Council required Jews and Muslims to wear distinctive clothing so they could be distinguished from Christians and avoided; it also prohibited Jews and Muslims from appearing in public over Easter weekend. This last prohibition explicitly claims that its purpose is to prevent Jews and Muslims from mocking Christians as they celebrate Christ's Passion, but it is probably also a tacit admission that Christian authorities could not protect them from popular violence at this particularly contentious time of year – a time when Christians were viscerally reminded through sermons and plays of the role that Jews had allegedly played in the trial and execution of Christ.

By the late thirteenth century, Christian anxieties had become focused on the miracle of transubstantiation and the Real Presence of Christ in the Eucharist, and the fears they projected onto Jews shifted as a result. According to the doctrine of transubstantiation, which had been re-emphasized by the Fourth Lateran Council, the wine and bread of the Eucharist are transformed into the body and blood of Christ when they are consecrated by the priest during the mass. This renewed emphasis on Christ being truly present in the Eucharist generated a wave of anxiety that Jews, or blasphemers and infidels as the Christians generally called them, might get hold of the consecrated host (the bread of the Eucharist) and use it for nefarious purposes. Christians began circulating stories about Jews procuring consecrated hosts and subjecting them to outrageous tortures in mockery of Christ's sacrifice, just as they were believed to kidnap and torture Christian children in mockery of Christ. The Jews were now portrayed not only as deicides, enemies of Christians, mockers of Christ, and murderers of children, they were also depicted as continually defiling Christ Himself in the form of the consecrated host. In all of these host desecration stories, the doctrine of transubstantiation is miraculously proven by the fact that the host bleeds or screams, or offers some other evidence that Christ is truly present in it, while the offending Jewish man is usually arrested and executed by the authorities, and his wife and children are normally converted to Christianity after witnessing these miraculous events.

Christians used these sensational charges of deicide, kidnapping, torture, murder, cannibalism, blasphemy, and host desecration to portray Jews as subhuman monsters and to justify a whole range of violence against them. Jews were massacred or subjected to forced conversion, segregated from Christians, forced to wear distinctive clothing, and, beginning in the late-twelfth century, they were expelled from various regions and kingdoms in western Europe – although the early expulsions were usually only temporary as Europe's rulers found that their economies could not function without the activity of Jewish moneylenders and permitted them to return, for a fee. By the Late Middle Ages, these expulsions were becoming more permanent as country after country in western Europe expelled its Jewish population and forced any remaining Jews to convert to Christianity.

If the tensions between Christians and Jews were largely characterized by Christian mistrust of Jews and unilateral violence against them, the tensions between Christians and Muslims were more equitable, in the sense that the violence went in both directions. After the death of Muhammed in 632 CE, Islam spread across the Arabian Peninsula and then across the Mediterranean world. Muslims invaded the Iberian Peninsula (modern Spain and Portugal) in 711, drove out the Christian Visigothic rulers, and by 750 they had established the Umayyad Caliphate of Cordoba. Muslims would continue to rule some portion of the Iberian Peninsula for the rest of the Middle Ages until the fall of the Kingdom of Granada in 1492. The Muslim advance into France through Spain was halted by Charles Martel in 732 at the Battle of Tours, and his descendant, Charlemagne, established a frontier on the border between his kingdom and the Caliphate of Cordoba to keep the Muslims confined to the Iberian Peninsula. Muslims also conquered Sicily in 827 and established small settlements on the Italian Peninsula as well. Unlike Judaism, which posed no military threat to Christendom and was not interested in proselytizing, Islam was an expansionist religion that had grown rapidly through military conquests and widespread voluntary conversions. Muslims had actively invaded western Europe and were regarded as a very real threat, but there was little Christian persecution of Muslims in the Early Middle Ages, largely because Europe's Muslims tended to live in Muslim-ruled territories.

The matter of the Holy Land further complicated Christian–Muslim relations. By the late eleventh century, the Seljuk Turks had converted to Islam and taken the

Holy Land from its previous Muslim rulers, the Fatimids. The Seljuks proved to be far less tolerant of Christians and Christian pilgrimage within their lands than their predecessors had been, and they were actively pushing into the Byzantine Empire. After repeated and increasingly urgent requests from Byzantine emperors to come to their assistance against the Seljuks, and hearing tales of Christians being brutally mistreated by Muslims in the Holy Land, western Europeans finally responded by launching the First Crusade. Pope Urban II called upon western Europe's Christians in 1095 to engage in an armed pilgrimage designed to drive the Muslims out from the Holy Land and return Jerusalem to Christian control for the first time in four centuries. Against very long odds, the First Crusade succeeded, largely because the Muslim world was divided and the Seljuks were at war with the Fatimids. The Christians exploited this opportunity, regained control of Jerusalem, and established four Latin Crusader Kingdoms; however, Muslims began to retake these territories almost immediately. For the next two centuries, Christians and Muslims would vie for control of sites that both faiths regarded as sacred until the fall of Acre, the last crusader outpost, in 1291.

From the beginning, relations between Christians and Muslims in western Europe were characterized by violence and mistrust. While there were areas where Christians and Muslims lived or worked together peacefully for long periods of time, such as Muslim Spain, southern Italy, and even the Crusader States themselves, Christian encounters with Muslims during the Middle Ages were often armed conflicts. It is also true that even against this backdrop of mutual distrust and violent aggression, Christians sometimes depicted their Muslim enemies as worthy adversaries. In *The Song of Roland* (c. 1100), for instance, the poet routinely praises the prowess of some of the Muslim warriors and calls them noble barons, before noting that demons come to collect their bodies once the Christians have killed them. For the most part, however, Christians viewed Muslims with antipathy and routinely portrayed them as blasphemous and idolatrous infidels, despite the fact that Islam strictly prohibits idolatry. Even the term Saracen, the name that medieval Christians used for all Muslims, regardless of their ethnicity, was a slur. Europeans claimed that Muslims called themselves *Saraceni* in order to pretend that they were descended from Abraham's legitimate wife Sarah, when in reality they were descended from her slave, Hagar. The term Saracen conveniently allowed Christians to brand Muslims with the humiliation of being descended from a bondswoman, and of lying to hide their resulting shame, when in fact the whole story was a Christian invention.

Both Jews and Muslims were regarded as monstrous by western Europeans primarily because of their religious difference. Christians viewed Jews as the enemies within; they were seen as dangerous threats to Christendom who challenged Christian doctrine and committed monstrous atrocities against Christ and Christians. Muslims, on the other hand, were viewed as external enemies. They were monstrous in their religion, in their behavior, and in the very real threat they posed to Christians in the form of potential conquest. While we will be examining how both groups were portrayed as monstrous in medieval Christian texts, it is worth noting that both Jews and Muslims were habitually depicted in medieval Christian art using the same monstrous iconography. In *Saracens, Demons, and Jews: Making Monsters in Medieval Art*, Debra Higgs Strickland demonstrates that all of these groups were represented in similar ways across a variety of medieval media, including stained glass and church sculptures that were regularly viewed by people from all ranks of medieval society. Western European Christians routinely represented Jews and Saracens with darkened skin that associated them with the blackness of demons, the models of monstrosity in medieval Europe, as well as monstrous features like hooked noses, beady eyes, and unruly beards. This common visual language was used by Christians not only to convey Jewish and Muslim perversity, moral degeneracy, barbarity, and their association with the demonic, but it also linked them to the monstrous races. In some cases, Muslims or Jews were even depicted with features derived from the monstrous races, like the images of dog-headed Saracens that equated Muslims with the monstrous, hybrid Cynocephali. The effect of this imagery was to associate these religious outsiders and enemies of Christians with a whole host of monstrous behaviors, vices, and habits. Like the monstrous races, Jews and Muslims were others against which Christians defined themselves and asserted their own humanity while depriving them of theirs.

This chapter will examine several western European Christian sources depicting Jews and then move on to some sources depicting Muslims. Our first source is Augustine of Hippo's *Contra Faustum* produced around 400. As we saw in Chapter 1, Augustine was revered as a Father of the Latin Church, and his works were enormously influential in western Europe throughout the Middle Ages. Augustine wrote *Contra Faustum* to rebut critiques of orthodox Christianity produced by Faustus, a Manichean heretic, who had attacked both the Old Testament and parts of the New Testament that disagreed with Manichean teachings. Augustine discusses the Jews in his defense of the Old Testament and begins by comparing the Jews to Cain, the first murderer, who killed his younger brother Abel in a jealous rage after God accepted Abel's sacrifice but rejected Cain's own. He asserts that the Jews were right to follow the Old Testament before the coming of Christ, but they were guilty of unbelief and disobedience to God when they refused to adopt Christianity. He compares this to Cain's disobedience and sin and argues that the Jews have become the servants of sin through their refusal to convert.

Augustine goes on to portray the Jews as inflamed with hatred against the Christians because God accepts the Christians' sacrifice but rejects that of the Jews. He asserts that this hatred inspired the Jews, the elder people, to kill Christ, the head of the younger people, and that Christ's blood cries out to God declaring their guilt. Like Cain, the Jews are cursed by God for their sin. Augustine declares that they are cut off from the Church and from salvation both for killing Christ and for stubbornly following the old law rather than following Christ. Augustine also connects their role in Christ's death to the loss of the Jewish kingdom and Jewish subjection to Christians. Like Cain, he says, the Jews are cursed to be outcasts and wanderers, living in constant fear that they might be killed. Augustine accuses the Jews of caring more about the death of the body than they do about God's anger with them and blames this on the fact that they are carnally minded. Still, God wants the Jews protected so that they can serve as a living reminder to Christians of the subjection they earned by killing Christ, and He promises a sevenfold vengeance to anyone who kills the Jews. Finally, Augustine compares the Jewish observance of the law to the mark of Cain. He says that no matter which nation has historically subjugated the Jews, they never ceased practicing their law and that no ruler has ever sought to kill them, by which he means that no ruler has forced them to abandon their faith. Only if a Jew converts to Christianity can he ever cease to be an outcast and return to God's presence.

Augustine's portrayal of the Jews repeats many themes that were already widely accepted by Christians by this time. He declares that the Jews are disobedient and impious, that their jealousy and hatred inspired them to kill Christ, and that their pride causes them to continue fruitlessly observing their law even in the face of God's wrath. Augustine explicitly compares the Jews to Cain the fratricide, calling them a cursed and marked people, but he also accuses them of the sin of pride and draws an implicit comparison with Lucifer, who rebelled against God and was cast out of heaven. Most importantly, Augustine portrays the Jews as the enemies of Christ and Christians and offers a rationale for their subjugation to Christians by arguing that it is part of God's curse for them to live in terrifying subjection to the people God favors. He also notes that the Jews are not to be killed or forcibly converted because God wants them to exist as a living memorial to the punishment they incurred for killing Christ. The monstrosity of the Jews consists of their religious disobedience, their willful sinfulness, and their monstrous behavior in re-enacting the sin of Cain by killing Christ – their sins have merited perpetual subjugation to Christians.

Augustine was not the only Christian author to portray the Jews in this way. Numerous treatises and homilies in the Early Middle Ages presented Jews in a very similar manner, accusing them of committing the most heinous crime in killing Christ, attributing a long list of sins to them, equating them with Cain, and finally reminding Christians that they were not to harm the Jews because God wanted them to live in infamy. It is unsurprising that violence against Jews broke out from time to time in the Early Middle Ages as Christians were constantly assured by religious authorities that Jews had killed Christ and were the enemies of Christians. Still, we have no records of large-scale Christian violence against Jews in western Europe until the First Crusade at the end of the eleventh century. Two main factors seem to have been driving this violence. The first is that the Church was going through a reforming period in the second half of the eleventh century. While these reforms focused on purifying the clergy by prohibiting activities like clerical marriage and simony (the buying and selling of spiritual things like church offices) that were now seen as serious abuses, the reformers also emphasized the need to purify the body of Christ, by which they meant the entire Christian community or Christendom. The Jews who lived in western Europe inhabited this Christian world and yet were not part of it. They were religious dissidents who refused to accept Christianity and who sometimes pointed out inconsistencies or implausibilities in Christian doctrine. They were believed to be responsible for the death of Christ, and they were increasingly viewed as a deviant and dangerous contaminant within the body of Christ.

The second factor behind the increase in anti-Jewish violence is the crusade mentality itself and the rhetoric that was used to authorize the crusade. As we will see in the section on Muslims later in the chapter, beginning in 1095, the papacy actively encouraged western European Christians to violently eliminate Muslims from the Holy Land to cleanse the Christian holy sites of infidels or nonbelievers. Crusaders and ordinary people were whipped into a frenzy of religious zeal and promised spiritual rewards for participating in this project. As the various contingents that made up the First Crusade wended their way east, some of them turned their violence on the unbelievers already residing among them – the Jews. We have many accounts of the violence these groups inflicted on Jews along the Rhine and Danube from both Christian and Jewish perspectives, but nothing that clearly indicates the crusaders' motives. What we do know is that the crusaders extorted Jewish communities, subjected them to forced conversion, and massacred any Jews who would not convert. Members of some Jewish communities, like the one at Mainz, chose to commit suicide to escape this violence. We also know that many Christian clerics tried to protect their local Jewish communities, but their efforts largely failed. It seems the Christians who made up these mobs had internalized the centuries-old Christian teaching that the Jews were the killers of Christ and the enemies of Christians, but discarded the Christian injunction not to harm the Jews when it suited them.

The violence perpetrated against Jews on the eve of the First Crusade clearly remained on the minds of the Christian clergy as they called for a second crusade in response to the County of Edessa being recaptured by Muslims in 1144. The great preacher of the Second Crusade, Abbot Bernard of Clairvaux (1090–1153), sent appeals to the leaders of western Europe entreating them to participate in this effort that specifically warned against harming Jews. In his "Letter to England to Summon the Second Crusade (1146)," for example, Bernard praises the zeal for God's glory that inspires the English but warns that their zeal needs to be restrained. He specifically says that the Jews are not to be persecuted or killed, that they are a living reminder to Christians of what Christ suffered, and that they have been scattered all over the world both as punishment for their crimes and so they can witness the redemption of the Christians. Like Augustine, Bernard asserts that the Jews are condemned to endure a hard captivity under Christian rulers, but unlike Augustine, he also emphasizes the apostle Paul's assurance that all living Jews will be converted and saved when Christ returns. He says that if the Muslims were similarly subjected to Christian rule, it would be unnecessary for Christians to go on the offensive against them, but since Muslims are attacking Christians, Christians are obliged to use force against them. He ends with a call to vanquish the proud Muslims but spare the subjected Jews who will be converted and saved when Christ returns and even reminds his readers that Christ himself was Jewish.

Bernard's portrayal of the Jews rehearses many of the same themes we saw in Augustine's *Contra Faustum*. The Jews are living reminders of Christ's suffering and have been dispersed and subjected to Christian rule as punishment for the crime of killing Christ. However, Bernard dispenses with comparing the Jews to Cain and instead emphasizes the fact that the Jews will be converted and saved when Christ returns and that they must be protected for this prophecy to be ful-filled. His change of emphasis and his tone reflect the lingering concern among the clergy over the anti-Jewish violence of the First Crusade. This is not to say, however, that the clergy stopped portraying the Jews in monstrous terms. For cler-ics like Bernard, the crusades were holy endeavors, and they required strict moral behavior from everyone involved, including the knights, if they were to succeed. Whenever any military action failed that the Christians believed should have had God's support, they blamed their own moral failings and rationalized their defeat by assuming that God was angry with them and punishing them by withholding victory until they corrected their behavior. Bernard's focus on portraying the Jews as a people who must be protected is not driven by any special compassion for the Jews; it has a clear motive, and that is to ensure that the Christian knights do not compromise their chance at victory by disobeying God.

There is one other element of Bernard's call to the Second Crusade that deserves comment, and that is his casual association of Jews with moneylending. By the mid-twelfth century when Bernard was writing, this association was already well-established. Jews were prohibited from loaning money at interest to other Jews, but many Jews in western Europe loaned money to their Christian neighbors and either earned a living or supplemented their income by charging interest. The stereotype of the Jewish moneylender arose in part due to the fact that the Church was trying to prevent Christians, especially monks, from lending money at interest to other Christians in the twelfth century. However, Bernard himself indicates that this did not prevent Christians from engaging in the business. There were still Christian moneylenders in Christendom. Although Bernard says this is only the case where there are no Jews, we have plenty of evidence that Christians engaged in money-lending alongside Jews and in spite of injunctions against it. Bernard goes on to say that Christian moneylenders behave worse than Jews and questions whether they can even be called Christians. This association between the Jews and money-lending, and between moneylending and immoral, unchristian behavior developed into the negative stereotype of the Jewish moneylender, which has often been used to explain anti-Jewish violence in the High Middle Ages. The problem with this explanation is that it ignores the long tradition of Christian anti-Jewish invective that had nothing to do with moneylending and focused on the Jews as the murder-ers of Christ, and it ignores the fact that Christian violence toward the Jews began long before the association between Jews and moneylending was established. By the twelfth century, Jewish participation in moneylending was certainly helping to fuel anti-Jewish resentment and violence among Christians in western Europe, but it did not cause it.

Peter the Venerable, the abbot of Cluny and a contemporary of Bernard of Clair-vaux, expands on many of the same themes in his anti-Jewish polemic, *Against the Inveterate Obduracy of the Jews*. Peter wrote both this work and his anti-Muslim polemic that we will examine later in this chapter, in the context of defending Christianity from the enemies of the Church and asserting the truth of Christian doctrine. Both works describe the other religion in monstrous terms meant to elicit disgust. In his prologue, Peter castigates the Jews for their refusal to accept

Christianity, calling them stiff-necked people and asserting that God has kindled His wrath against them in order to destroy them. He claims that the stubbornness of the Jews is so great, and their animosity toward Christians so boundless, that it drove them to kill Stephen, the first Christian martyr. Peter casually refers to the Jews as traitors and murderers, who have always resisted the Holy Spirit, and points out that the Jews have not only lost the heavenly kingdom as a result of their refusal to accept Christ, they have lost their earthly kingdom as well. Peter goes on to encourage the Jews to convert to Christianity, saying that they need not fear that they have slain Christ because he is not intent on avenging his death. He says that Christ's compassion is so great that he will receive even mockers and murderers. Even as Peter seemingly pleads with the Jews to convert, he describes them in monstrous terms and reminds his readers of their horrifying crimes.

Finally, Peter includes a reminder that Christ's coming was prophesized in Jewish scripture and that Christ himself was a Jew and not a member of a "barbarous" race. He rhetorically asks why the Jews are not moved by the fact that the Christian religion is a fulfillment of Jewish scripture and makes this point central to his argument about Jewish obduracy. By doing so, he effectively charges that the Jews do not believe in the truth of their own religious tradition and that their rejection of Christianity is also a rejection of Jewish scripture. Peter's depiction of the Jews in this passage reveals one of the aspects of Judaism that western Christians found most threatening – the Jewish refusal to accept the truth of Christianity and convert might cause Christians to reject, or at the very least question, their own religious beliefs. If the Jews did not accept Jesus as the Messiah predicted in their own scriptures, then perhaps it was the Christians who were mistaken. This possibility clearly motivated a great deal of Christian polemic against the Jews. It required Christians to vigorously assert the truth of their own beliefs and explain why the Jews refused to convert.

The sense that the Jews were the enemies of Christians intensified in the High and Late Middle Ages. About the time that Bernard of Clairvaux and Peter the Venerable were writing, a new charge against the Jews arose in England – ritual murder. The first alleged victim of this crime was William of Norwich, a 12-year-old boy whose corpse was discovered in 1144. Although the Christians of Norwich blamed William's death on the town's Jewish community and demanded justice, the local sheriff took the Jews into protective custody and none of them were ever charged with the crime. Most of the information we have about William's death comes from an account written by Thomas of Monmouth about 30 years later in 1173, *The Life and Miracles of Saint William of Norwich*, and its purpose was to record William's martyrdom for the benefit of the cult that had grown up around him at Norwich. In this version of events, Thomas asserts that the Jews of Norwich kidnapped William and tortured and killed him in mockery of Christ. Thomas' alleged informant, a converted Jew named Theobald, apparently also told him that the murder was ordered by a Jewish leader in Narbonne, France, that such human sacrifices were required by Jewish scripture and occurred annually, and that they were intended both to punish Christ for the persecution the Jews suffered at the hands of the Christians and enable the Jews to return to the Holy Land.

Despite the fact that there seems to have been no real evidence against the Jews of Norwich, and the fact that none of them were prosecuted, this tale of Jewish violence against Christians resonated. It incorporated almost every anxiety that western European Christians had about their Jewish neighbors. It claimed that there was a vast, international Jewish conspiracy to sacrifice a Christian child each year, that the Jewish scriptures required these murders, and that the Jews committed these murders partly as a form of revenge for their persecution by the Christians. The charges were custom-made to assuage the guilty consciences of Christians for persecuting the Jews and simultaneously assert that the Jews were monsters who deserved such persecution because their hatred of Christians ran so deep that they regularly kidnapped and killed Christian children.

By the end of the twelfth century, sensational ritual murder accusations were helping to fuel the persecution of Jews in England and France. Although the local sheriff protected the Jewish community of Norwich, other Jewish communities were not so lucky. Similar charges against the Jews of Blois in 1171, for instance, resulted in many of the town's Jewish inhabitants being burned to death, and spontaneous mob violence against the Jews became depressingly routine in England in the late-twelfth century. In his chronicle of Richard I's reign, the monk Richard of Devizes (fl. 1191) mentions the outbursts of anti-Jewish violence that surrounded the king's coronation. He says that the Londoners began immolating the Jews to their father, the Devil, on the day of Richard's coronation, that it took them almost two days to complete their work, and that the other towns and cities followed London's lead in killing their Jewish populations. Richard frames these massacres as acts of faith, as sacrifices or holocausts, and variously calls the Jews bloodsuckers, incorrigible, and worms. In fact, he seems to disapprove of the fact that the people of Winchester did not similarly exterminate their Jewish community at the time and notes that they waited until later when they could "cast out all the morbid matter once and for all." Richard's language here reflects the fact that the Jews were viewed as a disease within the body of Christ, a monstrous and malignant growth that posed a threat to the health of Christendom.

There has been a great deal of debate about whether Richard of Devizes meant this description of mob violence and the ritual murder accusation that we will examine next as satire, so we should be careful not to take his words as firm evidence of his own personal beliefs. I have included his descriptions in this collection because they are so vivid and because, whether they were intended as satire or not, they still tell us a great deal about Christian attitudes toward and beliefs about Jews. Even if Richard intended to mock the actions and beliefs of his fellow Christians in his presentation of these events (and he often has his tongue firmly in his cheek elsewhere in his chronicle), he would have to be exaggerating fairly common attitudes toward the Jews in order to satirize them. With this caveat in mind, we can look at Richard's depiction of a ritual murder accusation in Winchester, where he lived and wrote in the monastery of St. Swithun.

Richard begins his description of the ritual murder accusation by saying that the Jews of Winchester earned a reputation for martyring a boy. This boy was an orphan, an immigrant from France who was employed by a Jewish cobbler in

Winchester. Richard says that the cobbler, whom he refers to as a devil, seduced the boy with gifts and planned his murder in advance. He then details how this Christian boy came to be working for the Jewish cobbler in Winchester, saying that a certain French Jew had persuaded him to seek his fortune in England – a land flowing with milk and honey. After describing the vile inhabitants and disgusting conditions of other English cities, the French Jew directs the boy to settle in Winchester, which he describes as having the most merciful monks, the wisest clerics, the most courteous citizens, and the most beautiful women. He also calls Winchester the Jerusalem of the Jews, remarking that only there do the Jews enjoy perpetual peace. The only drawback to this otherwise delightful city is that all of its inhabitants lie like sentries. Richard clearly mocks the locals here, saying that no other place generates so many false rumors, but otherwise the people of Winchester are truthful in all things. Richard may in fact be referencing the rumor of this particular ritual murder in making these comments and implying that it was fabricated, but his account of the ritual murder accusation features elements that correspond to those found in other twelfth-century English ritual murder accusations.

After being tutored by the French Jew on where to seek his fortune in England, the boy and his companion set off for Winchester with a few tools and a letter of introduction to a certain Jew of Winchester written in Hebrew that they cannot read. The Jew of Winchester welcomes them with feigned kindness. One night near Passover, the boy fails to return home to his companion who fears something horrible has happened to his friend. After looking for his friend for several days, the companion goes to the Jew to ask if he knows of his friend's whereabouts. The Jew greets him harshly, and the boy loudly accuses him of having crucified his friend, calling the Jew a thief, traitor, and devil. When the neighbors come running to see what is happening, the boy accuses the Jew of cutting his friend's throat, and says he has probably eaten him too. He also charges that the French Jew, who he calls a son of the devil, gave his friend a letter to give to this man and implies that it must have led to his murder as he was last seen in the Jew's house. The boy's accusations were supported in part by a Christian woman who worked for the Jews and swore that she had last seen the other boy go into the Jew's storeroom and never return. Richard notes that the matter went to court, but the boy's testimony was rejected because he was under-age, and the woman's testimony was rejected because she was infamous for being employed by Jews. The matter was settled by a combination of bribery and the Jew swearing an oath to his innocence. Here, Richard seems to be both mocking the widely held assumption that Jews killed Christian children and blaming the legal system for failing to appropriately prosecute the ritual murder accusation, or at least pointing out that the legal system could be easily manipulated by bribing the judges.

This ritual murder accusation is unusual in some ways. Richard seems to mock his fellow Christians for their credulousness by playing upon established tropes. However, the story also echoes elements found in other contemporary stories and tells us a great deal about Christian attitudes toward the Jews in England in the 1190s. The Jews are portrayed as dangerous, conniving devils who routinely prey upon, and possibly eat, Christian children. They are evil incarnate. Even if Richard meant this as a caricature, it draws upon widely held assumptions about the Jews. Indeed, he portrays these assumptions about the Jews as being so pervasive by the late twelfth century that the missing boy's companion jumps to the conclusion that the Jewish cobbler must have crucified his friend when he realizes that he was last seen in the Jew's house. Finally, Richard's presentation of the way in which the case was prosecuted reveals some contempt for the legal system. His portrayal of the accused Jew manipulating the legal system and avoiding prosecution by bribing officials may indicate that he himself held anti-Jewish sentiments, and thus reframe our understanding of the preceding narrative, or it may simply be an admission that English judges were highly susceptible to bribery.

The next account of a ritual murder accusation against the Jews we will examine presents fewer challenges in that there is no question about whether the author is engaging in satire: it depicts the murder in painstaking and gruesome detail, it portrays the Jewish antagonist as purely evil, the Jews in general as enemies of Christ and Christians, and the murdered child as a martyr. *The Passion of Adam of Bristol* was written by an anonymous author, probably in the middle of the thirteenth century, and survives in a single manuscript dating from the early fourteenth century (BL Harleian MS 957, no. 7). The story centers on the ritual murder of a young boy, Adam of Bristol, by a certain Jew named Samuel who is assisted by his wife and son. Having been instructed by his father in procuring victims, Samuel's son lures Adam to their home, promising Adam that his father will give them apples and making sure that no one sees Adam with him. The family entertains Adam until the boy says he wants to go home, and then their loving welcome turns to vicious torment. Samuel strips Adam, binds him hand and foot, gags him, and finally nails him to a cross he has erected in their privy for this purpose. Samuel repeatedly states that he intends to take vengeance on Christ and his mother Mary by torturing and killing Adam and reveals that he has already murdered three local Christian boys in the same fashion. Samuel's explicit desire to avenge himself on Christ by killing Christians echoes many of the texts we have already examined that imputed this desire to Jews in general. However, the charge in the text that Samuel has already tortured and murdered three other boys for the same purpose heightens the monstrosity of his actions. Instead of committing a single ritual murder, Samuel is charged with being a serial torturer and killer of Christians whose hatred for Christ knows no bounds.

In the section that follows, the author lingers over describing the various tortures that Samuel and his family inflict on Adam. They strike Adam and spit on him, Samuel's wife cuts off Adam's nose and lips, they give him a bitter drink, drag him around the house, kick and stomp him, and roast him over a fire. Samuel, his wife, and their son all participate in the torture and are all portrayed as monstrous enemies of Christ. Throughout the prolonged description of the torture, Samuel is portrayed as variously addressing Adam as Christ, telling Adam that he will die on account of Christ, and daring Christ to free Adam and prove that He is God. As the family are roasting their victim, God finally responds. A deep voice issues from Adam's body declaring in Hebrew that he is the God of Abraham, Isaac, and Jacob and telling Samuel that he is persecuting God in killing these Christian boys. Notably, the voice of God reminds everyone that Samuel has already done this three times! At this point, Samuel's wife begins to have second thoughts about killing Adam and wants to put him to bed until he recovers enough that they can question him about the voice, but Samuel insists on returning him to the cross in the privy. After nailing Adam to the cross a second time, they question Adam, who tells them that Mary and Jesus came to comfort him in his tribulations but recalls nothing about the voice speaking in Hebrew. Completely unmoved, Samuel says that if this is so, why has Christ not healed Adam's wounds. He adds that if this boy Jesus that Adam claims to have seen shows up, he will nail him to the cross and punish him too! Finally, Samuel stabs Adam in the heart and kills him. There is an illumination for this section depicting Samuel stabbing Adam with a knife. Samuel is portrayed with a prominent hooked nose and has a gargoyle-like figure breathing fire above him. The image uses the iconography of monstrosity to convey the bestial nature of the Jews in general through the feature of the hooked nose, and the demonic influence behind Samuel's actions as the gargoyle-like figure is almost certainly a demon egging Samuel on to monstrous deeds.

At this point in the narrative, Samuel's wife realizes that they have sinned and expresses her remorse and her belief in Christ. Her husband, furious, says that Christ was nothing but a magician and an evil-doer. When his wife says that she wishes to be baptized, Samuel stabs her to death. Here, the voice of Christ is interpolated in the text to assure the reader that Christ has taken her soul to heaven along with Adam's because she died confessing her belief in him and asking him for mercy. Samuel's son undergoes a similar conversion, and Samuel also stabs him to death. Again, the text assures us that his soul is led to heaven by angels. Conversions like these are common in ritual murder accounts and in other miracle stories involving Jews. It was common for the wife and children of the Jewish antagonist to convert after witnessing miraculous events like these, but for the Jewish antagonist himself (and it is always a male) to remain stubbornly opposed to Christ, even in the face of miraculous evidence that should have convinced him of Christ's divinity. This stubbornness echoes the charge laid against the Jews by Peter the Venerable and other members of the Christian clergy who portrayed the Jews as implacably opposed to Christ and obdurate in their refusal to recognize the truth of the Christian faith. Samuel perfectly embodies this Christian caricature of Jewish obduracy. What is unusual is the fact that Samuel kills his own wife and son because they want to be baptized. It is more usual in these stories for the wife and child to survive and fulfill Christian fantasies of miraculous conversions, thereby proving the truth of Christianity and the falsity of Judaism. In this case, the fact that Samuel murders his own wife and son demonstrates just how monstrous and inhuman he is, and it provides the opportunity for the author to assure us that both Samuel's wife and son were received into heaven.

After murdering his wife and child, Samuel is still unmoved. As he buries Adam in the latrine, along with the nails and cross used to crucify him, he damns Christ for having taken his wife and son from him. The second half of the narrative recounts Samuel's efforts to conceal his monstrous crimes with the help of his sister and the complications presented by the fact that the privy where Adam is buried is now inhabited by an angel carrying a sword. Samuel's sister agrees to help him bury the bodies of his wife and son inside the house, while telling the neighbors that they have left him, and procure a discreet Christian priest to remove Adam's body from the latrine and take it far from Bristol. They shut up Samuel's house, Samuel goes to live with his sister, and they find an Irish priest who agrees to remove the body, reburies it in Ireland under angelic instruction, and miraculously forgets its location. The important components of this section for our purposes are that Samuel reaffirms his hatred for Christ in confessing his deeds to his sister, while she tells him to stop killing innocent Christians. At one point, Samuel's sister goes to see the angel in the privy and is awed by what she witnesses, but stops short of actual conversion. Samuel's sister presents an interesting counterpoint to Samuel himself. She agrees to help him only because the discovery of his deeds would put the whole Jewish community in danger, she recognizes that he is driven by irrational hatred, and although she also stubbornly refuses to believe in Christianity after witnessing a variety of miraculous events, she offers an alternative to Samuel's actions in her resolve to hold to Jewish law without perpetrating monstrous crimes against Christians.

Our final selection on Jews is an account of the first known accusation of host desecration against the Jews that occurred in Paris in 1290. The Italian author, Giovanni Villani, included this short description in the chronicle he wrote in the early fourteenth century. According to Villani, a certain Jewish moneylender in Paris agreed to return some clothes a Christian woman had pawned to him in exchange for a consecrated host. The woman, who Villani describes as greedy and gullible, agreed to the bargain. She went to communion on Easter morning, kept the host she received there, and brought it back to the Jew. The Jew then subjected the host to various tortures. He boiled it in water and, when this achieved nothing, he stabbed it with a knife. This caused the host to bleed and color the water red. Next, he removed the host from the boiling water and placed it in cold water, where it stained the water red again. At this point, some Christians arrived to borrow money, saw what the Jew had been doing, and witnessed the host miraculously spring up on to a table by itself. Villiani says that the Jew was captured and burned, the host was collected and preserved, and a church known as the Savior of the Boiling Water was built where the miracle had occurred.

This accusation of host desecration is short, but it includes some important details. First, the incident occurs at Easter, a time when Christian anxieties about Jews were particularly high. This reenactment of Christ's passion through torturing the consecrated host comes at precisely the same time that Christians were celebrating Christ's passion. Later host desecration stories often take place near the feast of Corpus Christi, which was formally established in 1264 to celebrate the Real Presence of Christ in the eucharist. Second, we can see that the association between Jews and moneylending is firmly set by the end of the thirteenth century and that the Jewish moneylender uses the fact that he holds Christian debts for nefarious purposes. Christians were particularly anxious about the fact that their indebtedness to Jewish moneylenders made them potentially vulnerable to deals such as the one we see in this story. In this case, the woman's simplicity and greed lead her to agree to deliver a consecrated host to the Jewish moneylender. Finally, this accusation emphasizes the miracle of transubstantiation. It asserts that the consecrated host is truly the body of Christ and that it bleeds when stabbed and moves of its own volition. Although the account is brief and early, it already contains elements that are repeated and embroidered in later stories. In fact, the only element missing is the miraculous conversion of the Jew's wife and child.

Although accusations of ritual murder still occurred, tales of host desecration surpassed them in the fourteenth century and spread throughout western Europe. By the fifteenth century, the Christian belief that Jews tortured the consecrated host in mockery of Christ's sacrifice was even being dramatized in morality plays like *The Croxton Play of the Sacrament*. These plays, which were probably performed during Easter or Corpus Christi celebrations, not only asserted the truth of the doctrine of transubstantiation, but they also vividly reminded Christians of alleged Jewish (and Muslim) monstrosity. In the Croxton play, for instance, the antagonists are described as five Jews who worship Muhammed, in an odd conflation of the Jewish and Islamic faiths. The men purchase the host from a greedy Christian merchant with the explicit intention of disproving transubstantiation, then pierce the host with five wounds in reenactment of the crucifixion. When the host bleeds from these wounds, they attempt to destroy it in boiling oil, but it stubbornly clings to the hand of the main antagonist, Jonathas. When they finally succeed in submerging it in the boiling oil, along with Jonathas' hand, the oil seethes with blood. Finally, they shut the host in an oven only to witness the Christ child miraculously emerge from the oven with five bloody wounds and rebuke them for their unbelief and cruelty. Christ heals Jonathas' hand and sends all five men to the local bishop to confess. In this case, the men are converted to Christianity by what they have witnessed, the Christian merchant repents for his part in the affair, and the miracle of transubstantiation is proven by Christ's actual appearance.

Western European Christians viewed Jews as monstrous primarily due to their religious difference, and the same is true of Muslims. The primary distinction between the two groups is that medieval Christians held Jews responsible for the death of Christ and believed Jews were driven to commit monstrous crimes against Christians by their hatred for Christ, while they viewed Muslims as an existential threat to Christendom and as defilers of Christian holy places. We can see this in the way Muslims are depicted in the call to the First Crusade. Our first source treating Muslims is Fulcher of Chartres' account of Pope Urban II's speech at Clermont in 1095 calling the First Crusade. Fulcher (c. 1059–1127) was a priest who participated in the First Crusade and may have been present at the Council of Clermont and witnessed Urban's speech. In Fulcher's version of Pope Urban's speech, he focuses on the fact that the Turks and Arabs have successfully invaded the Byzantine Empire. He charges that the Muslims have already killed many Christians and destroyed Christian churches and warns that more Christians will be attacked if the Muslims are not stopped. He urges Christians to destroy the Muslims and asserts that anyone who dies on this enterprise will have immediate remission of their sins. What is most notable for our purposes is the way in which Fulcher characterizes Muslims. In addition to calling them infidels, he also calls them a vile, despised, and base race, barbarians, pagans who worship demons, and enemies of the Lord. While we might expect Fulcher to use abusive language in characterizing a military enemy, the specific language he chooses is revealing. The Muslims are not just an existential threat to Christians, they are a monstrous threat. They are not just infidels or unbelievers, they are barbaric, demon-worshipping pagans. These terms are meant to elicit disgust and to portray Muslims as barely human. Fulcher describes the Christians, on the other hand, as friends of the Lord who Christ commands to destroy the vile Muslims.

In Robert the Monk's account of Urban II's speech, we see him expanding on the themes in Fulcher's account and lingering over the alleged monstrosity of the Muslims. Robert (c. 1055–1122) claims to have been present at the Council of Clermont but is reconstructing Urban's speech at least a decade after the event. Robert says that Urban began by calling the Franks, who were gathered to hear the speech, a race beloved and chosen by God. He then details the horrors that the Muslims have committed as a prelude to urging the Franks to come to the aid of their fellow Christians. He says a race from the kingdom of the Persians has been committing atrocities, and he calls them an accursed race that is utterly alienated from God. As for their atrocities, they not only kill Christians but also cruelly torture them by disemboweling them, flogging them, using them for archery practice, and hacking at their necks while attempting to decapitate them.

According to Robert, Urban reminds the Franks of the deeds of their ancestors, particularly their history of destroying pagans and extending the reach of the Christian church. He calls on them to live up to the legacy of their ancestors by driving out the Muslims who pollute Christian holy places with their filthiness and rescue Jerusalem from that wicked race. He reminds the Franks that Jerusalem is where Christ suffered, died, and was buried, and that it is now held by Christ's enemies. Robert reports that the Franks, roused by Urban's speech, responded, "it is the will of God!" Finally, Robert says that Urban issued instructions that everyone embarking on this holy pilgrimage should wear the sign of the cross on his forehead or breast, thus fulfilling Christ's injunction to take up the cross and follow him.

In Robert's account of Urban's speech, he presents the Franks as God's chosen people and champions, while portraying the Muslims as Christ's enemies. What is most interesting for our purposes is how Robert expands upon the theme of Muslims as the enemies of Christ and Christians to render them horrifyingly monstrous. He describes them not just as destroyers, but also as defilers who pollute Christian holy places with their filthiness. He asserts that they do not simply murder their victims, they gratuitously torture and rape them. He calls them not only a cursed race, but also one that is utterly alienated from God. Robert's anti-Muslim invective is intended to call the Franks to arms and present the Muslims as a monstrous affront to God who must be eradicated. Robert presents Islam as a false and vile religion and portrays Muslims as monsters who are violent, cruel, sexually depraved, filthy, and polluting.

One of the most notable aspects of Christian representations of Islam around the time of the First Crusade is just how inaccurate they are. In *The Song of Roland*, for instance, the anonymous Christian author portrays Muslims as inverted Christians who worship a trinity of gods: Mohammed, Termagant, and Apollo. He clearly misunderstands the role of the prophet Muhammed and includes him in this strange collection of deities. The author also continually refers to Muslims as idolators and pagans, despite the fact that Islam is one of the world's great monotheistic religions. While Christians living in close proximity to Muslims or under Muslim rulers were more familiar with Islam, many western European Christian texts depicting Muslims display a great deal of basic ignorance about the Islamic faith. Even as western European Christians became better informed about Islam during the twelfth century, their priority when writing about Islam was to depict it as a false religion and to demonstrate that Muhammed was a monstrous fraud, a heretic who had misled his followers and deprived them of salvation.

The Benedictine monk and historian, Guibert of Nogent (c. 1055–1124), develops these themes in his *Deeds of God through the Franks*, an account of the First crusade written about 1107/8. While Guibert did not participate in the First Crusade and his narrative largely relies on an earlier history written by an eye-witness, the *Gesta Francorum* (*Deeds of the Franks*), his work, contains an account of Muhammed and an explanation of Islam that, while much less inaccurate than the portrayal of Islam found in *The Song of Roland*, still monstrously perverts the Islamic faith and portrays Muhammed as a fraud who was eaten by pigs. Guibert correctly identifies Muhammed, whom he calls Mathomus or Mahomet, as the prophet who brought Islam to the world, and he correctly describes Muslims as monotheists who worship the same God as Jews and Christians. However, Guibert charges that Muhammed's teachings amount to little more than requiring circumcision and allowing every other kind of licentiousness. Guibert also reveals that he has not been able to find anything written about Muhammed's life and that he is basing his account of Muhammed entirely on what he has heard others say. He dismisses any questions about whether his information is accurate by saying that Muhammed already has such a terrible reputation that he can "safely speak ill of a man whose malignity transcends and surpasses whatever evil can be said of him."

Guibert describes Islam as heresy that originated in Alexandria. He says that when a certain patriarch of Alexandria died, a hermit was chosen to lead the church (this hermit figure is derived from Bahira, a Nestorian monk who, according to Islamic tradition, foretold that Muhammed would become a great prophet). When some of the local Christians visited the hermit and realized that he disagreed with them about the Catholic faith, they abandoned him and began condemning him. Scorned, the hermit determined to wreak his vengeance by spreading the poison of false belief and undermining Catholic teachings. At this point, Guibert says that Satan approached the hermit and told him that if he wanted to have greater power than even the patriarch, he should seek out Muhammed and fill his ears with his false teachings so they would be spread far and wide. The hermit then sought out Muhammed and did as the devil instructed. Guibert tells us that Muhammed was a poor man, and because wealthy men carry more authority, he set out to marry a wealthy widow (this is a reference to Muhammed's first wife Khadijah). The hermit advised this widow to remarry and told her that he had found a prophet for her who would provide for her in this life and the next. Through this marriage,

Muhammed was lifted to great wealth and power, but Guibert charges that it also gave him epilepsy. He says that the prophet contracted this disease through the couple's frequent sexual exchanges. Guibert asserts that Muhammed often suffered from terrible seizures that frightened his wife. Fearing her husband was insane, she went back to the hermit who assured her that the seizures were a sign that Muhammed was being visited by God. The hermit's words transformed how she saw her husband's illness, and she now regarded his seizures as being sacred and became his most devoted supporter.

As for Muhammed, Guibert charges that the hermit was filling him with diabolical teachings, and that his reputation as a prophet was growing. Once Muhammed had gained a following, Guibert says he decided to write a law (the Qur'an) that permitted every vice in order to gain even more followers. Guibert alleges that Muhammed hatched a plan to deceive his followers and ordered them to fast for three days while praying to God to grant them a law. He also told his followers that if God granted them a law, he would do so through an unusual sign. Meanwhile, Guibert tells us that Muhammed took the book he had written and tied it to the horns of a cow he had trained and hid her in his tent. On the third day of fasting and prayer, Muhammed climbed onto a high platform and began to speak in a loud voice. Hearing the voice of her master, the cow came running to him bearing the book that he had attached to her horns. Everyone was amazed, thinking that this was the sign from God that they had been waiting for. They removed the book from the cow's horns, and Muhammed read it to the crowd. Guibert says that the people happily accepted the license permitted by its foul law and goes on to allege that it allowed random copulation and condemned Christian morality. Guibert charges that the book allowed men to go beyond the sexual appetites of beasts and to fulfill their lusts with multiple whores under the pretense of procreating children. He also asserts that Muhammed's followers were not satisfied with these sexual acts, but engaged in other sexual acts so deviant they were not even known among animals.

Guibert follows this description of the depravity of Muhammed's law and the immorality of his followers with an account of the prophet's death, saying that one day he was walking alone when he fell down with a seizure. As he was writhing on the ground, some pigs came by and devoured his entire body, except for his heels. Guibert remarks that Muhammed was fittingly eaten by pigs because he himself was a pig, and that this master of filth died an appropriately filthy death. As for his heels, which the pigs did not devour, Guibert says they were left behind just as he had left behind his false belief and foulness in his followers. Guibert inserts an epitaph for Muhammed that reiterates his pig-like nature and the justice of his having been devoured by pigs, before joking that if the Manicheans are right, and everything we eat contains some part of the divine that is purified by digestion and then turned into angels, then the farts these pigs produced after eating Muhammed must have generated a huge number of angels. Adopting a more serious tone, Guibert adds that Muhammed's followers did not believe he was God, just that he was a leader who transmitted divine law. When they could not find his body, they imagined that he had been taken up into heaven, leaving only his heels behind as a monument for his adherents to venerate (this appears to be a misunderstanding of the reverence shown for the sandals Muhammed wore during his heavenly ascent). Finally, Guibert ascribes the Islamic prohibition against eating pork to the fact that their lord had been eaten by pigs.

Guibert next turns to the spread of Islam, calling it a pagan heresy and noting Islamic expansion into the Holy Land, Armenia, Syria, and Greece. He also notes that when the Seljuk Turks moved in, they defeated the other rulers in the region and began attacking the Byzantine Empire. The Byzantine Emperor then sent a letter to Count Robert of Flanders asking for aid against the Turks, which Guibert paraphrases. Guibert says that the emperor claimed that the Muslims, whom he calls pagans, turned some Christian churches into stables and others into temples where they carried out all kinds of filthy activities, making them brothels and theaters. Guibert also charges that they slaughtered many Catholics, but asserts that these martyrs attained eternal life and were better off than those who survived only to become enslaved. He then details how the Muslim Turks violated women, raping mothers in front of their daughters and then the daughters in front of their mothers. Guibert remarks that at least the raping of women was in accord with nature, before asserting that the Muslims became worse than animals and turned their lust on men, even killing a certain bishop by sodomizing him. Indeed, Guibert describes urgent lust as the dominant characteristic of Muslims and calls it worse than insanity since it causes them to commit sexual acts that beasts avoid and that Christians cannot even name. He concludes that even though these wretches are allowed to have intercourse with multiple women, they cannot refrain from having sex with men as well, and that God could not tolerate their wantonness, so he caused them to be cast out like excrement.

There is a great deal that is flatly incorrect in Guibert's account of the life of Muhammed and the spread of Islam, but we will focus on how he undermines Muhammed's status as a prophet, defames Islam, and portrays Muslims as subhuman monsters. Guibert's account of Muhammed deprives him of his role as prophet and denies him any divine revelations. It reduces Muhammed to being the puppet of a heretical Christian hermit who is himself the devil's instrument. In Guibert's telling, Islam was created by the devil and transmitted to this hermit who then conveyed it to Muhammed to carry to others. Guibert portrays Islam as a disease that spreads out from the hermit and his prophet and charges that the hermit's only purpose was to lead people away from Catholicism and fill them with the poison of his false teachings. Guibert's view of Islam as a heresy was widely shared by western European Christians in the Middle Ages, and, like other heresies, Islam was often portrayed as a spiritual disease. Like physical diseases, the spiritual disease of heresy could spread from one infected person to many, but heresy was more insidious as it deprived a person not only of their life, but of their salvation as well. Heresy was once of the great preoccupations of the High and Late Middle Ages, and the Roman Church was particularly concerned with eradicating all forms of heresy precisely because it was thought to be such a profound threat to human salvation. According to this framing, Muslims rejected Christianity, the true religion, and accepted a false religion concocted by the devil that would inevitably result in their damnation.

Furthermore, framing Islam as a heresy denies it the status of a religion that is co-equal with Christianity. While medieval Christians viewed Jews as stubbornly resistant to the truth of Christianity, they recognized Judaism as the more ancient religion and the forerunner of Christianity. Islam was different. Islam had arisen some seven centuries after the birth of Christ, and Muslims worshipped the same God as Jews and Christians. Although Muhammed had commended both Judaism and Christianity, he had rejected them in favor of Islam and explicitly rejected the divinity of Christ. This constellation of facts allowed western European Christians to view Islam as a heretical off-shoot of Christianity, a monstrous perversion of what they considered to be true religion. This understanding of Islam as a heresy was so widespread in western Europe that in the early fourteenth century, the Italian poet Dante placed Muhammed in the ninth bolgia of the eighth circle of his *Inferno*, a place reserved for those who had sown discord and schism during their time on Earth. In Dante's work, Muhammed is punished for creating this heresy by having his body split open, reflecting the split that he was thought to have caused in the church by introducing a false teaching and luring his followers away from Christ.

Aside from portraying Muhammed as the lacky of a Satanically inspired hermit, Guibert also alleges that the prophet was so lustful that he contracted epilepsy from this vice, that he was a charlatan who employed cheap tricks to convert people to his new religion, and that he died a fittingly filthy death when he was devoured by pigs. Guibert consistently associates Muhammed with filth and vice to dehumanize him, arouse his readers' disgust, and render him monstrous. One of Guibert's primary goals in this text is defaming Muhammed, but he is equally interested in detailing the alleged immorality of Islam and the purported sexual depravity of its adherents. Guibert spends a great deal of time condemning the licentiousness that Muhammed's new law allegedly unleashed and contrasting this with the strict morality and modesty he attributes to Christians. He lingers in particular over the variety of sexual perversions that Muslims allegedly engage in, including having intercourse with multiple women, indulging in sodomy, and partaking in sexual acts that even animals avoid and Christians cannot even name. Guibert also insists that Muslims use sexual acts to defile Christians, forcing mothers to watch as their daughters are raped, and vice versa, and even murdering a bishop by sodomizing him. Guibert's strategy of imputing outrageous acts of sexual perversion to Muslims and associating Islam with filth and degeneracy effectively render both the religion and its adherents monstrous; their excess, lack of restraint, and immorality make them more beasts than men. In fact, most accounts of Islam that emanated from medieval western Europe focused on its alleged carnality and associated Muslims with violence and sexual depravity.

Of all the sexual depravity that Guibert attributes to Muslims, the act that he describes with the greatest disgust is sodomy. While Guibert condemns the rape of women, he comments that this was at least in accord with nature. Sodomy, on the other hand, he calls an intolerable crime. Medieval Christian attitudes toward sex were ambivalent at best. The church tolerated heterosexual intercourse within the confines of marriage, but only just, and it was excused on the grounds that it was necessary for procreation. Sodomy, which technically encompassed all non-procreative sexual acts, whether committed between members of the opposite sex or the same sex, was viewed by the church as a crime against nature precisely because it did not result in procreation. In Guibert's account, however, he leaves no doubt that he is condemning penetrative sex between men as the most heinous perversion imaginable. Guibert is reflecting shifting cultural and clerical attitudes toward sodomy and male homosexuality here.

There is a great deal of evidence from penitentials (books that prescribe penances for various sins) that the early medieval church was not particularly concerned with male homosexuality and that it regarded sodomy as a sin on par with other sexual sins like fornication and adultery. However, that attitude was changing during the eleventh and twelfth centuries due to the efforts of reformers who were seeking to purify the Christian clergy by enforcing celibacy on its priests and bishops. One of the side effects of this new emphasis on clerical celibacy was a growing concern that men who had been forbidden to marry or have sexual relations with women might turn to having sexual encounters with other men, and this was accompanied by an increasingly strident condemnation of sodomy.

The western European condemnation of sodomy began in earnest in the eleventh century with the reformer Peter Damian (c. 1007–1073), a Benedictine monk and cardinal, whose *Book of Gomorrah* (c. 1050) was particularly vehement in condemning sodomy among the clergy, and it gathered steam during the twelfth and thirteenth centuries. Sodomy was specifically prohibited by the Third Lateran Council in 1179 and was to be punished by expulsion from the clergy or penance in a monastery if the perpetrator was a cleric, or by excommunication if the perpetrator was a lay person. By the thirteenth century, several secular jurisdictions in western Europe had criminalized sodomy, and some made the crime punishable by death. The rationale behind this legislation was the assumption that sodomy so angered God that He might destroy the whole polity if it was not eradicated.

Although Guibert was writing before sodomy was criminalized, sodomy was not a neutral act in the early twelfth century. It was not just considered a sin, it was understood as a crime against nature, and it was often attributed to groups that the church actively sought to demonize, such as heretics and Muslims. Indeed, sodomy and heresy became increasingly linked in the twelfth century because of the church's tendency to attribute sodomy to any group it deemed heretical. Guibert's focus on Islam as a heresy and Muslims as indiscriminate sexual violators of both women and men is designed to portray both the religion of Islam and its adherents as monstrous. As we saw with Fulcher of Chartres and Robert the Monk, Guibert's primary goal is to justify and encourage Christian violence against Muslims.

All of these Christian authors were writing about Muslims in the wake of the First Crusade, so it is unsurprising that their language is intended to dehumanize a military enemy and authorize violence against them. For the most part, they portray Islam as a false religion, whether they depict it as paganism or a heresy, and focus on describing the alleged atrocities of the Muslims. However, Guibert goes far beyond what was strictly necessary to convince western Christians of the righteousness of their cause; he also attempts to offer a detailed account of the religion of Islam and its origins, but, in doing so, he renders Islam even more monstrous than paganism. The ignorance that Guibert displays is in large part due to the fact that reliable sources about Islam were unavailable in western Europe. The materials that were available, like John of Damascus' *De Haeresibus* (Concerning Heresy), the *Storia de Mahometh* (History of Muhammed), and the *Tultusceptru* (another biography of Muhammed), all presented Islam as a Christian heresy, and the last two presented Muhammed as a dupe of the devil, just as Guibert does. Very importantly, all of these authors were writing before the Qur'an had been translated into Latin and made accessible to a western European Christian audience. That task was finally completed by a team of translators working under Abbot Peter the Venerable in 1143, probably using materials from Toledo in Spain which had only just returned to Christian control in 1085 after several centuries of Muslim rule. This Latin translation of the Qur'an, along with other materials translated from Arabic as part of this project, offered western European Christians their first real opportunity to understand Islam. Of course, having a better understanding of Islam did not necessarily lead to having a more positive view of it, or of Muhammed. Peter the Venerable subsequently used this translation of the Qur'an to produce a refutation of Islam that was grounded in a new familiarity with the religion, but still relied on old assumptions that Islam was a Christian heresy inspired by Satan himself.

Our final source in this chapter is Peter the Venerable's *Summa totius haeresis Saracenorum* (c. 1143/4), a summary of the entire Saracen heresy as he calls Islam. Peter wrote this polemic after overseeing the translation of the Qur'an, and, although his purpose is to refute what he considers a heresy, his work is at least grounded in an understanding of Islamic sources. Peter begins his refutation of Islam by pointing out that Muslims deny the Trinity, indicating that they are ignorant of God. He goes on to assert that they deny that God is the Father because they believe that no one can procreate without sexual intercourse. As for Christ, he asserts that Muslims believe he was conceived from a divine spirit and that Mary was a virgin when she gave birth to Him, but not that He is God or the Son of God. Rather, they believe that Christ is a prophet who never died as he escaped from the Jews who wanted to kill him and then ascended to heaven where he still lives in the presence of God and awaits the coming of Antichrist. When Antichrist comes, Christ will convert the Jews and teach his law perfectly to the Christians, then die and be resurrected with everyone else. Christ will not judge souls but will lead his followers to judgment and assist them. Peter then remarks that by teaching his followers this, the most wretched and impious Muhammed has condemned nearly a third of humanity to the devil and eternal death with his fables.

Peter next turns to explaining who Muhammed was so that Christians can learn how detestable his life and teachings were. Here, he points out some of the false beliefs that Christians held about the origins of Islam and seeks to correct them, but he only does so to more perfectly condemn both Muhammed and Islam. Peter notes that Muhammed lived during the time of Emperor Heraclius and calls him a pagan of low birth who was nearly illiterate. Peter does acknowledge that Muhammed was shrewd when it came to business, despite his lack of learning, and that he lifted himself to wealth and fame with his acumen. He also asserts that Muhammed inspired fear in those around him by attacking and sometimes killing his neighbors and kin and that he began to aspire to kingship over his race. Peter explains that people resisted Muhammed's efforts to acquire power because of his low birth, so he attempted to use the cloak of religion to advance his earthly ambitions. Peter also notes that because Muhammed was surrounded by idolatrous barbarians who were ignorant of human and divine law, this made them easy to seduce. He says that Muhammed set about convincing them that he was a prophet by pretending to be something good and trying to lead them away from their idolatry to his own false heresy rather than the true God.

Peter then goes on to assert that Satan sent a heretical Nestorian monk named Sergius to assist Muhammed (this is Bahira again). When Sergius arrived, he interpreted the scriptures for Muhammed, but did so in the heretical Nestorian fashion, explaining that Christ is not God and filling him with fables from apocryphal books. Once Muhammed had imbibed this Nestorian form of Christianity, which Catholic Christians like Peter viewed as abhorrently heretical, Peter says that the Jews came to Muhammed and taught him their fables so that nothing should be lacking for his damnation or that of his followers. The result was the Qur'an, which Peter calls a wicked confection of Jewish fables and heretical nonsense woven together in a barbarous fashion. Peter says that Muhammed created the lie that the book had been conveyed to him by the angel Gabriel and then poisoned the people of that miserable race with his scripture. Peter correctly asserts that Muhammed commended both Judaism and Christianity while rejecting them and points out that Muslims recognize Moses as a prophet, and recognize Christ as a great prophet born of a virgin, but reject and ridicule the teaching that Christ is the Son of God.

Peter then moves on to the Islamic conception of heaven. Peter cannot fathom that Muhammed's conception of heaven does not consist of angelic hosts or a vision of the divine and paints it as an entirely sensual paradise comprising feasts and sexual encounters with beautiful women. Peter severely disapproves of this, as Muhammed seems to promise his followers a heaven composed entirely of indulgence in the Christian vices of gluttony and lust. In fact, he says that Muhammed created Islam by vomiting up all the worst parts of ancient heresies under the devil's instruction and compares Islam to the heretical teachings of Sabellius, who rejected the Trinity; Nestorius, who rejected Christ's divinity; and Manichaeus, who denied the death and resurrection of Christ.

Peter goes on to give a description of Islamic law that sounds very similar to that given by Guibert. He says that Muhammed required circumcision, but allowed gluttony and sensuality in order to attract more followers. Peter also uses the fact that Muhammed had multiple wives to discredit him and charges that he committed adultery with the wives of many others as well. Peter follows this condemnation with the remark that Muhammed only commended almsgiving and prayer to avoid appearing completely disgraceful. In fact, Peter specifically calls Muhammed "utterly monstrous" here while describing how he joined licentiousness with prayer and almsgiving, just as someone might join a human's head with a horse's neck and birds' feathers. As Peter describes it, Islamic law is a monstrous hybrid of sexual license and gluttony, covered with a veneer of religiosity, as well as a monstrous confection of earlier heresies and Jewish fables. Peter contends that Muhammed used this formula to get people to abandon their previous idolatry and worship a single god, and because he was preaching to people who were ignorant, they believed he was God's prophet. Peter says that the people raised Muhammed as their king and then asserts that his teachings bore a nefarious harvest that should be burned by an everlasting fire. Peter says that God allowed the Saracens, who were infected with the plague of Muhammed's teachings, to rise to power by force of arms and spread their heresy.

Peter then turns back to the question of whether Islam should be considered a heresy. He says that he calls it a heresy because Muslims believe some things in common with Christians, but since they disagree in many things, it might be better for him to call them something worse, like pagans or heathens. He notes that they hold many false beliefs about Christ and that they do not accept any of the Christian sacraments, which even most heretics accept. According to Peter, the highest aspiration of Islam is to deny Christ's divinity and reduce him to the status of a prophet, a teaching that he asserts was conceived by the devil and first disseminated by Arius, then spread by "that Satan" Muhammed, and will ultimately be fulfilled through Antichrist. Here, Peter explicitly identifies Muhammed as a Satanically inspired forerunner of Antichrist. In fact, Peter goes on to say that Satan is particularly opposed to the Christian belief that God became man, that Satan has always tried to extinguish the Christian faith, and that, just as some heresies arose in the early church regarding these beliefs, God has now permitted the devil to seduce Muslims in the same way.

Peter goes on to note that the Muslim belief that Christ was a good man, but not divine, was also held by the apostate philosopher Porphyry. He marvels at how cunning the devil was to come up with such a lie, making sure to praise Christ while denying His divinity, the aspect of Christ that Christians believe makes salvation possible. He notes that anyone who consults Augustine's *City of God* and *The Harmony of the Evangelists* can see what the devil planned to do in circulating this lie, but was not able to execute until Muhammed spread it to an entire wretched race. He asserts that no mortal could have invented these fables without the devil's assistance and that Satan himself must have conceived this plot to ensure that Muslims would not believe that Christ was the Son of God and the Redeemer of humanity. Peter says that although Satan attempted to spread this falsehood in Porphyry's time, he was not able to do so until Muhammed came along, who Peter notes was reputed to be possessed by an evil spirit and suffer from epilepsy. With Muhammed, Satan was able to plunge nearly half of humanity into eternal damnation.

Peter ends his work with a reminder that he has written these things so Christians will have a better understanding of their enemy. He hopes that God will inspire someone to refute this heresy and free the Church of God from the disgrace it is suffering. According to Peter, the church has always confounded heresies by responding to them, but this one has been neglected until now because no one had bothered to learn about, and it poses a greater danger than previous heresies because it has infected so many. As Peter says, it has "caused the unbounded destruction of the human race, both in bodies and in souls." Finally, Peter closes with a short account of his trip to Spain where he had the Qur'an translated from Arabic into Latin along with some other texts. He notes that he expended great effort and expense to expose the impious doctrine and the accursed life of Muhammed so that everyone would know what a foul heresy it is. In a burst of frustration, Peter complains that he has waited a long time for someone else to take up the pen against Islam, and that he himself had even proposed to do this, but he would prefer that it was done better by someone else.

Peter's characterization of Islam may be based upon better familiarity with the Qur'an and the life of Muhammed than most previous Christian authors had enjoyed, but it still contains many claims that we have already seen in other texts produced by western Christians, especially its insistence that Islam is a demonically inspired heresy; that Muhammed was a charlatan and a convenient tool for the devil; that Islam encourages lust, gluttony, and violence; and that Muslims are the enemies of Christ and Christians. Like many earlier Christian authors, Peter portrays Muslims as heretics who share some beliefs with Christians but deny the Trinity and the divinity of Christ. He also asserts that Satan is the ultimate originator of these monstrous teachings and that they are designed to deprive people of salvation. To prove his point, he links Islam with earlier Christian heresies like Nestorianism, Arianism, and even the teachings of the apostate Porphyry, who also denied that Christ was divine, before linking them to the teachings that Antichrist will promote. In Peter's view, Islam is a product of Satan's malice toward humanity and a monstrous precursor of the reign of Antichrist.

As for Muhammed himself, Peter depicts him as a barbarian, a low-born pagan who aspired to worldly power and used the pretense of religion to acquire it. Like many other Christian writers, Peter emphasizes Muhammed's illiteracy in an effort to discount his teachings by portraying him as ignorant. Peter admits that Muhammed was shrewd in business, but he calls his teachings a barbaric confection of Nestorian heresy and Jewish fables. Like Guibert, Peter also emphasizes Muhammed's own alleged carnality and claims that he promoted the sins of gluttony and lust to acquire more adherents. Peter even accuses of Muhammed of not being satisfied with having 18 wives simultaneously and resorting to committing adultery with the wives of others. Like Guibert and many other Christian authors, Peter finds the Islamic acceptance of polygyny reprehensible, especially as it stands in direct contrast to the Christian emphasis on denying the flesh and remaining celibate if one is able. Finally, Peter brings up Muhammed's epilepsy and links it directly to demonic possession. Epilepsy was often associated with possession in ancient and medieval Europe, and both Peter and Guibert present this information to further discredit Muhammed and demonstrate that he was inspired by Satan rather than God.

Peter's portrayal of Muslims is a bit more complicated. On the one hand, he asserts that Muhammed attracted new followers by allowing them to engage in acts that Christians condemned as sinful, that Muslims spread their deadly heresy by force of arms, and that they deserve to be burned in everlasting fire. However, he also seems to show some pity for them when he calls them wretched, miserable, and doomed to damnation. He implies that they must have incurred some divine curse in order to have been afflicted with this deadly heresy, although he does not speculate as to what might have caused God to allow the devil to succeed in spreading false beliefs among Muslims when He had not permitted this in other cases. For example, just after he reports that Muhammed was possessed by an evil spirit and by epilepsy, Peter muses that Satan used Muhammed to damn an entire race and that only God knows why this was permitted. Whether Peter is expressing sincere sympathy for people he considers damned is difficult to say. He may well be engaging in mere rhetorical sympathy, but he certainly seems to indicate that Muhammed's followers are to some extent victims of a diabolical plot to deprive them of salvation.

Finally, Peter states several times that his goal in writing this work, and in overseeing the translation of Islamic texts from Arabic into Latin, is to furnish Christians with information that they can use to confound their Muslim enemies and potentially eliminate this heresy. He presents Muslims not only as military enemies, but also as spiritual enemies. For Peter, Muslims are Christ's enemies because they deny His divine nature and are aligned with Satan, and they are the enemies of Christians and humanity in general because their teachings have the potential to lead the faithful astray and fool the gullible into damnation. Just as Christians feared that the Jewish rejection of Christian doctrine might cause some Christians to question or reject their faith, they harbored similar fears that some Christians might be drawn away from their religion by the influence of Islam, and they saw it as a moral duty to combat what they considered a damnable heresy.

While Christian anxieties about Jews shifted considerably during the course of the Middle Ages, at first focusing on the Jews as monstrous deicides and a cursed race who were being punished by God, and then focusing on Jews as perpetrators of ritual murder and host desecration, the western European Christian view of Muslims remained fairly stable. Muhammed was most often portrayed as a demonically inspired fraud, a poor, illiterate man who craved power and obtained it by foisting a monstrous deception upon his followers. He was routinely slandered as a charlatan, and Christian authors used a variety of tactics to deprive him of moral authority, from connecting his epilepsy with sexual excess or demonic possession to accusing him of being nothing more than a mouthpiece for a heretical hermit. Likewise, Christian authors portrayed Islam as a particularly nasty Christian heresy, a monstrous hybrid of earlier heresies and Jewish fables designed by Satan himself to deprive humanity of salvation. As for Muslims, the same Christian authors depicted them as lewd, filthy, lascivious, violent, cruel, and dangerous to Christians. Christians viewed both Jews and Muslims as monstrous primarily on account of their religion, but Christian fears about Jews revolved around the idea that Jews hated Christians and were secretly attacking Christian children and the consecrated host, while Christian fears about Muslims were clearly linked to the possibility that the Islamic world might ultimately triumph over Christendom.

PRIMARY SOURCES

Jews

**Augustine of Hippo, "Contra Faustum," in *The Works of Aurelius
Augustine: A New Translation*, trans. Richard Stothert (T & T Clark,
1872), vol. V, XII.9–13, pp. 240–2.**

9. As Cain's sacrifice of the fruit of the ground is rejected, while Abel's sacrifice of
his sheep and the fat thereof is accepted, so the faith of the New Testament praising
God in the harmless service of grace is preferred to the earthly observances of the
Old Testament. For though the Jews were right in practising these things, they were
guilty of unbelief in not distinguishing the time of the New Testament when Christ
came, from the time of the Old Testament. God said to Cain, "If you offer well, yet
if you divide not well, you have sinned." If Cain had obeyed God when He said,
"Be content, for to you shall be its reference, and you shall rule over it," he would
have referred his sin to himself, by taking the blame of it, and confessing it to God;
and so assisted by supplies of grace, he would have ruled over his sin, instead of
acting as the servant of sin in killing his innocent brother. So also the Jews, of
whom all these things are a figure, if they had been content, instead of being turbulent, and had acknowledged the time of salvation through the pardon of sins by
grace, and heard Christ saying, "They that are whole need not a physician, but they
that are sick; I came not to call the righteous, but sinners to repentance;" Matthew
9:12–13 and, "Every one that commits sin is the servant of sin;" and, "If the Son
make you free, you shall be free indeed," John 8:34, 36 – they would in confession
have referred their sin to themselves, saying to the Physician, as it is written in the
Psalm, "I said, Lord, be merciful to me; heal my soul, for I have sinned against
You." And being made free by the hope of grace, they would have ruled over sin as
long as it continued in their mortal body. But now, being ignorant of God's righteousness, and wishing to establish a righteousness of their own, proud of the works
of the law, instead of being humbled on account of their sins, they have not been
content; and in subjection to sin reigning in their mortal body, so as to make them
obey it in the lusts thereof, they have stumbled on the stone of stumbling, and have
been inflamed with hatred against him whose works they grieved to see accepted
by God. The man who was born blind, and had been made to see, said to them,
"We know that God hears not sinners; but if any man serve Him, and do His will,
him He hears;" John 9:31 as if he had said, God regards not the sacrifice of Cain,
but he regards the sacrifice of Abel. Abel, the younger brother, is killed by the elder
brother; Christ, the head of the younger people, is killed by the elder people of the
Jews. Abel dies in the field; Christ dies on Calvary.

10. God asks Cain where his brother is, not as if He did not know, but as a
judge asks a guilty criminal. Cain replies that he knows not, and that he is not his
brother's keeper. And what answer can the Jews give at this day, when we ask them

with the voice of God, that is, of the sacred Scriptures, about Christ, except that they do not know the Christ that we speak of? Cain's ignorance was pretended, and the Jews are deceived in their refusal of Christ. Moreover, they would have been in a sense keepers of Christ, if they had been willing to receive and keep the Christian faith. For the man who keeps Christ in his heart does not ask, like Cain, Am I my brother's keeper? Then God says to Cain, "What have you done? The voice of your brother's blood cries unto me from the ground." So the voice of God in the Holy Scriptures accuses the Jews. For the blood of Christ has a loud voice on the earth, when the responsive Amen of those who believe in Him comes from all nations. This is the voice of Christ's blood, because the clear voice of the faithful redeemed by His blood is the voice of the blood itself.

11. Then God says to Cain: "You are cursed from the earth, which has opened its mouth to receive your brother's blood at your hand. For you shall till the earth, and it shall no longer yield unto you its strength. A mourner and an abject shall you be on the earth." It is not, Cursed is the earth, but, Cursed are you from the earth, which has opened its mouth to receive your brother's blood at your hand. So the unbelieving people of the Jews is cursed from the earth, that is, from the Church, which in the confession of sins has opened its mouth to receive the blood shed for the remission of sins by the hand of the people that would not be under grace, but under the law. And this murderer is cursed by the Church; that is, the Church admits and avows the curse pronounced by the apostle: "Whoever are of the works of the law are under the curse of the law." Galatians 3:10 Then, after saying, Cursed are you from the earth, which has opened its mouth to receive your brother's blood at your hand, what follows is not, For you shall till it, but, You shall till the earth, and it shall not yield to you its strength. The earth he is to till is not necessarily the same as that which opened its mouth to receive his brother's blood at his hand. From this earth he is cursed, and so he tills an earth which shall no longer yield to him its strength. That is, the Church admits and avows the Jewish people to be cursed, because after killing Christ they continue to till the ground of an earthly circumcision, an earthly Sabbath, an earthly passover, while the hidden strength or virtue of making known Christ, which this tilling contains, is not yielded to the Jews while they continue in impiety and unbelief, for it is revealed in the New Testament. While they will not turn to God, the veil which is on their minds in reading the Old Testament is not taken away. This veil is taken away only by Christ, who does not do away with the reading of the Old Testament, but with the covering which hides its virtue. So, at the crucifixion of Christ, the veil was rent in two, that by the passion of Christ hidden mysteries might be revealed to believers who turn to Him with a mouth opened in confession to drink His blood. In this way the Jewish people, like Cain, continue tilling the ground, in the carnal observance of the law, which does not yield to them its strength, because they do not perceive in it the grace of Christ. So too, the flesh of Christ was the ground from which by crucifying Him the Jews produced our salvation, for He died for our offenses. But this ground did not yield to them its strength, for they were not justified by the virtue of His resurrection, for He arose again for our justification. As the apostle says: "He was crucified in weakness, but He lives by the power of God." 2 Corinthians 13:4

This is the power of that ground which is unknown to the ungodly and unbelieving. When Christ rose, He did not appear to those who had crucified Him. So Cain was not allowed to see the strength of the ground which he tilled to sow his seed in it; as God said, "You shall till the ground, and it shall no longer yield unto you its strength."

12. "Groaning and trembling shall you be on the earth." Here no one can fail to see that in every land where the Jews are scattered they mourn for the loss of their kingdom, and are in terrified subjection to the immensely superior number of Christians. So Cain answered, and said: "My case is worse, if You drive me out this day from the face of the earth, and from Your face shall I be hid, and I shall be a mourner and an outcast on the earth; and it shall be that every one that finds me shall slay me." Here he groans indeed in terror, lest after losing his earthly possession he should suffer the death of the body. This he calls a worse case than that of the ground not yielding to him its strength, or than that of spiritual death. For his mind is carnal; for he thinks little of being hid from the face of God, that is, of being under the anger of God, were it not that he may be found and slain. This is the carnal mind that tills the ground, but does not obtain its strength. To be carnally minded is death; but he, in ignorance of this, mourns for the loss of his earthly possession, and is in terror of bodily death. But what does God reply? "Not so," He says; "but whosoever shall kill Cain, vengeance shall be taken on him sevenfold." That is, It is not as you say, not by bodily death shall the ungodly race of carnal Jews perish. For whoever destroys them in this way shall suffer sevenfold vengeance, that is, shall bring upon himself the sevenfold penalty under which the Jews lie for the crucifixion of Christ. So to the end of the seven days of time, the continued preservation of the Jews will be a proof to believing Christians of the subjection merited by those who, in the pride of their kingdom, put the Lord to death.

13. "And the Lord God set a mark upon Cain, lest any one finding him should slay him." It is a most notable fact, that all the nations subjugated by Rome adopted the heathenish ceremonies of the Roman worship; while the Jewish nation, whether under Pagan or Christian monarchs, has never lost the sign of their law, by which they are distinguished from all other nations and peoples. No emperor or monarch who finds under his government the people with this mark kills them, that is, makes them cease to be Jews, and as Jews to be separate in their observances, and unlike the rest of the world. Only when a Jew comes over to Christ, he is no longer Cain, nor goes out from the presence of God. . . .

Bernard of Clairvaux, "Letter to England to Summon the Second Crusade, 1146 (Letter 391)," in *The Letters of St. Bernard of Clairvaux*, trans. Bruno Scott James (Burns Oates, 1953), pp. 460–3.

. . . I have heard with great joy of the zeal for God's glory which comes in your midst, but your zeal needs the timely restraint of knowledge. The Jews are not to be persecuted, killed or even put to flight. Ask anyone who knows the Sacred Scriptures what he finds foretold of the Jews in the psalm. "Not for their destruction do I pray," it says. The Jews are for us the living words of Scripture, for they remind us always of what our Lord suffered. They are dispersed all over the world so that by expiating their crime they may be everywhere the living witnesses of our redemption. Hence the same psalm adds, "only let thy power disperse them." And so it is: dispersed they are. Under Christian princes they endure a hard captivity, but "they only wait for the time of their deliverance." Finally we are told by the Apostle that when the time is ripe all Israel shall be saved. But those who die before will remain in death. I will not mention those Christian money lenders, if they can be called Christian, who, where there are no Jews, act, I grieve to say, in a manner worse than any Jew. If the Jews were utterly wiped out, what will become of our hope for their promised salvation, their eventual conversion? If the pagans were similarly subjugated to us then, in my opinion, we should wait for them rather than seek them out with swords. But as they have now begun to attack us, it is necessary for those of us who do not carry a sword in vain to repel them with force. It is an act of Christian piety both "to vanquish the proud" and also "to spare the subjected," especially those for whom we have a law and a promise, and whose flesh was shared by Christ whose name is forever blessed.

Peter the Venerable, *Against the Inveterate Obduracy of the Jews*, trans. Irven M. Resnick (Catholic University of America Press, 2013), pp. 49–51.

Here Begins the Book of Lord Peter the Venerable, Abbot of Cluny, Against the Inveterate Obduracy of the Jews.

Prologue

I APPROACH YOU, O Jews – you, I say, who even to this day deny the Son of God. How long, wretches, will you fail to believe the truth? How long will you reject God? How long will you fail to soften [your] iron hearts? Behold that since antiquity almost the entire world has acknowledged Christ, while you alone do not acknowledge him; while all peoples submit to him, you alone do not listen to him; every tongue confesses him, while you alone deny him; others see him, hear him, understand him, but you alone remain blind, deaf, like stones. Clearly your eyes are blind, your ears are deaf, your hearts are stone.

Nor is this something new for you. Everywhere this world reads and recites in frequent readings what God says about you to Moses: "I see that this people is stiff-necked: Let me alone, that my wrath may be kindled against them, and that I may destroy them." And again he says to you: "You are a stiff-necked people; once I shall come down in your midst, I shall destroy you." [The world] also reads of your Moses, or rather ours, arguing against you in this manner: "I know your obstinacy," he says, "and your most stiff neck. While I am yet living, and going in with you, you have always been rebellious against the Lord: how much more when I shall be dead?" It also reads Isaiah, a prophet of singular excellence, to whom God said of you: "Blind the heart of this people," he said, "and make their ears heavy, and shut their eyes, lest they see with their eyes, and hear with their ears, and understand with their heart, and be converted and I heal them." It reads and hears its own Stephen, whom your stones, O stone-like race, made the first witness to Christ after Christ. It reads and surely it hears him, filled with the Holy Spirit, upbraiding in you the spirit of most wicked stubbornness: You, "uncircumcised in hearts and ears," you traitors and murderers, "you have always resisted the Holy Spirit even as your fathers did."

But will you always do so? Will you always make of yourselves a public spectacle throughout all the lands of the world because of such great obduracy? Come to your senses, now at last come to your senses; "return to the heart, O transgressors," as one prophet says to you. "Return to the heart" now, at least, when by the just judgment of the Most High you have fallen not only from heavenly glory but even from the earthly glory that alone you loved. Observe that those very things have been fulfilled among you that the Christ, whom you deny, spoke to your fathers and predicted for you if you did not come to your senses: "The kingdom of God will be taken away from you and given to a people yielding its fruit." Having lost, then, the heavenly kingdom, and now having lost a very long time ago even an earthly kingdom, acknowledge that this has happened to you because of this impiety. Acknowledge that the cause of your very harsh condemnation is this: that you did not recognize, did not receive, did not worship the messiah once he came, the one that for such a long time you sang, read, and preached would come, but instead you spurned him, mocked him, slew him, in your detestable fashion.

But what else? If you decide to convert, you need not fear that you have slain him. He is not intent upon avenging his death, if the correct outcome of your conversion follows. Previously, while hanging from the cross as the man that he had assumed, he prayed for the very ones who crucified him, and he did not pray only while he suffered but even later, after he had risen from the dead, he granted his favor to those who repented and converted. He was not unmindful that he had suffered death for the sake of the life of men and, once they had converted, he received those whom he regarded as mockers and murderers with that very evident and truly bountiful divine compassion which is upon every man. This same infinite bounty will not be lacking for you, nor will that bounty that embraces almost the entire world reject your small number from among the number of the saved, if you do not reject it.

Believe, then, your law, and not another's; believe your prophets and not those of others; believe your own Scriptures and not those of others. Why does this barely move you? Why does it not move you that the entire strength of the Christian faith, that the entire hope for human salvation, originates in your texts? Why does it not move you that we have received the patriarchs, the prophets, the harbingers, the apostolic preachers, the highest and supercelestial Virgin mother of Christ, and Christ himself, the author of our salvation – who was called the "expectation of the nations" by your own prophet – not from the barbarous races, not from just any nations whatsoever, but from your race, as descendants from the great stock of Abraham? I refer you, then, to men of your own race, I refer you to your own Scriptures that you received from God, and I offer testimonies from them to which, however often there is a Jewish disputation, it will be compelled to surrender.

Richard of Devizes, "The Chronicle of Richard of Devizes,"
in *Chronicles of the Crusades: Contemporary Narratives of the*
***Crusade of Richard Coeur de Lion* (George Bell and Sons, 1888),**
Sections 79–83, pp. 48–52.

Sect. 79. Because Winchester ought not to be deprived of its due reward for keeping peace with the Jews, as in the beginning of this book is related, the Winchester
Jews (after the manner of the Jews), studious of the honour of their city, procured
themselves notoriety by murdering a boy in Winchester, with many signs of the
deed, although, perhaps, the deed was never done. The case was thus: – A certain Jew engaged a Christian boy, a pretender to the art of shoemaking, into the
household service of his family. He did not reside there continually to work, nor
was he permitted to complete any great thing all at once, lest his abiding with
them should appraise him of the fate intended for him; and, as he was renumer-
ated better for a little labor there, than for much elsewhere, allured by his gifts and
wiles, he frequented the more freely the wretch's house. Now, he was French by
birth, under age, and an orphan, of abject condition and extreme poverty. A certain
French Jew, having unfortunately compassioned his great miseries in France, by
frequent advice persuaded him that he should go to England, a land flowing with
milk and honey; he praised the English as liberal and bountiful, and that there no
one would continue poor who could be recommended for honesty. The boy, ready
to like whatever you may wish, as is natural with the French, having taken a certain
companion of the same age as himself, and of the same country, got ready to set
forward on his foreign expedition, having nothing in his hands but a staff, nothing
in his wallet but a cobbler's awl.

Sect. 80. He bade farewell to his Jewish friend; to whom the Jew replied, "Go
forth as a man. The God of my fathers lead thee as I desire." And having laid his
hands upon his head, as if he had been the scapegoat, after certain muttering of the
throat and silent imprecations, being now secure of his prey, he continued – "Be of
good courage; forget your own people and native land, for every land is the home
of the brave, as the sea is for the fish, and as the whole of the wide world is for the
bird. When you have entered England, if you should come to London, you will
quickly pass through it, as that city greatly displeases me. Every race of men, out
of every nation which is under heaven, resort thither in great numbers; every nation
has introduced into that city its vices and bad manners. No one lives in it without
offense; there is not a single street in it that does not abound in miserable, obscene
wretches; there, in proportion as any man has exceeded in wickedness, so much is
he the better. I am not ignorant of the disposition I am exhorting; you have, in addition to your youth, an ardent disposition, a slowness of memory, and a soberness
of reason between extremes. I feel in myself no uneasiness about you, unless you
should abide with men of corrupt lives; for from our associations our manners are
formed. But let that be as it may. You will come to London. Behold! I warn you,
whatever of evil or of perversity there is in any, whatever in all parts of the world,
you will find in that city alone. Go not to the dances of panders, nor mix yourself
up with the herds of the stews [public bath houses]; avoid the talus and the dice,

the theatre and the tavern. You will find more braggadocios there than in all France, while the number of flatterers is infinite. Stage-players, buffoons, those that have no hair on their bodies, Garamantes, pick-thanks, catamites, effeminate sodomites, lewd musical girls, druggists, lustful persons, fortune-tellers, extortioners, nightly strollers, magicians, mimics, common beggars, tatterdemalions, – this whole crew has filled every house. So if you do not wish to live with the shameful, you will not dwell in London. I am not speaking against the learned, whether monks or Jews; although, still, from their very dwelling together with such evil persons, I should esteem them less perfect there than elsewhere.

Sect. 81. "Nor does my advice go so far, as that you should betake yourself to no city; with my counsel you will take up your residence nowhere but in a town, though it remains to say in what. Therefore, if you should land near Canterbury, you will have to lose your way, if even you should but pass through it. It is an assemblage of the vilest entirely devoted to their – I know not whom, but who has been lately canonized, and had been the archbishop of Canterbury [Thomas Becket, who had recently been canonized], as everywhere they die in open day in the streets for want of bread and employment. Rochester and Chichester are mere villages, and they possess nothing for which they should be called cities, but the sees of their bishops. Oxford scarcely, I will not say satisfies, but sustains, its clerks. Exeter supports men and beasts with the same grain. Bath is placed, or rather buried, in the lowest parts of the valleys, in a very dense atmosphere and sulphury vapour, as it were at the gates of hell. Nor yet will you select your habitation in the northern cities, Worcester, Chester, Hereford, on account of the desperate Welshmen. York abounds in Scots, vile and faithless men, or rather rascals. The town of Ely is always putrefied by the surrounding marshes. In Durham, Norwich, or Lincoln, there are very few of your disposition among the powerful; you will never hear anyone speak French. At Bristol, there is nobody who is not, or has not been, a soapmaker, and every Frenchman esteems soapmakers as he does night-men [people who cleaned cesspools, sewers, and privies at night]. After the cities, every market, village, or town, has but rude and rustic inhabitants. Moreover, at all times, account the Cornish people for such as you know our Flemish are accounted in France. For the rest, the kingdom itself is generally most favoured with the dew of heaven and the fatness of the earth; and in every place there are some good, but much fewer in them all than in Winchester alone.

Sect. 82. "This [Winchester] is in those parts the Jerusalem of the Jews, in it alone they enjoy perpetual peace; it is the school of those who desire to live well and prosper. Here they become men, here there is bread and wine enough for nothing. There are therein monks of such compassion and gentleness, clergy of such understanding and frankness, citizens of such civility and good faith, ladies of such beauty and modesty, that little hinders but I should go there and become a Christian with such Christians. To that city I direct you, the city of cities, the mother of all, the best above all. There is but one fault, and that alone in which they customarily indulge too much. With the exception I should say of the learned and of the Jews, the Winchester people tell lies like watchmen, but it is in making up reports. For in no place under heaven so many false rumours are fabricated so easily as there; otherwise they are true in everything. I should have many things too still to tell you about business; but for fear you should not understand or should forget, you will place this familiar note in the hands of the Jew my friend, and I think, too, you may some time be rewarded by him." The short note was in Hebrew. The Jew made an end of his speech, and the boy having understood all things for good, came to Winchester.

Sect. 83. His awl supplied him, and his companion as well, with food, and the cruel courtesy and deceitful beneficence was by the letter unfortunately obtained to their relief. Wherever the poor fellows worked or eat apart by day, they reposed every night in one little bed in the same old cottage of a certain old woman. Days follow days, and months months, and in the same way as we have hitherto so carefully described, the boys hasten the time of their separation that they may meet again. The day of the Holy Cross had arrived, and the boy that same day, whilst working at his Jew's, being by some means put out of the way, was not forthcoming. Now the Passover, a feast of the Jews, was at hand. His companion, during the evening, greatly surprised at his absence, not returning home to bed, was terrified that night with many visions and dreams. When he had sought him several days in all corners of the city without success, he came to the Jew and simply asked if he had sent his benefactor anywhere; whom when he found violently enraged beyond his general disposition, from having been so courteous the day before, and noticed the incoherence of his words and change of countenance, he presently fired up, and as he was of a shrill voice and admirable readiness of speech, he broke out into abuse, and with great clamour challenged him with taking his companion away. "Thou son of a sordid harlot," said he; "thou robber, thou traitor, thou devil, thou hast crucified my friend. Alas, me! wherefore have I not now the strength of a man! I would tear you to pieces with my hands." The noise of his quarrelling in the house is heard in the street, Jews and Christians come running together from all quarters. The boy persists, and now, deriving courage from the crowd, addressing those present, he alleged his concern for his companion as an excuse. "O you good people," said he, "who are assembled, behold if there is any sorrow like my sorrow. That Jew is a devil; he has stolen away my heart from my breast – he has butchered my only companion, and I presume too that he has eaten him. A certain son of the devil, a Jew of French birth, I neither know nor am acquainted with; that Jew gave my comrade letters of his death-warrant to that man. To this city he came, induced, or rather seduced. He often gave attendance upon this Jew, and in his house he was last seen." He was not without a witness to some points, inasmuch as a Christian woman, who, contrary to the canons, had nursed up the young Jews in the same house, constantly swore that she had seen the boy go down into the Jew's store, without coming up again. The Jew denies it – the case is referred to the judges. The accusers are defective; the boy because he was under age, the woman because the service of Jews had rendered her ignominious. The Jew offered to clear his conscience of the evil report. Gold contented the judges. Phineas gave and pleased, and the controversy ceased.

The Passion of Adam of Bristol, British Library, Harleian MS. 957, no. 7, trans. Robert Stacey (by Permission of the Author).

"Hear, o islands, and give heed, people from far away.'" Thus says the lord God.

"I, the only begotten son, who speaks to the entire world through the strength of my arm, hear men of Judah, hear, rebels and unbelievers, with pity and great compassion," what the Jews have done to me in idolatrous and garrulous England."

There was a certain Jew in the city of Bristol in the western part of the city, and he had one sister and she was a widow, for her husband was dead. This particular Jew, in the days of King Henry, father of the other Henry, went to his sister and said to her: "Come, my sister, and I will speak with you in secret." And the woman arose and they went into a secret place.

And when they had come to the place, the Jew said: "O my beloved sister, I want to tell you about a wonderous event."

"It happened that one day when my young son, having left the house, went into the city he found himself a certain young boy, and he said to him, as I had previously taught him, "Come home with me so that we can play together and my mother will give you and me lots of apples."

To whom the Christian boy: "Where is your house and who is your father and who is your mother?"

To this the Jewish boy, prudently instructed by his father: "My father and my mother are Christians."

To whom the Christian boy: "Let us go to your house but afterwards you shall go with me to my house and my mother will give me white bread and I will give you a portion along with me."

To whom the Jewish boy: "Come first with me to my house and afterwards I will go back with you. But I will go first with quick steps and you follow behind me, and where you see me enter, you enter and quickly." And he added: "Cover your face with your hood." "And so it was done," says the lord God.

When the Christian boy had entered the Jews' house he said to the Jewish boy: "What game do you want to play?" At this the elder Jew, whose name was Samuel: "Go, my little sons, and play in our chamber and I will buy you a penny's worth of apples." These things said, the boys entered the house. They having entered, the Jew shut the outer door and said to his wife: "Send the Christian maidservant to fetch a penny's worth of apples, so that we can give them to this Christian boy, because we want to crucify him and mock him in outrageous insult to Christ and His mother."

To whom the woman: "Let us take care that no one saw the coming of that boy into our house."

To whom the Jew: "Do not fear. This boy was not raised in this part of the city. For he has been led to us from a long distance away, so prudent is our son."

"But go quickly and fetch what I said." And the woman went and brought the apples as the man had commanded.

To whom the man: "Go into our strongroom and bring them the apples, and give them food and drink. And inquire carefully as to the names of each of his parents, and where their house is, and in what parish."

"Meanwhile, I will stand in the street to hear whether anyone says anything to me about the entry of this boy [into our house]." And the woman went and entered the strongroom, [and] gave the boys the apples.

And approaching, she deceitfully kissed the Christian boy three times, saying: "You are welcome, son."

To whom the boy: "Thank you". At that the woman immediately arose, brought a clean tablecloth, and white bread, and meat, and beer, and said: "Eat and drink and after supper eat our apples." And she added: "O beloved boy, what is your name?" And he: "I am called Adam and my father is called William of Wales in the parish which is called St Mary of Redcliff."

To whom the Jewish woman: "Son, does your mother not live?" To this the boy: "She lives, and this night just past gave birth to a son, and so is still very sick."

To whom the Jewish woman: "What brothers and sisters do you have?" And he: "My mother has none except me alone and that one to whom this night she has given birth. But my father has in this city two young sons, by another woman, whom he fathered before he took my mother in marriage. And they are shoemakers." And then the woman, hearing this, went to her husband walking outside on the street with some Christians.

And she said to him in secret: "Did anyone see the boy?"

To whom he: "No." Then she recounted to him all the boy's words. And then he said joyfully: "Go back to the boy and give him drink, to make him drunk." And the woman went and made the boy drink with her.

When he had drunk over and over again, he said to the woman: "O lady, I want to go home lest I anger my father."

To whom the woman: "I am your father's niece."

"You are, thus, with your other brothers, my blood and my flesh, and I will lead you home to your father and mother."

To whom the boy: "No way, I want to go right now." To whom the Jewish woman: "This entire night *I will hold you in my arms* [literally, "lodge you in my bosom"]', and tomorrow you will bring gifts with me to your mother." To whom the boy: "I do not want to be here tonight; rather, I want to go home."

To whom the woman: "I will go and tell my lord that you want to go." And the woman went and called her husband and said: "This boy wants to leave." These things said, the Jew went and brought a small piece of wood which he had prepared for this purpose, the length of one palm and the thickness of a young boy's arm. And approaching the boy, he said: "Stay with us tonight and I will buy you nuts and a belt and a knife."

To whom the boy: "I do not want to; rather, I will go home." Then the Jew said in the Hebrew language to the woman: "Close the doors, and sing loudly in the front of the house." "And so it was done as it was said," said the lord God.

And immediately the Jew grabbed the boy's throat with both hands, and in the boy's opened mouth placed in it crossways the piece of wood prepared for this purpose, and he bound it on each side with a small piece of rope, adapted for this purpose, around the head and neck of the boy. And he bound his hands and feet, [and] covered him with a linen sheet. And the man and the woman with their son went out and sat together outside the door of their house in the street as they were accustomed to do.

And when the shadows began to cover the face of the earth, the man said: "Arise, woman, and light the fire and fetch wood, and prepare supper for us, and we will rejoice this night and exult." And he added in the Hebrew language: "And we will take vengeance now on the god of the Christians and on his most base mother." And when the fire was lit, the man said: "Woman, bring me a light and I will go see my piglet."

And when the Jew uncovered the boy's head and saw his face he spat in the boy's mouth and in his open eyes, saying in a low voice: "May your Christ be damned." And he returned to the front of the house. And he said: "Give us food and drink for a feast." And they ate until they were stuffed, and they drank, and they talked about how they would cruelly inflict punishment upon the innocent and consign him to death.

At last the Jew arose and said to the son: "Bring a light and an adequate supply of candles with you and follow me." And the father and son went out, and they prepared a cross in their privy, in which, the year before, he had crucified three boys, two born and raised within the walls of the city and the third from the parish of St Mary of Bedminster, whom that same Jew, amazingly, had murdered by various punishments unheard of throughout the ages, nailing them to the cross. "The suffering (literally, the passion) of whom I will reveal to the sons of men," thus says the lord God.

When everything had been prepared, the Jew went out, preceded by the boy with the light. And he took the boy, with his hands and feet bound to his sides, and violently threw him to the ground in front of the cross in the privy, saying: "This is the god of the Christians." And he untied the bound hands and feet of the boy and placed the boy on the cross, affixing him with nails prepared for this purpose. "By the hands and feet, in the manner of my cross," says the lord God.

Through all of this the innocent could not speak one single word because his mouth was blocked by the wood placed crossways in his mouth.

And when the boy was crucified, and bound by a rope around the neck to the cross, and naked was punished by excessive cold and the excruciating nails, he groaned wordlessly, insofar as he could.

To whom the Jew: "You groan from this? You shall die a much more evil death on account of your god Christ, and his mother a most base whore."

"I, a Jew, will punish you this night to death."

And when the boy understood this man to be a Jew, he said to himself: "Woe, woe, I am dead, for he is a Jew." And he added in his heart, saying: "Have mercy on me, Holy Mary, that I might not die," understanding nothing except the death of the body.

For he was a boy of seven and a half years, except for a few days. And the Jew spat again and again in the face of the boy saying: "Such honor is owed to your Christ and his mother." And he gave him a slap, saying: "You are Christ, the son of God, descend from the cross so that we might believe in you as in our God."

But the boy did not understand these words. And with the boy put back on the cross and bound, the Jew and his son went into the front of the house to the fire and sat together. And the Jew said: "O woman, rejoice and be glad; behold, we have this night affixed the fourth god of the Christians to the cross, eyes open, like the insane God of the Christians. Give me drink!" And drink was brought to him.

And when he had drunk he said: "And you drink!" And each of them drank. And the woman said to the man:

"What shall we do now?" To whom the man: "Light a great and most excellent [fire must be intended here, although the ms. omits the word], with wood and charcoal, and the body of the Christians' god will be roasted next to the fire like a fat chicken." And arising, he brought a large pole, two cubits and three feet and one palm in length, and the thickness of a staff and more.

He also brought another, larger pole, like a beam joined together, prepared already with a point, and yet nonetheless of a length of four cubits. And the man said to the woman: "Place a great stone next to the fire and another stone next to that one, so that it will stay firm."

"In the middle, place our tripod to support the body, and I will turn the body of the Christians' god on the fire because he is cold."

At this the woman smiled and said: "May such a god be damned." And the man added: "Let us all go and mock him before he is burned." And the man and the woman and their little son went into the privy.

And when they had entered with the light they cried out, saying: "Behold the god of the Christians." And Samuel said: "Let us strike him and spit on him." And the woman went up to him, and with the knife with which she was accustomed to cut bread she cut off the boy's nose and his lips as far as the teeth. And she said: "Behold how beautifully the Christian god smiles." And the boy streamed with blood.

Then Samuel said: "Let us give this boy a drink because he is drying out." At this the woman: "I will make him a drink." And the man, approaching, took from the boy's mouth the wood placed crossways and offered the steaming drink to him, saying in the French language: "Drink." To whom the boy in the English language: "I will drink, lord, and do not kill me, for the love of Saint Mary of Redcliff." At this utterance the Jew spat in his face and said: "For the love of that whore you will die a most cruel death this night." And again he offered him the drink, saying: "Drink quickly or else I will strike you." And when the innocent had tasted it, he said: "I can drink no more, for it is bitter." These things accomplished, Samuel said to his son: "Go and strike Christ, our adversary." To whom the boy: "I cannot reach his face to strike him." To this Samuel: "Take the knife from your mother's hand and I will lift you up so you can strike him." And so it was done. Lifted-up, with the knife in his hand, the Jewish boy struck the Christian boy in the middle of the head with the sharp iron. And the Christian boy cried out, insofar as he could: "Woe, I am dead." At this Samuel: "Not yet! But if you are the god of the Christians, *descend from the cross* "and go home." To whom the boy: "Let me go home and I will give you my tunic and my hood."

To this Samuel: "Give them to your God so that he may free you." These things said, they took the boy from the cross and threw him to the ground and kicked him with their feet and stomped on him.

At last the man, with a rope tied to the boy's feet, dragged him into the front of the house. But the boy, naked and with his vilely mutilated face, seeing the great fire said, insofar as he could with his lips cut off: "Lord, let me go to the fire, for I die from cold." To whom the Jew: "Do you hope to have enough fire on your sides?" To whom the boy, insofar as he could: "Lord, thank you." For he thought the Jew would have pity on him. Then Samuel said: "Woman, take up the light and go into the privy, and bring me the little piece of wood that was in the boy's mouth." And the woman went and brought it, as the man had ordered her. And approaching, the woman said: "*Here is the wood.* Meanwhile the innocent had warmed himself almost to death. And Samuel said to the woman: "Put wood on the fire." And so it was done. Then the Jew grabbed the boy's face, or rather the countenance of the innocent, and put the wood in his mouth crossways, as previously, and bound it as he had done before. And he said: "Woman, lift up the feet of this Christian and stretch him out." And with the boy's feet and hands extended, Samuel placed the larger pole that he had already prepared under the boy's belly and bound him firmly, starting at the head and so down to the feet, saying: "This god is well bound."

And when he was bound from the top of his head to the soles of his feet, Samuel said: "Woman, lift up the end of the pole at the head and place it on the stone next to the fire, and I will turn." "And so it was done as it was said," says the lord God.

And when he turned the boy over the great fire, his hands bound to the pole, a deep voice came forth from the boy's throat, saying in a great voice: "Samuel, why do you burn me all night? I am the God of Abraham and the God of Isaac and the God of Jacob, whom for the fourth time now you have affixed to the cross, and still you burn me. Desist, wretch, desist! It is God *whom you persecute*." And the voice was silent. And the man and woman were stupefied, and they said: "Now whose voice was that?" And the man said: "O woman, take the boy from the fire and take the wood out of his mouth and let him be freed from his bonds so that he can speak to us, if he lives." And immediately the boy was set free from his bonds and the body fell as if lifeless. And Samuel said: "This one is dead." And the woman said: "Who then has spoken to us in the Hebrew language? Have we not clearly heard the words of our own language?"

To this Samuel: "We have heard wonders this night."

To whom the woman: "Take beer and pour it in his mouth, so that he might speak to us, if there should still be a vital spirit in him."

And when they had poured in his mouth a small portion of the beer, the boy breathed as if awakening from sleep. He said nothing, however, but fell as if sleeping in a bed. And the woman, approaching on bended knees, placed her mouth at the left ear of the boy and said three times: "Little Adam, Little Adam, Little Adam, speak with me and I will lead you home to your father and your mother." And the boy responded to her not a word.

Then Samuel, marveling at what lay beyond his understanding, said: "Not one single person in this entire town knows how to deliver a sermon in our Hebrew language, and this little boy, almost lifeless, roasted in the fire, said this with cut-off lips. This [boy] has in no way spoken. Perhaps *it was a phantasm.*"

To whom the woman: "It was no phantasm that we heard a voice like a man's clearly saying in a clear and distinct voice 'Samuel, why do you burn me this night? I am the God of Abraham and the God of Isaac and the God of Jacob whom for the fourth time now you have affixed to the cross, and still you burn me. Desist, wretch, desist! It is God whom you persecute.' That was not in any way a phantasm." To whom the man: "Now what shall we do concerning this wonderous event?"

To whom the woman: "Do not burn the boy, but put him back in bed until he can speak to us." And the man said, "No way; instead I shall put him back on the cross again, *and we will see if his Christ comes to free him* from our hands."

To whom the woman: "Do as you wish." And the man carried the innocent in his hands, preceded by his wife with the son with the light.

And when they had bound him on the cross up to the point that they affixed him with nails, the woman said, "Take the rope away, the nails are enough." And so it was done. But the boy, fastened on the cross again with nails again fixed in his feet and hands through new wounds, as if awakened from sleep said:

"Holy Mary help me." The Jew had pierced the boy's wounds through with wounds, and so the boy had eight wounds from the fixed nails.

And when the Jew heard the name of Mary, he spat in the boy's face and said: "Call on that whore to help you". At this the woman:

"Lord, let me speak to the boy."

To whom the man: "Speak."

Then the woman, approaching the cross, said: "Little Adam, speak to me and tomorrow I will lead you home to your father and mother."

To whom the boy, as well as he could with his cut-off lips: "What shall I say to you?" To whom the woman: "What did you see when you were in the blazing heat of the fire? And what did you hear?" To whom the boy, as well as he could with cut-off lips:

"When you placed me next to the great fire, an exceedingly beautiful lady came to me and sat between me and the fire, and said in the English language, kissing me for as long as I was next to the fire: "Son, this night you will come to your father and mother and you will rejoice with them."

To whom the woman: "Did you hear anyone speaking with us when you were in the fire?" And he: "I saw on my right a boy kissing the wounds of my hands and feet and saying to me, '*You are my beloved brother*'."

To whom the woman: "And what did you respond?" To whom the innocent: "My mouth was blocked by the wood, so I could not speak."

To this the woman: "You heard nothing that boy said to us? "And he: "I did not understand the words of those whom I saw."

At this the woman: "Who did you see?" "I saw many men around me with that boy who kissed me."

To whom she: "What did they say to you about us?" And he: "Nothing".

To whom she: "Where now is that boy who said all this?"

To this the boy: "He is with me on the cross and he kisses me." At this the woman: "My beloved son, ask of him and say "What is your name?"

To whom the boy: "I will ask him". And he said, "Boy, what is your name?"

To whom the Lord said in a clear voice with all hearing: "Jesus Christ the Naza-rene is my name." And they all fell to the ground and were greatly stupified. The Jews' son, however, trembled for fear and said to his mother: "Mother, let us go from here and go to sleep." Then the man and woman arose from the ground. And the man said: "It is a phantasm that this boy saw." To whom the woman: "It was no phantasm that we heard. We all heard the voice on the cross beside the boy saying: 'Jesus Christ the Nazarene is my name.'"

To whom the man: "If he is God as the Christians say, why does he not heal the wounds of the boy, snatching him from our hands?" And Samuel added: "If this boy Jesus whom the Christian sees should come to me, I will affix him to the cross and punish him."

To whom the woman: "What more should we do to this boy?" This said, the Jew grabbed the knife which he had at his belt and he struck the boy in the side to the heart, and immediately the innocent *gave up his spirit*. And they all heard the voice of thousands and thousands of thousands saying: "*Blessed are all the works of the lord God*," etc.

[This folio begins in the upper left corner with an illuminated initial, showing a younger male figure dressed identically to the Jewish male in the larger illumina-tion, but with pleasant features, a conical cap, a very pointed and prominent nose, but not a hooked one. He is holding up the hem of his outer garment, revealing green leggings underneath. Kneeling before him on the left is a female figure wear-ing a green dress and a green hat. These figures are meant to represent Samuel's wife and son, who are about to convert to Christianity. In the upper right hand corner of the folio there is an illustration showing Samuel, caricatured as a Jew with a prominent hooked nose, stabbing Adam on the cross in his right side with a knife. The cross is erected in a two-hole privy, which is clearly displayed in the illustration. Samuel's knife looks like a shochet, a knife used by Jews for the kosher slaughtering of animals. Adam is naked except for a loincloth. Samuel is wearing green leggings and a russet overgarment, with a mustard-colored hood and a green, closely fitted cap. The cross is also green. Adam's body is white, as is his loincloth. The background is red, with a gargoyle-like figure breathing fire over the head of the Jew, and another beast to Adam's right, whose tail becomes a branch from which flowers are growing, and from whose mouth another flower emerges.]

And when the woman heard this she said, "*We have sinned, we have done wrong. Jesus Christ the Nazarene is the creator of all.*"

At this the enraged Jew struck her, saying: "Lying whore, he was a magician and an evildoer." Then the woman withdrew, saying: "Tomorrow I will receive baptism in the name of our lord Jesus Christ, believing in him."

And when the man heard this he ran after her and struck her with the knife saying: "Now believe in Jesus." But struck mortally in the side, she said in a great voice: "Jesus son of Mary, have mercy upon me." Then the man struck her mortally a third and a fourth time, and so the woman *gave up the spirit*. "And I, Jesus Christ, the son of God and of the Virgin Mary, led the soul of the woman with the soul of the crucified boy to the kingdom of eternal joy," says the lord God.

And when the boy, the son of the Jew, saw his murdered mother: "Woe is me, my mother is dead."

To whom the father: "Do you wish, beloved, to believe in Jesus Christ the evil-doer and to be baptized in the Christian manner?"

To whom the boy: "I believe in Jesus Christ the god of the Christians, as my mother believed, and I want to be baptized in the Christian manner." These things said, immediately the father struck him with a knife to the death of the flesh. And immediately his soul was led by angels to heaven.

Then the Jew, sorrowful unto death, said "Woe to me that ever I was born. My wife and my son are dead and I alone am left." And he wept with great tears, saying: "Woe, woe, it goes badly for me tonight." And he went out raging. And made a deep pit, with tools excellently prepared for this purpose, to a depth of almost two and a half feet, and a length of four feet, and a width of almost two feet. And he took the precious martyr from the cross and placed him in the grave and said with tears:

"May your Christ be damned, because he has taken from me this night son and wife."

And together with the body of the martyr he threw into the grave the nails by which the boy was transfixed to the cross.

And he also threw into the grave the wood of the holy cross, disassembled into three parts, thinking to himself: "Never again will I affix a Christian to the cross, because of this misfortune which has befallen me this night." And he replaced the earth over the body of the martyr, almost levelling the ground. And he went to the bodies of his son and wife.

The entire area, indeed, was soaked with the blood of the son and the mother.

And the Jew sat weeping and wailing and saying: "Woe, what shall I do now? I shall take both bodies and hide them under woolen cloth until day comes, so that I can take counsel concerning such a misfortune." And he took the body of the woman and hid it under the cloth and dirt. And then he took the son's body and hid it under the mother's shroud. And he covered the fire with ashes, as the woman had customarily done, and he went to sleep, dressed and shod as he had been throughout the day. *And immediately the cock crowed.*

And when it was day the wretch arose from his bed and went to the privy to purge his bowels. "And he saw, upon the grave of the martyr, my angel," says the lord God, "holding a fiery sword in his hands and saying to him: 'Wretch, you shall not purge your bowels here!'" But the Jew, astonished, fell backward out the door of the privy and with quick steps returned to the front of the house, and said: "I shall flee from this town, so as to be no further confounded." And going out, he closed the door of the house.

And when he looked at his tunic and shoes stained with blood, he returned to his house, and washed the tunic inside and the shoes outside, along with his hands and all the other things soaked with blood. And so he went out, closing the outer door with a very strong bar.

This done, he decided to tell these wonders to his sister.

And when he had fully related the death of the Christian boy, the sister said: "O beloved brother, where is the body of that boy whom you killed?". To whom the brother: "I buried the body of that boy in the privy, and then I saw with my eyes, in a clear light, a most terrifying angel of God upon the grave of that boy, at the head, threatening me with a great sword in his hand extended against me, and saying to me in a voice most lofty and terrible, 'Wretch, you shall not purge your bowels here!' And terrified with horrible fear, I fled and came here to you." To whom the sister: "What appearance had that one whom you saw?" And he: "A most terrible appearance, *and eyes* that seemed to me *like two flaming fires*."

To this the sister: "What clothing had he?" And he, "O sister, because of the exceeding splendor and light in the latrine, surpassing all to which human creatures are accustomed, I could not look at him any more."

To whom the sister: "Where is your wife with your son?" And he, "Woe, sister, they are dead." To whom the sister: "How, and by what death?" To this, he: "I killed her with my son because they said, 'we want to be baptized in the Christian manner' and 'we believe in Jesus Christ the Nazarene."

To whom the sister: "Where have you buried them?" And he with tears said: "I have not yet buried them." To this the sister: "Do not cry so greatly, and let us act carefully concerning such a misfortune." And she added: "Let us go individually, in silence, to your house and there let us see together what should be done." And they went together, the man going first, and having unbarred the door, they entered the house. And the man said to his sister: "O sister, come and see my wife and my beloved son." And they went and uncovered each of the bodies. The which seen, the woman said: "Brother, you have done very badly," and the woman wept with great tears. And the man wept. Then the sister said to the brother, "Let us bury these bodies in this house, and we shall say to our people that your wife has left you with the son, and we do not know where they went." And these things said, the man agreed. And they prepared together a deep pit in the west corner of the strongroom, to a depth of three feet and a length of seven feet and a width of two cubits and more.

These things done, the sister said: "Take the bodies as quickly as possible and we shall bury them so that none of our brothers shall know. And with them bury all of their clothing."

And so it was done. And the mother and son were placed in the pit with all their clothing and shoes, and the earth quickly replaced, although he could not level the ground.

To whom the sister: "Don't worry about the levelling of the ground, because no one will suspect you of their deaths."

To whom the brother: "O sister, I do not want to remain here so long as that boy whom I crucified is in the privy with that angel, whom I saw with my eyes and heard with my ears. Nor do I dare look at the door of the latrine for fear."

To whom the sister: "I will go and see that angel."

To whom the brother: "I adjure you by the living god, sister, do not approach him because he is truly terrible." To this the sister: "I will not go because you have adjured me by the living god." "The woman was indeed blindly faithful to her law," says the lord God. Leaving, the man went before his sister, *because of his horrible fear*. Having exited through the door into the street, the sister said to the brother:

"Be comforted, brother, and do not fear. I will gather some neighbors from amongst our people and I will tell them that your son and your wife have left you, you know not where."

To whom the brother: "Do as you have said, sister, and returning let us take all the goods which are in my house to your house, because I will live with you." "And so it was done as it was said," said the lord God.

And when all but the tools had been carried away, the brother said to the sister: "Sister, close that door with an inner bar, so that no one shall enter and see our misfortune." And everything was barred as the man commanded. And Samuel lived with his sister, fearing and trembling, day and night, from all that had come to pass.

To whom the sister in secret: "Brother, why did you crucify that little boy?" And he: "To the outrageous insult of Jesus Christ the Nazarene, his god, for whom and for whose mother I have always held a vehement hatred."

To whom the sister: "Why do you hate him and his mother? What evil has he done to you?"

To whom Samuel: "No evil has he done me, but I hold a hatred towards him because he said, 'I am Christ the son of the living God." And she: "What is it to us if he said that? Let us hold to our law, which Jesus gave to us by the hand of Moses and Aaron, and that is enough for us."

To whom Samuel: "Let us provide together how that boy whom I killed on the cross can be transferred from the place in which he is buried to a Christian cemetery, because I fear and abhor to look at my house so long as that boy is buried there."

To this the sister: "I will go and see whether the angel whom you saw is there as you say, or not."

To whom Samuel: "O sister I beg you, do not go near that place." To whom the sister: "I will go and see."

To whom the brother: "I beg you, whatever you may see or hear, do not believe in Jesus the god of the Christians."

To this the sister, smiling, said: "The sight of a thousand angels will not turn me away from the law of our fathers." This said, the woman went and having unbolted the door, entered the house. And immediately a remarkably fragrant odor infused her nostrils, and she said to herself: "From where does this fragrance come to me?" And she approached the door of the privy. She looked inside and saw within a boundless light.

Her eyes, indeed, failed her from the extraordinary clarity of the light. And she said: "I shall not enter, lest I die from a powerful blow by the angel." And returning with quick steps she closed the door with a bar as she had done before. And entering her own house she said to her brother: "Woe, Samuel, woe beloved brother, you have done badly. You have killed a holy friend of God. Oh what a w*onderous light* I have seen with my eyes today*! Oh ho*w sw*eet, how g*lorious is the fragrant odor in your house."

To this, that wretch: "Did you not see the angel of God with a sword?" And she, "Not at all. But when I stood outside the door of the privy, with lowered head I looked for a moment and saw a wonderful light and one beyond the bounds of human and created nature, and terrified with fear I retreated. Never will I go there any more, nor will I enter that house so long as that friend of God is buried there."

"If the Christians should perceive it, they will burn us and our houses and so the memory of our people will be obliterated from the earth. You have done miserably." To this he: "O sister, do not be angry with me, lest I lose my life."

To this the sister: "I grieve for you, brother, because you wanted to kill an innocent on account of some hatred, and to condemn him to a most cruel death."

To whom Samuel: "O sister, I have 40 marks in this house under your care. Those marks and whatever I have I will give to some faithful Christian, either a priest or a cleric of the Christian law, to transfer to the Christian cemetery the body of that boy whom I killed."

The woman responded: "Samuel, brother, for a smaller price I can find a priest of the Christian law to transfer the boy's body to a Christian cemetery."

To this Samuel: "It is true that for a smaller price you could find a priest to do this, but not all can be trusted. Because certain of them, if they knew this secret, in their drunkenness would pass it on to their whores or to others, and so our people would be confounded." And the man added: "And there is another thing that worries me. If we should perhaps choose by common agreement a holy and religious priest of the Christian law, as soon as the secret was revealed to him he would disclose it to the bishop and clergy, to our confusion and death."

"If we tell that secret to a self-indulgent and gluttonous priest, he in his drunkenness will pass it on to his whore and she to the entire people, and so there will be no hope to us of life, and so much the more worrisome and threatening will this be to us. The boy's father, William of Wales, will seek his son throughout the city, and if he should come to know the death of his son at our hands, he will avenge it, and then there will come upon us tribulation and most severe persecution."

The woman responded: "It is as you have said." To whom Samuel: "Let us go, sister, through the city and search for some needy priest, who does not have his whore in his house, so that, hired for a fee, he will transfer the boy's body from the privy." To this, the woman responded: "Today is a feast for the Christians, and they all eat and drink."

"For that day was the day of the Assumption of my most pious mother Mary, through Me and to Me," says the lord God.

And indeed no work was done in the city on so extremely solemn a day. And the woman added: "First let us eat and drink, and afterwards we will go into the city. And the lord God of our fathers will provide us a priest of the Christian law, faithful to us in all our secret doings." "And so it was done as it was said," says the lord God. And the Jews ate and drank in sorrow and trembling of soul.

And when they had eaten and drunk, Samuel said: "This entire night I have not slept. I will go and sleep a little while, because my eyes are heavy." And the woman said: "Go and rest a little while." Meanwhile that woman went into the city and encountered a priest from Ireland, and the woman said: "Are you a priest?" To whom he: "I am indeed a priest, from Ireland." And she: "Where are you going?" And he: "I travel to Rome by reason of a pilgrimage and for other reasons."

To whom she said joyfully: "When did you arrive in this town?" And he: "I came now and as yet I do not have lodgings and I have not eaten nor drunk today." To this she responded:

"Follow me at a distance and enter the house when I enter." And he: "Thanks be to you, lady I will follow." And having followed the woman and entered the house, he said, "We seek hospitality, hospitably, with thanks." He had in his party two men and two women. To whom the woman: "I will give you excellent hospitality and I will give you meat and drink sufficient for this night and tomorrow."

To whom the priest said, in the English language insofar as he knew it: "May Holy Mary bless you and repay you." And she fell silent.

And when the pilgrims had sat down together, the Jewish woman said: "What meat would you like to have to eat?" To whom the priest: "O lady, pig meat." And she: "Pig meat is neither good nor healthy in this city because many are leprous, and they eat human shit in the streets. But I will give you beef meat and three fat chickens for you and for us. And I don't want you to leave this house."

To this the priest, giving thanks, said: "We will not go out." And the woman said to her maidservant, who was of her people, "Go quickly into the city and buy three fat and excellent chickens for 3 pence and I meanwhile will prepare the fire and put the meat in the pot." And so it was done, and the chickens were brought.

And when all was prepared, the woman went out to her brother, saying: "Samuel, arise and we shall go eat because our lord God has sent us an excellent priest." And Samuel, rejoicing, said: "Where is he from?" And she: "He is from Ireland." At this Samuel: "Does he know either the English or French language?" And she: "He knows and understands both."

To whom Samuel: "Let us give thanks, sister, to God." And he added with tears: "All that I have is yours if you can free me from this misfortune." The woman responded, "Do not fear, excellent brother, I will free you. Above all, take care that they do not perceive us to be Jews." And he: "I will do, sister, what you ask."

And when all was prepared, all the Christians sat down together at the table, and the Jews sat apart from them a little ways.

And when the priest blessed the meat and drink by making the sign of the cross, saying: "May the son of God bless the meat and drink of his servants, in the name of the father and of the son and of the holy spirit, amen," the Jew, hearing this, spat three times on the ground. "In hatred towards me," says the lord God.

The Christians ate and drank and got drunk. The drunken priest even asked the maidservant of the house to sleep with him that night. But she told her lady the priest's request.

To whom she: "I beseech you, my beloved girl, that you do whatever he may wish."

The maidservant responded: "In no way will I do what you ask, because I am a virgin." To this the lady: "Go, then, and make up the bed of the priest and the other Christians." And so it was done.

And when all were asleep the woman said to her brother: "How shall we proceed concerning the boy whom you killed?" And he: "He cannot be buried in a cemetery in this city on account of the multitude of men walking around here and there."

To this the woman responded: "It would be better for us to give these Christians some of our wealth, so that they will carry the boy's body outside the city and bury it there, either in the cemetery or outside it." This said, the man praised the prudence of the woman. And the woman added: "Let us say, then, that the dead boy is our son, crucified and killed by Jews in this city, and that we do not want anyone in this world to know this on account of the royal officials, who will despoil us of our money."

"These and similar things we will say so that they do not perceive us to be Jews."

"I will speak of everything with the priest, you listening. We will also give the priest five marks of the finest silver and each of the others one mark, the promise of the priest and of the others confirmed by an oath, that he will carry the boy's body in his bosom, wrapped in new linen cloth which we will give him. And when he shall have left the city, he will bury it in some secret place, as shall seem most expedient." To whom the man: "You have given us excellent advice. So shall it be. Amen." And they slept until morning.

And when the day began to grow light, the woman said: "Arise, everyone, and let us go to church to hear mass." This said, the priest quickly got up, and dressed and shod, he said to the woman: "Lady, thank you for the good things you have bestowed charitably upon us. We will go on our way now and we will pray for you."

To whom the woman: "Take three pence, and give them to three priests, and ask that they sing a mass of the Holy Spirit that all shall go well for us. And you sing mass, if you can, because today I will feed all of you excellently." To this the priest, giving thanks, said: "I will do as you have said." And receiving three coins from the woman, he went to three churches, and to three priests he offered each a penny, saying to each: "Sing a mass of the Holy Spirit." And he, as the fourth, celebrated mass, while his companions waited at the house with their luggage.

And when the priestly office was completed, the pilgrim priest returned to his lodging, and the Jewish woman said to him: "Come, good priest, I want to confess to you our secrets, which if you should reveal to anyone, we will tell the bishop and clergy, and convicted by us, you will be imprisoned and punished by a just judgment."

To whom the priest: "Never have I revealed a sin to anyone, nor will I reveal one."

For he was a simple and religious man and one who feared God, except when drunk. And these three went into a secret place, that is, the priest, and the woman, and Samuel. And the woman said to the priest: "To the lord God and to you we render up our secret." And he: "Render it up." To whom she: "I will not render it up to you unless first you swear to me, by your faith, that you will not reveal our secret; also, at the same time, your companions, by your hand, shall swear that along with you they will keep our secret. And we will give you five marks of excellent silver, and to each of your companions one mark of silver, if you assent to our counsel." These things said, the priest swore for himself, and upon his own faith on behalf of his companions.

Then the woman said: "Lord priest, I had one son, and he went out yesterday to the house of a certain most base Jew, our neighbor. And this evil Jew in secret seized my son and, affixing him to the cross, killed him by a cruel death. And having found the boy's body, we buried him in a certain privy, because if the royal officials of the city found out, they would despoil us of all our money, by blaming us for the crime of having murdered the boy. Wherefore we beseech you, take from our money what you please, and carefully carry the body of our son out of the city and bury it in some secret place, wherever you please. Because if anyone finds out, we shall be destroyed and despoiled."

To this the priest: "If you give to me and my companions what you have promised, I will do as you have said." To whom the woman: "I shall give you and your companions seven marks right now, and I will count them before you. You, meanwhile, should speak with your companions so that they will remain faithful in keeping all our secrets. But nonetheless do not tell them that the boy was crucified by Jews. You can keep that from them." And seven marks of silver were counted out and placed in the priest's sack. And the woman said: "Take this linen cloth, and wrap that boy in this cloth, because he was buried naked. And whatever you may see or hear, reveal it to no one except me alone. And when you have wrapped the boy's entire body, put the linen cloth back in the front of the house, and close the door to the street as the maidservant will show you. Quickly return to me and tell me everything. But you will find through the open windows whatever tools you will need with which to dig."

To this the priest: "Who will go with me and who will show me the burial place?"

To this Samuel: "When you have entered the front of the house, go into the strongroom, and on the right you will find the door of the privy. Go into the western part and you will find beneath your feet and hands the burial place, because the earth is not solidly compacted. And in the same privy you will find prepared instruments, upon the naked body of the boy. You will find wood and eight iron nails. Replace all that in the ground and level the dirt of the ground just as it was before. But take care that the maidservant does not enter with you." And summoning the maidservant, the woman said, "Go and open the door of my brother's house and do not enter. The lord priest, however, will follow close behind you, and he will enter through the door that he shall see you open. And close the inner door so that no one shall enter." And the maidservant went first and opened the door of the house as the woman had commanded. The door unbarred, the maidservant returned and encountered the priest. And she said, "Go and enter the house. I heard the sweetest song in that house." To whom the terrified priest said, "Who are those who sing in that house?"

To this the maidservant: "I don't know." And immediately the priest returned, saying to the woman: "Lady, tell me who those are who sing in that house to which I am going."

"I do not want to enter alone. Two of my companions shall enter with me." To whom the woman: "Angels of God sing around the most holy body of my son."

To this the priest responded: "I will not enter without my companions." To whom the woman: "Do as you wish."

For the woman was frightened almost to death. And the priest said to his companions: "You two men come with me. The women shall sit here for the time being." And the priest went out and the two men followed him. And they entered Samuel's house, the priest going first. And the Christians who were standing nearby said to the pilgrims entering the house: "Don't go in there for that is a Jew's house." But they did not understand the English language; they were from Ireland. All having entered, the priest closed the inner door.

And having gone inside with the two men, he heard singing from the right of the house like a choir of monks singing with thousands of thousands of boys singing the treble in three parts, one among the thousands of thousands above all the others, singing with thousands *in organo,* with ineffable sweetness, and saying, "*To God alone be honor and glory, now and forever.*" And one of the laymen who had come with the priest said in the Irish language: "Where is this song of the clergy? And where is the church?"

To whom the priest: "Take care not to speak one single word. Sit here until I return to you, and say the *Pater Noster,* that is, the Lord's prayer, and the *Ave Maria* that is, the Hail Mary; and I do not want you to leave this spot." And the two men sat down together weeping for joy on account of the sweet song of the angels. "They were truly faithful men," says the lord God.

And when the priest came near the door of the privy he heard a voice saying to him: "Go, priest chosen by God, to some neighboring priest in this city and confess to him all your sins, in thought and in deed, and correct the moral depravities of your drunkenness. And afterwards come here to us. You must leave this place until you are cleansed. These men of Ireland, your companions, shall remain in peace here until you come back, because they are clean. You, however, are full of sordidness. Go and repent and confess, and be fully cleansed, and then you will be told what you are to do."

"Depart quickly, for you stink powerfully before God!" And the voice was silent, nor did he hear any more the sound of singing as before. And the priest, going in to his companions, said: "Wait here until I come back. Say nothing, but pray to God that he will remit to you your sins." And immediately he went out to a neighboring priest, who was sitting with his wife. And on bended knees, he [the Irish priest] said in the French language: "I want to speak with you."

To whom he: "Where do you wish us to speak together?" And he: "In the church of God." And when they had entered the church, the pilgrim fell at his feet, [saying]: "Lord, I will confess to you all my sins." And when he had fully confessed to him everything, with contrite heart, in tears and great sobbing, and penance had been enjoined upon him, the pilgrim departed, absolved from the stain of crime. And he returned to Samuel's house to his companions and said: "Has no one said anything to you?" And they: "No, not at all."

"But we saw most beautiful youths standing around us." To which the priest: "What did they say to you?" And they responded: "Nothing". And he: "What more did you see?" To whom they: "We saw a certain woman exiting and entering, dressed in a purple cloak, with a certain little boy with clothing of the same color. All entered and exited from the right side of the house. Their appearance was truly like the sun." To which the priest: "Did any one of those whom you saw look at you?" And they: "That woman dressed in purple clothing, with her son following behind her, blessed us, showing us three wounds in her body, two in the chest and the third in the side. The little boy, however, following behind her, showed one wound beneath the breast. But many processed with them, following them. But a w*onderous light* arose from the right side of the house. O what joyful thing is there? What exalted and delightful habitation is there?" These things said, the priest, by himself, went out towards the door of the privy in great fear, saying: "Lord Jesus Christ have mercy upon me; that I may not be destroyed." And he heard a voice saying: "Enter, do not fear. For you are indeed clean." Having heard this, he entered the privy. And he said in the Irish language: "Hail to you, good men." To which all the body of saints in a clear voice: "*Amen, Amen, Amen.*" And all the angelic citizens stood in a circle around the precious martyr. There were, indeed, *among the elder*s, thousands of thousands of angels singing, *"Glory and honor be to God the father and to the Holy S*on *and to the Paraclete for ever and ever."* The chorus responded: "A*men, Amen, Amen."*

The priest, however, astonished by the vision of the angels and the voice and the immense light, fell to the ground *among the elders.* And one of them *touched him, saying:* "*Arise quickly.* Do not fear. And take the linen cloth which you have at your waist, beneath your belt, and wrap the body of the martyr in it." And he, having forgotten the cloth out of excessive wonder, said: "Lord, I do not have linen cloth under my belt." And immediately it was responded to him: "You have it under your belt. Take it and wrap the boy completely in cloth." And he, recalling to memory the cloth which he had placed under his belt, quickly took it from his waist and said: "Where is the boy?" And immediately three angels offered the body to the priest, holding it in their hands high in the air. And one of the angels holding the body of the martyr said to the priest: "Cover the body with the cloth and take your needle and thread and sew it all the way up, lest the saint be seen naked." And he placed the cloth upon the body. And he covered the boy, the angels helping and holding the body high in the air above the ground, and he wrapped it in cloth. And taking his needle and thread from his pouch, he immediately did as he had been commanded.

The cloth completely sewn together around the body of the martyr, the angels with the elders sang continuously in parts (*in organo*) with astonishing sweetness: *"Blessed are all the w*orks *of the Lord. Praise the Lord and exalt him forever, who deigned to be born from the glorious Virgin Mary,"* the choir singing the lower part in a softer voice, the angels, in three parts, singing *in organ*o in a high voice most sweetly above all the others. And so they sang all the verses of the hymn distinctly and clearly.

And when they had come to that verse, *"Blessed be the land of the Lord,"* they said the hymn *"Declare and praise and exalt him forever, who deigned to be born of the glorious Virgin Mary."*

Similarly at the other verse, *"Blessed be the Lord of Israel,"* [they said] the hymn *"Declare and praise and exalt him forever, who deigned to be born from the glorious Virgin Mary."* At the final verse they said: *"Blessed art thou, Lord, in the firmament of heaven, most praiseworthy and glorious and exalted forever, who deigned to be born from the glorious Virgin Mary."* Then the angel said to the priest:

"Take the body of the martyr and bear it into the front of the house. And put your brothers on their knees and they shall hold in their hands the body of the precious martyr. You, meanwhile, shall go to the house of the Jewish woman, and make from wood a modest container appropriate to the body, in length four feet, in width a foot and a half. And say to that man, the brother of the woman who spoke with you today, that, truly penitent, he should confess all his sins fully, and truly believing, be baptized in the name of our lord Jesus Christ. And I will come with you to fully complete this and he shall be our friend. And at the same time, [speak] to the aforesaid woman in the name of our lord Jesus Christ, that she may be converted and live. Tell your brothers, however, waiting in the front of the house with the body, that they should sit in silence, praying. Go and carry together with us the body of the martyr. And put your brothers on their knees until you return with a container appropriate to the body of the martyr, as I have said. For you shall carry the precious body to your church in Ireland and bury it there."

Lift up the body together with us and let us carry it into the front of the house, and place it on the knees of the men." And the priest put his hands at the boy's feet. The angels, however, carried the head and body. Preceded by the body, a choir of elders followed with a multitude of angels singing this psalm without rank (*sive/sine ordinem*) and saying: *"Praise the lord from the heavens, praise him in the highest."* And so they sang the psalm up to the end. And when the body was placed in the laps of the men, the priest said to them: "Sit here and hold this most holy body on your knees. And do not speak to each other, but pray intently, and wait until I come back."

And they, seeing the multitude of angels singing with the choir of elders, were terrified with fear.

The angel said to them, *"Do not fear.* For we will go with you to Ireland. Sit in peace, and do not move from this spot." And the priest quickly went out. And having entered the house of the woman, he said: "O good woman, I have seen wonders today."

To whom the woman: "What have you seen?" And he: "I will not tell you unless, believing in our lord Jesus Christ, you are baptized in the Christian manner in the name of the Father and the Son and the Holy Spirit, amen."

To this the woman: "I do not believe in the mortal man Jesus." Samuel, approaching, said to the sister:

"Withdraw from here, woman, lest perhaps through the deceptive words of the priest you should believe in Jesus."

To whom the priest: "O good man, believe in Jesus Christ, God omnipotent, and be baptized in true penitence, and confess to me your sins and I will bring you to God."

To whom the Jew: "Who revealed to you that I am a Jew?" "An angel of God showed me that you are an unbeliever." And he added: "Bring me wood so that I can prepare myself a modest container in which to carry the body of the boy with me to Ireland."

Joyful, Samuel went into the city and bought four pieces of wood, and borrowed from certain Christians tools with which to work the wood, and he gave them to the priest, saying "Behold I have brought you everything." And the priest prepared, as well as he knew how, a modest container as the angel had commanded. And the woman said to the priest: "When you want to eat I will prepare you your food." The priest responded: "I will not eat in this house." These things said, the woman was silent; nor did she dare to question the priest concerning all that he had heard or seen.

And when the container was prepared and the wood fastened together with nails, he said to the [Christian] women: "Pick up your luggage and come with me quickly." And so it was done, and the women followed him. To whom, having exited, [he said]: "Wait here outside. I will come right back to you." And the priest went into the house toward the gathering of angels, bearing in his arms that container that he had prepared.

To whom the angel: "Work quickly!" And the container opened, three angels together with the priest placed the boy's body in the container. And the container closed, the angel said to the priest, "Take off your cape and cover the entire container, and bind the container at the bottom with the cape. Depart quickly from this city, because now you shall find a ship ready in which you shall cross the sea to Ireland and prosperously return to your country. Buy yourselves what you need. All of us whom you have seen this day will be with you until you are in Ireland. We will be the leaders of your journey until you return to your houses and residences. Take care that you do not become drunk; this container is never to be uncovered. Place your head upon it at night." These things said, one of the angels took the nails, by which the boy had been affixed to the cross, and the wood of the cross, and said to the priest: "Your companions shall bear this holy wood and these precious nails. Everything must be covered."

"Tell no one of this vision, lest by chance you die." The priest, taking up the wood and the nails from the hands of the angel, handed all to one of the men and said: "Carry all this most excellently, and cover it with your clothing insofar as you can, and we shall go." The priest took up in his arms the container with the body. And going first, he went out into the street, his companions following. And calling to the women, they returned to the ships, necessities purchased, and prosperously returned to their country.

And when the priest had returned home, the angel appeared to him in the middle of that night, saying: "*Arise quickly* and come with me. And bring the body of the precious martyr in your arms, and tools with which to open the earth." And so it was done with all speed. And preceded by an immense light he came and showed the priest the spot and said: "Open the earth. I, meanwhile, with my fellow servants, will hold the precious body." And having made a small grave, the angel said to the priest: "Come quickly and we shall place the container with the body of the martyr, beloved by God, in the ground, as God has commanded us." The angel together with the priest placed the most holy body in the ground, inside the container. And the earth was replaced in that spot.

These things finished, the angel said to the priest: "Go to your house and love and fear the Lord your God in your heart. Bury the wood of the holy cross that you have in your house, with the nails, in a cemetery this night. On the third day, go with your companions to Rome as you vowed to do, blessing God all the time, *because he is pious and clement and merciful and he will triumph over evil.* This place, however, shall be unknown to you and to all human creatures until the day predetermined by God the Father." These things said, the angels appeared no more.

And as the priest stood there astonished, he heard the voices of innumerable angels in the highest heaven, singing *"Te Deum laudamus"* in full, up to this verse: *"Deign, lord, this day, etc."* And the priest went and buried the wood of the cross with the nails in the cemetery beneath the church, and he went back to his house, praising God all the time, and he went on his way rejoicing and exulting.

And when he returned from Rome with his companions he went through many places looking for the grave of the martyr, and not finding that most holy place, he was intensely sorrowful, and said with tears: "Woe, where is the place where I put the martyr?" For he had forgotten the words that the angel had spoken to him: "This place shall be unknown to you and to all human creatures until the day predetermined by God the Father."

Giovanni Villani, "The Story of the Jewish Desecration of the Eucharist (Paris 1290)," in *Nuova Cronica*, trans. W.L. North from the Edition of G. Porta, *Nuova Cronica* (Parma, 1990), 3 vols, VIII. 143, I. 616.

Concerning a great miracle concerning the body of Christ that happened in Paris.

In the aforesaid year [1290] there was a Jew who had loaned money at interest to a Christian woman who had pawned her clothes, and she wished to recover them in order to have them to wear on Easter day. The Jew said to her: If you bring me the body of your Christ, I will return your clothes without payment. The simple and covetous woman promised him [to do so], and on the morning of Easter, when she went to receive communion, she kept the sacrament and brought it to the Jew. He put a pot on the fire with boiling water and threw the body of Christ in, but it could not consume it. Seeing this, he stabbed it many times with a knife and it poured forth a copious amount of blood so that the water turned all vermillion. Then, he removed it [from the boiling water] and put it in cold water, and it became vermillion in a similar manner. When some Christians arrived to borrow money, they realized the Jew's sacrilege, and the holy body sprung onto a table all by itself. When this was learned, the Jew was captured and burned, and the holy body was collected by the priest with great reverence. Of that house where the miracle occurred, a church was built which is called the Savior of the Boiling Water.

Muslims (Saracens)

Fulcher of Chartres, "Speech of Urban II at Clermont," in *A Source Book for Medieval History*, ed. Oliver J. Thatcher and Edgar Holmes McNeal (Scribners, 1905), pp. 513–7.

". . . your brethren who live in the east are in urgent need of your help, and you must hasten to give them the aid which has often been promised them. For, as the most of you have heard, the Turks and Arabs have attacked them and have conquered the territory of Romania [the Greek empire] as far west as the shore of the Mediterranean and the Hellespont, which is called the Arm of St. George. They have occupied more and more of the lands of those Christians, and have overcome them in seven battles. They have killed and captured many, and have destroyed the churches and devastated the empire. If you permit them to continue thus for awhile with impurity, the faithful of God will be much more widely attacked by them. On this account I, or rather the Lord, beseech you as Christ's heralds to publish this everywhere and to persuade all people of whatever rank, foot-soldiers and knights, poor and rich, to carry aid promptly to those Christians and to destroy that vile race from the lands of our friends. I say this to those who are present, it is meant also for those who are absent. Moreover, Christ commands it.

"All who die by the way, whether by land or by sea, or in battle against the pagans, shall have immediate remission of sins. This I grant them through the power of God with which I am invested. O what a disgrace if such a despised and base race, which worships demons, should conquer a people which has the faith of omnipotent God and is made glorious with the name of Christ! With what reproaches will the Lord overwhelm us if you do not aid those who, with us, profess the Christian religion! Let those who have been accustomed unjustly to wage private warfare against the faithful now go against the infidels and end with victory this war which should have been begun long ago. Let those who for a long time, have been robbers, now become knights. Let those who have been fighting against their brothers and relatives now fight in a proper way against the barbarians. Let those who have been serving as mercenaries for small pay now obtain the eternal reward. Let those who have been wearing themselves out in both body and soul now work for a double honor. Behold! on this side will be the sorrowful and poor, on that, the rich; on this side, the enemies of the Lord, on that, his friends. Let those who go not put off the journey, but rent their lands and collect money for their expenses; and as soon as winter is over and spring comes, let them eagerly set out on the way with God as their guide."

Robert the Monk, "Speech of Urban II at Clermont," in Dana C. Munro, "Urban and the Crusaders," in *Translations and Reprints from the Original Sources of European History* (University of Pennsylvania Press, 1895), vol. 1:2, pp. 5–8.

Oh, race of Franks, race from across the mountains, race chosen and beloved by God as shines forth in very many of your works set apart from all nations by the situation of your country, as well as by your catholic faith and the honor of the holy church! To you our discourse is addressed and for you our exhortation is intended. We wish you to know what a grievous cause has led us to Your country, what peril threatening you and all the faithful has brought us.

From the confines of Jerusalem and the city of Constantinople a horrible tale has gone forth and very frequently has been brought to our ears, namely, that a race from the kingdom of the Persians, an accursed race, a race utterly alienated from God, a generation forsooth which has not directed its heart and has not entrusted its spirit to God, has invaded the lands of those Christians and has depopulated them by the sword, pillage and fire; it has led away a part of the captives into its own country, and a part it has destroyed by cruel tortures; it has either entirely destroyed the churches of God or appropriated them for the rites of its own religion. They destroy the altars, after having defiled them with their uncleanness. They circumcise the Christians, and the blood of the circumcision they either spread upon the altars or pour into the vases of the baptismal font. When they wish to torture people by a base death, they perforate their navels, and dragging forth the extremity of the intestines, bind it to a stake; then with flogging they lead the victim around until the viscera having gushed forth the victim falls prostrate upon the ground. Others they bind to a post and pierce with arrows. Others they compel to extend their necks and then, attacking them with naked swords, attempt to cut through the neck with a single blow. What shall I say of the abominable rape of the women? To speak of it is worse than to be silent. The kingdom of the Greeks is now dismembered by them and deprived of territory so vast in extent that it cannot be traversed in a march of two months. On whom therefore is the labor of avenging these wrongs and of recovering this territory incumbent, if not upon you? You, upon whom above other nations God has conferred remarkable glory in arms, great courage, bodily activity, and strength to humble the hairy scalp of those who resist you.

Let the deeds of your ancestors move you and incite your minds to manly achievements; the glory and greatness of king Charles the Great, and of his son Louis, and of your other kings, who have destroyed the kingdoms of the pagans, and have extended in these lands the territory of the holy church. Let the holy sepulchre of the Lord our Saviour, which is possessed by unclean nations, especially incite you, and the holy places which are now treated with ignominy and irreverently polluted with their filthiness. Oh, most valiant soldiers and descendants of invincible ancestors, be not degenerate, but recall the valor of your progenitors.

But if you are hindered by love of children, parents and wives, remember what the Lord says in the Gospel, "He that loveth father or mother more than me, is not worthy of me." "Every one that hath forsaken houses, or brethren, or sisters, or father, or mother, or wife, or children, or lands for my name's sake shall receive an hundredfold and shall inherit everlasting life." Let none of your possessions detain you, no solicitude for your family affairs, since this land which you inhabit, shut in on all sides by the seas and surrounded by the mountain peaks, is too narrow for your large population; nor does it abound in wealth; and it furnishes scarcely food enough for its cultivators. Hence it is that you murder one another, that you wage war, and that frequently you perish by mutual wounds. Let therefore hatred depart from among you, let your quarrels end, let wars cease, and let all dissensions and controversies slumber. Enter upon the road to the Holy Sepulchre; wrest that land from the wicked race, and subject it to yourselves. That land which as the Scripture says "floweth with milk and honey," was given by God into the possession of the children of Israel Jerusalem is the navel of the world; the land is fruitful above others, like another paradise of delights. This the Redeemer of the human race has made illustrious by His advent, has beautified by residence, has consecrated by suffering, has redeemed by death, has glorified by burial. This royal city, therefore, situated at the centre of the world, is now held captive by His enemies, and is in subjection to those who do not know God, to the worship of the heathens. She seeks therefore and desires to be liberated, and does not cease to implore you to come to her aid. From you especially she asks succor, because, as we have already said, God has conferred upon you above all nations great glory in arms. Accordingly undertake this journey for the remission of your sins, with the assurance of the imperishable glory of the kingdom of heaven.

When Pope Urban had said these and very many similar things in his urbane discourse, he so influenced to one purpose the desires of all who were present, that they cried out, "It is the will of God! It is the will of God!" When the venerable Roman pontiff heard that, with eyes uplifted to heaven he gave thanks to God and, with his hand commanding silence, said:

Most beloved brethren, today is manifest in you what the Lord says in the Gospel, "Where two or three are gathered together in my name there am I in the midst of them." Unless the Lord God had been present in your spirits, all of you would not have uttered the same cry. For, although the cry issued from numerous mouths, yet the origin of the cry was one. Therefore I say to you that God, who implanted this in your breasts, has drawn it forth from you. Let this then be your war-cry in combats, because this word is given to you by God. When an armed attack is made upon the enemy, let this one cry be raised by all the soldiers of God: It is the will of God! It is the will of God!

And we do not command or advise that the old or feeble, or those unfit for bearing arms, undertake this journey; nor ought women to set out at all, without their husbands or brothers or legal guardians. For such are more of a hindrance than aid, more of a burden than advantage. Let the rich aid the needy; and according to their wealth, let them take with them experienced soldiers. The priests and clerks of any order are not to go without the consent of their bishop; for this journey would profit them nothing if they went without permission of these. Also, it is not fitting that laymen should enter upon the pilgrimage without the blessing of their priests.

Whoever, therefore, shall determine upon this holy pilgrimage and shall make his vow to God to that effect and shall offer himself to Him as a, living sacrifice, holy, acceptable unto God, shall wear the sign of the cross of the Lord on his forehead or on his breast. When,' truly',' having fulfilled his vow he wishes to return, let him place the cross on his back between his shoulders. Such, indeed, by the twofold action will fulfill the precept of the Lord, as He commands in the Gospel, "He that taketh not his cross and followeth after me, is not worthy of me."

Guibert of Nogent, *The Deeds of God through the Franks*, trans. Robert Levine (Boydell Press, 1997), pp. 32–7.

According to popular opinion, there was a man, whose name, if I have it right, was Mathomus, who led them away from belief in the Son and in the Holy Spirit. He taught them to acknowledge only the person of the Father as the single, creating God, and he said that Jesus was entirely human. To sum up his teachings, having decreed circumcision, he gave them free rein for every kind of shameful behavior. I do not think that this profane man lived a very long time ago, since I find that none of the church doctors has written against his licentiousness. Since I have learned nothing about his behavior and life from writings, no one should be surprised if I am willing to tell what I have heard told in public by some skillful speakers. To discuss whether these things are true or false is useless, since we are considering here only the nature of this new teacher, whose reputation for great crimes continues to spread. One may safely speak ill of a man whose malignity transcends and surpasses whatever evil can be said of him.

An Alexandrian patriarch died, I'm not sure when, and the leaderless church was divided, as usual, into various factions; the more eagerly each argued for the person whom he favored, the more strongly he argued against the person whom he opposed. The choice of the majority was a hermit who lived nearby. Some of the more discerning men often visited him, to find out what he was really like, and from these conversations they discovered that he disagreed with them about the Catholic faith. When they found this out, they immediately abandoned the choice they had made, and, with the greatest regret, set about condemning it. Scorned, torn apart by bitter grief, since he had been unable to reach what he had striven for, like Arius, he began to think carefully how to take vengeance by spreading the poison of false belief, to undermine Catholic teachings everywhere. Such men, whose whole aim in life is to be praised, are mortally wounded, and bellow unbearably, whenever they feel that their standing in the community is diminished in any way. Seeing his opportunity with the hermit, the Ancient Enemy approached the wretch with these words: "If," he said, "you want certain solace for having been rejected, and you want power far greater than that of a patriarch, look very carefully at that young man who was with those who came to you lately – I shall recollect for you his clothing, his face, his physical appearance, his name – fill his vigorous, receptive mind with the teaching that lies near to your heart. Pursue this man, who will listen faithfully to your teachings and propagate them far and wide." Encouraged by the utterance, the hermit searched among the groups that visited him for the identifying signs of the young man. Recognizing him, he greeted him affectionately, then imbued him with the poison with which he himself was rotting. And because he was a poor man, and a poor man has less authority than a rich one, he proceeded to procure wealth for himself by this method: a certain very rich woman had recently become a widow; the filthy hermit sent a messenger to bring her to him, and he advised her to marry again. When she told him that there was no one appropriate for her to marry, he said that he had found her a prophet who was appropriate, and that, if she consented to marry him, she would live in perfect happiness. He persisted steadily in his blandishments, promising that the prophet would provide for her both in this life and in the next, and he kindled her feminine emotions to love a man she did not know. Seduced, then, by the hope of knowing everything that was and everything that might be, she was married to her seer, and the formerly wretched Mahomet, surrounded by brilliant riches, was lifted, perhaps to his own great stupefaction, to unhoped-for power. And since the vessel of a single bed frequently received their sexual exchanges, the famous prophet contracted the disease of epilepsy, which we call, in ordinary language, falling sickness; he often suffered terribly while the terrified prophetess watched his eyes turning upward, his face twitching, his lips foaming, his teeth grinding. Frightened by this unexpected turn of events, she hurried to the hermit, accusing him of the misfortune which was happening to her. Disturbed and bitter in her heart, she said that she would prefer to die rather than to endure an execrable marriage to a madman. She attacked the hermit with countless kinds of complaints about the bad advice he had given her. But he, who was supplied with incomparable cleverness, said, "You are foolish for ascribing harm to what is a source of light and glory. Don't you know, blind woman, that whenever God glides into the minds of the prophets, the whole bodily frame is shaken, because the weakness of the flesh can scarcely bear the visitation of divine majesty? Pull yourself together, now, and do not be afraid of these unusual visions; look upon the blessed convulsions of the holy man with gratitude, especially since spiritual power teaches him at those moments about the things it will help you to know and to do in the future." Her womanly flightiness was taken in by these words, and what she had formerly thought foul and despicable now seemed to her not only tolerable, but sacred and remarkable. Meanwhile the man was being filled with profane teaching drawn by the devil's piping through the heretical hermit. When the hermit, like a herald, went everywhere before him, Mahomet was believed by everyone to be a prophet. When far and wide, in the opinion of everyone, his growing reputation shone, and he saw that people in the surrounding as well as in distant lands were inclining towards his teachings, after consulting with his teacher, he wrote a law, in which he loosened the reins of every vice for his followers, in order to attract more of them. By doing this he gathered a huge mob of people, and the better to deceive their uncertain minds with the pretext of religion, he ordered them to fast for three days, and to offer earnest prayers for God to grant a law. He also gives them a sign, because, should it please God to give them a law, he will grant it in an unusual manner, from an unexpected hand. Meanwhile, he had a cow, whom he himself trained to follow him, so that whenever she heard his voice or saw him, almost no force could prevent her from rushing to him with unbearable eagerness. He tied the book he had written to the horns of the animal, and hid her in the tent in which he himself lived. On the third day he climbed a high platform above all the people he had called together, and began to declaim to the people in a booming voice. When, as I just said, the sound of his words reached the cow's ears, she immediately ran from the tent, which was nearby, and, with the book fastened on her horns, made her way eagerly through the middle of the assembled people to the feet of the speaker, as though to congratulate him. Every-one was amazed, and the book was quickly removed and read to the breathless people, who happily accepted the license permitted by its foul law. What more? The miracle of the offered book was greeted with applause over and over again. As though sent from the sky, the new license for random copulation was propa-gated everywhere, and the more the supply of permitted filth increased, the more the grace of a God who permitted more lenient times, without any mention of turpitude, was preached. All of Christian morality was condemned by a thousand reproofs, and whatever examples of goodness and strength the Gospel offered were called cruel and harsh. But what the cow had delivered was considered uni-versal liberty, the only one recommended by God. Neither the antiquity of Moses nor the more recent Catholic teachings had any authority. Everything which had existed before the law, under the law, under grace, was marked as implacably wrong. If I may make inappropriate use of what the Psalmist sings, "God did not treat other nations in this fashion, and he never showed his judgements to any other people." The greater the opportunity to fulfill lust, and, going beyond the appetites of beasts, by resorting to multiple whores, was cloaked by the excuse of procreating children. However, while the flow of nature was unrestrained in these normal acts, at the same time they engaged in abnormal acts, which we should not even name, and which was unknown even to the animals. At the time, the obscu-rity of this nefarious sect first covered the name of Christ, but now it has wiped out his name from the furthest corners of the entire East, from Africa, Egypt, Ethiopia, Libya, and even the more remote coasts of Spain – a country near us. But now to describe how this marvelous law-giver made his exit from our midst. Since he often fell into a sudden epileptic fit, with which we have already said he struggled, it happened once, while he was walking alone, that a fit came upon him and he fell down on the spot; while he was writhing in this agony, he was found by some pigs, who proceeded to devour him, so that nothing could be found of him except his heels. While the true Stoics, that is, the worshipers of Christ, killed Epicurus, lo, the greatest law-giver tried to revive the pig, in fact he did revive it, and himself a pig, lay exposed to be eaten by pigs, so that the master of filth appropriately died a filthy death. He left his heels fittingly, since he had wretchedly fixed the traces of false belief and foulness in wretchedly deceived souls. We shall make an epi-taph for his heels in four lines of the poet:

Aere perennius,
Regalique situ pyramidum altius:
(I have built a monument) more lasting than brass, taller than the royal site of
   the Pyramids . . .

So that the fine man, happier than any pig, might say with the poet:

Non omnis moriar, multaque pars mei
Vitabit Libitiam
I shall not die entirely, a great part of me shall avoid Hell.

That is:

> Manditur ore suum, qui porcum vixerat, hujus
> Membra beata cluunt, podice fusa suum.
> Quum talos ori, tum quod sus fudit odori,
> Digno qui celebrat cultor honore ferat.
> He who has lived by the pig is chewed to death by the pig and the limbs which
>   were called blessed have become pigs' excrement. May those who wish to
>   honor him carry to their mouths his heels, which the pig has poured forth in
>   stench.

What if there is some truth in what the Manicheans say about purification, that in every food something of God is present and that part of God is purified by chewing and digesting, and the purified part is turned into angels, who are said to depart from us in belching and flatulence: how many angels may we believe were produced by the flesh eaten by these pigs and by the great farts they let go? But, laying aside the comic remarks intended to mock his followers, my point is that they did not think that he was God, but a just man and leader, through whom divine laws might be transmitted. They imagined that he had been taken up into heaven, with only his heels left as a monument for his faithful adherents, who visit them with great veneration, and condemn eating pork, because pigs consumed their lord with their bites.

After the pagan heresy had grown strong over a long time, and for many generations, the people whom we have mentioned above invaded Palestine, Jerusalem, and the Holy Sepulchre, and captured Armenia, Syria, and the part of Greece that extends almost to the sea which is called the Arm of Saint George. Among all the Eastern kingdoms, the Babylonian empire was from ancient times the most powerful, and ruled over many kingdoms. However, the kingdom of the Parthians, whom we, because of changes in the language, call the Turks, is preeminent in military matters, in horsemanship, and in courage, although it is a very small country. And so the Babylonian emperor occupied the areas we just mentioned with a large army, but in the course of time he lost them, as the Turks grew in number, and the Assyrians were defeated. More energetic, and in command of an astute boldness, they were attacking the empire of Constantinople and seemed about to besiege the city, when the Emperor of the Greeks, frightened by their frequent and relentless incursions, sent a letter to France, written to the elder Robert, Count of Flanders, offering him reasons that might urge him to defend endangered Greece. He did not approach him because he thought that Robert, although extremely wealthy, and capable of raising a large force, could alone supply enough troops for the task, but because he realized that if a man of such power went on such a journey, he would attract many of our people, if only for the sake of a new experience, to support him. This count was truly as wise in military matters as he was perspicacious and discriminating in literary matters. He had once before gone to Jerusalem, for the sake of prayer, and, happening to pass through Constantinople on the way, had spoken with the emperor; as a result, on the basis of the great feeling of trust he had developed for him, the emperor was impelled to call upon him for aid. Since inserting the letter itself in this little work would produce a tedious effect, I have preferred to offer some of what was said, but clothed in my own words.

He complained that, "After Christianity was driven out, the churches which the pagans held had been turned into stables for horses, mules, and other animals. It was also true that they had set up in them temples, which they called Mahomeries, and they carried out all kinds of filthy activity in them, so that they had become not cathedrals, but brothels and theaters. Moreover, there would be no purpose to my mentioning the slaughter of Catholics, since the faithful who died received in exchange eternal life, while those who survived led lives wretchedly bound by the yoke of slavery, harsher, I believe, than what those who died endured. They took virgins and made them public prostitutes, since they were never deterred by shame or feeling for marital fidelity. Mothers were violated in the presence of their daughters, raped over and over again by different men, while their daughters were compelled, not only to watch, but to sing obscene songs and to dance. Then they changed places, and the suffering, which is painful and shameful to speak of, was inflicted upon the daughters, while the filthy activity was adorned by the obscene songs of the unfortunate mothers. Finally reverence for all that was called Christian was handed over to the brothel. When the female sex was not spared (an action which might be excused since it is at least in accord with nature), they became worse than animals, breaking all human laws by turning on men. Their lust overflowed to the point that the execrable and profoundly intolerable crime of sodomy, which they committed against men of middle or low station, they also committed against a certain bishop, killing him. How can this urgent lust, worse than any insanity anywhere, which perpetually flees wisdom and modesty, and is enkindled more powerfully the more it is quenched, control itself among human beings, whom it befouls with couplings unheard of among beasts, actions to which Christians may not give a name. And although, according to their own judgement, these wretches may have many women, that is not enough, but they must stain their dignity at the hog-trough of such filth by using men also. It is not surprising that God could not tolerate their ripe wantonness, and turned it into grief, and the earth, in its ancient way, cast out the excrement of such destructive inhabitants."

**Peter the Venerable, "Summa Totius Haeresis Saracenorum,"
in *Writings Against the Saracens*, trans. Irven M. Resnick (The
Catholic University of America Press, 2014), pp. 34–50.**

This is a summary of the entire heresy and of the diabolical teaching of the Saracens, that is, the Ishmaelites.

1. First and foremost, their first and greatest error that ought to be cursed is that they deny the Trinity in the unity of the deity, and in this way, while shunning number in unity, they do not believe in a triune number of persons in the one essence of divinity, while I say that the beginning and end of all forms is ternary; and thus they do not receive the cause and origin and goal of all things that are formed;

although confessing God with their lips, they do not know him in a profound way. These foolish ones, these inconstant ones, confess that there is a principle for change and for every difference, to wit one that is only binary in unity, namely the divine essence itself, and its life (*anima*). For this reason the Qur'an – by which name they call their law, and Qur'an, translated from Arabic, means a collection of precepts – always introduces God speaking in the plural.

2. Furthermore, these blind ones deny that God the Creator is the Father, because, according to them, no one becomes a father without sexual intercourse. And although they accept that Christ was conceived from a divine spirit, they do not believe that he is the Son of God nor, moreover, that he is God, but that he is a good, most truthful prophet, free from all deceit and sin, the son of Mary, begotten without a father; he never died, because he did not deserve death – instead, although the Jews wanted to slay him, he slipped through their hands, ascended to the stars, and lives there now in the flesh in the presence of the Creator, until the advent of the Antichrist. When the Antichrist comes, this same Christ will slay him himself with the sword of his virtue, and he will convert the remaining Jews to his law. Moreover, he will teach his law perfectly to the Christians, who a long time ago lost his law and Gospel owing, on the one hand, to his departure, and on the other hand owing to the death of the apostles and disciples, by which [law] all Christians at that time will be saved, just like his first disciples. Even Christ himself will die with them and with all creatures at one and the same time, when Seraphim – who they say is one archangel – sounds the trumpet; and afterward he will rise with the rest, and he will lead his disciples to judgment, and he will assist them and pray for them, but he will not himself judge them. Indeed, God alone will judge. The prophets and the individual messengers, however, will be present among them as their intercessors, and to assist them. Thus, to be sure, the most wretched and impious Mohammad has taught them, he who, denying all the sacraments of Christian piety by which men are especially saved, has condemned already nearly a third of the human race to the devil and to eternal death with the unheard-of foolishness of fables – by what judgment of God, we do not know.

3. It seems that one must speak about who he [Mohammad] was, and what he taught, for the sake of those who will read that book, so that they might better understand what they read, and come to know how detestable both his life and teaching were. For some think that he was that Nicholas who was one of the first seven deacons, and that this law (*lex*) of the modern Saracens is the teaching of the Nicolaitans, who were named after him, which is denounced in the Apocalypse of John. And others dream up other individuals and, as they are careless in reading and unacquainted with the actual events, so here, just as in other cases, they conjecture every manner of falsehood.

4. This one [Mohammad], however, as even the chronicle translated from Greek into Latin by Anastasius the Librarian of the Roman church clearly relates, lived during the age of the Emperor Heraclius, a little after the time of the great Roman Pope, Gregory I, almost 550 years ago; he was one who was of the Arab nation, of low birth, at first a worshiper of the old idolatry – just as the other Arabs still were at that time – unlearned, nearly illiterate, active in business

affairs, and, being very shrewd, he advanced from low birth and from poverty to riches and fame. And here, increasing little by little, and by frequently attacking neighbors and especially those related to him by blood with ambushes, robberies, and incursions – killing by stealth those whom he could, and killing publicly those whom he could – he increased fear of him, and because he often came out on top in these encounters, he began to aspire to kingship over his race.

5. And when, with everyone equally resisting [him] and condemning his low birth, he saw that he could not pursue this path for himself as he had hoped, he attempted to become king under the cloak of religion and under the name of a divine prophet, because he was unable to do so by the power of the sword. And since he lived as a barbarian among barbarians, and as an idolater among idolaters, and among those who, more than all races, were unacquainted with and ignorant of law both human and divine, he knew that they were easy to seduce, and he began to undertake the iniquitous task he had conceived. And since he had heard that God's prophets were great men, and saying that he is His prophet so as to pretend to be something good, he attempted to lead them partly away from idolatry, yet not to the true God but rather to his own false heresy, which he had already begun to bring forth.

6. Meanwhile, with the judgment of Him who is said to be "terrible in his counsels over the sons of men" and who "has mercy on whomever he chooses, and hardens the heart of whomever he chooses," Satan bestowed success upon error, and he sent the monk Sergius, a sectarian follower of the heretical Nestorius, who had been expelled from the Church, to those parts of Arabia, and united the monk-heretic with the false prophet. Accordingly Sergius joined with Mohammad, supplied what he lacked and, explicating for him the Sacred Scriptures – of both the Old and the New Testament – in accord with the understanding of his master, Nestorius, who denied that our Savior is God, [and] partly in accord with his own conception, and at the same time completely filling him up with fables from apocryphal books, he made him into a Nestorian Christian.

7. And, in order that the complete fullness of iniquity should coalesce in Mohammad, and so that nothing should be lacking for his damnation or for that of others, Jews were joined to the heretic, and lest he become a true Christian, the Jews whispered to Mohammad, shrewdly providing to the man who was eager for novelties not the truth of the Scriptures but their fables, which still today they have in abundance. And in this way, taught by the best Jewish and heretical teachers, Mohammad created his Qur'an, and having confected it from both Jewish fables and the foolish nonsense of heretics, he wove together that wicked scripture in his own barbarous fashion. Having created the lie that gradually this was conveyed to him in a book by Gabriel, whose name he knew already from Sacred Scripture, he poisoned a people that was ignorant of God with a lethal draught, and, in the manner of men such as this, coating the rim of the chalice with honey, with the deadly poison following after, he destroyed – O woe! – the souls and bodies of that miserable race.

8. Clearly that impious man did so when, while commending both the Christian and the Jewish religion (*lex*), confirming that neither one ought to be embraced,

he rejected them while proving himself reprobate. For this reason he confirms that Moses was the best prophet, that Christ the Lord was greater than all, proclaims that he [Christ] was born of a virgin, confesses that he was the messenger of God, the word of God, the spirit of God, yet he does not understand or confess [Christ as] the messenger, Word, or Spirit as we do. Actually, he ridicules [the Christian teaching] that he is said or believed to be the Son of God. And, measuring the eternal birth of the Son of God in comparison to human generation, the bovine man denies and mocks with as much effort as he can that God could have either begotten or been begotten. With frequent repetition he affirms the resurrection of the flesh; he does not deny that there is a general judgment at the end of time, but it must be carried out not by Christ but by God. He insanely affirms that Christ, as the greatest of all after God, will be present at that judgment and that he himself will be present to assist his people.

9. He describes the torments of hell such as it pleased him to do, and such as it was fitting for the great false prophet to invent. He painted a paradise that is not of the company of angels, nor of a vision of the divine, nor of that highest good that "no eye has seen, nor ear heard, nor has it entered into the human heart," but painted one such as truly flesh and blood desired, or rather the dregs of flesh and blood, and one which he desired to have prepared for himself. There, he promises to his followers a meal of meats and of every kind of fruit, rivers of milk and honey, and of sparkling waters; there promises the embrace and sexual satisfaction of the most beautiful women and virgins, in which the whole of his paradise is defined. Vomiting up again among these nearly all of the dregs of the ancient heresies, which he had absorbed from the devil's instruction, he denies the Trinity with Sabellius, rejects the deity of Christ with his own Nestorius, [and] repudiates the death of the Lord along with Manichaeus, although he does not deny his return to the heavens.

10. Instructing the people in these and similar teachings not for improvement but for damnation, he completely turned away from God, and, lest a Gospel word besides could have a place among them – just as it does for those who know everything that pertains to the Gospel and Christ – he blocked entry to their hearts with the iron barrier of impiety. He decreed, moreover, that circumcision ought to be observed, just as it had been adopted by Ishmael, the father of that people; and, in addition to all these things, so that he could attract to himself more easily the carnal minds of men, he relaxed the reins on gluttony and libidinal pleasure; and, having himself eighteen wives at one and the same time, and the wives of many others, committing adultery as if in response to divine command, he joined a larger number of the damned to himself just as if by prophetic example. And lest he appear completely disgraceful, he commended a zeal for almsgiving and certain acts of mercy, he praised prayer, and in this way the utterly monstrous one joined "to a human head a horse's neck, and the feathers" of birds, as a certain one says. Seeing that, at the persuasion of the monk already mentioned and the aforementioned Jews, he [Mohammad] completely abandoned idolatry, and persuaded those whom he could that it ought to be abandoned, and proclaimed that there is one God that ought to be worshiped, having abandoned a multiplicity of gods, he seemed to say what

had not been heard before by those that are rude and unschooled. And because, in the first place, this preaching was in harmony with their reason, they believed him to be God's prophet.

11. From then, in the progress of time and of error, he was raised up by them to the kingship that he had desired. Thus, mixing good things with evil, confusing true things with false, he sowed the seeds of error, and, partly during his time and partly and especially in the time after him, he produced a nefarious harvest that should be burned up by an everlasting fire. Immediately thereafter, as the Roman Empire was declining or rather nearly ceased to exist, with the permission of Him "through whom kings reign," the dominion of the Arabs or the Saracens arose, infected with this plague, and, little by little occupying by force of arms the largest parts of Asia with the whole of Africa and part of Spain, just as it transferred its rule upon those subject to it, so too did it transfer error.

12. Although I would name them heretics because they believe some things with us, in most things they depart from us; perhaps more correctly I should name them pagans or heathens, which is worse. For although they say some things about the Lord that are true, nonetheless they proclaim many others that are false, and they participate neither in baptism, nor the sacrifice [of the Mass], nor penance, nor any Christian sacrament, which everyone other than these heretics has done.

13. The highest aspiration of this heresy is to have Christ the Lord believed to be neither God, nor the Son of God, but, although a great man and beloved by God, nonetheless a mere man, and certainly a wise man and a very great prophet. What once, indeed, were conceived by the devil's device, first disseminated by Arius and then advanced by that Satan, namely Mohammad, will be fulfilled completely according to diabolical design through the Antichrist. In fact, since the blessed Hilary said that the origin of the Antichrist was in Arius, then what he began, by denying that Christ is the true Son of God and by calling him a creature, the Antichrist will at last consummate by asserting that in no way was he God or the Son of God, but also that he was not a good man; this most impious Mohammad seems properly to be provided for and prepared by the devil as the mean between both of them, as one who became in a certain sense both an extension of Arius and the greatest support for the Antichrist who will say worse things before the minds of the unbelievers.

14. To be sure, nothing is so contrary to the Enemy of the human race as the faith of God Incarnate, by which we are particularly aroused to piety; and, renewed by the heavenly sacraments with the operative grace of the Holy Spirit, we hope to return again to that place from which he [the Enemy] took pride that we were cast out, namely, to the vision of the King and of our fatherland, with the King himself and the Creator God descending to our place of exile, recalling us to himself with mercy. From the beginning he endeavored to extinguish equally the faith and love of piety and of the divine dispensation in the hearts of men, and he attempted to eradicate this also at the beginning of the still nascent Church, if then it were permitted, by the most ingenious subtlety, and almost in the same way in which, later, he was permitted to seduce that most unhappy race.

15. To be sure, the blessed Augustine says that the philosopher Porphyry, after he had wretchedly become an apostate from Christianity, reported this in his books that he produced against the Christians: to wit, that he consulted the oracles of the gods and asked, concerning Christ, what he was. The reply to him was, actually, from the demons, that Christ was indeed a good man, but that his disciples had sinned gravely when, ascribing divinity to him, they invented something that he had never said about himself. This opinion is very often found among those fables [of the Saracens], almost in the same words. How great was this subtlety of the devil that he said something good about Christ, when he knew that if he spoke only evil of him, in no way would one believe him, not caring what Christ was thought to be so long as divinity, which especially saves men, was not believed to be in him; if anyone wishes to understand more fully, let him read the eighteenth book and the nineteenth book of *The City of God* by this same father Augustine, and the first [book] of *The Harmony of the Evangelists*. In fact therein, if one has a good and studious talent, he should be able to surmise with certainty both what the devil planned to do then but was not allowed to do, and what at length he did in this single most wretched race, with a hidden judgment allowing it, once he was unleashed.

16. In no way, in fact, could any mortal have invented such fables as the written ones that are singled out here, unless by the assistance of the devil's presence, through which [fables], after many ridiculous and insane absurdities, Satan planned particularly and in every way to bring it to pass that Christ would not be believed to be Lord, the Son of God and True God, the Creator and Redeemer of the human race. And in reality this is what he wanted to introduce persuasively at that time through Porphyry, but through God's mercy he was blown away from the Church, which at that time was burning still with the first fruits of the Holy Spirit; [but] at length, [he] used that most wretched man Mohammad (and as it is reported by many, one who is possessed by an evil spirit and by epilepsy) as an instrument and implement, as it were, most suited to him; alas, he plunged into eternal damnation, along with himself, a very large race and one which at present can be reckoned as nearly a half part of the world. Why this was permitted to him He alone knows to whom no one can say, "Why do you do this?" and who said, "Even from among the many that are called, few are chosen."

17. For this reason I, choosing to tremble all over rather than debate, have briefly noted down these things so that the one who reads them will understand, and if there is such a one as wishes to and can write against this entire heresy, he will know with what kind of enemy he will do battle. Perhaps there yet will be one whose spirit the Lord will awaken, in order to free the Church of God from the great disgrace that it suffers therefrom, because although up until our own time, you may be sure, it has confounded all heresies – both ancient and modern – by responding to them, not only has it not replied at all to this one alone, which, beyond all others, has caused the unbounded destruction of the human race, both in bodies and in souls, but neither has it attempted to inquire – even a little or inadequately – how great a plague it is or whence it came.

18. It was for this entire reason that I, Peter, humble abbot of the holy church of Cluny, when I tarried in Spain for the visitation of our properties that exist there, had translated from Arabic into Latin, with great effort and at great expense, that entire impious doctrine and the accursed life of its terrible inventor, and, once it was laid bare, I had it come to our acquaintance, so that one would know how foul and frivolous a heresy it is, and so that some servant of God, with the Holy Spirit enkindling him, would be spurred on to refute it with a written composition. O shame! that there is no one who will do this, because with nearly all ardor for these efforts of the saints everywhere grown cool already in the Church, I actually have waited a long time, and [because] there was no one who would open [his] mouth and move the pen and growl with the zeal of holy Christianity, I myself, at all events, proposed for some time to undertake this, if my extensive occupations permitted, with the Lord assisting. Nonetheless, I would always prefer that this be done better by someone else, rather than worse by me.

Bibliography

Akbari, Suzanne. "Placing the Jews in Late Medieval English Literature." In *Orientalism and the Jews*. Eds. Ivan Davidson Kalmar and Derek J. Penslar. Brandeis University Press, 2005.32–50.

Altschul, Nadia. "Saracens and Race in *Roman de la Rose* Iconography: The Case of Dangier in Bodleian Douce 195." *Digital Philology* 2/1 (2013): 1–15.

Bale, Anthony. *The Jew in the Medieval Book: English Antisemitisms 1350–1500*. Cambridge University Press, 2006.

Bale, Anthony. *Feeling Persecuted: Christians, Jews, and Images of Violence in the Middle Ages*. Reaktion Books, 2011.

Beal, Timothy. *Religion and its Monsters*. Routledge, 2002.

Berger, David. "The Attitude of St. Bernard of Clairvaux toward the Jews." *Proceedings of the American Academy for Jewish Research* 40 (1972): 89–108.

Cohen, Jeffrey J. "The Flow of Blood in Medieval Norwich." *Speculum* 79 (2004): 26–65.

Cohen, Jeffrey J. "The Future of the Jews of York." In *Christians and Jews in Angevin England*. Eds. Sarah Rees Jones and Sethina Watson. Boydell and Brewer, 2013.278–93.

Cohen, Jeremy. *The Friars and the Jews: The Evolution of Medieval Anti-Judaism*. Cornell University Press, 1982.

Dorin, Rowan. *No Return: Jews, Christian Usurers, and the Spread of Mass Expulsion in Medieval Europe*. Princeton University Press, 2023.

Frakes, Jerold, Ed. *Contextualizing the Muslim Other in Medieval Christian Discourse*. Palgrave Macmillan, 2011.

Franklin, Arnold, Roxani Eleni Margariti, Marina Rustow, and Uriel Simonsohn, Eds. *Jews, Christians, and Muslims in Medieval and Early Modern Times: A Festschrift in Honor of Mark R. Cohen*. Brill, 2014.

Frassetto, Michael. "Medieval Attitudes towards Muslims and Jews." In *Misconceptions about the Middle Ages*. Eds. Stephen J. Harris and Bryon L. Grigsby. Routledge, 2008.76–82.

Gow, Andrew. *The Red Jews: Antisemitism in an Apocalyptic Age, 1200–1600*. Brill, 1995.

Green, Monica. "Conversing with the Minority: Relations among Christian, Jewish, and Muslim Women in the High Middle Ages." *Journal of Medieval History* 34/2 (2008): 105–18.

Green, Monica and Daniel Lord Smail. "The Trial of Floreta d'Ays (1403): Jews, Christians, and Obstetrics in Later Medieval Marseille." *Journal of Medieval History* 34/2 (2008): 185–211.

Heng, Geraldine. *Empire of Magic: Medieval Romance and the Politics of Cultural Fantasy.* Columbia University Press, 2003.

Heng, Geraldine. "Jews, Saracens, 'Black Men', Tartars: England in a World of Difference." In *A Companion to English Literature and Culture c. 1350–c. 1500.* Ed. Peter Brown. Wiley-Blackwell, 2007.247–69.

Heng, Geraldine. "England's Dead Boys: Telling Tales of Christian-Jewish Relations Before and After the First European Expulsion of the Jews." *MLN* 127/5 (December 2012): S5—85.

Heng, Geraldine. "Reinventing Race, Colonizations, and Globalisms Across Deep Time: Lessons from la Longue Durée." *PMLA* 130/2 (2015): 358–66.

Heng, Geraldine. *The Invention of Race in the European Middle Ages.* Cambridge University Press, 2018.

Hess, Cordelia and Jonathan Adams, Eds. *Fear and Loathing in the North: Jews and Muslims in Medieval Scandinavia and the Baltic Region.* De Gruyter, 2015.

Hsia, R. Po-Chia. *The Myth of Ritual Murder: Jews and Magic in Reformation Germany.* Yale University Press, 1988.

Johnson, Hannah. *Blood Libel: The Ritual Murder Accusation at the Limit of Jewish History.* University of Michigan Press, 2012.

Jones, Sarah Rees and Sethina Watson, Eds. *Christians and Jews in Angevin England: the York Massacre of 1190, Narratives and Contexts.* Boydell, 2013.

Kaplan, M. Lindsay. "The Jewish Body in Black and White in Medieval and Early Modern England." *Philological Quarterly* 92/1 (2013): 41–65.

Kaplan, M. Lindsay. *Figuring Racism in Medieval Christianity.* Oxford University Press, 2018.

Kennedy, M.J. "'Faith in the One God Flowed Over You From the Jews, the Sons of the Patriarchs and the Prophets': William of Newburgh's Writings on Anti-Jewish Violence." *Anglo-Norman Studies* 25 (2003): 139–52.

Kim, Dorothy. "Reframing Race and Jewish/Christian Relations in the Middle Ages." *transversal* 13/1 (2015): 52–64.

Kinoshita, Sharon. "'Pagans are Wrong and Christians are Right': Alterity, Gender, and Nation in the *Chanson de Roland.*" *Journal of Medieval and Early Modern Studies* 31/1 (2001): 79–111.

Kruger, Steven. *The Spectral Jew: Conversion and Embodiment in Medieval Europe.* University of Minnesota Press, 2005.

Krummel, Miriamne. "The Pardoner, the Prioress, Sir Thopas, and the Monk: Semitic Discourse and the Jew(s)." In *The Canterbury Tales, Revisited: 21st-Century Interpretations.* Ed. Kathleen Bishop. Cambridge Scholars, 2008.88–110.

Krummel, Miriamne. *Crafting Jewishness in Medieval England: Legally Absent, Virtually Present.* Palgrave, 2011.

Krummel, Miriamne and Tison Pugh, Eds. *Jews in Medieval England: Teaching Representations of the Other.* Palgrave, 2017.

Lampert-Weissig, Lisa. "'Why is This Knight Different from All Other Knights?' Jews, Anti-Semitism, and the Old French Grail Narratives." *Journal of English and Germanic Philology* 106/2 (2007): 224–7.

Langmuir, Gavin. *Toward a Definition of Antisemitism*. University of California Press, 1990.

Lapina, Elizabeth. "Anti-Jewish rhetoric in Guibert of Nogent's Dei gesta per Francos." *Journal of Medieval History* 35/3 (2009): 239–53.

Limor, Ora. "Christians and Jews." In *Christianity in Western Europe, c. 1100–c. 1500*. Eds. Miri Rubin and Walter Simons. Cambridge University Press, 2009.133–48.

Lipton, Sara. "Christianity and its Others: Jews, Muslims, and Pagans." In *The Oxford Handbook of Medieval Christianity*. Ed. John H. Arnold. Oxford University Press, 2014.413–35.

Matteoni, Francesca. "The Jew, the Blood and the Body in Late Medieval and Early Modern Europe." *Folklore* 119/2 (August 2008): 182–200.

Mittman, Asa Simon. "'In Those Days': Giants and the Giant Moses in the Old English Illustrated Hexateuch." In *Imagining the Jew: Jewishness in Anglo-Saxon Literature and Culture*. Ed. Samantha Zacher. Cornell University Press, 2016.237–63.

Mittman, Asa Simon. "Mandeville's Jews, Colonialism, Certainty, and Art History." In *Post-colonising the Medieval Image*. Eds. Eva Frojmovic and Catherine Karkov. Ashgate, 2017.

Nirenburg, David. *Communities of Violence: Persecution of Minorities in the Middle Ages*. Princeton University Press, 1996.

Nirenburg, David. "Christendom and Islam." In *Christianity in Western Europe, c. 1100–c. 1500*. Eds. Miri Rubin and Walter Simons. Cambridge University Press, 2009.149–69.

Nirenburg, David. *Anti-Judaism: The Western Tradition*. W.W. Norton, 2013.

Nirenburg, David. *Neighboring Faiths: Christianity, Islam, and Judaism in the Middle Ages and Today*. University of Chicago Press, 2014.

Resnik, Irven M. "Medieval Roots of the Myth of Jewish Male Menses." *The Harvard Theological Review* 93/3 (2000): 241–63.

Resnik, Irven M. "Odo of Tournai and the Dehumanization of Medieval Jews: A Reexamination." *Jewish Quarterly Review* 98/4 (2008): 471–84.

Resnik, Irven M. *Marks of Distinction: Christian Perceptions of Jews in the High Middle Ages*. Catholic University of America Press, 2012.

Resnik, Irven M. "Peter the Venerable on the Talmud, the Jews, and Islam." In *Medieval Encounters: Jewish, Christian and Muslim Culture in Confluence and Dialogue*. Brill, 2018.510–29.

Resnik, Irven M. "Cruentation, Medieval Anti-Jewish Polemic, and Ritual Murder." *Antisemitism Studies* 3/1 (2019): 95–131.

Resnik, Irven M. "Jews and Abuse of the Cross in the Middle Ages: A Cross Desecration Libel?" *Jewish Quarterly Review* 111/4 (2021): 582–604.

Resnik, Irven M. "Medieval Automata and Later Medieval Judeophobia." *Journal of Medieval Religious Cultures* 48/2 (2022): 1–20.

Rose, Emily. *The Murder of William of Norwich: The Origins of the Blood Libel in Medieval Europe*. Oxford University Press, 2015.

Rubenstein, Jay. "Cannibals and Crusaders." *French Historical Studies* 31/4 (2008): 525–52.

Rubin, Miri. "Desecration of the Host: The Birth of an Accusation." *Studies in Church History* 29 (1992): 169–85.

Rubin, Miri. *Gentile Tales: The Narrative Assault on Late Medieval Jews*. Yale University Press, 1999.

Scheil, Andrew. *The Footsteps of Israel: Understanding Jews in Anglo-Saxon England*. University of Michigan Press, 2004.

Signer, Michael A. and John Van Engen, Eds. *Jews and Christians in Twelfth-Century Europe*. University of Notre Dame Press, 2001.

Stacey, Robert. "The Conversion of Jews to Christianity in Thirteenth-Century England." *Speculum* 67/2 (1992): 263–83.

Stacey, Robert. "From Ritual Crucifixion to Host Desecration: Jews and the Body of Christ." *Jewish History* 12/1 (1998): 11–28.

Strickland, Debra Higgs. *Saracens, Demons, and Jews: Making Monsters in Medieval Art.* Princeton University Press, 2003.

Taylor, Julie Anne. "Lucera Sarracenorum: A Muslim Colony in Medieval Christian Europe." *Nottingham Medieval Studies* 43 (1999): 110–25.

Thomas, James. "The Racial Formation of Medieval Jews: A Challenge to the Field." *Ethnic and Racial Studies* 30/10 (2010): 1737–55.

Utterback, Kristine and Merrall Llewelyn Price, Eds. *Jews in Medieval Christendom: 'Slay them not'.* Brill, 2013.

3   The Monstrous Female Body, Monstrous Women, and Monstrous Births

Women occupied a special place in medieval Europe in that they were at once part of Christian society and marked out within it as being more sinful than men and a source of temptation capable of luring even otherwise virtuous men into sin. This made them both monstrous and dangerous, and medieval moralists seem to have taken special delight in crafting sermons castigating women for these qualities. Not only did women bear the burden of being regarded as the daughters of Eve, who had been misled by Satan and then led Adam astray in the Garden of Eden, but women were also viewed as being fundamentally more prone to sin due to their physical and intellectual qualities. The ancient Greeks and Romans had regarded women as not only physically weaker than men, but morally and intellectually inferior as well, and less able to control their emotions – their cultural descendants in medieval western Europe inherited these beliefs. Men were associated with positive qualities like the intellect, the soul, moderation, and restraint, while women were associated with baser qualities like emotion, the body, excess, and a lack of self-control. Even worse, medieval medical theories, which relied on ancient authors like Aristotle and Galen, viewed women's bodies as deficient and deformed male bodies. Some authorities, like Isidore of Seville, even asserted that menstrual blood was poisonous, corrosive, and could make dogs rabid. Women were regarded as human, but, like the monstrous races examined in Chapter 1, they were deficient; deformed; excessive in their appetites, vices, and emotions; and potentially harmful to men.

Ancient anti-feminist beliefs and medical theories were incorporated into a Christian framework during the early Middle Ages where they were combined with negative Christian attitudes toward sex and a preference for celibacy as the surest path to salvation. These negative attitudes toward women and female bodies were ingrained in western European culture, and they provided the foundations for the virulent misogyny of the High and Late Middle Ages. Women had long been viewed as dangerous to men, but they became the particular target of Christian moralists during the eleventh century as reformers within the Church attempted to impose celibacy on a not entirely willing clergy. In their attempts to separate the clergy from their wives and girlfriends, the reformers took aim at women in general, portraying them in ever more monstrous terms to make women as unappealing as possible. For these moralists and reformers, women were little more

DOI: 10.4324/9780429243004-4

than sources of temptation and the embodiment of practically every vice. By the twelfth century, monks like Bernard of Clairvaux and Peter Abelard were arguing that even nuns, who took vows of chastity, had the potential to lead men astray and were better avoided by any man who valued his immortal soul.

All women were physically monstrous, at least theoretically, by virtue of their sex, and anxiety over the temptation they posed to men increased over time. Some women, however, also engaged in behaviors that were considered monstrous. Women who transgressed gender norms or engaged in witchcraft, for example, were often singled out as being particularly heinous; although women who took on more masculine attributes could sometimes be viewed with admiration, depending on the context. Female saints who dressed as men to live as monks stand out as admirable examples of gender transgression, as do the noble women clerical authors singled out for their masculine virtue, by which they usually meant that the women had good sense or had efficiently performed their husbands' duties in their absence and safeguarded their family's possessions and honor. Even so, women who failed to observe gender norms generally earned opprobrium rather than praise, as we will see later in this chapter.

The sources in this chapter are roughly grouped into three categories that sometimes overlap: the female body, monstrous women, and monstrous births. The material on the female body is drawn from Aristotle and Galen, whose works shaped medieval medicine. This is followed by selections from clerical authors who routinely presented women as being more prone to sin and a source of temptation for men. Finally, there are several texts that present either female monsters, monstrous women, or monstrous births. Some of the monstrous births included in this chapter were regarded as omens, as we saw in Chapter 1, while others served as evidence of the barbarity of an entire people, in this case the Irish, and were used to justify their conquest.

We begin with Aristotle's (384–322 BCE) views on the female body in his *Generation of Animals*. Although much of Aristotle's work was known only indirectly in western Europe in the early Middle Ages, Aristotelian physiology profoundly influenced western European medical theories after his works were rediscovered in the twelfth century. Together with Galen, Aristotle provided the basis for medieval medical theory. Aristotle's description of human procreation begins with the assertion that the female body is weaker and colder than the male body and that females produce menstrual blood in place of semen. He goes on to state that women contribute nothing to procreation other than "matter" and an empty vessel in which the fetus gestates. Following this reasoning, he believes that the male alone contributes the soul to the fetus while the female contributes only the body. Most importantly, Aristotle contends that females are deformed males. He makes this claim in explaining why women bear children that are sometimes male and sometimes female. He says that women contribute material that contains all of the potential parts of the body, but just as deformed parents sometimes produce deformed children, women sometimes produce offspring that are female (deformed) like them. He goes on to explain that this is because "the female is as it were a deformed male." Later, he explains that the female body is a deformity, but one that occurs in the ordinary course of nature.

Aristotle also addresses the causes of monstrosities in his treatise. He says that they are produced when the material provided by the mother is not fully mastered or shaped by the semen provided by the father. When this happens, it results in deformed offspring that are called monstrosities. He adds that people with extra body parts, misshapen body parts, or both male and female sexual organs, which he notes are also called monstrosities, are the result of more material being set during gestation than is needed. According to Aristotle, monstrosity is a type of deformity, and both are produced in a similar fashion. Finally, he clarifies that most monstrosities, strictly speaking, are the result of two or more embryos that have grown together.

For Aristotle, the male body was the perfect or default human form. It was the male who contributed the most important material to the fetus, the male semen that "mastered" the mere matter contributed by the female, and the male who imparted a soul to his offspring. Women, on the other hand, were reduced to providers of raw material and incubators for the gestating fetus. The female body itself was viewed as an aberration, a deformity and deviation from the perfect male body, but one that was nonetheless essential to procreation and occurred in the ordinary course of nature. Aristotle's explanation of the cause of monstrosities and deformities also implicates the female body, as it is the material provided by the female and gestated by her that fails to "set" correctly. Aristotle's works had a profound influence on High and Late Medieval medicine. While some medieval physicians and thinkers challenged his view of women as deformed men, it remained widespread and shaped medieval conceptions about women.

The second-century Greek physician and philosopher Galen (129–216 CE), who served as physician to Emperor Marcus Aurelius, also profoundly shaped medieval understandings of medicine and the body. In his *On the Usefulness of the Parts of the Body*, Galen reinforces Aristotle's hierarchy of the sexes, explaining that just as man is the most perfect of all the animals, man is more perfect than woman due to his excess heat, which is nature's primary instrument. Since women are colder than men, they are necessarily less perfect, and female sexual organs are less perfect because they fail to emerge from the body due to the lack of heat. Although Galen regards women as incomplete men who failed to fully develop and describes the uterus as being formed by the scrotum remaining inside the body and failing to emerge, he presents this in a positive light. He asserts that the Creator has made half of the human race "imperfect" and "mutilated" because it provided humans with a great advantage by allowing them to reproduce. He adds that God designed this defect in women to ensure that human fetuses have an appropriate place to develop.

While Galen views the female body as imperfect and mutilated by divine design, he does allow women a greater role in reproduction than Aristotle who asserted that women provided only matter for male semen to act upon. Galen notes that women have ovaries (which he calls smaller, less perfect testes) and says that they produce semen that contributes to the fetus; however, Galen describes this female semen as far inferior to male semen as it is colder, wetter, and there is less of it. Moreover, he asserts that it is only the more perfect male semen that is capable of generating an animal. The female's real contributions to procreation are having a hollow receptacle to receive the male semen and accumulating an excess of nutrients that nourish the fetus. Although they differed in their views of what females contributed to the fetus, Aristotle and Galen fundamentally agreed on the inferiority, imperfection, and deformity of the female body. Whether this deformity was viewed as the beneficial product of nature or the gift of a benevolent Creator, the female body was viewed as being inherently monstrous in its deficiency.

Not only were women largely viewed as deformed men in medieval western European medicine, their menstrual blood was widely regarded as monstrous as well. Isidore of Seville (c. 560–636), the Spanish scholar, theologian, and archbishop of Seville, discusses menses in his great collection of ancient knowledge known as the *Etymologies*. He repeats the widely held belief that contact with menstrual blood could cause a whole host of calamities, from causing fruit crops to fail to giving dogs rabies. Isidore's description of the menses also erroneously asserts that woman is the only menstruating animal, thereby implying that her body is more disordered and dangerous than that of other female animals. Isidore was not alone in his concern over menstrual blood. It was regarded as polluting and ritually impure in most pre-modern cultures, and there were numerous taboos surrounding it. Roman writers like Pliny the Elder in his *Natural History* (books VII, XIX, and XXVIII) and Columella in *On Agriculture* (XI.3 50 and 51) catalogued the harmful and negative qualities associated with this blood, as well as some of its beneficial properties. According to Pliny, menstrual blood was not only a dangerous substance capable of killing crops and bees and driving dogs mad, it could also be protective, and menstruating women could actually drive off natural disasters like hailstorms and whirlwinds. Columella asserted that menstrual blood was so powerful, a menstruating woman could kill a young plant just by looking at it. Menstrual blood was also an issue of great concern in the Judeo-Christian religious tradition. The Old Testament (Leviticus 15:9–13) declared that menstruating women were ritually unclean and that anyone who touched them was ritually unclean as well. It subjected women to ritual exclusion during their menses and required a purifying bath before they were readmitted to society. While Christians were less strict about excluding menstruating women from certain activities, they did forbid sexual intercourse while women were menstruating, and there was some debate in western Europe in the Early Middle Ages over whether menstruating women could attend mass and receive communion (this question was finally settled affirmatively in 735).

These beliefs around menstruation added to the sense that women's bodies were monstrous. Not only was the female body regarded as less perfect than the male, it exuded blood that was believed to be incredibly powerful and dangerous on a monthly basis as well. The Hippocratic belief that the womb was capable of wandering around the female body and causing a variety of ailments also persisted into the Middle Ages; although this was disputed by a number of ancient and medieval physicians, it still contributed to the sense that women's bodies were particularly unruly. Ancient and medieval physicians and philosophers may have regarded women as human and as necessary to the survival of the human race, but in many ways women were viewed as inferior to men: their bodies were deformed reflections of perfected male bodies, and female bodies behaved in monstrous and dangerous ways. Women were regarded as intimate others who could not be dispensed with altogether, but they could not be entirely trusted either. This becomes extremely clear when we look at the rhetoric that was used to describe women in medieval Europe.

Medieval western Europeans inherited many of their beliefs about the unruliness of women's bodies and behaviors from the ancient Greeks and Romans, but the Christian preference for celibacy added a new dimension to their anti-feminist rhetoric. Of course, even this preference for celibacy among Christians was inherited from the Greeks and Romans, but the new religious context added a new twist. In ancient Greece and Rome, celibacy was regarded as an ideal state for philosophers because it freed them from mundane concerns and allowed them to focus their attention on higher things. Even for non-philosophers, romantic love and sexual intercourse were both potentially dangerous because they could cause a man to become irrational and immoderate, and even drive him to madness; both romantic love and sex had to be treated with caution in order to maintain one's rationality, which was considered the hallmark of man's superiority to beasts. Early Christians, who were Greco-Romans themselves, were certainly influenced by these beliefs, but they were even more influenced by the fact that both Jesus and Paul of Tarsus had been celibate and had recommended celibacy as a more perfect state than marriage and a surer path to salvation since it allowed one to focus on God. As for sex, that was now a potentially sinful act that could imperil one's salvation. Sex outside of marriage was undoubtedly sinful, but even enjoying sex too much within marriage could be categorized as indulging in the sin of lust.

There are some important distinctions between the older, pagan Greco-Roman preference for celibacy and the new Christian preference. First, not everyone in the ancient world was advised to remain celibate, only philosophers, who were almost exclusively male. Sex was not viewed as sinful, marriage was the normal and acceptable state for most people, and procreation was encouraged for the good of the state. Falling madly in love or becoming too obsessed with sex could endanger one's reason, but it could not endanger one's soul. Christianity, however, linked sex with sinfulness and celibacy with virtue and salvation, and all Christians were necessarily concerned about the state of their souls. Of course, even within Christianity, there was a clear understanding that not everyone could maintain a perfect celibate state, hence Paul's advice that it was better to marry than to burn if one could not remain celibate (1 Corinthians 7:7–9). Still, the link between celibacy and salvation, and the corresponding link between sex and sin, made sexuality a profoundly urgent matter for all Christians. The new focus on sex as an activity with the potential to imperil one's salvation is clear in both Paul's epistles and the writings of the Latin Church Fathers who frequently expounded upon Paul's words.

In his treatise, *Against Jovinian* (c. 393), Saint Jerome (d. 420) asserts the superiority of celibacy by going back to the words of Paul. We know very little about

Jovinian, other than the fact that he published a treatise claiming that virginity was not preferable to marriage. This work so provoked Jerome, the great theologian and translator of the Latin vulgate version of the Bible, that he produced a forceful defense of celibacy and critique of marriage as a source of worldly distraction. In his defense of celibacy, Jerome argues that marriage is inferior to celibacy and is only offered as an alternative to something worse, namely fornication. To drive home his point, he compares celibacy to fine wheat flour, marriage to barley, and fornication to excrement. He observes that while we would allow a starving man to eat barley so he is not forced to consume dung, that does not make barley superior to wheat. He also returns to Paul's words, "it is good not to touch a woman" (1 Corinthians 7:1), to demonstrate that women are an inherent source of danger to men, capable of igniting lust and endangering their souls. As Jerome points out, Paul did not say that " 'it is good not to have a wife', but 'it is good not to touch a woman,' as though there were danger even in the touch." Jerome then recounts how Joseph fled as if from a mad dog when the Egyptian woman wanted to touch him and even threw away the cloak she had touched as though it was contaminated. Jerome not only argues that celibacy is superior to marriage, he also identifies women as a source of danger and potential peril to men's salvation.

Jerome's focus on the danger that women posed to men as potential sources of lust and sin is not surprising. Greek and Roman philosophers, who were almost all men, had focused solely on the danger that women posed to masculine higher pursuits. Even the Apostle Paul had focused mainly on the danger that women posed to men. While Paul had also recommended that women should remain celibate to focus on God (1 Corinthians 7:32–40), he never said it is good not to touch a man. That warning was exclusively focused on avoiding women. Although women had played important roles in the early Church, by the time Jerome was writing in the late fourth century, all of the leaders of the Church were men and it was with male celibacy that they were most concerned. Women were enjoined to be celibate too, but they were more often portrayed by male authors as impediments to male perfection than as individuals who could attain perfection themselves.

Not only were women regarded as potentially hazardous to men, but they were also believed to share with Eve the responsibility for unleashing sin into the world. The charge was suggested by the Apostle Paul (1 Timothy 2:8–15), who connected Eve's transgression in the garden of Eden with the subordinate and obedient position he prescribed for women in the church. The great Christian apologist from Roman North Africa, Tertullian (c. 155–220), makes this connection more forcefully in his treatise *On the Apparel of Women*, which he wrote to remind women in the early Church of the importance of modesty. According to Tertullian, women should go about perpetually dressed in mourning to atone for the sin they share with Eve – namely, being the cause of human perdition. Tertullian reminds women that they are all Eve and share her guilt. He goes on to castigate women as the devil's gateway and the first deserters of divine law and reminds them that woman was responsible for destroying the man made in God's image and that Christ died for their crime. The enormity of the crimes attributed to women in this single paragraph is breathtaking. They are collectively responsible for abandoning God, causing the fallen state of humanity, and for necessitating Christ's sacrifice. Tertullian was writing specifically to chastise women who wore ostentatious clothing in this work, but he himself was married and he has positive things to say about women elsewhere. Like many Christian authors, he could also praise women for their virtue. Even so, here he underscores the monstrosity of Eve's behavior and insists that all women share her guilt. Tertullian was not alone in this belief either. Countless other Christian authors repeated this charge to the point that it became a mainstay of medieval moralists, a charge leveled against women so frequently that it was practically taken for granted. Women were not only regarded as inferior to men and easier to lead astray, which is why the devil had approached Eve rather than Adam in the first place, but as the cause of man's perdition and Christ's death. It is difficult to conceive of a more monstrous crime, and all women were branded with it.

Just as there was a whole range of monstrous and uncivilized behaviors that were attributed to the monstrous races, there was a whole range of monstrous behaviors that were regularly attributed to women by Christian moralists. Most of these stereotypes about women go back to the ancient Greeks and Romans. There is an enormous corpus of ancient invective against women that includes works by Roman writers like Terence, Juvenal, Horace, Ovid, Martial, Catullus, and Petronius, just to name a few. Medieval Christian writers inherited these negative stereotypes, incorporated them into their own polemics against women, and added examples from biblical history. The French theologian and bishop, Marbod of Rennes (c. 1035–1123), for example, rehearses many of the vices women were believed to possess in the third chapter of book of Christian advice, the *Book of Ten Chapters* (*Liber decem capitulorum*). This chapter, entitled either "The Whore" (*De meretrice*) or "The Evil Woman" (*De muliere mala*), is inspired by the biblical image of the temptress or wicked woman (Proverbs 7:21–27 and Ecclesiasticus 25:22–27) and is followed by a chapter praising the virtues of good women. In this chapter, however, Marbod focuses on the evils associated with women. He asserts that women are scheming, the root of evil and dissension, and the cause of wars and slaughter. They are deceptive, vengeful, envious, greedy, capricious, gluttonous, drunkards, arrogant, and lustful. Marbod says that there is no evil in the world that woman does not have some hand in.

Marbod claims that woman subverts the world with her vices and provides examples by recounting the crimes of specific biblical women, starting with Eve. Women not only commit their own heinous crimes, but they also drive men to commit the most monstrous crimes imaginable: incest, adultery, sacrilege, and murder. They deprive men of their strength and lead the holy astray. Marbod then gives a few examples of monstrous Greek and Roman women mentioned by ancient historians and poets, before turning to mythological monsters. He interprets the Chimaera, for instance, as signifying the harlot, with the front of a lion, the tail of a scorpion, and a mid-section of hot flames. He explains that the harlot uses her lion's face to deceive the world into believing she is noble as she carries off her ill-gotten spoils, she consumes her captives in the burning flames of "irrational, furious lust," and the poison in her scorpion's tail signifies the death and damnation awaiting those who engage in sensual pleasures. He goes on to describe how Charybdis and the Sirens lure men to their deaths. Marbod notes that Ulysses avoided the fate of his crew by blocking his ears to resist the Sirens' song and then eluded Circe's poisons. His men, however, were not so lucky, and Marbod says they represent degenerates who live like animals in being entirely subject to their lusts. Marbod warns his readers to beware of women, not to underestimate their danger, to flee from them and not even look back, lest they be turned to stone. Finally, he advises his readers to imitate the example of Ulysses and to block their ears with sound doctrine and lash themselves to the timber of the cross with the rope of divine fear in order to attain salvation.

Marbod's presentation of the vices of women not only associates them with every possible type of crime, but it also highlights the danger that women were believed to pose to men and their salvation. Women were monstrous in their viciousness, in their propensity to sin, and in their potential to lure men into perdition. Marbod draws upon a variety of sources, mixing ancient stereotypes of women with examples of evil women drawn from the Bible, classical history, and mythology, before ending with a list of female monsters. The effect is to link all women with vice in general, then with particular crimes, and then with the explicitly monstrous. The chapter may be called "On Evil Women," but Marbod makes no distinction here between good women and bad women; he effectively presents all women as monstrous.

Marbod's work is but one example of a vast corpus of medieval European invective against women that used historical, biblical, and legendary women to illustrate the viciousness and monstrosity of all women. The Christian tradition of wicked women stretched all the way back to the early church and became increasingly common after the reform movements of the eleventh century with their renewed emphasis on enforcing celibacy among the clergy. Medieval European invectives against women formed their own genre that included works like Petrus Pictor's *On Wicked Women* (*De Muliere Mala*), Bernard of Cluny's *On Scorn for the World* (*De contemptu mundi*), and Walter Map's *Letter of Valerius to Rufinus*, and attacks on women were a widespread trope that appeared in practically every literary genre produced in the European Middle Ages. While the image of the wicked woman was often accompanied by an account of virtuous women, as it is in Marbod's work, it was the wicked women that seem have excited the imaginations of the clerical authors who produced these works, and their main interest was to present women in such negative terms that celibacy would appear preferable to contact with them. By the Late Middle Ages, the body of literature treating wicked women was so vast that Chaucer referred to it as the cause of marital discord between the Wife of Bath and her abusive fifth husband, Jankyn, as he was constantly reading tales of deceitful wives and reproaching his own wife for the sins associated with her sex. It also inspired Christine de Pizan to attempt to counter its influence by producing *The Book of the City of Ladies* in the early fifteenth century, which focuses exclusively on virtuous women and positive female examples.

The image of the wicked woman was a mainstay of medieval moralists, but it also appeared in courtly literature that was produced by mostly clerical authors.

One of the most notable examples is Queen Guinevere, King Arthur's unfaithful wife, who makes her first appearance in medieval romance in the late twelfth-century *Knight of the Cart* (*Le chevalier de la Charette*), written by the French cleric Chrétien de Troyes. Chrétien tells us that he wrote the work for Countess Marie of Champagne, and another book written for Marie continues the tradition of invective against women under the guise of instructing men in the art of love. Andreas Capellanus, a French chaplain attached to Marie's court, wrote his *Art of Courtly Love* (*De amore*, c. 1185) at Marie's request. The book purports to be a manual of sorts for the author's friend Walter, but the treatise is a satirical work that owes a great debt to Ovid's *Ars Amatoria*. In his first two books, the cleric Capellanus explains love to his young friend and gives him advice on how to woo women and retain their love. After two books extolling the virtues that love inspires in men, Capellanus reverts to condemning the entire female sex in book three, "The Rejection of Love." He advises Walter that he cannot possibly find mutual love with a woman because no woman ever truly loves; their only concern is enriching themselves. According to Capellanus, all women are gold-diggers who are driven by avarice. Their greed makes them unfaithful, capricious, and ready to trade their virtue for wealth. They are stained with every vice and prone to every evil. They are envious, slanderers, liars, drunkards, gluttons, vain, and proud, and they also lack wisdom, believe everything they hear, and insist on being praised.

Of course, no Christian invective against women would be complete without bringing up Eve, whom Capellanus uses to illustrate woman's gluttony. He then uses Delilah to illustrate woman's duplicity, asserting that women can never be trusted with secrets and that men must always hide their true intentions from them, before moving on to woman's disobedience. This vice he illustrates with the example of a man who hated his wife but did not want to murder her with his own hands, so he put poison in a flask of wine and told his wife not to drink it because it was filled with poison. As soon as the man left, the woman drank the poison and died. Capellanus compares Eve to the disobedient wife who drank the poison, saying that Eve destroyed herself and sentenced all her descendants to death by disobeying God. He concludes that if you want a woman to do anything, you should order her to do the opposite.

Capellanus is intentionally implicating all women in these monstrous behaviors. At the end of many of his paragraphs, he asserts that there are no exceptions to this rule, or this rule applies to all women without exception, or that no woman has been found who is an exception to these rules. Even after exhausting the stock of possible vices that could be attributed to women, he goes on to repeat the charges and elaborate them a second time. After rehashing these, he adds a final vice. He charges that all women are preoccupied with auguries and compares them to heathens (non-Christians). The charge is almost lost in the avalanche of evils attributed to women, but it is telling. He says that women sin again and again by resorting to practitioners of divination and that they will not do anything without consulting these witches. The comparison of women to heathens and the insistence that they consult witches before doing anything associate women with monstrous practices like idolatry and witchcraft, even if Capellanus does not directly accuse women of engaging in these things themselves. Capellanus closes his work by quoting Solomon's declaration that "there is no good woman" and asking his friend Walter why he wants to love something that is bad.

Most scholars believe that Capellanus' work was intended as satire. However, the satirical material here seems to be the first two chapters in which he describes the virtues associated with love and gives advice on how to acquire and retain it. The language he uses in describing the vices of women in chapter three, while certainly the type of hyperbole associated with satire, also relies on what was by now a very old Christian tradition of associating women with vice and sin to emphasize the danger they posed to men. Whatever Capellanus' intentions were, the charges he lays against women in chapter three follow a venerable pattern of defaming women and portraying them as monstrous, and anyone reading or listening to his work would have recognized these tropes.

While medieval medical discourses portrayed the female body as monstrous, and both clerical and secular literature routinely depicted women's behavior, vices, and appetites as monstrous, there were also some medieval accounts of female monsters and more explicitly monstrous women. We have already seen that there was a tradition among some clerical authors of employing female monsters from Greco-Roman mythology to illustrate their assertions about the monstrous behavior of women in general, but there are relatively few explicitly female monsters in medieval literature. One of the few is Mélusine from Jean d'Arras' fourteenth-century *Roman de Mélusine*, which features her as the cursed, fairy matriarch of the Lusignan family who transforms into a serpent every Saturday. Another is Grendel's mother from *Beowulf*, an Old English poem that likely circulated orally before it was written down around 1000 by an anonymous Christian author. Grendel's mother is an interesting example because she is monstrous in a variety of ways. She is the mother of a monster, she is recognizably shaped like a monster, she lives in a liminal space under a lake, and she transgresses gender boundaries by avenging the death of her son. Although the poem is set in the pre-Christian past, the Christian author describes Grendel's mother as devil-shaped and both her and her son as descendants of Cain, the son of Adam and Eve who killed his brother Abel and introduced murder into the world. She is also portrayed as a fearsome threat to men, although she is described as less powerful than her son on account of her sex.

Grendel's mother is the second monster that Beowulf faces in the poem. After killing Grendel, the monster who had haunted Hrothgar's hall and killed his men, Beowulf believes that he has restored peace to Heorot. However, Grendel's mother still lives and is bent on avenging her son. The obligation to exact vengeance for Grendel's death should have fallen on a male relative, but since Grendel has none, his mother takes up this duty. She sneaks into Heorot under the cover of night while Beowulf is lodged elsewhere. When she is discovered, she takes her son's bloody hand that Beowulf had kept as a trophy and kills Hrothgar's retainer Aeschere before fleeing back to the fen. The murder of Aeschere requires that vengeance be exacted again, and Hrothgar once again asks Beowulf for help. Beowulf has to seek Grendel's mother out under the water, the dwelling place of monsters. Despite her sex, Grendel's mother proves to be a formidable opponent. She grabs Beowulf as soon as he reaches her den, and his sword proves to be of no use in the fight as it cannot harm her. They grapple, and at one point Beowulf stumbles. Grendel's mother pins him down and draws her blade, but she fails to harm him due to the strength of his mail shirt. At this point Beowulf spots an enormous, old sword that was forged by giants and manages to lift it. He uses the sword to kill Grendel's mother by cutting into her neck, but Beowulf does not take a trophy from her body as he did with Grendel. Instead, he uses the charmed sword to decapitate Grendel's corpse, who had made his way back to his mother's lair before dying. After making contact with Grendel's poisonous blood, the blade of the sword dissolves, and Beowulf returns to the water's surface carrying just the sword's hilt and Grendel's head.

Beowulf's battle with Grendel's mother contributes to his heroism. Although she is female, she is still a fearsome monster whose body resists Beowulf's blade, and several times the men back on the water's surface think that Beowulf must have lost his life to her as they see the water churning with blood. Grendel's mother may be a fearsome opponent, but the fact that she is female makes her problematic. First, vengeance was typically a male business. Women normally participated in the feud by encouraging their male relatives to seek vengeance, not by seeking it themselves. In this case, the poet tells us that there is no one else to avenge Grendel's death as he has no father or other kin, and there is a certain respect for the actions of Grendel's mother in avenging her only child, even if she is transgressing accepted gender norms. It was sometimes acceptable for women to pursue vengeance, but only when there was no male relative to do so. Second, although Beowulf faces real danger in fighting Grendel's mother and is almost killed by her, triumphing over a woman (or a female monster) was different from defeating a male enemy. Women were generally protected from the violence of the feud, and defeating a woman generated some unease. This unease is expressed in the fact that Beowulf does not take a trophy from the body of Grendel's mother after killing her. Instead, he takes Grendel's head back to the surface, along with the sword hilt, to prove his victory over Grendel's mother.

Grendel's mother, although fearsome, is less fearsome than her son, and in some sense she is simply an extension of Grendel himself. She serves as a device to draw out the narrative tension and emphasize Beowulf's heroism in defeating Grendel by requiring him to triumph over a second, slightly less terrifying, version of Grendel. The honor derived from this second triumph turns out to be problematic as well. There was little honor to be gained in defeating a woman, even though there was certainly shame in being defeated by one. The only honorable elements in Beowulf's victory over Grendel's mother are the fact that he has avenged the death of Aeschere and ended this particular cycle of violence by ensuring that Grendel has no kin left to continue prosecuting the feud.

While female monsters like Mélusine and Grendel's mother are fairly rare in medieval literature, medieval texts are littered with examples of women doing monstrous things, exhibiting monstrous physical characteristics, and having monstrous offspring. William of Malmesbury's *Chronicle of the Kings of England* (c. 1125) contains two notable examples that he presents as marvels in the midst of his historical narrative. The first is the story of the witch of Berkely, and the second is the story of conjoined twins who were regarded as a prodigy. William (c. 1095–1143) was a Benedictine monk at Malmesbury Abbey in Wiltshire, about thirty miles from Berkley, and he tells us that a certain woman who lived in Berkely practiced augury and was addicted to witchcraft. He adds that she was gluttonous, lustful, and debauched as well, very much like some of the wicked women we have already seen. One day, the witch noticed that her favorite was chattering more loudly than usual, and she took this as an omen that she would suffer a catastrophe and her own demise in short order. A little later, a messenger arrived to inform her of the sudden death of her son and his family. Stricken with grief, she took to her bed and summoned her other children, a monk and a nun. She told her children that she had practiced witchcraft with the assistance of demonical arts and indulged in every vice during her life, and that she now feared she would be called to account. While she despaired of saving her soul, she hoped that they might be able to save her body, and she asked them to sew up her corpse in a deer hide and place it in a stone coffin secured with lead, iron, another stone, and three huge iron chains. In addition, they were to ensure that 50 psalms were sung for her for 50 nights, along with an equal number of masses for an equal amount of time. If her body remained in the coffin for three nights, on the fourth day they were to bury it in the ground. Her children complied with her request as best they could, but her guilt so was great that, during the first two nights, two of the enormous chains securing her coffin were broken open by demons as terrified priests attempted to sing psalms around her body. On the third night, the monastery where her body was laying suffered an attack by demons, and the largest of them broke open the gate. The demon commanded the woman to rise, broke the remaining chain, opened the coffin, dragged her out of the church, and placed her on a black horse. Accompanied by a host of demons, the whole party vanished while the woman's cries were heard for miles. William then asserts the truth of this marvel and compares it to the stories of greedy men who were taken from their tombs by evil spirits as punishment for their sins.

The witch of Berkley's story is very similar to the stories of revenants recounted by William of Newburgh and Walter Map that are covered in Chapter 4, and who are invariably male. In those cases, the reanimated corpses of sinful men rise from the tomb to terrify and harass the living, sometimes causing disease and death. In the cases of the most sinful among them, their corpses are specifically reanimated by demonic forces. While the witch of Berkley does not return as a revenant to haunt the living, she is escorted from her tomb by a demonic host who presumably dragged her down to hell due to the enormity of her sins. In this case, the woman's main sins are witchcraft and practicing augury, both of which were monstrous acts associated with pagans. While she is also described as having engaged in every vice, witchcraft and augury stood in direct opposition to Christianity, and William even has her admit that they are demonical arts. The proof of their association with the demonic, which was by definition monstrous, comes in the form of the actual demons who come to collect her after her death and forcibly drag her from the monastery. Not all of the people accused of practicing magic in the European

Middle Ages were female, but the vast majority of them were, and this association between women and witchcraft was reinforced by stories like the witch of Berkley. In this case, the author is focused on the fact that practicing witchcraft and augury has rendered the woman so monstrous that her body cannot rest quietly. Indeed, the witch's body is even more disruptive after death than it was in life, threatening the clergy of the monastery with the violence of demonic attacks before it is finally taken to hell by a band of demons.

The second marvel from William of Malmesbury's *Chronicle of the Kings of England* is more prosaic as it concerns the birth of female conjoined twins. William describes the women as twins joined at the navel, who had two heads and four arms, but shared a single trunk and a single pair of legs, as well as a single digestive system. When one of the twins died, the other carried the body of her dead sister for three years, until she finally died from fatigue. As we saw in Chapter 1, conjoined twins were regarded as monstrous in ancient and medieval Europe not only in the sense that their appearance deviated from the norm, but also in the sense that they were regarded as portents or omens, and this is precisely how William treats them. He tells us the women were regarded as a prodigy that represented England and Normandy, which had been joined together in 1066 when William the Conqueror, the Duke of Normandy, conquered England and united them under a single ruler. William says that whatever these countries consumed flowed into a common receptacle, which he identifies as the greed of the ruler or the need to defend the realm from external enemies. The important point for William is that Normandy is regarded as the dead twin, who contributes nothing herself but puts additional pressure on England who may collapse internally or fall to her enemies under the weight. At the time William of Malmesbury was writing, the Anglo-Norman kings routinely used English resources to fund their wars, and the English bitterly resented these exactions as well as the fact that their king's attention was usually occupied by his French possessions. The image of the conjoined twins, one dead and one struggling to live on but burdened by the decaying corpse of her sister, was a fitting metaphor for the attitude of some of the English toward Normandy.

Our final selections regarding monstrous women and monstrous births come from Gerald of Wales (c. 1146 – c. 1223), an Anglo-Cambrian cleric who wrote his *History and Topography of Ireland* in 1187 as the English were attempting to conquer Ireland. Gerald incorporates descriptions of the marvels found in Ireland into his history, which largely focuses on depicting the Irish as a savage people who need to be civilized by the English. He uses the rhetoric of monstrosity against the Irish in general, but there are several chapters in which he pays special attention to Irish women as a means of illustrating Irish barbarity. For example, in his second book, which contains an account of the marvels and prodigies found in Ireland, he describes a bearded woman from Limerick who also had a crest that reached down her back, calling these physical characteristics "monstrous deformities." He remarks that she followed the customs of her country in wearing a long beard, even though it was "unnatural." Gerald uses his description of the bearded woman to underscore how the Irish failed to conform to English gender expectations. He implies that although the woman is afflicted with two monstrous deformities, she could mitigate one of them by shaving her beard, but she refuses to do so and wears it long, like an Irish man. Gerald singles out the Irish custom of wearing long, unruly beards as particularly barbaric in book three, so this attribute is doubly monstrous in a woman. In fact, he refers to the woman's choice to wear a beard as unnatural. The woman's beard is unnatural to Gerald not so much in the sense that a woman having facial hair was unnatural, but in the sense that she insisted on wearing it like a man, and like an Irish man at that! She refused to make every effort to appear female and conform to gender standards by shaving her beard.

Gerald asserts that this bearded woman was not a hermaphrodite and follows her description with that of an actual hermaphrodite from Connaught, who appeared male and had a beard on the right side of their face, but appeared female on the left side. In this case, Gerald genders the person as female, perhaps because they presented as female, but asserts that she "partook of the nature of both sexes." Although he does not directly comment on whether this is monstrous, we saw in Chapter 1 that intersex individuals, and specifically hermaphrodites, were routinely grouped among examples of monstrous births in ancient and medieval Europe. Gerald may assume that the person's monstrosity is obvious, and he certainly indicates that this is the case by linking this individual with the bearded woman he explicitly describes as monstrous earlier in the same paragraph. Like the bearded woman who refuses to shave, the hermaphrodite who wears a beard on the left side of their face presents a challenge to gender norms.

Gerald also notes that both of these women routinely attended royal courts and that the bearded woman specifically was regarded as an object of ridicule and wonder. The fact that these women were associated with entertainment at royal courts reflects the ancient custom of displaying monstrosities as a form of entertainment as discussed in Chapter 1, but here Gerald uses it to link these women to the Irish kings of Limerick and Connaught in an effort to further discredit them and illustrate their lack of civilization. This becomes clear a couple of chapters later, when Gerald again credits the king of Connaught with keeping a tame white goat who had intercourse with the woman who took care of it. Gerald uses this example of monstrous behavior to illustrate the bestial and irrational nature of the woman who sank to the level of a beast in her lust, but the king and the rest of the Irish appear to be implicated as well. Gerald indirectly connects the king of Connaught with the woman's bestiality since it was his pet goat, and Gerald's lament over the fact that the woman has abandoned reason in satisfying her lust seems to be a condemnation of the Irish more generally, who Gerald describes in book three as savages who need to be conquered by the English so they can be civilized. In addition to claiming that the Irish neglect their children, wear hideously rough clothing, fail to exploit their natural resources due to laziness, and go into war unarmored with crude weapons, Gerald pointedly says that they "are a rude people" who "live like beasts." This story about an Irish woman engaging in actual bestiality appears designed to prove that point.

Gerald goes on to illustrate the horrifying monstrosity of bestiality in the next chapter, where he recounts that a lion owned by Prince Philip of France was in the habit of having intercourse with a girl named Joan. Gerald says that "both of these brutes merited a shameful death" and notes that such abominations are not just products of modern times, but the ancient society was polluted with these vices as well. He quotes Leviticus 20:16 on this point and asserts that while both the human and animal involved in bestiality are ordered to be put to death for the crime, the animal is not killed for its guilt because it lacks reason; the animal is killed to remind everyone of the enormity of the crime. Imputing the crime of bestiality to the Irish not only reinforces the sense that the Irish are brutes themselves, but it also renders them worthy of death.

Throughout *The History and Topography of Ireland*, Gerald presents the human inhabitants and animals of Ireland as wonders akin to those found in the east. He presents the Irish in terms that are very similar to what we saw with the monstrous races. In book three where Gerald focuses on the Irish and their customs, he takes a break from recounting their allegedly barbaric behavior to muse upon the number of people in Ireland who are born with some birth defect. He says that he has never seen as many individuals in any other country who are born with some natural defect as there are among the Irish, and he attributes this to the fact that the Irish are an adulterous and incestuous people. In other words, the behavior of the Irish is so monstrous that it produces people who have monstrous physical attributes in the form of birth defects. He goes on to say that these defects are part of God's plan and that nature sometimes produces beings that are contrary to her own laws among people who refuse to honor God. As we saw in Chapter 1, there was a long history of regarding people born with birth defects as "monstrous" and of interpreting these monstrous births as divine warnings or products of divine wrath. Here, Gerald is claiming that the Irish suffer from an usually high number of birth defects as people not only due to their immoral behavior, but also due to the defectiveness of their faith. Gerald is remarkably thorough in attributing monstrous characteristics to the Irish in this work, and using the rhetoric of monstrosity to argue that the barbaric Irish must be conquered and subjected to the civilizing influence of the English.

There were a variety of discourses in medieval Europe that portrayed women as monstrous. Ancient and medieval medical discourses viewed women as deformed or mutilated men whose bodies were defective and whose menstrual blood was a powerful source of contamination and poison. This view of female bodies helped to justify the subordination of women as part of a natural and divinely established order in both ancient and medieval Europe. There was also a huge ancient and medieval corpus of invective against women that portrayed women as monstrously excessive in their appetites and emotions, and medieval moralists were particularly keen to encourage male celibacy with tales of the danger that women posed to male salvation. Even secular literature repeated these charges against women, charging that women were inherently vicious and eager to commit or encourage the most monstrous crimes. Like the medical discourses around the female body, this literature asserted that women were defective, potentially dangerous, and had to be contained, subordinated to men, or simply avoided. Finally, the monstrosity of whole peoples, like the Irish, could be distilled into stories about the barbaric behavior of their women and mobilized to justify their conquest and subjection.

PRIMARY SOURCES

**Aristotle, *Generation of Animals*, trans. A.L. Peck, Loeb Classical
Library (Harvard University Press, 1942), pp. 91–3, 97, 101–3, 109,
173–5, 185, 417–9, 425, 441, 443, and 459–61.**

1. (726[b]) Semen is pretty certainly a residue from that nourishment which is in the form of blood and which, as being the final form of nourishment, is distributed to the various parts of the body. This, of course, is the reason why semen has great potency – the loss if it from the system is just as exhausting as the loss of pure healthy blood . . .

2. Now (i) the weaker creature too must of necessity produce a residue, greater in amount and less thoroughly concocted; and (ii) this, if such is its character, must of necessity be a volume of bloodlike fluid. (iii) That which by nature has a smaller share of heat is weaker; and (iv) the female answers to this description. . . .

3. (727[a]) Now it is impossible that any creature should produce two seminal secretions at once, and as the secretion in females which answers to semen in males is the menstrual fluid, it obviously follows that the female does not contribute any semen to generation; for if there were semen, there would be no menstrual fluid; but as menstrual fluid is in fact formed, therefore there is no semen. . . .

4. (727[b]) By now it is plain that the contribution which the female makes to generation is the *matter* used therein, that this is to be found in the substance constituting the menstrual fluid, and finally that the menstrual fluid is a residue. (728a) . . . A woman is as it were an infertile male; the female, in fact, is female on account of inability of a sort, viz., it lacks the power to concoct semen out of the final state of nourishment . . . because of the coldness of its nature. . . .

5. (729[a]) The male provides the 'form' and the 'principle of the movement', the female provides the body, in other words, the material. Compare the coagulation of milk. Here, the milk is the body, and the fig-juice or the rennet contains the principle which causes it to set. . . .

6. (737[a]) When the semen has entered the uterus it 'sets' the residue produced by the female and imparts to it the same movement with which it is itself endowed. The female's contribution, of course, is a residue too, . . . and contains all the parts of the body *potentially*, though none in *actuality*; and 'all' includes those parts which distinguish the two sexes. Just as it sometimes happens that deformed offspring are produced by deformed parents, and sometimes not, so the offspring produced by a female are sometimes female, sometimes not, but male. The reason is that the female is as it were a deformed male; and the menstrual discharge is semen, though in an impure condition; i.e. it lacks one constituent, and one only, the principle of Soul.

7. (738[b]) An animal is a living body, a body with a Soul in it. The female always provides the material, the male provides that which fashions the material into

shape; this, in our view, is the specific characteristic of each of the sexes: that is what it means to be male or female. Hence, necessity requires that the female should provide the physical part, i.e. a quantity of material, but not that the male should do so, since necessity does not require that the tools should reside in the product that is being made, nor that the agent which uses them should do so. Thus the physical part, the body, comes from the female, and the Soul from the male, since the Soul is the essence of a particular body.

8. (769ᵇ) And indeed this is what comes next to be treated . . . the causes of monstrosities, for in the end, when the movements (that came from the male) relapse and the material (that came from the female) does not get mastered, what remains is that which is most "general," and this is the (merely) "animal." People say that the offspring which is formed has the head of a ram or an ox, and similarly with other creatures, that one has the head of another, e.g., a calf has a child's head or sheep an ox's head. . . . This, then, is one sort of "monstrosity" we hear spoken of. There are others which quality for the name in virtue of having additional parts to their body, being formed with extra feet or extra heads. The account of the cause of monstrosities is very close and in a way similar to that of the cause of deformed animals, since a monstrosity is really a sort of deformity. . . . (770ᵇ) A monstrosity, of course, belongs to the class of "things contrary to nature," although it is contrary not to Nature in her entirety but only to Nature *in the generality of cases*!

9. (772ᵇ) With regard to the redundance of parts which occurs contrary to Nature, the cause of this is the same as that of the production of twins, since the cause occurs right back in the fetations, whenever more material gets "set" than the nature of the part requires; the result then is that the embryo has some part larger than the other, e.g. a finger or a hand or a foot, or some other extremity or limb; or, if the fetation has been split up, several come to be formed – just as eddies are formed in rivers . . . Some creatures develop in such a way that they have two generative organs (one male, the other female). Always, when this redundancy happens, one of the two is operative the other inoperative, since the latter, being contrary to Nature, always gets stunted so far as nourishment is concerned. . . . (773ᵃ) Monstrosities differ from redundant growths in that most monstrosities are instances of embryos growing together.

10. (775ᵃ) Once birth has taken place everything reaches its perfection sooner in females than in males – e.g. puberty, maturity, old age, – because females are weaker and colder in their nature; and we should look upon the female state as being as it were a deformity, though one which occurs in the ordinary course of nature. While it is within the mother, then, it develops slowly on account of its coldness, since development is a sort of concoction, concoction is effected by heat, and if a thing is hotter its concoction is easy; when, however, it is free from the mother, on account of its weakness it quickly approaches its maturity and old age, since inferior things all reach their end more quickly.

Galen, *On the Usefulness of the Parts of the Body*, trans. Margaret Tallmadge May (Cornell University Press, 1968), pp. 630–2.

1   (II. 299) Now just as mankind is the most perfect of all animals, so within mankind the man is more perfect than the woman, and the reason for his perfection is his excess of heat, for heat is Nature's primary instrument. Hence in those animals that have less of it, her workmanship is necessarily more imperfect, and so it is no wonder that the female is less perfect than the male by as much as she is colder than he. In fact, just as the mole has imperfect eyes, though certainly not so imperfect as they are in those animals that do not have any trace of them at all, so too the woman is less perfect than the man in respect to the generative parts. For the parts were formed within her when she was still a foetus, but could not because of the defect in the heat emerge and project on the outside, and this, though making the animal itself that was being formed less perfect than one that is complete in all respects, provided no small advantage for the race; for there needs must be a female. Indeed, you ought not to think that our Creator would purposely make half the whole race imperfect and, as it were, mutilated, unless there was to be some great advantage in such a mutilation.

2   (II. 300) Let me tell what this is. The foetus needs abundant material both when it is first constituted and for the entire period of growth that follows. . . . Accordingly, it was better for the female to be made enough colder so that she cannot disperse all the nutriment which she concocts and elaborates. . . . This is the reason why the female was made cold, and the immediate consequence of this is the imperfection of the parts, which cannot emerge on the outside on account of the defect in the heat, another very great advantage for the continuance of the race. For, remaining within, that which would have become the scrotum if it had emerged on the outside was made into the substance of the uteri, an instrument fitted to receive and retain the semen and to nourish and perfect the foetus.

3   (II. 301) Forthwith, of course, the female must have smaller, less perfect testes, and the semen generated in them must be scantier, colder, and wetter (for these things too follow of necessity from the deficient heat). Certainly such semen would be incapable of generating an animal. . . . The testes of the male are as much larger as he is the warmer animal. The semen generated in them, having received the peak of concoction, becomes the efficient principle of the animal. Thus, from one principle devised by the Creator in his wisdom, that principle in accordance with which the female has been made less perfect than the male, having stemmed all these things useful for the generation of the animal: that the parts of the female cannot escape to the outside; that she accumulates an excess of useful nutriment and has imperfect semen and a hollow instrument to receive the perfect semen; that since everything in the male is the opposite [of what it is in the female], the male member has been elongated to be most suitable for coitus and the excretion of semen; and that his semen itself has been made thick, abundant, and warm.

Isidore of Seville, "Etymologies," in *Woman Defamed and Defended*, trans. Alcuin Blamires (Oxford University Press, 1992), XI.i.140, p. 44.

The Menses

4 (XI i. 140) The *menstrua* are the superfluous blood of women. They are called *menstrua* after the cycle of the moon, in accordance with which this flow usually comes – the moon being named *mene* in Greek. They are also called 'womanish things' [*muliebria*], since woman is the only menstruating animal. (141) From contact with this blood, fruits fail to germinate, grape-must goes sour, plants die, trees lose their fruit, metal is corroded with rust, and bronze objects go black. Any dogs which consume it contract rabies. The glue of bitumen, which resists both metal and water, dissolves spontaneously when polluted with that blood.

Jerome, "Against Jovinian," in *The Principal Works of St. Jerome*, trans. W.H. Fremantle, Select Library of Nicene and Post-Nicene Fathers, V (James Parker and Co, 1893), pp. 64–5.

1 (1.7) . . . Let us turn to the main point of the evidence: 'It is good', St. Paul says, 'for a man not to touch a woman.' If it is good not to touch a woman, it is bad to touch one: for there is no opposite to goodness but badness. If however it is bad and the evil is pardoned, it is for this reason that the allowance is made, namely to prevent a worse evil. But surely, a thing which is only allowed because there may be something worse has only a slight degree of goodness. He would never have added 'let each man have his own wife', unless he had previously used the words 'to avoid fornication'. Do away with fornication, and he will not say 'let each man have his own wife'. Just as though one were to lay it down: 'It is good to feed on wheaten bread, and to eat the finest wheat flour' and yet, to prevent a person pressed by hunger from devouring cow-dung, I may allow him to eat barley. Does it follow that the wheat will not have its peculiar purity, if barley is preferred to excrement? That is naturally good which does not admit of comparison with what is bad, and is not eclipsed because something else is preferred.

2 At the same time, we must take note of the Apostle's good sense. He did not say, 'it is good not to have a wife', but 'it is good not to touch a woman': as though there were danger even in the touch; as though he who touched her would not escape from her who 'hunts for the precious life,' who causes the young man's judgement to fly away. 'Who can hold fire firmly to his chest and not be burnt or can walk upon burning coals and not be scorched?' Just as he who touches fire is instantly burned, so by mere touch the peculiar nature of man and woman is perceived, and the difference of sex is understood. Heathen fables relate how Mithras and Ericthonius were begotten of the soil, in stone or earth, by raging lust. Hence it was that our Joseph, because the Egyptian woman wished to touch him, fled from her hands, and, as if he had been bitten by a mad dog and feared the spreading poison, threw away the cloak which she had touched.

Tertullian, "On the Apparel of Women," in *Ante-Nicene Fathers*, trans. S. Thelwall (Christian Literature Publishing Co, 1885), vol. 4, I.i.

If there dwelt upon earth a faith as great as is the reward of faith which is expected in the heavens, no one of you at all, best beloved sisters, from the time that she had first "known the Lord," and learned (the truth) concerning her own (that is, woman's) condition, would have desired too gladsome (not to say too ostentatious) a style of dress; so as not rather to go about in humble garb, and rather to affect meanness of appearance, walking about as Eve mourning and repentant, in order that by every garb of penitence she might the more fully expiate that which she derives from Eve, – the ignominy, I mean, of the first sin, and the odium (attaching to her as the cause) of human perdition. "In pains and in anxieties dost thou bear (children), woman; and toward thine husband (is) thy inclination, and he lords It over thee." And do you not know that you are (each) an Eve? The sentence of God on this sex of yours lives in this age: the guilt must of necessity live too. *You* are the devil's gateway: *you* are the unsealer of that (forbidden) tree: *you* are the first deserter of the divine law: *you* are she who persuaded him whom the devil was not valiant enough to attack. *You* destroyed so easily God's image, man. On account of *your* desert – that is, death – even the Son of God had to die. And do you think about adorning yourself over and above your tunics of skins?

Marbod of Rennes, "Liber Decem Capitulorum," in *Woman Defamed and Defended*, trans. Alcuin Blamires (Oxford University Press, 1992), pp. 100–3.

1 Countless are the traps which the scheming enemy has set throughout the world's paths and plains: but among them the greatest – and the one scarcely anybody can evade – is woman. Woman the unhappy source, evil root, and corrupt off-shoot, who brings to birth every sort of outrage throughout the world. For she instigates quarrels, conflicts, dire dissensions; she provokes fighting between old friends, divides affections, shatters families. But these are trivia I speak of: she dislodges kings and princes from the throne, makes nations clash, convulses towns, destroys cities, multiples slaughters, brews deadly poisons. She hurls conflagration as she rampages through farmsteads and fields. In sum, there lurks in the universe no manifestation of evil in which woman does not claim some part for herself.

2 (15) Her sex is envious, capricious, irascible, avaricious, as well as intemperate with drink and voracious in the stomach. She relishes revenge and is always panting for the upper hand, without the slightest qualm about crime or deceit so long as she wins; she is intent on achieving whatever she wants by fair means or foul. To her nothing seems illicit if it is pleasurable. She belies her own appearance as she goes, concealing her squalid secrets, a shameless liar who is by no means innocent of the crime of intrigue. Here gaping at wealth, there burning with the flames of lust, she is a babbler, and unreliable, and – on top of so much evil – arrogant.

3   (25) Armed with these vices woman subverts the world; woman the sweet evil, compound of honeycomb and poison, spreading honey on her sword to transfix the hearts of the wise. Who urged the first parent to taste what was forbidden? A woman (Eve). Who drove a father to corrupt his daughters? A woman (Lot's daughters). Who eliminated a man's strength when his hair was cut off? A woman (Delilah). Who lopped off the sacred head of a righteous man with a sword? A woman (Salome), who piled crime on her mother's (Herodias) crime, and branded shocking incest with yet more shocking murder.

4   (34) Who led astray David the holy and who led wise Solomon astray with sweet charm so that one turned adulterer and the other committed sacrilege – who but seductive woman? I pass over many women catalogued on the sacred page: the horrifying Jezebel, Athalia who dared to commit heinous sin, and more whom it is unnecessary to enumerate. I mention only in passing many who are traditionally spoken of in the work of poets and historians: Eriphyle, Clytemnestra, Belides, Procne, and that harlot bred by Leda who was fought over in the ten-year Trojan war of nations, and others too whose stories the tragic poets often rehearse for the people.

5   (45) As exemplar of this dire monster to be avoided, ancient wisdom contrived the terrifying Chimaera. Not undeservedly, it is said a threefold shape was given to it: the front part lion, the rear a serpent's tail, and the middle parts nothing but red hot flame. This image mimics the nature of a harlot, in that she seizes spoil to carry off in her lion's mouth, while feigning to be something with an impressive, quasi-noble appearance. With this façade she consumes her captives in the flames of love in which nothing of substance or weight is seen; only frivolous, irrational, furious lust. The back parts are crammed with deadly poison because death and damnation terminate sensual pleasures.

6   (58) Turbulent Charybdis, who sucks in and draws to its death everything near her, bears female form. The Siren is also like this: she entices fools by singing lovely melodies, draws them towards her once they are enticed, and when they are drawn in she plunges them into the annihilating abyss. But Ulysses evaded this fate. He closed his crew's ears to the notorious songs while physically restraining himself from being able to change course, by being lashed with ropes to the mast of the speeding ship. No less successfully did he elude evil Circe's sweet poisons. Those who drank them took on the shapes of wild beasts, transformed into the likeness of dogs and filthy swine. They signify degenerates and sensualists living the life of a herd of animals under the sway of lust.

7   (71) Oh race of men! Beware the honied poisons, the sweet songs and the pull of dark depths. Do not let the charm of contrived appearances seduce you; be in dread of the destructive flames and the fierce serpent. If a beautiful woman courts you aiming to deceive you, and if you have such confidence in yourself that you stout-heartedly prepare to enter the fray, you will deceive yourself with ignorance, if you scorn the darts of the enemy. It is not the rule in this type of struggle that you can win by close combat. It is better to undertake retreat and attain safety with your feet. If you run, you will get away: if you approach, you will be caught. But I warn you not to look back at her, since anyone who toys with desire can be turned to stone by the very sight of the Gorgon.

8 (84) Whoever seeks earth's calm seas in the home of the Church in order to arrive at the desired harbour of the homeland – avoiding sweet-sounding songs and dangerous attractions – should block up and protect the hearing with lawful doctrine and stay fastened to the timber with rope of divine fear. The timber is the cross our salvation, like a ship's mast, Nor is it without sailyards, which are the arms of the cross.

Andreas Capellanus, *The Art of Courtly Love*, trans. John Jay Parry (Columbia University Press, 1960), pp. 200–9.

Again we confound lovers with another argument. The mutual love which you seek in women you cannot find, for no woman ever loved a man or could bind herself to a lover in the mutual bonds of love. For a woman's desire is to get rich through love, but not to give her lover the solaces that please him. Nobody ought to wonder at this, because it is natural. According to the nature of their sex all women are spotted with the vice of a grasping and avaricious disposition, and they are always alert and devoted to the search for money or profit. I have traveled through a great many parts of the world, and although I made careful inquiries I could never find a man who would say that he had discovered a woman who if a thing was not offered to her would not demand it insistently and would not hold off from falling in love unless she got rich gifts in one way or another. But even though you have given a woman innumerable presents, if she discovers that you are less attentive about giving her things than you used to be, or if she learns that you have lost your money, she will treat you like a perfect stranger who has come from some other country, and everything you do will bore her or annoy her. You cannot find a woman who will love you so much or be so constant to you that if somebody else comes to her and offers her presents she will be faithful to her love. Women have so much avarice that generous gifts break down all the barriers of their virtue. If you come with open hands, no women will let you go away without that which you seek; while if you don't promise to give them a great deal, you needn't come to them and ask for anything. Even if you are distinguished by royal honors, but bring no gifts with you, you will get absolutely nothing from them; you will be turned away from their doors in shame. Because of their avarice all women are thieves, and we say they carry purses. You cannot find a woman of such lofty station or blessed with such honor or wealth that an offer of money will not break down her virtue, and there is no man, no matter how disgraceful and low-born he is, who cannot seduce her if he has great wealth. This is so because no woman ever has enough money – just as no drunkard ever thinks he has had enough to drink. Even if the whole earth and sea were turned to gold, they could hardly satisfy the avarice of a woman.

Furthermore, not only is every woman by nature a miser, but she is also envious and a slanderer of other women, greedy, a slave to her belly, inconstant, fickle in her speech, disobedient and impatient of restraint, spotted with the sin of pride and desirous of vainglory, a liar, a drunkard, a babbler, no keeper of secrets, too much given to wantonness, prone to every evil, and never loving any man in her heart.

Now woman is a miser, because there isn't a wickedness in the world that men can think that she will not boldly indulge in for the sake of money, and, even if she has an abundance she will not help anyone who is in need. You can more easily scratch a diamond with your finger-nail than you can by any human ingenuity get a woman to consent to giving you any of her savings. Just as Epicurus believed that the highest good lay in serving the belly, so a woman thinks that the only things worthwhile in this world are riches and holding on to what she has. You can't find any woman so simple and foolish that she is unable to look out for her own property with a greedy tenacity, and with great mental subtlety get hold of the possessions of someone else. Indeed, even a simple woman is more careful about selling a single hen than the wisest lawyer is in deeding away a great castle. Furthermore, no woman is ever so violently in love with a man that she will not devote all her efforts to using up his property. You will find that this rule never fails and admits of no exceptions.

That every woman is envious is also found to be a general rule, because a woman is always consumed with jealousy over another woman's beauty, and she loses all pleasure in what she has. Even if she knows that it is the beauty of her own daughter that is being praised, she can hardly avoid being tortured by hidden envy. Even the neediness and the great poverty of the neighbor woman seem to her abundant wealth and riches, so that we think the old proverb which says

> The crop in the neighbor's field is always more fertile,
> And your neighbor's cow has a larger udder.

seems to refer to the female sex without any exceptions. It can hardly come to pass that one woman will praise the good character or the beauty of another, and if she should happen to do so, the next minute she adds some qualification that undoes all she has said in her praise.

And so it naturally follows that a woman is a slanderer, because only slander can spring from envy and hate. That is a rule that no woman ever wanted to break; she prefers to keep it unbroken. It is not easy to find a woman whose tongue can ever spare anybody or who can keep from words of detraction. Every woman thinks that by running down others she adds to her own praise and increases her own reputation – a fact which shows very clearly to everybody that women have very little sense. For all men agree and hold it as a general rule that words of dispraise hurt only the person who utters them, and they detract from the esteem in which he is held; but no woman on this account keeps from speaking evil and attacking the reputation of good people, and so I think we must insist that no woman is really wise. Every quality that a wise man has is wholly foreign to a woman, because she believes, without thinking, everything she hears, and she is very free about insisting on being praised, and she does a great many other unwise things which it would be tedious for me to enumerate.

Every woman, likewise, is sullied by the vice of greediness, because every woman tries with all her might to get everything good for herself, not only from other men but even from a husband who is very suitable for her, and when she gets them she tries to keep them so that they are of no use to anybody. So great is the avarice by which women are dominated that they think nothing of running counter to the laws, divine and human, and they try to enrich themselves at the expense of others. Indeed, women think that to give to no one and to cling with all their might to everything, whether rightly or wrongly acquired, is the height of virtue and that all men ought to commend it. To this rule there are no exceptions, not even in the case of the Queen.

Woman is also such a slave to her belly that there is nothing she would be ashamed to assent to if she were assured of a fine meal, and no matter how much she has she never has any hope that she can satisfy her appetite when she is hungry; she never invites anybody to eat with her, but when she eats she always seeks out hidden and retired places and she usually likes to eat more than normal. But although in all other respects those of the feminine sex are miserly and hold with might and main to what they have, they will greedily waste their substance to gobble up food, and no one ever saw a woman who would not, if tempted, succumb to the vice of gluttony. We can detect all these qualities in Eve, the first woman, who, although she was created by the hand of God without man's agency, was not afraid to eat the forbidden fruit and for her gluttony was deservedly driven from her home in Paradise. So if that woman who was created by the hand of God without sin could not refrain from the vice of gluttony, what about the others whom their mothers conceived in sin and who never live free from fault? Therefore let it be laid down for you as a general rule that you will rarely fail to get from a woman anything you desire if you will take the trouble to feed her lavishly and often.

Woman is commonly found to be fickle, too, because no woman ever makes up her mind so firmly on any subject that she will not quickly change it on a little persuading from anyone. A woman is just like melting wax, which is always ready to take a new form and to receive the impress of anyone's seal. No woman can make you such a firm promise that she will not change her mind about the matter in a few minutes. No woman is ever of the same mind for an hour at a time, so that Martianus had good reason to say, "Come now, cease your delay, for a woman is always fickle and changeable." Therefore you must not hope to get any satisfaction from any woman's promise unless you are sure you already have the thing she promises you; it is not expedient to rely upon the civil law for what a woman promises, but you should always bring your bag with you, ready to take it. When dealing with women there seems to be no exception to that old saying, "Don't delay; putting off things you are ready for always does harm."

We know that everything a woman says is said with the intention of deceiving, because she always has one thing in her heart and another on her lips. No man can pride himself on knowing a woman so well or on being on such good terms with her that he can know her secret thoughts or when she means what she says. No woman ever trusts any of her men friends, and she thinks every one of them is a downright deceiver; so she always keeps herself in the mood for deception, and everything she says is deceitful and uttered with a mental reservation. Therefore never rely upon a woman's promise or upon her oath, because there is no honesty in her; always be careful to keep your intentions hidden from her, and never tell her your secrets; in that way you may cheat one trick with another and forestall her frauds. Samson's good character is well enough known to everybody, but because he couldn't keep his secrets from a woman he was, we read, betrayed by her in the duplicity of her heart, was overcome by a troop of his enemies, and was captured and deprived of both his bodily strength and his eyesight. We learn, too, of innumerable other women who, according to the stories, have shamefully betrayed husbands or lovers who were not able to keep secrets from them.

Every woman is likewise stained by the sin of disobedience, because there isn't in the world a woman so wise and discreet that, if anyone forbids her to misuse anything she will not strive against this prohibition with all her might and do what she is told not to. Therefore the remark of the wise man, "We strive for what is forbidden, and always want what is denied us," should be applied to all women without exception.

We read, too, of a very wise man who had a wife whom he hated. Because he wanted to avoid the sin of killing her with his own hand, and he knew that women always strive eagerly after what is forbidden them, he prepared a very valuable flask into which he put wine of the best and most fragrant kind, mixed with poison, and he said to his wife, "My sweetest wife, be careful not to touch this vessel, and don't venture to taste any of this liquor, because it is poisonous and deadly to human beings." But the woman scorned her husband's prohibition, for no sooner had he gone away than she drank some of the forbidden liquor and so died of the poison. But why should we mention this, since we know of worse cases? Wasn't it Eve, the first woman, who, although she was formed by the hand of God, destroyed herself by the sin of disobedience and lost the glory of immortality and by her offense brought all her descendants to the destruction of death? Therefore if you want a woman to do anything, you can get her to do it by ordering her to do the opposite.

The feminine sex is also commonly tainted by arrogance, for a woman, when incited by that, cannot keep her tongue or her hands from crimes or abuse, but in her anger she boldly commits all sorts of outrages. Moreover, if anybody tries to restrain an angry woman, he will tire himself out with a vain labor; for though you may bind her, hand and foot, and fasten her into any kind of instrument of torture, you cannot keep her from her evil design or soften her arrogance of soul. Any woman is incited to wrath by a mild enough remark of little significance and indeed at times by nothing at all, and her arrogance grows to tremendous proportions; so far as I can recall no one ever saw a woman who could restrain it. And no woman has been found who is an exception to these rules.

Furthermore, every woman seems to despise all other women – a thing which we know comes only from pride. No man could despise another unless he looked down upon him because of pride. Besides, every woman, not only a young one but even the old and decrepit, strives with all her might to exalt her own beauty; this can come only from pride, as the wise man showed very clearly when he said, "There is arrogance in everybody and pride follows beauty." Therefore it is perfectly clear that women can never have perfectly good characters, because, as they say, "A remarkable character is soiled by an admixture of pride."

Vainglory also mightily possesses woman, since you cannot find a woman in the world who does not delight in the praise of men above everything else and who does not think that every word spoken about her has to do with her praise. This fault can be seen even in Eve, the first woman, who ate the forbidden food in order to have knowledge of good and evil. Furthermore, you cannot find a woman so lowly-born that she will not tell you she has famous relatives and is descended from a family of great men and who will not make all sorts of boasts about herself. These are the things that vainglory seeks for its own.

You will find, too, that every woman is a liar, because there isn't a woman living who doesn't make up things that are untrue and who doesn't boldly declare what is false. Even for a trifle a woman will swear falsely a thousand times, and for a tiny gain she will make up innumerable lies. Women indeed try by every means to support their lies, and they usually cover up the sin of one with that of others that are elaborately concocted. No man can have such a strong case against a woman that she will confess her fault unless she is caught in the very act.

Again, every woman is a drunkard, that is, she likes to drink wine. There is no woman who would blush to drink excellent Falernian with a hundred gossips in one day, nor will she be so refreshed by that many drinks of undiluted wine that she will refuse another if it is brought her. Wine that is turned she considers a great enemy, and a drink of water usually makes her sick. But if she finds a good wine with no water in it, she would rather lose a good deal of her property than forgo drinking her fill of that; therefore there is no woman who is not often subject to the sin of drunkenness.

Every woman is also loud-mouthed, since no one of them can keep her tongue from abuses, and if she loses a single egg she will keep up a clamor all day like a barking dog, and she will disturb the whole neighborhood over a trifle. When she is with other women, no one of them will give the others a chance to speak, but each always tries to be the one to say whatever is to be said and to keep on talking longer than the rest; and neither her tongue nor her spirit ever gets tired out by talking. We even see many women who are so anxious to talk that when they are alone they talk to themselves and speak out loud. A woman will boldly contradict everything you say, and she can never agree with anything, but she always tries to give her opinion on every subject.

Moreover, no woman knows how to keep a secret; the more she is told to keep it to herself, the harder she tries to tell it to everybody. No one to this day has been able to find a woman who could keep hidden anything confided to her, no matter how important it was or how much it seemed that to tell it would be the death of somebody. Whatever you intrust as a secret to the good faith of a woman seems to burn her very vitals until she gets the harmful secrets out of her. You cannot avoid this in a woman by ordering her to do the opposite, as in the case mentioned above, because every woman takes great pleasure in gossip; therefore be careful to keep your secret from every woman.

Every woman in the world is likewise wanton, because no woman, no matter how famous and honored she is, will refuse her embraces to any man, even the most vile and abject, if she knows that he is good at the work of Venus; yet there is no man so good at the work that he can satisfy the desires of any woman you please in any way at all.

Furthermore, no woman is attached to her lover or bound to her husband with such pure devotion that she will not accept another lover, especially if a rich one comes along, which shows the wantonness as well as the avarice of a woman. There isn't a woman in this world so constant and so bound by pledges that, if a lover of pleasure comes along and with skill and persistence invites her to the joys of love, she will reject his entreaties – at any rate if he does a good deal of urging – or will defend herself against his importunity. No woman is an exception to this rule either. So you can see what we ought to think of a woman who is in fortunate circumstances and is blessed with an honorable lover or the finest of husbands, and yet lusts after some other man. But that is what a woman does who is too much troubled with wantonness.

Woman is also prone to every sort of evil. Whatever evil in this world is great-est, that any woman will commit without fear and for a trivial reason; by a little persuading anyone can easily incline her mind toward any evil. Besides there is not a woman living in this world, not even the Empress or the Queen, who does not waste her whole life on auguries and the various practitioners of divination, as the heathen do, and so long as she lives she persists in this credulousness and sins without measure again and again with the art of astrology. Indeed, no woman does anything without considering the proper day and hour for beginning it and without inaugurating it with incantations. They will not marry, or hold funeral rites for the dead, or start their sowing, or move into a new house, or begin anything else without consulting this feminine augury and having their actions approved by these witches. Therefore Solomon, that wisest of men, who knew all the evils and the misdeeds of womankind, made a general statement concerning their crimes and wickednesses when he said, "There is no good woman." Why therefore, Walter, are you striving so eagerly to love that which is bad?

Beowulf, trans. Lesslie Hall (D. C. Heath & Co, 1892), pp. 44–57.

XX.
THE MOTHER OF GRENDEL.

They sank then to slumber. With sorrow one paid for
His evening repose, as often betid them
While Grendel was holding the gold-bedecked palace,
Ill-deeds performing, till his end overtook him,
Death for his sins. 'Twas seen very clearly,
Known unto earth-folk, that still an avenger
Outlived the loathed one, long since the sorrow
Caused by the struggle; the mother of Grendel,
Devil-shaped woman, her woe ever minded,
Who was held to inhabit the horrible waters,
The cold-flowing currents, after Cain had become a

Slayer-with-edges to his one only brother,
The son of his sire; he set out then banished,
Marked as a murderer, man-joys avoiding,
Lived in the desert. Thence demons unnumbered
Fate-sent awoke; one of them Grendel,
Sword-cursed, hateful, who at Heorot met with
A man that was watching, waiting the struggle,
Where a horrid one held him with hand-grapple sturdy;
Nathless he minded the might of his body,
The glorious gift God had allowed him,
And folk-ruling Father's favor relied on,
His help and His comfort: so he conquered the foeman,
The hell-spirit humbled: he unhappy departed then,
Reaved of his joyance, journeying to death-haunts,
Foeman of man. His mother moreover
Eager and gloomy was anxious to go on
Her mournful mission, mindful of vengeance
For the death of her son. She came then to Heorot
Where the Armor-Dane earlmen all through the building
Were lying in slumber. Soon there became then
Return to the nobles, when the mother of Grendel
Entered the folk-hall; the fear was less grievous
By even so much as the vigor of maidens,
War-strength of women, by warrior is reckoned,
When well-carved weapon, worked with the hammer,
Blade very bloody, brave with its edges,
Strikes down the boar-sign that stands on the helmet.
Then the hard-edged weapon was heard in the building,
The brand o'er the benches, broad-lindens many
Hand-fast were lifted; for helmet he recked not,
For armor-net broad, whom terror laid hold of.
She went then hastily, outward would get her
Her life for to save, when some one did spy her;
Soon she had grappled one of the athelings
Fast and firmly, when fenward she hied her;
That one to Hrothgar was liefest of heroes
In rank of retainer where waters encircle,
A mighty shield-warrior, whom she murdered at slumber,
A broadly-famed battle-knight. Beowulf was absent,
But another apartment was erstwhile devoted
To the glory-decked Geatman when gold was distributed.
There was hubbub in Heorot. The hand that was famous
She grasped in its gore; grief was renewed then
In homes and houses: 'twas no happy arrangement
In both of the quarters to barter and purchase

With lives of their friends. Then the well-aged ruler,
The gray-headed war-thane, was woful in spirit,
When his long-trusted liegeman lifeless he knew of,
His dearest one gone. Quick from a room was
Beowulf brought, brave and triumphant.
As day was dawning in the dusk of morning,
When then that earlman, champion noble,
Came with comrades, where the clever one bided
Whether God all gracious would grant him a respite
After the woe he had suffered. The war-worthy hero
With a troop of retainers trod then the pavement
(The hall-building groaned), till he greeted the wise one,
The earl of the Ingwins; asked if the night had
Fully refreshed him, as fain he would have it.

XXI.
HROTHGAR'S ACCOUNT OF THE MONSTERS.

Hrothgar rejoined, helm of the Scyldings:
"Ask not of joyance! Grief is renewed to
The folk of the Danemen. Dead is Æschere,
Yrmenlaf's brother, older than he,
My true-hearted counsellor, trusty adviser,
Shoulder-companion, when fighting in battle
Our heads we protected, when troopers were clashing,
And heroes were dashing; such an earl should be ever,
An erst-worthy atheling, as Æschere proved him.
The flickering death-spirit became in Heorot
His hand-to-hand murderer; I can not tell whither
The cruel one turned in the carcass exulting,
By cramming discovered. The quarrel she wreaked then,
That last night igone Grendel thou killedst
In grewsomest manner, with grim-holding clutches,
Since too long he had lessened my liege-troop and wasted
My folk-men so foully. He fell in the battle
With forfeit of life, and another has followed,
A mighty crime-worker, her kinsman avenging,
And henceforth hath 'stablished her hatred unyielding,
As it well may appear to many a liegeman,
Who mourneth in spirit the treasure-bestower,
Her heavy heart-sorrow; the hand is now lifeless
Which availed you in every wish that you cherished.
Land-people heard I, liegemen, this saying,
Dwellers in halls, they had seen very often
A pair of such mighty march-striding creatures,

Far-dwelling spirits, holding the moorlands:
One of them wore, as well they might notice,
The image of woman, the other one wretched
In guise of a man wandered in exile,
Except he was huger than any of earthmen;
Earth-dwelling people entitled him Grendel
In days of yore: they know not their father,
Whe'r ill-going spirits any were borne him
Ever before. They guard the wolf-coverts,
Lands inaccessible, wind-beaten nesses,
Fearfullest fen-deeps, where a flood from the mountains
'Neath mists of the nesses netherward rattles,
The stream under earth: not far is it henceward
Measured by mile-lengths that the mere-water standeth,
Which forests hang over, with frost-whiting covered,
A firm-rooted forest, the floods overshadow.
There ever at night one an ill-meaning portent
A fire-flood may see; 'mong children of men
None liveth so wise that wot of the bottom;
Though harassed by hounds the heath-stepper seek for,
Fly to the forest, firm-antlered he-deer,
Spurred from afar, his spirit he yieldeth,
His life on the shore, ere in he will venture
To cover his head. Uncanny the place is:
Thence upward ascendeth the surging of waters,
Wan to the welkin, when the wind is stirring
The weathers unpleasing, til the air growth gloomy,
And the heavens lower. Now is help to be gotten
From thee and thee only! The abode thou know'st not,
The dangerous place where thou'rt able to meet with
The sin-laden hero: seek if thou darest!
For the feud I will fully fee thee with money,
With old-time treasure, as erstwhile I did thee,
With well-twisted jewels, if away thou shalt get thee."

XXII.
BEOWULF SEEKS GRENDEL'S MOTHER.

Beowulf answered, Ecgtheow's son:
"Grieve not, O wise one! For each it is better,
His friend to avenge than with vehemence wail him;
Each of us must the end-day abide of
His earthly existence; who is able accomplish,
Glory ere death! To battle-thane noble
Lifeless lying, 'tis at last most fitting.

Arise, O king, quick let us hasten
To look at the footprint of the kinsman of Grendel!
I promise thee this now: to his place he'll escape not,
To embrace of the earth, nor to mountainous forest,
Nor to depths of the ocean, wherever he wanders.
Practice thou now patient endurance
Of each of thy sorrows, as I hope for thee soothly!"
Then up sprang the old one, the All-Wielder thanked he,
Ruler-Almighty, that the man had outspoken.
Then for Hrothgar a war-horse was decked with a bridle,
Curly-maned courser. The clever folk-leader
Stately proceeded: stepped then an earl-troop
Of linden-wood bearers. Her footprints were seen then
Widely in wood-paths, her way o'er the bottoms,
Where she faraway fared o'er fen-country murky,
Bore away breathless the best of retainers
Who pondered with Hrothgar the welfare of country.
The son of the athelings then went o'er the stony,
Declivitous cliffs, the close-covered passes,
Narrow-passages, paths unfrequented,
Nesses abrupt, nicker-haunts many;
One of a few of wise-mooded heroes,
He onward advanced to view the surroundings,
Till he found unawares woods of the mountain
O'er hoar-stones hanging, holt-wood unjoyful;
The water stood under, welling and gory.
'Twas irksome in spirit to all of the Danemen,
Friends of the Scyldings, to many a liegeman
Sad to be suffered, a sorrow unlittle
To each of the earlmen, when to Æschere's head they
Came on the cliff. The current was seething
With blood and with gore (the troopers gazed on it).
The horn anon sang the battle-song ready.
The troop were all seated; they saw 'long the water then
Many a serpent, mere-dragons wondrous
Trying the waters, nickers a-lying
On the cliffs of the nesses, which at noonday full often
Go on the sea-deeps their sorrowful journey,
Wild-beasts and wormkind; away then they hastened
Hot-mooded, hateful, they heard the great clamor,
The war-trumpet winding. One did the Geat-prince
Sunder from earth-joys, with arrow from bowstring,
From his sea-struggle tore him, that the trusty war-missile
Pierced to his vitals; he proved in the currents
Less doughty at swimming whom death had offcarried.

Soon in the waters the wonderful swimmer
Was straitened most sorely with sword-pointed boar-spears,
Pressed in the battle and pulled to the cliff-edge;
The liegemen then looked on the loath-fashioned stranger.
Beowulf donned then his battle-equipments,
Cared little for life; inlaid and most ample,
The hand-woven corslet which could cover his body,
Must the wave-deeps explore, that war might be powerless
To harm the great hero, and the hating one's grasp might
Not peril his safety; his head was protected
By the light-flashing helmet that should mix with the bottoms,
Trying the eddies, treasure-emblazoned,
Encircled with jewels, as in seasons long past
The weapon-smith worked it, wondrously made it,
With swine-bodies fashioned it, that thenceforward no longer
Brand might bite it, and battle-sword hurt it.
And that was not least of helpers in prowess
That Hrothgar's spokesman had lent him when straitened;
And the hilted hand-sword was Hrunting entitled,
Old and most excellent 'mong all of the treasures;
Its blade was of iron, blotted with poison,
Hardened with gore; it failed not in battle
Any hero under heaven in hand who it brandished,
Who ventured to take the terrible journeys,
The battle-field sought; not the earliest occasion
That deeds of daring 'twas destined to 'complish.
Ecglaf's kinsman minded not soothly,
Exulting in strength, what erst he had spoken
Drunken with wine, when the weapon he lent to
A sword-hero bolder; himself did not venture
'Neath the strife of the currents his life to endanger,
To fame-deeds perform; there he forfeited glory,
Repute for his strength. Not so with the other
When he clad in his corslet had equipped him for battle.

XXIII.
BEOWULF'S FIGHT WITH GRENDEL'S MOTHER.

Beowulf spake, Ecgtheow's son:
"Recall now, oh, famous kinsman of Healfdene,
Prince very prudent, now to part I am ready,
Gold-friend of earlmen, what erst we agreed on,
Should I lay down my life in lending thee assistance,
When my earth-joys were over, thou wouldst evermore serve me

In stead of a father; my faithful thanemen,
My trusty retainers, protect thou and care for,
Fall I in battle: and, Hrothgar beloved,
Send unto Higelac the high-valued jewels
Thou to me hast allotted. The lord of the Geatmen
May perceive from the gold, the Hrethling may see it
When he looks on the jewels, that a gem-giver found I
Good over-measure, enjoyed him while able.
And the ancient heirloom Unferth permit thou,
The famed one to have, the heavy-sword splendid
The hard-edged weapon; with Hrunting to aid me,
I shall gain me glory, or grim-death shall take me."
The atheling of Geatmen uttered these words and
Heroic did hasten, not any rejoinder
Was willing to wait for; the wave-current swallowed
The doughty-in-battle. Then a day's length elapsed ere
He was able to see the sea at its bottom.
Early she found then who fifty of winters
The course of the currents kept in her fury,
Grisly and greedy, that the grim one's dominion
Some one of men from above was exploring.
Forth did she grab them, grappled the warrior
With horrible clutches; yet no sooner she injured
His body unscathed: the burnie out-guarded,
That she proved but powerless to pierce through the armor,
The limb-mail locked, with loath-grabbing fingers.
The sea-wolf bare then, when bottomward came she,
The ring-prince homeward, that he after was powerless
(He had daring to do it) to deal with his weapons,
But many a mere-beast tormented him swimming,
Flood-beasts no few with fierce-biting tusks did
Break through his burnie, the brave one pursued they.
The earl then discovered he was down in some cavern
Where no water whatever anywise harmed him,
And the clutch of the current could come not anear him,
Since the roofed-hall prevented; brightness a-gleaming
Fire-light he saw, flashing resplendent.
The good-one saw then the sea-bottom's monster,
The mighty mere-woman; he made a great onset
With weapon-of-battle, his hand not desisted
From striking, that war-blade struck on her head then
A battle-song greedy. The stranger perceived then
The sword would not bite, her life would not injure,

But the falchion failed the folk-prince when straitened:
Erst had it often onsets encountered,
Oft cloven the helmet, the fated one's armor:
'Twas the first time that ever the excellent jewel
Had failed of its fame. Firm-mooded after,
Not heedless of valor, but mindful of glory,
Was Higelac's kinsman; the hero-chief angry
Cast then his carved-sword covered with jewels
That it lay on the earth, hard and steel-pointed;
He hoped in his strength, his hand-grapple sturdy.
So any must act whenever he thinketh
To gain him in battle glory unending,
And is reckless of living. The lord of the War-Geats
(He shrank not from battle) seized by the shoulder
The mother of Grendel; then mighty in struggle
Swung he his enemy, since his anger was kindled,
That she fell to the floor. With furious grapple
She gave him requital early thereafter,
And stretched out to grab him; the strongest of warriors
Faint-mooded stumbled, till he fell in his traces,
Foot-going champion. Then she sat on the hall-guest
And wielded her war-knife wide-bladed, flashing,
For her son would take vengeance, her one only bairn.
His breast-armor woven bode on his shoulder;
It guarded his life, the entrance defended
'Gainst sword-point and edges. Ecgtheow's son there
Had fatally journeyed, champion of Geatmen,
In the arms of the ocean, had the armor not given,
Close-woven corslet, comfort and succor,
And had God most holy not awarded the victory,
All-knowing Lord; easily did heaven's
Ruler most righteous arrange it with justice;
Uprose he erect ready for battle.

XXIV.
BEOWULF IS DOUBLE-CONQUEROR.

Then he saw mid the war-gems a weapon of victory,
An ancient giant-sword, of edges a-doughty,
Glory of warriors: of weapons 'twas choicest,
Only 'twas larger than any man else was
Able to bear to the battle-encounter,
The good and splendid work of the giants.

He grasped then the sword-hilt, knight of the Scyldings,
Bold and battle-grim, brandished his ring-sword,
Hopeless of living, hotly he smote her,
That the fiend-woman's neck firmly it grappled,
Broke through her bone-joints, the bill fully pierced her
Fate-cursed body, she fell to the ground then:
The hand-sword was bloody, the hero exulted.
The brand was brilliant, brightly it glimmered,
Just as from heaven gemlike shineth
The torch of the firmament. He glanced 'long the building,
And turned by the wall then, Higelac's vassal
Raging and wrathful raised his battle-sword
Strong by the handle. The edge was not useless
To the hero-in-battle, but he speedily wished to
Give Grendel requital for the many assaults he
Had worked on the West-Danes not once, but often,
When he slew in slumber the subjects of Hrothgar,
Swallowed down fifteen sleeping retainers
Of the folk of the Danemen, and fully as many
Carried away, a horrible prey.
He gave him requital, grim-raging champion,
When he saw on his rest-place weary of conflict
Grendel lying, of life-joys bereaved,
As the battle at Heorot erstwhile had scathed him;
His body far-bounded, a blow when he suffered,
Death having seized him, sword-smiting heavy,
And he cut off his head then. Early this noticed
The clever carles who as comrades of Hrothgar
Gazed on the sea-deeps, that the surging wave-currents
Were mightily mingled, the mere-flood was gory:
Of the good-one the gray-haired together held converse,
The hoary of head, that they hoped not to see again
The atheling ever, that exulting in victory
He'd return there to visit the distinguished folk-ruler:
Then many concluded the mere-wolf had killed him.
The ninth hour came then. From the ness-edge departed
The bold mooded Scyldings; the gold-friend of heroes
Homeward betook him. The strangers sat down then
Soul-sick, sorrowful, the sea-waves regarding:
They wished and yet weened not their well-loved friend-lord
To see any more. The sword-blade began then,
The blood having touched it, contracting and shriveling
With battle-icicles; 'twas a wonderful marvel

That it melted entirely, likest to ice when
The Father unbindeth the bond of the frost and
Unwindeth the wave-bands, He who wieldeth dominion
Of times and of tides: a truth-firm Creator.
Nor took he of jewels more in the dwelling,
Lord of the Weders, though they lay all around him,
Than the head and the handle handsome with jewels;
The brand early melted, burnt was the weapon:
So hot was the blood, the strange-spirit poisonous
That in it did perish. He early swam off then
Who had bided in combat the carnage of haters,
Went up through the ocean; the eddies were cleansed,
The spacious expanses, when the spirit from farland
His life put aside and this short-lived existence.
The seamen's defender came swimming to land then
Doughty of spirit, rejoiced in his sea-gift,
The bulky burden which he bore in his keeping.
The excellent vassals advanced then to meet him,
To God they were grateful, were glad in their chieftain,
That to see him safe and sound was granted them.
From the high-minded hero, then, helmet and burnie
Were speedily loosened: the ocean was putrid,
The water 'neath welkin weltered with gore.
Forth did they fare, then, their footsteps retracing,
Merry and mirthful, measured the earth-way,
The highway familiar: men very daring
Bare then the head from the sea-cliff, burdening
Each of the earlmen, excellent-valiant.
Four of them had to carry with labor
The head of Grendel to the high towering gold-hall
Upstuck on the spear, till fourteen most-valiant
And battle-brave Geatmen came there going
Straight to the palace: the prince of the people
Measured the mead-ways, their mood-brave companion.
The atheling of earlmen entered the building,
Deed-valiant man, adorned with distinction,
Doughty shield-warrior, to address King Hrothgar:
Then hung by the hair, the head of Grendel
Was borne to the building, where the beer-thanes were drinking,
Loth before earlmen and 'eke for the lady:
The warriors beheld then a wonderful sight.

**William of Malmesbury, *Chronicle of the Kings of England*, trans.
J.A. Giles (Henry G. Bohn, 1847), pp. 230–2 and 235–6.**

[A.D. 1065.] Story of the Berkely Witch

At the same time something similar occurred in England, not by divine miracle, but by infernal craft; which when I shall have related, the credit of the narrative will not be shaken, though the minds of the hearers should be incredulous; for I have heard it from a man of such character, who swore he had seen it, that I should blush to disbelieve. There resided at Berkeley a woman addicted to witchcraft, as it afterwards appeared, and skilled in ancient augury: she was excessively glut-tonous, perfectly lascivious, setting no bounds to her debaucheries, as she was not old, though fast declining in life. On a certain day, as she was regaling, a jack-daw, which was a very great favourite, chattered a little more loudly than usual. On hear-ing which the woman's knife fell from her hand, her countenance grew pale, and deeply groaning, "This day," said she, "my plough has completed its last furrow; to-day I shall hear of, and suffer, some dreadful calamity." While yet speaking, the messenger of her misfortunes arrived; and being asked, why he approached with so distressed an air? "I bring news," said he, "from that village," naming the place, "of the death of your son, and of the whole family, by a sudden accident." At this intelligence, the woman, sorely afflicted, immediately took to her bed, and per-ceiving the disorder rapidly approaching the vitals, she summoned her surviving children, a monk, and a nun, by hasty letters; and, when they arrived, with faltering voice, addressed them thus: "Formerly, my children, I constantly administered to my wretched circumstances by demoniacal arts: I have been the sink of every vice, the teacher of every allurement: yet, while practising these crimes, I was accus-tomed to soothe my hapless soul with the hope of your piety. Despairing of myself, I rested my expectations on you; I advanced you as my defenders against evil spir-its, my safeguards against my strongest foes. Now, since I have approached the end of my life, and shall have those eager to punish, who lured me to sin, I entreat you by your mother's breasts, if you have any regard, any affection, at least to endeavor to alleviate my torments; and, although you cannot revoke the sentence already passed upon my soul, yet you may, perhaps, rescue my body, by these means: sew up my corpse in the skin of a stag; lay it on its back in a stone coffin; fasten down the lid with lead and iron; on this lay a stone, bound round with three iron chains of enormous weight; let there be psalms sung for fifty nights, and masses said for an equal number of days, to allay the ferocious attacks of my adversaries. If I lie thus secure for three nights, on the fourth day bury your mother in the ground; although I fear, lest the earth, which has been so often burdened with my crimes, should refuse to receive and cherish me in her bosom." They did their utmost to comply with her injunctions: but alas! vain were pious tears, vows, or entreaties; so great was the woman's guilt, so great the devil's violence. For on the first two nights, while the choir of priests was singing psalms around the body, the devils, one by one, with the utmost ease bursting open the door of the church, though closed with an immense bolt, broke asunder the two outer chains; the middle one being more laboriously wrought, remained entire. On the third night, about cock-crow, the whole monastery seemed to be overthrown from its very foundation, by the clamour of the approaching enemy. One devil, more terrible in appearance than the rest, and of loftier stature, broke the gates to shivers by the violence of his attack. The priests grew motionless with fear, their hair stood on end, and they became speechless. He proceeded, as it appeared, with haughty step towards the coffin, and calling on the woman by name, commanded her to rise. She replying that she could not on account of the chains: "You shall be loosed," said he, "and to your cost:" and directly he broke the chain, which had mocked the ferocity of the others, with as little exertion as though it had been made of flax. He also beat down the cover of the coffin with his foot, and taking her by the hand, before them all, he dragged her out of the church. At the doors appeared a black horse, proudly neighing, with iron hooks projecting over his whole back; on which the wretched creature was placed, and, immediately, with the whole party, vanished from the eyes of the beholders; her pitiable cries, however, for assistance, were heard for nearly the space of four miles. No person will deem this incredible, who has read St. Gregory's Dialogues; who tells, in his fourth book, of a wicked man that had been buried in a church, and was cast out of doors again by devils. Among the French also, what I am about to relate is frequently mentioned. Charles Martel, a man of renowned valour, who obliged the Saracens, when they had invaded France, to retire to Spain, was, at his death, buried in the church of St. Denys; but as he had seized much of the property of almost all the monasteries in France for the purpose of paying his soldiers, he was visibly taken away from his tomb by evil spirits, and has nowhere been seen to his day. At length this was revealed to the bishop of Orleans, and by him publicly made known.

[A.D. 1065.] Prodigy Near Normandy

At that time too, on the confines of Brittany and Normandy, a prodigy was seen in one, or more properly speaking, in two women: there were two heads, four arms, and every other part two-fold to the navel; beneath, were two legs, two feet, and all other parts single. While one was laughing, eating, or speaking, the other would cry, fast, or remain silent: though both mouths ate, yet the excrement was discharged by only one passage. At last, one dying, the other survived, and the living carried about the dead, for the space of three years, till she died also, through the fatigue of the weight, and the stench of the dead carcass. Many were of opinion, and some even have written, that these women represented England and Normandy, which, though separated by position, are yet united under one master. Whatever wealth these countries greedily absorb, flows into one common receptacle, which is either the covetousness of princes, or the ferocity of surrounding nations. England, yet vigorous, supports with her wealth Normandy now dead and almost decayed, until she herself perhaps shall fall through the violence of spoilers. Happy, if she shall ever again breathe that liberty, the mere shadow of which she has long pursued! She now mourns, borne down with calamity, and oppressed with exactions. . . .

Gerald of Wales, *The Historical Works of Giraldus Cambrensis, Containing the Topography of Ireland and the History of the Conquest of Ireland*, trans. Thomas Forester (Bell, 1887), II.xx–xxi and xxiii–xxiv and III.xxxv, pp. 84–7 and 147–8.

Book II

Chapter XX. Of a Woman Who had a Beard, and a Hairy Crest and Mane on her Back

Duvenald, king of Limerick, had a woman with a beard down to her navel, and, also, a crest like a colt of a year old, which reached from the top of her neck down her backbone, and was covered with hair. The woman, thus remarkable for two monstrous deformities, was, however, not an hermaphrodite, but in other respects had the parts of a woman; and she constantly attended the court, an object of ridicule as well as of wonder. The fact of her spine being covered with hair neither determined her gender to be male or female; and in wearing a long beard she followed the customs of her country, though it was unnatural in her. Also, within our time, a woman was seen attending the court in Connaught, who partook of the nature of both sexes, and was an hermaphrodite. On the right side of her face she had a long and thick beard, which covered both sides of her lips to the middle of her chin, like a man; on the left, her lips and chin were smooth and hairless, like a woman.

Chapter XXIII. Of a Goat Which had Intercourse with a Woman

Roderic, king of Connaught, had a white tame goat, remarkable for its flowing hair and the length of its horns. This goat had intercourse, bestially, with the woman to whose care it had been committed; the wretched creature having seduced it to become the instrument of gratifying her unnatural lust, rather than that the animal was the guilty actor. O foul and disgraceful deed! How dreadfully has reason given the reins to sensuality! How brutally does the lord of brutes, discarding his natural privileges, descend to the level of brutes, when he, rational animal, submits to such intercourse with a beast! For although on both sides it is detestable and abominable, it is by far the least that brutes should be entirely submissive to rational creatures. But though brutes are destined by nature for the service of men, they were created for use, not abuse. The indignation of nature, strongly repudiating it, thus vents itself in verse:

"Omnia jam novitate placent, nova grata voluptas,
Et naturalis inveterata Venus.
Arte minus natura placet, consumitur usus;
In reprobos ratio, jam ratione carens.
Vis genitiva gemit, violata cupidinis arte;
Et violans vindex publicat ira scelus.
Pandit enim natura nefas, proditque pudorem
Criminis infandi, prodigiosa creans."

Chapter XXIV. Of a Lion that was Enamoured of a Woman

I saw at Paris a lion which some cardinal had presented, when it was a whelp, to Philip, the son of king Louis. This lion was in the habit of having bestial intercourse with a silly girl, whose name was Joan. If, by any chance, it broke out of its den, and became so infuriated that no one dared to approach it, Joan was called, and instantly disarmed its malice and pacified its rage. Soothed by female allurements, it followed her where she pleased, and immediately changed its fury to love. Both of these brutes merited a shameful death. But not only in modern times have these abominations been attempted, but in the earliest ages, remarkable for their greater innocence and simplicity of manners, society was polluted by these infamous vices. Thus we find it written in Leviticus: "If a woman approach unto any beast and lie down thereto, thou shalt kill the woman, and the beast shall be put to death. Their blood shall be upon them." The beast was commanded to be slain, not for its guilt, of which its nature as a brute exculpated it, but as a memorial, to recall to the mind the enormity of the sin. It is also the opinion of many persons, that the story of Pasiphae being leaped (raped) by a bull was not a mere fable, but an actual fact.

Book III

Chapter XXXV. Of the Number of Persons in this Nation Who have Bodily Defects

Moreover, I have never seen in any other nation so many individuals who were born blind, so many lame, maimed, or having some natural defect. The persons of those who are well-formed are indeed remarkably fine, nowhere better; but as those who are favoured with the gifts of nature grow up exceedingly handsome, those from whom she withholds them are frightfully ugly. No wonder if among an adulterous and incestuous people, in which both births and marriages are illegitimate, a nation out of the pale of the laws, nature herself should be foully corrupted by perverse habits. It should seem that by the just judgments of God, nature sometimes produces such objects, contrary to her own laws, in order that those who will not regard Him duly by the light of their own consciences, should often have to lament their privations of the exterior and bodily gift of sight.

Bibliography

Acker, Paul. "Horror and the Maternal in *Beowulf.*" *PMLA* 121/2 (2006): 702–16.
Bates, A.W. *Emblematic Monsters: Unnatural Conceptions and Deformed Births in Early Modern Europe*. Brill, 2016.
Brown, Judith and Robert Davis. *Gender and Society in Renaissance Italy*. Longman, 1998.
Bruckner, Matilda. "Natural and Unnatural Woman: Melusine Inside and Out." In *Founding Feminisms in Medieval Studies: Essays in Honour of E. Jane Burns*. Eds. Laine Doggett and Daniel O'Sullivan. Brewer, 2016.21–31.
Buckle, Henry. *History of Civilization in England*. Cambridge University Press, 2011.

Bullough, Vern and James Brundage, Eds. *Handbook of Medieval Sexuality*. Garland, 2000.

Burns, Jane. "A Snake-Tailed Woman: Hybridity and Dynasty in the *Roman de Mélusine*." In *From Beasts to Souls: Gender and Embodiment in Medieval Europe*. Eds. Jane Burns and Peggy McCracken. University of Notre Dame Press, 2013.185–220.

Cadden, Joan. *Meanings of Sex Difference in the Middle Ages: Medicine, Science, and Culture*. Cambridge University Press, 1993.

Campbell, Josie. *Popular Culture in the Middle Ages*. Bowling Green State University Popular Press, 1986.

Chadwick, Nora. "The Monsters and Beowulf." In *The Anglo-Saxons: Studies in Some Aspects of Their History*. Ed. Peter Clemoes. Bowes & Bowes, 1959.171–203.

Chance, Jane. "The Structural Unity of Beowulf: The Problem of Grendel's Mother." *Texas Studies in Literature and Language* 22/3 (1980): 287–303.

Chance, Jane. *Woman as Hero in Old English Literature*. Syracuse University Press, 1986.95–111.

Chance, Jane. "Reading Grendel's Mother." In *New Readings on Women and Early Medieval English Literature and Culture: Cross-Disciplinary Studies in Honour of Helen Damico*. Eds. H. Scheck and C. Kozikowski. Amsterdam University Press, 2019.209–26.

Clark, Robert. "Eve and her Audience in the Anglo-Norman *Adam*." In *Crossing Boundaries: Issues of Cultural and Individual Identity in the Middle Ages and the Renaissance*. Ed. Sally McKee. Brepols, 1999.27–39.

Clover, Carol. "Maiden Warriors and Other Sons." *The Journal of English and Germanic Philology* 85/1 (1986): 35–49.

Cockburn, David. *Human Beings*. Cambridge University Press, 1991.

Colwell, Tania. "Mélusine: Ideal Mother or Inimitable Monster?" In *Love, Marriage, and Family Ties in the Later Middle Ages*. Eds. Isabel Davis, Miriam Müller, and Sarah Rees Jones. Brepols, 2003.181–203.

Fletcher, R.A. *Bloodfeud*. Oxford University Press, 2003.

Friðriksdóttir, J. *Women in Old Norse Literature*. Springer, 2013.

Fries, Maureen. "The Evolution of Eve in Medieval French and English Drama." *Studies in Philology* 99/1 (2002): 1–16.

Getz, Faye. *Medicine in the English Middle Ages*. Princeton University Press, 1998.

Green, Monica. "The Transmission of Ancient Theories of Female Physiology and Disease Through the Early Middle Ages." PhD dissertation. Princeton University, 1985.

Green, Monica. "Women's Medical Practice and Health Care in Medieval Europe." *Signs* 14/2 (1989): 434–74.

Green, Monica. *Women's Healthcare in the Medieval West: Texts and Contexts*. Ashgate, 2000.

Green, Monica. "Bodies, Gender, Health, Disease: Recent Work on Medieval Women's Medicine." *Studies in Medieval and Renaissance History* 3/2 (2005): 1–46.

Green, Monica. *Making Women's Medicine Masculine: The Rise of Male Authority in Pre-Modern Gynaecology*. Oxford University Press, 2008.

Hennequin, M. "We've Created a Monster: The Strange Case of Grendel's Mother." *English Studies* 89/5 (2008): 503–23.

Jesch, J. *Women in the Viking Age*. Boydell Press, 1991.

Kiernan, Kevin. "Grendel's Heroic Mother." *Geardagum: Essays on Old English Language and Literature* 6 (1984): 13–33.

King, Helen. "Once Upon a Text: Hysteria from Hippocrates." In *Hysteria Beyond Freud*. Eds. Sander Gilman, Helen King, Roy Porter, George Rousseau, and Elaine Showalter. University of California Press, 1993.3–90.

Krahmer, Shawn. "Adam, Eve, and Original Sin in the Works of Bernard of Clair-vaux." *Cistercian Studies Quarterly: An International Review of Monastic and Contemplative Spirituality* 37/1 (2002): 3–12.

Margolis, Nadia and Katharina Wilson, Eds. *Women in the Middle Ages: An Encyclopedia*, 2 vols. Greenwood, 2004.

McCracken, Peggy. *The Curse of Eve, the Wound of the Hero: Blood, Gender, and Medieval Literature.* University of Pennsylvania Press, 2003.

Miller, Sarah Alison. *Medieval Monstrosity and the Female Body.* Routledge, 2010.

Miller, William Ian. "Choosing the Avenger: Some Aspects of the Bloodfeud in Medieval Iceland and England." *Law and History Review* 1/2 (1983): 159–204.

Mitchell, Linda. "Gender(ed) Identities? Anglo-Norman Settlement, Irish-ness, and The Statutes of Kilkenny of 1367." *Historical Reflections* 37/2 (2011): 8–23.

Monson, Don. *Andreas Capellanus, Scholasticism, and the Courtly Tradition.* Catholic University Press of America, 2005.

Moore, Rebecca. *Women in Christian Traditions.* NYU Press, 2015.

Niles, John. "Pagan Survivals and Popular Belief." In *The Cambridge Companion to Old English Literature.* Eds. Malcolm Godden and Michael Lapidge. Cambridge University Press, 2012.123–8.

Nitzsche, Jane. "The Structural Unity of *Beowulf*: The Problem of Grendel's Mother." *Texas Studies in Literature and Language* 22/3 (1980): 287–303.

Overing, Gillian. "The Women of *Beowulf*: A Context for Interpretation." In *The Beowulf Reader.* Ed. Peter Baker. Routledge, 2000.219–60.

Pairet, Ana. "Melusine's Double Binds: Foundation, Transgression, and the Genealogical Romance." In *Reassessing the Heroine in Medieval French Literature.* Ed. Kathy Krause. University Press of Florida, 2001.71–86.

Park, Katharine. *Secrets of Women: Gender, Generation, and the Origins of Human Dissection.* Zone Books, 2006.

Pinson, Yona. "The Femme Fatale – Eve/Venus/*Luxuria*." In *Pictorial Languages and their Meanings. Liber Amicorum in Honor of Nurith Kenaan-Kedar.* Eds. Christine Verzar and Gil Fishhof. Tel Aviv University, 2006.339–52.

Puhvel, Martin. "The Might of Grendel's Mother." *Folklore* 80/2 (1969): 81–8.

Rawcliffe, Carole. *Medicine and Society in Later Medieval England.* Sutton, 1995.

Riddle, John. *Contraception and Abortion from the Ancient World to the Renaissance.* Harvard University Press, 1992.

Sayers, William. "Grendel's Mother, Icelandic Grýla, and Irish Nechta Scéne: Eviscerating Fear." *Proceedings of the Harvard Celtic Colloquium* 16/17 (1996/7): 256–68.

Schaus, Margaret, Ed. *Women and Gender in Medieval Europe: An Encyclopedia.* Routledge, 2006.

Siraisi, Nancy. *Medieval & Early Renaissance Medicine: An Introduction to Knowledge and Practice.* University of Chicago Press, 2007.

Stauton, Michael. *The Historians of Angevin England.* Oxford University Press, 2017.

Taylor, Keith. "Beowulf 1259a: The Inherent Nobility of Grendel's Mother." *English Language Notes* 31/3 (1994): 13–25.

Temple, Mary Kay. "Beowulf 1258–66: Grendel's Lady Mother." *English Language Notes* 23/3 (1986): 10–15.

Tervahauta, Ulla, Ivan Miroshnikov, Outi Lehtipuu, and Ismo Dunderberg, Eds. *Women and Knowledge in Early Christianity.* Brill, 2017.

Trilling, Renée Rebecca. "Beyond Abjection: The Problem with Grendel's Mother Again." *Parergon* 24/1 (2007): 1–20.

Tuana, Nancy. *The Less Noble Sex: Scientific, Religious and Philosophical Conceptions of Women's Nature*. Indiana University Press, 1993.

Van De Walle, Etienne and Elisha Renne, Eds. *Regulating Menstruation: Beliefs, Practices, Interpretations*. University of Chicago Press, 2001.

4   Revenants

Revenants are the walking dead, people who bodily return from the grave to haunt and harass the living. These reanimated corpses are sometimes called ghosts in modern translations of medieval sources, which can be confusing for modern readers as we commonly think of ghosts as disembodied apparitions. While revenants and ghosts both haunt the living, revenants are distinctly corporeal, and their physicality sets them apart from modern ghosts. Revenants also resemble both modern zombies and vampires in some respects, but, again, there are important differences between these medieval monsters and their modern cousins. Medieval revenants are the products of historical periods and cultures very different from our own, and we need to approach them on their own terms rather than examining them for traces of our favorite modern monsters.

This chapter covers two sets of revenant stories originating from northern Europe in the High Middle Ages: one set comes to us from twelfth-century England and the other from thirteenth-century Iceland. The first cluster of revenant stories was produced by a handful of clerical authors working in twelfth-century England: Geoffrey of Burton, the abbot of Burton Abbey in Staffordshire (we lack firm dates for Geoffrey, but he became abbot of Burton in 1114 and composed his *Life of Saint Modwenna* between 1118 and 1150); William of Malmesbury (c. 1095–1143), a Benedictine monk at Malmesbury Abbey in Wiltshire; William of Newburgh (1136–1198), an Augustinian canon at Newburgh Priory in Yorkshire; and Walter Map (c. 1130–1210), a royal clerk who held prebends at Lincoln, London, Hereford, and Oxford.

The earliest of these works is likely Geoffrey of Burton's *Life of Saint Modwenna*, which contains a marvelous and detailed story about two peasants who fled lands belonging to the monastery of Burton to live under the jurisdiction of a neighboring count, Roger the Poitevin. After causing an armed conflict between the abbot of Burton and Count Roger, the runaway peasants were struck dead as they were sitting down to eat one day and were buried the next day in the village of Stapenhill, where they had lived before fleeing from the abbot's jurisdiction. On the day of their burial, they were seen carrying their coffins in the neighboring town of Drakelow, which belonged to Count Roger. The reanimated corpses of the two peasants spent the next several nights disturbing the villagers of Drakelow

DOI: 10.4324/9780429243004-5

by walking around; shape-shifting into dogs, bears, and other animals; hanging on to the walls of their houses; and shouting at them to get going. After these disturbances had gone on for some time, a disease spread through Drakelow that sickened the villagers and killed all but three of them.

These dramatic events caused Count Roger to repent of the evils he had inflicted on the monastery of Burton. He begged the pardon of the abbot, the monks, and their patron, the holy virgin Modwenna, and even paid them double restitution for the damage he had inflicted on the monastery's property, but this did not stop the nightly wanderings of the two dead peasants. The dead men continued to terrorize the village of Drakelow until the local bishop granted permission for their corpses to be exhumed. When the corpses were dug up, the villagers found that the linen cloths covering their faces were covered in blood. They decapitated the corpses, put their heads between their legs, removed their hearts, and reburied them. They then burned their hearts and saw an evil spirit shaped like a crow fly out of the flames. This finally put an end to the revenants' nocturnal antics, as well as the disease that had devastated Drakelow. The villagers who had been languishing with this mysterious illness recovered, and they picked up their families and possessions and moved to the village of Gresley, leaving Drakelow completely deserted.

Geoffrey of Burton presents his revenant tale both as a property dispute and as an example of the vengeance meted out by Saint Modwenna. The peasants who become revenants are monastic resources, and their attempt to leave Stapenhill for Count Roger's village of Drakelow threatens to deprive the monastery and the saint of an important source of labor and revenue. When the runaway peasants lodge false charges against the abbot of Burton in front of Count Roger, the count sends armed troops against the monks and seizes some of their crops, then destroys the crops in the abbey's fields near Blackpool. When the runaway peasants die, they are returned to their home village of Stapenhill for burial, but they return as revenants to terrorize Count Roger's village of Drakelow, and the disease they spread kills only the count's peasants. At the end of the tale, Geoffrey makes it clear that the remaining villagers abandoned Drakelow out of fear at the vengeance that God had worked through Saint Modwenna. The tale thus demonstrates Modwenna's sanctity and power and serves as a warning to anyone else thinking of depriving the saint and the monks of their property.

Although Geoffrey is primarily interested in conveying Saint Modwenna's power, he also provides us with some exceptional details about revenants. The corpses of the two runaway peasants are not only reanimated, they can also shape-shift, and we learn that their post-mortem wandering was the result of an evil spirit lodged in their hearts that was finally released through burning. Sinfulness is often what causes the dead to return as revenants in the English accounts, and we are given several indications that the two peasants committed grievous sins by leaving the monastic village of Stapenhill and rousing Count Roger's anger against the abbot of Burton. Their actions caused the theft and destruction of the abbey's crops and the armed conflict between the abbot and the count. Once they were struck dead for their sins, they not only terrorized the villagers of Drakelow, they also spread a disease that killed most of them. They were only stopped when their bodies were exhumed and decapitated, their severed heads were placed between their legs in a ritual humiliation, and their hearts were burned.

William of Malmesbury provides far less detailed accounts of revenants, but he mentions them in his *Gesta regum Anglorum* (Deeds of the Kings of the English) and records a ghostly haunting in his *Gesta pontificum Anglorum* (Deeds of the English Bishops), both of which were composed around 1125. The *Gesta regum Anglorum* contains an account of King Alfred's ghost returning to his body at night to corporeally haunt the canons of Winchester Cathedral until his son had his remains reinterred at the newly completed Hyde Abbey, which Alfred had established. Two features stand out in William's account. This first is the fact that he links Alfred's return as a revenant to tensions between the monks of Hyde Abbey and the canons of Winchester Cathedral and implies that Alfred's post-mortem activity was due to his having been laid to rest in the cathedral rather than in the abbey since his haunting stopped once his body was relocated. The other remarkable feature is that William calls the canons of Winchester deluded for claiming that Alfred's body wandered around the cathedral. He characterizes the whole story as nonsense and compares it to other beliefs maintained by the credulous English, particularly the belief that the corpses of criminals can be possessed and reanimated by demons. William seems to blame Alfred both for spending so much money on the construction of the abbey and for placing it so close to the cathedral that it generated trouble between the monks and canons. He then appears to dismiss the story altogether.

William of Malmesbury mentions another variety of ghostly activity in the slightly later *Gesta Pontificum Anglorum*. He recounts a story about Abbot Brihtwald of Malmesbury in which he recalls that Brihtwald impoverished the abbey by alienating some of its estates and blames him for a lack of foresight. He also notes that Brihtwald was prone to doing evil and died in the middle of a drinking bout. After the abbot was buried, the church watchmen thought they saw shadowy shapes until Brihtwald's body was dug up and buried in a marsh far away from the monastery. However, even this did not completely stop Brihtwald's post-mortem activity as his body seems to have regularly produced an exceptionally noxious stench that afflicted the surrounding countryside. While William expresses skepticism about the supernatural activity here by saying that the watchmen thought they saw something, this time he does not dismiss it out of hand.

Whether William of Malmesbury believed spectral activity was possible but drew the line at the idea of corpses returning bodily, or believed that neither of these was possible, we may never know. Still, he took the trouble to record these stories, both which contain details that conform to the general sketch of revenant beliefs found in Geoffrey of Burton. For example, William portrays both Alfred and Brihtwald as blameworthy. William mocks Alfred for his lavish spending on Hyde Abbey and blames him for placing it so close to the cathedral that it caused tensions between the monks and canons. He portrays Abbot Brihtwald as more clearly sinful for alienating the abbey's property, being prone to evil, and dying during a drunken bender. Although William discounts the veracity of these stories, he also tells us quite a bit about contemporary revenant beliefs. He tells us, for instance, that both the canons of Winchester Cathedral and the watchmen of Malmesbury Abbey thought that they were experiencing hauntings, that the English people generally believed that people who were criminals, and thus sinful, were susceptible to demonic possession after they died, and that relocating the body of the deceased was one means of dealing with such activity – although it was not always entirely successful, as the example of Brihtwald demonstrates.

We can see similar features in a group of revenant stories that William of Newburgh included in his *Historia rerum Anglicarum* (History of English Affairs) in the second half of the twelfth century. William records a total of four tales about the walking dead. The first is a story about a man from Buckinghamshire who returned after death to annoy his wife, family, and neighbors, first at night and then during the day. Although the local people were terrorized, no one was actually hurt by the revenant, and he was finally put to rest after the community sought the assistance of the Church. The bishop of Lincoln wrote a letter of absolution and had the man's tomb opened and the letter placed on his breast. Once the tomb was closed back up, the man's wandering ceased. Notably, during the bishop of Lincoln's investigation into the possibility of revenant activity, his companions tell him that such things often happen in England and that popular wisdom holds that the only way to restore tranquility is to dig up the man's corpse and burn it.

William next tells a story about very sinful and wealthy man from Berwick who returned from the tomb to terrorize his neighbors each night accompanied by a pack of barking dogs. William states twice that people believed this particular corpse was reanimated by Satan and that they feared being physically harmed by the revenant or afflicted by disease if it was not stopped. In this case, the townspeople did not seek the assistance of the Church. Instead, they chose ten men to dig up the corpse, dismember it, and burn it to ashes (the solution that the bishop of Lincoln rejected in the previous story). Once this was done, the revenant activity stopped, but a disease still arose that killed a great number of the people of Berwick.

William then interrupts his revenant stories briefly to inject some skepticism by reflecting on the fact that these tales would be completely unbelievable if there were not so much evidence of them happening in his own day and so many reliable witnesses testifying to their veracity. Interestingly, he says that he cannot find evidence of such things in the works of ancient authors, implying that this revenant activity is new. He then moves on to narrate the tale of the "Hundeprest," a sinful priest who was known for his love of hunting and who returned as a revenant after death. After an unsuccessful attempt to haunt the monastery of Melrose where he was buried, the priest resorted to terrorizing a noble lady he had served as chaplain. When the lady revealed this to one of the friars of Melrose, he assembled three companions and waited in the cemetery for the revenant to make his appearance. Sometime after midnight, three of the men left to warm themselves at a nearby house, leaving the friar on his own. As soon as the other men had left, William says that the devil roused up his chosen vessel (the Hundeprest) and charged at the friar, who struck him with an axe. Wounded, the monster fled back to his tomb. Meanwhile, the friar's three companions returned, and they dug up the corpse, carried it outside the walls of the monastery, burned it to ash, and scattered the ash to the winds.

William's final revenant tale is the story of another sinner, this time a jealous husband from Anantis. This man was renowned for his evil propensities in life and died after falling from the rafter in his bedroom during an attempt to catch his wife with her lover. The whole episode is reminiscent of the fabliaux as the jealous husband deceives his wife by telling her that he is going on a trip then hides himself on the beam in their bedroom. When he witnesses his wife having sex with her lover, he falls out of the rafters in a jealous rage. The lover escapes in the confusion, and when the jealous husband threatens to punish his wife, she tells him that he is talking nonsense because he is unwell. Things take a more serious turn shortly afterward when the husband refuses the advice of a priest to make confession and receive the Eucharist and then dies. William specifically notes that the man received a Christian burial, although he was unworthy of it, and that this did not benefit him much as Satan still caused him to return from the grave accompanied by a pack of barking dogs. He terrorized the town, causing everyone to stay indoors after dusk, and spread a pestilence that killed many of the residents and caused others to flee. William's informant on this occasion, the priest whose salutary advice was ignored by the jealous husband, tried to console the remaining people as best he could. However, some of the townspeople decided to take matters into their own hands. They dug up the corpse, dragged it outside the village, tore out its heart saying the body would not burn if the heart was not removed, and burned the body to ashes. This stopped the jealous husband's wandering, as well as the pestilence that afflicted the town.

William of Newburgh's revenants are all portrayed as sinners who return to annoy and terrify the living. He clearly links the deceased person's sinfulness with the level of damage and disease their reanimated corpse inflicts, and the most sinful corpses are portrayed as demonically possessed and accompanied by barking dogs. The means by which the revenant is stopped varies according to the degree of sinfulness as well. The revenant from Buckinghamshire causes no damage or disease, is not thought to be demonically possessed or accompanied by dogs, and is put to rest by the bishop of Lincoln's written absolution. Likewise, the Hundeprest tries to harm the monks of Melrose but fails due to their holiness and only succeeds in terrorizing his former employer. However, he is still thought to be animated by Satan and has to be dispatched by burning. The two most notable sinners, the wealthy man from Berwick and the jealous husband from Anantis, are both thought to be demonically possessed, both are accompanied by packs of barking dogs, both kill people by spreading disease, and both are stopped by dismemberment and burning.

Finally, Walter Map recounts three revenant stories in his *De nugis curialium* (Courtier's Trifles) from the late twelfth century. In the first story, an English soldier named William Laudun seeks Bishop Gilbert Foliot's advice about a Welsh malefactor and unbeliever who died in his house and has returned to haunt it for four consecutive nights. Each night, the revenant returns and summons another person staying at William's house, causing them to become ill and die. Bishop Foliot responds that God must have given the devil the power to reanimate the

Welshman's corpse and advises William to exhume the body, sprinkle it with holy water, and rebury it. William does this, but the blessing fails and the Welsh revenant continues to return and summon the house's inhabitants, including William himself. Desperate to stop the revenant, William rushes after it, pursues it to the grave, and decapitates it with his sword. The decapitation works, and the revenant activity ceases.

Map's second story concerns another unbeliever who was seen wandering about day and night for over a month after his death. In this case, Bishop Roger of Worcester advised that a cross be raised over the corpse's grave to stop it. Like Bishop Foliot's advice in the preceding story, this solution fails, at least initially. When the revenant returns to his grave, he jumps back at the sight of the cross and flees. The townspeople have to remove the cross, allow the revenant to return to his grave, and then raise the cross back over it in order to put him to rest. In this case, the power of the cross is sufficient both to frighten the revenant and to keep it in the tomb.

Map's final story is about a solider from Northumbria whose father returns as a revenant, reassures him that he will not harm him, and begs him to send for a priest. When the priest arrives, the revenant reveals that he was excommunicated along with a group of others for having withheld tithes and has returned to seek absolution. The priest grants him absolution, and the revenant peacefully returns to his grave accompanied by a huge procession of people.

There are some fascinating details in Map's revenant tales. His first two stories concern unbelievers who are thought to be demonically possessed. In the first story, Bishop Foliot's advice to bless the corpse fails to stop it, and, in the second, Bishop Roger's advice to erect a cross over the man's grave initially fails as it prevents the corpse from returning to the grave. The sprinkling of the corpse with holy water in the first story may be a blessing or an attempt to exorcise the demon from the man's corpse. In either case, it does not work, and William of Laudun has to decapitate the revenant. The erection of a cross over the grave in the second story proves to be more effective, but even this has to be timed correctly in order to work. In the third story, we see a sentient revenant asking his son to call for a priest, then confessing and seeking absolution. In this case, the man is a Christian who appears truly penitent and is following the prescribed process for putting his soul to rest; the result is that the solution works without issue, and the implication, as we saw in William of Newburgh's story of the Berwick revenant, is that absolution is both necessary and available post-mortem.

The English revenants share a common feature: they are invariably men whose sinfulness predisposed them to returning from the dead to haunt the living. For twelfth-century English clerical writers, revenants were either men who had been particularly sinful in life or who had rejected Christianity altogether. Once dead, they were unable to rest and returned corporeally, almost always at night, to haunt their families, friends, and neighbors. Often the revenants merely terrified people, but, in some cases, the revenants killed people by attacking them or spreading disease. One thing that the English sources all agree on is that the customary way to stop a revenant is to destroy the body, either by burning or decapitation, but we also see some interesting experiments taking place. In one of William of Newburgh's stories, he tells us that the bishop of Lincoln rejected advice to burn the body of a revenant and instead provided a written absolution to place on its breast. To everyone's joy and amazement, the bishop's novel solution worked, and the corpse stopped its nightly wandering. In a similar story recorded by Walter Map, however, we see quite the opposite happening. When the body of a revenant is dug up and sprinkled with holy water in an attempt to stop it, the ritual completely fails, and the revenant has to be dispatched by means of decapitation. Interestingly, Map contrasts the failure of this blessing with the successful use of the power of the cross to stop a revenant in his next tale.

In some of these stories, we also see evidence that revenants were sometimes believed to feed on blood, although whether that blood was thought to be human or animal is unclear. While none of the sources specifically state that the revenants consume blood, Geoffrey of Burton, William of Newburgh, and Walter Map all note that some of these revenants are discovered to have mouths that are covered in blood, linen clothes over their faces that are covered in blood, or that the corpse itself is engorged with blood. Several scholars have argued that these revenants are early antecedents of modern vampires, and while we certainly see some elements of the vampire myth in these accounts, these revenants do not fit neatly into the modern category of the vampire. Viewing them solely as precursors to modern vampires minimizes their importance as unique cultural creations that are worthy of study in their own right and glosses over the fact that their historical context, attributes, and cultural functions are all very different from modern vampires. These are not the sexy undead creatures of nineteenth-century novels or modern movies; the cultural work that they do and the anxieties they embody are those of their own time and place.

In these twelfth-century English accounts, we have clerical writers recounting stories of sinners and criminals whose evil deeds or lack of Christian belief caused them to return from the grave to terrify or harm those around them. These clerical authors are also particularly interested in determining how these dead men were reanimated. They report that most of the returning corpses were possessed by demons and that these revenants caused death and disease and required decapitation and/or burning. However, not all revenants were thought to be demonically possessed. Some of them caused no harm and merely required priestly intervention to stop their nocturnal wandering, indicating that they had been less sinful in life than other revenants. These revenants and their defining features are the products of the authors' clerical culture and reflect contemporary concerns about morality. The stories function on one level as morality tales that offer a warning to the living about the wages of sin and the importance of faith, penance, and absolution. Not only does the unrepentant sinner risk returning as a revenant, his sinfulness may also result in post-mortem demonic possession and manifest itself as a deadly contagion that kills his family, friends, and neighbors.

If we compare these twelfth-century English revenant accounts with their closest analogs from the thirteenth-century Icelandic sagas, we can see some similarities and some important cultural differences. Included in this chapter are the story of Glam from *Grettir's Saga* and the stories of Thorolf and Thorgunna from *Eyrbyggja Saga*. These family sagas were produced in the thirteenth century and describe events in Iceland that occurred between the nineth and twelfth centuries. Although we do not know the identity of the author of either work, they are clearly Christian authors recounting a pagan past and the period of conversion to Christianity in Iceland. In the Icelandic sagas, the revenant or *draugr* (often misleadingly translated as ghost) displays even more destructive behavior than those in the English sources, and those who become *draugar* are either people who were difficult in life, foreigners who had recently moved to Iceland, or people who retained their pagan beliefs even as most Icelanders converted to Christianity. Finally, the Icelandic *draugr* tends to spread illness that not only kills its victims, but causes them to return as *draugar* as well, a feature we do not see in the English sources.

One example of an Icelandic revenant who displays these features is Glam from *Grettir's Saga*. Glam was a recent immigrant to Iceland who was known for his massive frame and abrasive character. He takes a job as a shepherd on a notoriously haunted farm where most of the other people dislike him because of his surliness, but he proves to be a good worker and he looks after the sheep for several months without incident. On a Christmas morning, however, Glam goes into the kitchen and demands his breakfast from his employer's wife who tells him that whole household is fasting until after mass. Glam mocks her Christian beliefs, demands his breakfast again, eats, and goes out to work. When he does not return that evening, everyone fears that the *draugr* that haunts the farm has attacked him. When they finally find Glam, he is dead, apparently killed in a violent struggle with the *draugr*.

In spite of several attempts to carry him to the church for burial, Glam's body resists being moved or even blessed by a priest. In the end, the people decide to bury Glam where he is and erect a pile of stones, or cairn, over the body. Glam then returns as a *draugr* himself, haunting the farm where he had previously worked. Glam returns bigger, stronger, and meaner than he had been in life. He attacks and kills his employer's livestock, rides the roof of the farmhouse so that its walls shake, terrifies the farm's inhabitants, and kills the farmer's daughter. Glam is finally stopped by the hero Grettir, who arrives at the farm looking for an adventure. After a violent struggle in which Glam curses Grettir with bad luck and a fear of the dark, Grettir decapitates Glam, and he and the farmer burn Glam's corpse. This puts an end to Glam's haunting, but Grettir had the misfortune to look into Glam's eyes during their fight and so suffers a form of bewitchment that manifests itself as a fear of the dark. Glam's curse hangs over Grettir until his own death.

A similar story occurs in *Eyrbyggja Saga*, where the ill-tempered Thorolf returns as a *draugr* to haunt his former farm and the surrounding countryside. Thorolf dies suddenly, consumed with rage, after fighting with his son Arnkel. Due to the circumstances of Thorolf's death and his notoriously bad temper, Arnkel immediately takes precautions to prevent anyone in the household from becoming bewitched by having them avoid walking in front of the corpse until after its eyes had been closed. He also attempts to prevent his father from returning to the house as a *draugr* by cutting a hole in the wall through which to remove the corpse. It was believed that the dead could only re-enter a house the way they had left it, and these "corpse-doors" were commonly cut into walls to remove a body and then sealed up to prevent their return. Arnkel also makes sure to build a solid cairn, or stone mound, over his father's grave in the hope of keeping him in the ground.

Despite Arnkel's precautions, Thorolf predictably returns from the dead. Like Glam, Thorolf's *draugr* rides the roof of the house, kills livestock, and terrorizes the local people. Thorolf even drives his own widow to an early grave. With Thorolf killing any animal that came near his grave and amassing a company of people he had killed to join him in his haunting, he made the entire valley uninhabitable and drove off the living. Remarkably, Thorolf and his band of revenants caused no harm when Arnkel was around. The local people finally charge Arnkel with moving his father's body to put an end to the haunting. When Arnkel exhumes his father's body, he is surprised to see the corpse uncorrupted (*draugar* were typically described as having a grotesque blackish or bluish appearance, like Glam). Arnkel and his men are able to move Thorolf's body, but only with great difficulty as the corpse becomes heavier and heavier as they move away from the farm. Finally, they can move the body no further. Arnkel buries his father on a hillside sufficiently far from human settlement and builds a wall around the site to prevent Thorolf from leaving. Unlike Glam, Thorolf was not a foreigner, but he was a quarrelsome person in life, and this quality, along with the circumstances of his death, predisposed him to return as a revenant. Thorolf, who was also decidedly greedy in life, refuses to vacate his farm after his death and ensures that no one else can enjoy it.

This end to Thorolf's haunting turns out to be temporary. Once Arnkel dies, Thorolf resumes his attacks, clearing out the living from whole swaths of land and moving on to other farms. Eventually, Thorolf begins haunting land belonging to Thorodd Thorbrandsson and becomes his problem. Thorodd and his servants exhume Thorolf's body, which is still uncorrupted but now described as black as death (much like Glam's). They burn the body with difficulty, and the wind scatters much of Thorolf's ashes around before the men can carefully dispose of them in the sea. This leads to Thorolf shape-shifting. He reappears as a ghostly dapple-grey bull roaming the shore where Thorolf was cremated and mates with a cow who has licked Thorolf's malignant ashes off the stones near the shore. The cow eventually gives birth to a cursed bull, Glaesir, who becomes the vehicle through which Thorolf continues his violence. Although Thorodd is warned multiple times by his foster-mother that Glaesir is a monster and should be destroyed, he refuses to kill the calf and is finally killed by it. As for Glaesir and the last vestiges of Thorolf, they vanish when the bull runs into a quagmire, sinks down, and disappears.

Eyrbyggja Saga also contains a story about a rare female revenant, Thorgunna. Like Glam, Thorgunna is a recent arrival to Iceland who has trouble fitting in. When Thorgunna arrives from the Hebrides with her foreign finery, she arouses the envy of Thurid, a local woman, who offers to purchase some of her things and is particularly interested in her fine English bedding. Thorgunna refuses to sell any of her belongings and on her deathbed orders that all her bedding must be destroyed, warning that she does not want to be responsible for what may happen to anyone who keeps it. Thurid, however, talks her husband, Thorodd, into disregarding Thorgunna's wishes and allowing her to keep the dead woman's bedding. Thurid and Thorodd then prepare Thorgunna's corpse for burial and begin the journey to her final resting place. When Thorgunna's funeral cortege is refused hospitality by a farmer along the way, a naked Thorgunna rises from her coffin to prepare a meal and shame the farmer into more neighborly behavior. This is the last we see of Thorgunna's corpse. Once Thorgunna is buried at the church in Skalholt, she does not reappear, but there are still serious consequences for those who ignored her last wishes.

When the funeral party returns to Thorodd's farm, they are accompanied by bad omens, and members of the household soon begin to die. First, a shepherd who appears to have been bewitched dies and begins to haunt the farm, then Thorir Wood-Leg dies and joins him as a *draugr*. Before long, six people have died and are all haunting the farm, along with a seal that rises up from the floor of the farm-house (*draugar* were believed to be able to shape-shift and sometimes appeared in the form of seals). Thorodd himself eventually drowns at sea, along with his fishing party, and they all begin to haunt the farmhouse as well. This company of revenants make themselves at home by the fire each evening throughout the Christmas season, driving the living out of the room, while a mysterious creature makes noises in the store-room. After a final round of deaths caused by the haunting, a total of eighteen members of the household have died and are returning each night to haunt the farm.

The haunting at Thorodd's farm is finally ended by Kjartan with the help of his uncle, Snorri, who advises that Thorgunna's bedding must be burnt, then the revenants must be summoned to a door-court and tried by the living for trespassing, and finally a priest must sprinkle holy water around the farmhouse and say mass. This tripartite ritual to end the haunting confirms that Thorgunna's bedding and the injury done to the dead woman by ignoring her final wishes were believed to be the original cause of the trouble, but just destroying the bedding was insufficient to end the haunting. The dead must be tried for trespassing according to regular judicial procedure and sentenced before they will leave. It is this act of legal eviction, which is unique among revenant tales, that banishes the dead from the spaces inhabited by the living. Finally, the Christian rituals undertaken by the priest are supplementary to eliminating the original cause of the haunting by burning Thorgunna's bedding and evicting the dead through legal means, but they appear to provide some measure of protection against future revenant activity.

The story of Thorgunna is unusual in several ways. Revenants are rarely women, Thorgunna does not personally return to haunt Thorodd's farm, and the legal eviction of the dead for trespassing is unique. However, there are many elements that do appear in other Icelandic revenant stories. Thorgunna is a foreigner who was difficult in life, and whose final wishes were not respected. These qualities predispose her to return as a revenant. Additionally, the features of the haunting are familiar. First, a shepherd is bewitched, dies, and returns as a *draugr*, then illness and death spread throughout the household with the newly deceased also returning as spooks.

As in the other Icelandic tales, Thorgunna's story demonstrates that *draugar* were believed to cause bewitchment and that those who died during the haunting were likely to return as *draugar* themselves.

The Icelandic revenant stories were formed in a different cultural matrix than the twelfth-century English stories reviewed earlier. Although these stories were written in the thirteenth century by Christian authors, they record events that occurred two to three centuries earlier, when Iceland was newly settled and still in the process of conversion. As a result, they reflect the Christian attitudes of their authors, as well as a concern with newly arrived foreigners and an emphasis on the necessity of neighborly cooperation in an inhospitable environment. In Glam, we see a recent pagan arrival to Iceland who mocks the Christianity of his employer's wife and refuses to get along with his fellows. Similarly, Thorgunna is a new arrival to Iceland who, although a Christian herself, does not get on well with most of the members of her new community. As for Thorolf, he may be a native Icelander, but he is known for his bad temper and terrible interpersonal relationships. In the Icelandic sources, the difficult, the irascible, the greedy, the wronged, the pagan, and the foreigner are all prime candidates for returning from the dead. While these qualities differ somewhat from the sinfulness that was believed to predispose people to returning from the dead in the English sources, the Icelandic sources also emphasize the fact that the personal qualities of the recently deceased determine who will return as a revenant and who will rest quietly in their grave.

As we saw in the twelfth-century English sources, Icelandic revenants were also believed to be a source of contagion. In the English sources, the disease spread by the revenant kills his friends, neighbors, and family, but in the Icelandic sources, the contagion not only kills other members of the community, but it also causes them to become revenants as well and join in the haunting. The activities that the English and Icelandic revenant engage in are also similar. The English revenants return to harass their communities, and occasionally the local animals, as do the Icelandic *draugar*. In fact, the primary distinction between the hauntings is that the English revenants tend to cause fewer deaths and less destruction, while the Icelandic revenants tend to kill larger numbers of animals and people and are more likely to drive the living out of larger regions.

Icelandic and English culture had a great deal in common in the twelfth and thirteenth centuries, so it is not surprising to find similar revenants in both cultures. About a third of England had been settled by Scandinavians in the ninth and tenth centuries, precisely the same period that Scandinavians were settling in Iceland, so some of beliefs about revenants may have made their way into England from Scandinavia at this time. However, there were some important differences between the two cultures. England's inhabitants were distinctly diverse and included large Celtic, Anglo-Saxon, and Norman populations, as well as Scandinavians, while Iceland was settled almost entirely by Norwegians. Moreover, the English had been converted to Christianity in the seventh century, while Iceland did not begin the process of conversion until the end of the tenth century. These differences help to account for the differences in the revenants that each culture produced. The English authors are not concerned with foreigners at all, they are primarily interested in sin and morality. The Icelandic preoccupation with foreigners derives from the fact that Iceland had a small, homogenous population, and the hostile conditions on the island meant that survival required a high degree of community cooperation. Icelandic revenants therefore tended to be difficult, greedy, or foreign people, who did not get along well with others. While the Icelandic revenants were sometimes pagans who rejected Christianity entirely, they are not cast specifically as sinners as they are in the English sources. These features reflect both the specific conditions of the Icelandic settlement and the island's more recent conversion to Christianity.

Revenants in both cultures are destructive, but none of the Icelandic *draugar* are thought to be demonically possessed. In fact, demons are only mentioned in passing in *Eyrbyggja Saga* when the author comments that the oxen used to haul Thorolf's corpse were ridden to death by demons. Since the English sources link demonic possession (as well as disease) specifically to the degree of sinfulness exhibited by the people who become revenants, it makes sense that the demonic element is largely missing from the Icelandic accounts where sin is not a primary concern.

Finally, both cultures had similar approaches to dispatching revenants. In the English sources, the most sinful revenants have to be destroyed by decapitation and/or burning, and in many of the Icelandic sources, including *Grettir's Saga*, *draugar* are dispatched by decapitating and burning the corpse. Grettir takes the additional step of placing Glam's decapitated head between the dead man's own thighs in a ritual act of humiliation intended to ensure that Glam is too ashamed to return before burning Glam's body. At first, Arnkel simply relocates Thorolf's body far from the habitations of the living to stop his destruction, but, after Arnkel dies, Thorolf returns and his body is finally burned. However, even burning fails to put an end to Thorolf's haunting as the wind blows his ashes around the field, and these ashes are consumed by a cow who gives birth to the possessed bull, Glaesir. It is only when Glaesir sinks into a quagmire and disappears that Thorolf's haunting truly ceases. None of the Icelandic accounts mention attempts to stop a *draugr* by absolving the corpse. This appears to be a uniquely English approach rooted in the fact that the monastic English authors explicitly connected revenants with sinfulness, while the Icelandic authors did not. English revenant stories functioned as Christian morality tales warning people about the wages of sin and encouraging them to lead more moral lives, whereas Icelandic revenant stories functioned as warnings about uncooperative, selfish, and often foreign people who endangered the already precarious lives of Icelanders.

PRIMARY SOURCES

Geoffrey of Burton: Life and Miracles of St Modwenna, trans. Robert Bartlett (Clarendon Press, 2002), ch. 47, pp. 191–9.

47. The Evildoer Who Put Out his Own Eye and the Runaways Who Suffered a Wonderful Example of Vengeance Which Befell Them On Their Own Account

There was a royal official, an enemy of the church, called Ælfwine of Hopwas, who had often done much harm to the monastery of Burton and continually threatened and plotted worse things. He had no reverence for the virgin, wished to injure her monks as much as he could, and took a foolish delight in his wicked acts. One day, when he had returned from the courts where he had ordered judgement to be given against the saint's men, he was sitting in his house and, resting his chin on his hand, boasted in front of his wife and family about his wicked deeds. He was gleefully threatening to do even worse things to the monks in contempt of the virgin whose bones they watched over, when he suddenly put out his own eye with a thrust of his thumb. Thus he demonstrated before everyone that divine judgement had been visited upon him for his sin. He spent the rest of his life with one eye and was thereafter a milder man, learning from such a punishment, even though late, that it is not good to do evil to the monastery of the servants of God.

Again, an injury was committed against the church which the Lord, on account of the virgin's merits, avenged in a terrifying way. There were two villagers living in Stapenhill under the jurisdiction of the abbot of Burton who ran away to the neighboring village called Drakelow, wrongfully leaving their lords, the monks, and wishing to live under the authority of count Roger the Poitevin. The father of the monastery ordered that their crops, which had not yet been taken out of the barns, should be seized and taken to his own barns, hoping in this way to induce them to return to their own dwellings. But these men went off to count Roger and brought a false charge before him, stirring him up and speaking wickedly. The count's anger was aroused against the abbot, so much that he threatened to kill him wherever he might find him. Violently angry, he gathered a great troop of knights and peasants with weapons and carts and sent them in a great company to the monks' barns at Stapenhill and had them seize by force all the crops stored there, those belonging to the abbey which should supply the monks' food as well as those of the wicked fugitives. Not content with this, count Roger sent many men and knights to the abbey's fields near Blackpool, commanding them to lay waste the church's crops with all their might and encouraging them to especially lure into battle the ten knights of the abbot's own family whom he had in his company. The abbot heard about this and forbade his knights from going out. He and his monks entered into the church barefoot and groaning and, in tears, set on the ground the shrine of the blessed virgin containing her most holy bones. In unison they addressed a desperate appeal to the Lord, beseeching His boundless power with all their hearts that He should deign to help His servants in His goodness, if that were His will, and that He should make known with manifest miracle His aid to those who were struggling in such difficulty.

Meanwhile, as those inside were praying with one voice, the ten knights decided to ignore the prohibition and, arming themselves with one accord, without the knowledge of the abbot or the monks, mounted their horses boldly and set out to do battle in the field, few against many. One of the abbot's knights immediately spurred his horse into a gallop, struck the count's steward and hurled him to the ground so forcefully that the power of the blow broke his leg. Now another of the abbot's knights likewise spurred his horse to a gallop and struck a knight who was a relative of the count, knocking him into a nearby stream, hurling him with tremendous force into the mud far from his horse. The rest of the monks' knights each acted so bravely in this fight that ten men put more than sixty to flight and a few drove very many from the field, to their great shame, through the merit of the virgin and the power of God.

The very next day, at the third hour, the two runaway peasants who were the cause of this evil were sitting down to eat, when they were both suddenly struck down dead. Next morning they were placed in wooden coffins and buried in the churchyard at Stapenhill, the village from whence they had fled. What followed was amazing and truly remarkable. That very same day on which they were interred they appeared at evening, while the sun was still up, at Drakelow, carrying on their shoulders the wooden coffins in which they had been buried. The whole following night they walked through the paths and fields of the village, now in the shape of men carrying wooden coffins on their shoulders, now in the likeness of bears or dogs or other animals. They spoke to the other peasants, hanging on the walls of their houses and shouting, 'Move, quickly, move! Get going! Come!' When these astonishing events had taken place every evening and every night for some time, such a disease afflicted the village that all the peasants fell into desperate straits and within a few days all except three (whom we shall discuss later) perished by sudden death in a remarkable way.

The count, seeing these remarkable occurrences, was stunned and terrified. He repented and came with his knights to the monastery, where he begged humble pardon, made a firm concord with the abbot and monks, and entreated them with prayers that they should placate God and the virgin whom he had offended. Before them all, with faithful devotion, he gave command to Drogo the reeve of the village that there should be double restitution for all the damages he had inflicted, and so, in peace of mind, he left the monastery and hastened without delay to his other lands. Drogo then quickly returned and restored double to the abbey as he had been ordered and, after seeking pardon yet again, left for other parts with all haste, desiring to escape that lethal scourge. The two peasants who still remained in the village (Drogo was the third) fell sick and languished for a long time. Men were living in terror of the phantom dead men who carried their wooden coffins on their shoulders every evening and night, as has been described, and they received permission from the bishop to go to their graves and dig them up. They found them intact, but the linen cloths over their faces were stained with blood. They cut off the men's heads and placed them in the graves between their legs, tore out the hearts from their corpses, and covered the bodies with earth again. They brought the hearts to the place called *Dodecrossefora/Dodefreseford* and there burned them from morning until evening. When they had at last been burned up, they cracked with a great sound and everyone saw an evil spirit in the form of a crow fly from the flames. Soon after this was done both the disease and the phantoms ceased. The two peasants sick in their beds recovered their health as soon as they saw the smoke rising from the fire where the hearts were burned. They got up, gathered together their sons and wives and all their possessions, and, giving thanks to God and to the holy virgin that they had escaped, they departed to the next village, which was called Gresley, and settled there. Drakelow was thus abandoned and for long thereafter no one dared to live there, fearing the vengeance of the Lord that had struck there and wondering at the prodigies that God omnipotent had worked through the holy virgin.

We have talked of these acts of vengeance after dealing with benefits, now, after dealing with vengeance, we shall speak again of benefits.

William of Malmesbury: Gesta Regum Anglorum (Deeds of the Kings of the English), ed. and trans. R.A.B. Mynors, R.M. Thomson, and M. Winterbottom (Oxford University Press, 1998), vol. I, ii. 124, pp. 195–7.

124. Alfred, having paid the debt of nature, was buried at Winchester in his own monastery. To construct its buildings, he purchased a sufficient space of ground from the bishop and canons of the day, paying for every foot a mancus of gold by the public weight. The king's self-denial was really extraordinary – to be willing to be milked of so much money! No doubt he meant not to offer God a sacrifice derived from the robbery of the poor. And the two churches were so close, the walls actually touching, that the voices of those chanting in either interfered with the other. For this and many other reasons bad feeling unfortunately arose, and many pretexts were brought to the surface which could be developed into serious trouble. This monastery has therefore been moved lately to a site outside the city, and has become a more healthy, as well as a more conspicuous, residence. They say that Alfred was buried first in the cathedral, because his own monastery was still unfinished; but that not long after, the deluded canons maintained that the king's ghost returned to his dead body and wandered at night through their lodgings, and so his son and successor took up his father's remains and laid them in peace in the new monastery. This nonsense and the like (it is believed, for example, that the corpse of a criminal after death is possessed by a demon, and walks) wins credit among the English from a sort of inborn credulity; they borrow it, no doubt, from the pagans, as in Virgil's line: 'Such shapes are said to wander after death.'

William of Malmesbury: Gesta Pontificum Anglorum (Deeds of the English Bishops), ed. and trans. M. Winterbottom and R.M. Thomson (Oxford University Press, 2007), vol. I, ch. 258, p. 615.

Chapter 258 Cyneweard to Brihtwald II (980–1067)

Aethelred died after ruling for thirty-seven years, and was followed by Cnut for twenty years, by Harold, Cnut's son, for four years, by Harthacnut for one year and by Edward for twenty-four years. In these eighty-six years the abbots of Malmesbury after Aethelweard were Cyneweard, Brihthelm, Beihtwald, Ederic, and Wulsine. We know from English documents that Brihtwald did many things that were disadvantageous to the monastery, completely alienating some of its estates, and making inroads on others for a small price. But we should not blame him for he could find no other remedy for his troubles when under the burden of providing those big sums of gold which were then given to the Danes. He did not see that his lack of thought for the future could bring trouble to those coming after him.

Wulsine restored to its former healthy state the religious life of the monks, which had been much weakened by the advent of the Danes. There were still monks alive in our own day who saw Wulsine in the flesh, and who found it sweet to go through their memories of the man and to pass them on to others. Relying on the tales told me by these monks, I have stored away in my mind many marvelous doings of Wulsine, but I hesitate to relate them, as they do not fit in with the scheme of my work. Wulsine was followed by Aethelweard, who was abbot for ten years. Later Aelfwine was abbot for a year and a half, then Brihtwald for seven years. Ancient tradition has it that Brihtwald, being slow to do good but quick to do evil, came to a pitiful end, dying in the town surrounded by the materials for a drinking bout, and was buried among his predecessors in the church of St Andrew, which is right next to the big church. It is generally believed that the watchmen at the church were disturbed by dreamlike shadowy shapes, until they dug up Brihtwald's body and sunk it in a deep marsh far away from the monastery. At intervals a noxious smell rose up from the marsh and it spread its noisome stench over the surrounding countryside. But I will leave these unpleasant matters and roll up my sleeves to write of the miracles which during these years were revealed by the Godhead at the tomb of the blessed confessor.

William of Newburgh, "Historia Rerum Anglicarum," in *The Church Historians of England*, trans. Joseph Stevenson (Seeley's, 1861), vol. IV, part II, Bk. V, ch. 22–4, pp. 656–61.

Chapter 22: Of the Prodigy of the Dead Man, Who Wandered About after Burial

In these days a wonderful event befell in the county of Buckingham, which I, in the first instance, partially heard from certain friends, and was afterwards more fully informed of by Stephen, the venerable archdeacon of that province. A certain man died, and, according to custom, by the honorable exertion of his wife arid kindred, was laid in the tomb on the eve of the Lord's Ascension. On the following night, however, having entered the bed where his wife was reposing, he not only terrified her on awaking, but nearly crushed her by the insupportable weight of his body. The next night, also, he afflicted the astonished woman in the same manner, who, frightened at the danger, as the struggle of the third night drew near, took care to remain awake herself, and surround herself with watchful companions. Still he came; but being repulsed by the shouts of the watchers, and seeing that he was prevented from doing mischief, he departed. Thus driven off from his wife, he harassed in a similar manner his own brothers, who were dwelling in the same street; but they, following the cautious example of the woman, passed the nights in wakefulness with their companions, ready to meet and repel the expected danger. He appeared, notwithstanding, as if with the hope of surprising them should they be overcome with drowsiness; but being repelled by the carefulness and valor of the watchers, he rioted among the animals, both indoors and outdoors, as their wildness and unwonted movements testified.

Having thus become a like serious nuisance to his friends and neighbors, he imposed upon all the same necessity for nocturnal watchfulness; and in that very street a general watch was kept in every house, each being fearful of his approach unawares. After having for some time rioted in this manner during the night-time alone, he began to wander abroad in daylight, formidable indeed to all, but visible only to a few; for oftentimes, on his encountering a number of persons, he would appear to one or two only though at the same time his presence was not concealed from the rest. At length the inhabitants, alarmed beyond measure, thought it advisable to seek counsel of the church; and they detailed the whole affair, with tearful lamentation, to the above-mentioned archdeacon, at a meeting of the clergy over which he was solemnly presiding. Whereupon he immediately intimated in writing the whole circumstances of the case to the venerable bishop of Lincoln, who was then resident in London, whose opinion and judgment on so unwonted a matter he was very properly of opinion should be waited for: but the bishop, being amazed at his account, held a searching investigation with his companions; and there were some who said that such things had often befallen in England, and cited frequent examples to show that tranquility could not be restored to the people until the body of this most wretched man were dug up and burnt. This proceeding, however, appeared indecent and improper in the last degree to the reverend bishop, who shortly after addressed a letter of absolution, written with his own hand, to the archdeacon, in order that it might be demonstrated by inspection in what state the body of that man really was; and he commanded his tomb to be opened, and the letter having been laid upon his breast, to be again closed: so the sepulcher having been opened, the corpse was found as it had been placed there, and the charter of absolution having been deposited upon its breast, and the tomb once more closed, he was thenceforth never more seen to wander, nor permitted to inflict annoyance or terror upon any one.

Chapter 23: Of a Similar Occurrence at Berwick

In the northern parts of England, also, we know that another event, not unlike this and equally wonderful, happened about the same time. At the mouth of the river Tweed, and in the jurisdiction of the king of Scotland, there stands a noble city which is called Berwick. In this town a certain man, very wealthy, but as it afterwards appeared a great rogue, having been buried, after his death sallied forth (by the contrivance, as it is believed, of Satan) out of his grave by night, and was borne hither and thither, pursued by a pack of dogs with loud barkings; thus striking great terror into the neighbors, and returning to his tomb before daylight. After this had continued for several days, and no one dared to be found out of doors after dusk – for each dreaded an encounter with this deadly monster – the higher and middle classes of the people held a necessary investigation into what was requisite to be done; the more simple among them fearing, in the event of negligence, to be soundly beaten by this prodigy of the grave; but the wiser shrewdly concluding that were a remedy further delayed, the atmosphere, infected and corrupted by the constant whirlings through it of the pestiferous corpse, would engender disease and death to a great extent; the necessity of providing against which was shown by frequent examples in similar cases. They, therefore, procured ten young men renowned for boldness, who were to dig up the horrible carcass, and, having cut it limb from limb, reduce it into food and fuel for the flames. When this was done, the commotion ceased. Moreover, it is stated that the monster, while it was being borne about (as it is said) by Satan, had told certain persons whom it had by chance encountered, that as long as it remained unburned the people should have no peace. Being burnt, tranquility appeared to be restored to them; but a pestilence, which arose in consequence, carried off the greater portion of them: for never did it so furiously rage elsewhere, though it was at that time general throughout all the borders of England, as shall be more fully explained in its proper place.

Chapter 24: Of Certain Prodigies

It would not be easy to believe that the corpses of the dead should sally (I know not by what agency) from their graves, and should wander about to the terror or destruction of the living, and again return to the tomb, which of its own accord spontaneously opened to receive them, did not frequent examples, occurring in our own times, suffice to establish this fact, to the truth of which there is abundant testimony. It would be strange if such things should have happened formerly, since we can find no evidence of them in the works of ancient authors, whose vast labor it was to commit to writing every occurrence worthy of memory; for if they never neglected to register even events of moderate interest, how could they have suppressed a fact at once so amazing and horrible, supposing it to have happened in their day? Moreover, were I to write down all the instances of this kind which I have ascertained to have befallen in our times, the undertaking would be beyond measure laborious and troublesome; so I will fain add two more only (and these of recent occurrence) to those I have already narrated, and insert them in our history, as occasion offers, as a warning to posterity.

A few years ago the chaplain of a certain illustrious lady, casting off mortality, was consigned to the tomb in that noble monastery which is called Melrose. This man, having little respect for the sacred order to which he belonged, was excessively secular in his pursuits, and – what especially blackens his reputation as a minister of the holy sacrament – so addicted to the vanity of the chase as to be designated by many by the infamous title of "Hundeprest," or the dog-priest; and this occupation, during his lifetime, was either laughed at by men, or considered in a worldly view; but after his death – as the event showed – the guiltiness of it was brought to light: for, issuing from the grave at night-time, he was prevented by the meritorious resistance of its holy inmates from injuring or terrifying any one with in the monastery itself; whereupon he wandered beyond the walls, and hovered chiefly, with loud groans and horrible murmurs, round the bedchamber of his former mistress. She, after this had frequently occurred, becoming exceedingly terrified, revealed her fears or danger to one of the friars who visited her about the business of the monastery; demanding with tears that prayers more earnest than usual should be poured out to the Lord in her behalf as for one in agony. With whose anxiety the friar – for she appeared deserving of the best endeavors, on the part of the holy convent of that place, by her frequent donations to it – piously and justly sympathized, and promised a speedy remedy through the mercy of the Most High Provider for all.

Thereupon, returning to the monastery, he obtained the companionship of another friar, of equally determined spirit, and two powerful young men, with whom he intended with constant vigilance to keep guard over the cemetery where that miserable priest lay buried. These four, therefore, furnished with arms and animated with courage, passed the night in that place, safe in the assistance which each afforded to the other. Midnight had now passed by, and no monster appeared; upon which it came to pass that three of the party, leaving him only who had sought their company on the spot, departed into the nearest house, for the purpose, as they averred, of warming themselves, for the night was cold. As soon as this man was left alone in this place, the devil, imagining that he had found the right moment for breaking his courage, incontinently roused up his own chosen vessel, who appeared to have reposed longer than usual. Having beheld this from afar, he grew stiff with terror by reason of his being alone; but soon recovering his courage, and no place of refuge being at hand, he valiantly withstood the onset of the fiend, who came rushing upon him with a terrible noise, and he struck the axe which he wielded in his hand deep into his body. On receiving this wound, the monster groaned aloud, and turning his back, fled with a rapidity not at all inferior to that with which he had advanced, while the admirable man urged his flying foe from behind, and compelled him to seek his own tomb again; which opening of its own accord, and receiving its guest from the advance of the pursuer, immediately appeared to close again with the same facility. In the meantime, they who, impatient of the coldness of the night, had retreated to the fire ran up, though somewhat too late, and, having heard what had happened, rendered needful assistance in digging up and removing from the midst of the tomb the accursed corpse at the earliest dawn. When they had divested it of the clay cast forth with it, they found the huge wound it had received, and a great quantity of gore which had flowed from it in the sepulchre; and so having carried it away beyond the walls of the monastery and burnt it, they scattered the ashes to the winds. These things I have explained in a simple narration, as I myself heard them recounted by religious men.

Another event, also, not unlike this, but more pernicious in its effects, happened at the castle which is called Anantis, as I have heard from an aged monk who lived in honor and authority in those parts, and who related this event as having occurred in his own presence. A certain man of evil conduct flying, through fear of his enemies or the law, out of the province of York, to the lord of the before-named castle, took up his abode there, and having cast upon a service befitting his humor, labored hard to increase rather than correct his own evil propensities. He married a wife, to his own ruin indeed, as it afterwards appeared; for, hearing certain rumors respecting her, he was vexed with the spirit of jealousy. Anxious to ascertain the truth of these reports, he pretended to be going on a journey from which he would not return for some days; but coming back in the evening, he was privily introduced into his bedroom by a maid-servant, who was in the secret, and lay hidden on a beam overhanging, his wife's chamber, that he might prove with his own eyes if anything were done to the dishonor of his marriage-bed. Thereupon beholding his wife in the act of fornication with a young man of the neighborhood, and in his indignation forgetful of his purpose, he fell, and was dashed heavily to the ground, near where they were lying.

The adulterer himself leaped up and escaped; but the wife, cunningly dissembling the fact, busied herself in gently raising her fallen husband from the earth. As soon as he had partially recovered, he upbraided her with her adultery, and threatened punishment; but she answered, "Explain yourself, my lord," said she; "you are speaking unbecomingly which must be imputed not to you, but to the sickness with which you are troubled." Being much shaken by the fall, and his whole body stupefied, he was attacked with a disease, insomuch that the man whom I have mentioned as having related these facts to me visiting him in the pious discharge of his duties, admonished him to make confession of his sins, and receive the Christian Eucharist in proper form: but as he was occupied in thinking about what had happened to him, and what his wife had said, put off the wholesome advice until the morrow – that morrow which in this world he was fated never to behold! – for the next night, destitute of Christian grace, and a prey to his well-earned misfortunes, he shared the deep slumber of death. A Christian burial, indeed, he received, though unworthy of it; but it did not much benefit him: for issuing, by the handiwork of Satan, from his grave at night-time, and pursued by a pack of dogs with horrible barkings, he wandered through the courts and around the houses while all men made fast their doors, and did not dare to go abroad on any errand whatever from the beginning of the night until the sunrise, for fear of meeting and being beaten black and blue by this vagrant monster. But those precautions were of no avail; for the atmosphere, poisoned by the vagaries of this foul carcass, filled every house with disease and death by its pestiferous breath.

Already did the town, which but a short time ago was populous, appear almost deserted; while those of its inhabitants who had escaped destruction migrated to other parts of the country, lest they too should die. The man from whose mouth I heard these things, sorrowing over this desolation of his parish, applied himself to summon a meeting of wise and religious men on that sacred day which is called Palm Sunday, in order that they might impart healthful counsel in so great a dilemma, and refresh the spirits of the miserable remnant of the people with consolation, however imperfect. Having delivered a discourse to the inhabitants, after the solemn ceremonies of the holy day had been properly performed, he invited his clerical guests, together with the other persons of honor who were present, to his table. While they were thus banqueting, two young men (brothers), who had lost their father by this plague, mutually encouraging one another, said, "This monster has already destroyed our father, and will speedily destroy us also, unless we take steps to prevent it. Let us, therefore, do some bold action which will at once ensure our own safety and revenge our father's death. There is no one to hinder us; for in the priest's house a feast is in progress, and the whole town is as silent as if deserted. Let us dig up this baneful pest, and burn it with fire."

Thereupon snatching up a spade of but indifferent sharpness of edge, and hastening to the cemetery, they began to dig; and whilst they were thinking that they would have to dig to a greater depth, they suddenly, before much of the earth had been removed, laid bare the corpse, swollen to an enormous corpulence, with its countenance beyond measure turgid and suffused with blood; while the napkin in which it had been wrapped appeared nearly torn to pieces. The young men, however, spurred on by wrath, feared not, and inflicted a wound upon the senseless carcass, out of which incontinently flowed such a stream of blood, that it might have been taken for a leech filled with the blood of many persons. Then, dragging it beyond the village, they speedily constructed a funeral pile; and upon one of them saying that the pestilential body would not burn unless its heart were torn out, the other laid open its side by repeated blows of the blunted spade, and, thrusting in his hand, dragged out the accursed heart. This being torn piecemeal, and the body now consigned to the flames, it was announced to the guests what was going on, who, running thither, enabled themselves to testify henceforth to the circumstances. When that infernal hell-hound had thus been destroyed, the pestilence which was rife among the people ceased, as if the air, which had been corrupted by the contagious motions of the dreadful corpse, were already purified by the fire which had consumed it. These facts having been thus expounded, let us return to the regular thread of history.

Walter Map, *Master Walter Map's Book, De Nugis Curialium (Courtier's Trifles),* trans. Frederick Tupper and Marbury Ogle (Chatto & Windus, 1924), ch. 27, 28, and 30, pp. 125–8.

Concerning A Certain Marvel. XXVII

The greatest marvel that I know happened in Wales. William Laudun, an English soldier, sturdy in his strength and of established courage, went to Gilbert Foliot, at that time Bishop of Hereford, but now of London, and said to him, 'Master, I fly to thee for advice; a certain Welsh malefactor died in my house not long ago, a non-believer; [20] after an interval of four nights he hath never failed to return each night, and hath not ceased summoning forth, one by one and by name, all his fellow-lodgers. As soon as they are summoned, they grow ill and die within three days, so that now only a few survive.' The bishop on his wonderment replied, 'Power, perchance, was given by God to the evil angel of that wretch to render him restless in his dead body. However, dig up the corpse, cut the neck, and besprinkle the body and the grave [30] with holy water, and then rebury it.' Although this was done, none the less were the survivors assailed by the restless spirit. On a certain night, therefore, William himself, since now but a few were left, was summoned thrice, and he, bold and active as he was, knowing full well what he summons signified, drew his sword and rushed out. As the demon fled he pursued it to the very grave, and as it lay therein, he clave its head to the neck. From that hour ceased the persecution from this ghostly wanderer, nor henceforth did William or any other suffer harm therefrom. The manner of this thing we know, of its cause we are ignorant.

Another Marvel. XXVIII

We also know that, in the time of Bishop Roger of Worcester, a certain man who, it was said, died in unbelief, for a month or even longer, both day and night, wandered about, seen of all, in his hair-shirt, until he was surrounded in an orchard by all the people of the neighborhood. He was seen there, it is said, for three days. We know, moreover, that this same Bishop Roger bade a cross be raised over the grave of this wretch and his spirit to be laid. When the demon had come to the grave, followed by a crowd of people, he leaped back, seemingly at the sight of the cross, and fled elsewhere. Then the people, acting upon wise advice, removed the cross, and the demon fell into the grave, covered himself with earth, and, after the cross was raised again, lay in peace.

Another Marvel. XXX

A soldier from Northumbria was seated alone in his house one day in summer after his lunch about the tenth hour (or three o'clock) when, lo, there appeared, clad in a cheap and ragged cloak, his father who had died some time before. The solider, thinking him a demon, drove him from the door. Then to him said his father: 'Dearest son, have no fear, for I am thy father, and bring thee no harm; but summon a priest that thou mayest learn the reason for my coming.' A priest was [30] thereupon called and came with a great crowd, and the man, falling down at the priest's feet, cried out, 'I am that unhappy wretch on whom thou long since didst lay a curse because I wrongfully held back my tithes, and whom thou, without calling me by name, didst excommunicate along with a crowd of others; but of such avail to me have, by God's grace, been the general prayers of the Church and the alms of the faithful that I may now seek absolution.' He was thereupon absolved, and, attended by a great procession, he came to the grave into which he fell and of its own accord closed over him. This strange hap introduced a new discussion of Holy Writ.

The Saga of Grettir the Strong, trans. G.A. Hight (J.M. Dent & Sons Ltd, 1929), ch. 32–5.

Chapter 32 – Spook at Thorhallsstad. Glam the Shepherd Killed by a Fiend. His Ghost Walks

There was a man named Thorhall living in Thorhallsstad in Forsaeludal, up from Vatnsdal. He was the son of Grim, the son of Thorhall, the son of Fridmund, who was the first settler in Forsaeludal. Thorhall's wife was named Gudrun; they had a son named Grim and a daughter named Thurid who were just grown up. Thorhall was fairly wealthy, especially in live-stock. His property in cattle exceeded that of any other man. He was not a chief, but an honest bondi nevertheless. He had great difficulty in getting a shepherd to suit him because the place was haunted. He consulted many men of experience as to what he should do, but nobody gave him any advice which was of any use. Thorhall had good horses, and went every summer to the Thing. On one occasion at the All-Thing he went to the booth of the

Lawman Skapti the son of Thorodd, who was a man of great knowledge and gave good counsel to those who consulted him. There was a great difference between Thorodd the father and Skapti the son in one respect. Thorodd possessed second sight, but was thought by some not to be straight, whereas Skapti gave to every man the advice which he thought would avail him, if he followed it exactly, and so earned the name of Father-betterer.

So Thorhall went to Skapti's booth, where Skapti, knowing that he was a man of wealth, received him graciously, and asked what the news was.

"I want some good counsel from you," said Thorhall.

"I am little fit to give you counsel," he replied; "but what is it that you need?"

"It is this: I have great difficulty in keeping my shepherds. Some get injured and others cannot finish their work. No one will come to me if he knows what he has to expect."

Skapti answered: "There must be some evil spirit abroad if men are less willing to tend your flocks than those of other men. Now since you have come to me for counsel, I will get you a shepherd. His name is Glam, and he came from Sylgsdale in Sweden last summer. He is a big strong man, but not to everybody's mind."

Thorhall said that did not matter so long as he looked after the sheep properly. Skapti said there was not much chance of getting another if this man with all his strength and boldness should fail. Then Thorhall departed. This happened towards the end of the Thing.

Two of Thorhall's horses were missing, and he went himself to look for them, which made people think he was not much of a man. He went up under Sledaass and south along the hill called Armannsfell. Then he saw a man coming down from Godaskog bringing some brushwood with a horse. They met and Thorhall asked him his name. He said it was Glam. He was a big man with an extraordinary expression of countenance, large grey eyes and wolfgrey hair. Thorhall was a little startled when he saw him, but soon found out that this was the man who had been sent to him.

"What work can you do best?" he asked.

Glam said it would suit him very well to mind sheep in the winter.

"Will you mind my sheep?" Thorhall asked. "Skapti has given you over to me."

"My service will only be of use to you if I am free to do as I please," he said. "I am rather crossgrained when I am not well pleased."

"That will not hurt me," said Thorhall. "I shall be glad if you will come to me."

"I can do so," he said. "Are there any special difficulties?"

"The place seems to be haunted."

"I am not afraid of ghosts. It will be the less dull."

"You will have to risk it," said Thorhall. "It will be best to meet it with a bold face."

Terms were arranged and Glam was to come in the autumn. Then they parted. Thorhall found his horses in the very place where he had just been looking for them. He rode home and thanked Skapti for his service.

The summer passed. Thorhall heard nothing of his shepherd and no one knew anything about him, but at the appointed time he appeared at Thorhallsstad. Thorhall treated him kindly, but all the rest of the household disliked him, especially the mistress. He commenced his work as shepherd, which gave him little trouble.

He had a loud hoarse voice. The beasts all flocked together whenever he shouted at them. There was a church in the place, but Glam never went to it. He abstained from mass, had no religion, and was stubborn and surly. Everyone hated him.

So the time passed till the eve of Yule-tide. Glam rose early and called for his meal. The mistress said: "It is not proper for Christian men to eat on this day, because to-morrow is the first day of Yule and it is our duty to fast to-day."

"You have many superstitions," he said; "but I do not see that much comes of them. I do not know that men are any better off than when there was nothing of that kind. The ways of men seemed to me better when they were called heathen. I want my food and no foolery."

"I am certain," she said, "that it will fare ill with you to-day if you commit this sin."

Glam told her that she should bring his food, or that it would be the worse for her. She did not dare to do otherwise than as he bade her. When he had eaten he went out, his breath smelling abominably. It was very dark; there was driving snow, the wind was howling and it became worse as the day advanced. The shepherd's voice was heard in the early part of the day, but less later on. Blizzards set in and a terrific storm in the evening. People went to mass and so the time passed. In the evening Glam did not return. They talked about going out to look for him, but the storm was so violent and the night so dark that no one went. The night passed and still he had not returned; they waited till the time for mass came. When it was full day some of the men set forth to search. They found the animals scattered everywhere in the snow and injured by the weather; some had strayed into the mountains. Then they came upon some well-marked tracks up above in the valley. The stones and earth were torn up all about as if there had been a violent tussle. On searching further they came upon Glam lying on the ground a short distance off. He was dead; his body was as black as Hel and swollen to the size of an ox. They were overcome with horror and their hearts shuddered within them. Nevertheless they tried to carry him to the church, but could not get him any further than the edge of a gully a short way off. So they left him there and went home to report to the bondi what had happened. He asked what could have caused Glam's death. They said they had tracked him to a big place like a hole made by the bottom of a cask thrown down and dragged along up below the mountains which were at the top of the valley, and all along the track were great drops of blood. They concluded that the evil spirit which had been about before must have killed Glam, but that he had inflicted wounds upon it which were enough, for that spook was never heard of again. On the second day of the festival they went out again to bring in Glam's body to the church. They yoked oxen to him, but directly the downward incline ceased and they came to level ground, they could not move him; so they went home again and left him. On the third day they took a priest with them, but after searching the whole day they failed to find him. The priest refused to go again, and when he was not with them they found Glam. So they gave up the attempt to bring him to the church and buried him where he was under a cairn of stones.

It was not long before men became aware that Glam was not easy in his grave. Many men suffered severe injuries; some who saw him were struck senseless and some lost their wits. Soon after the festival was over, men began to think they saw him about their houses. The panic was great and many left the neighbourhood. Next he began to ride on the house-tops by night, and nearly broke them to pieces. Almost night and day he walked, and people would scarcely venture up the valley, however pressing their business. The district was in a grievous condition.

Chapter 33 – *Doings of Glam's Ghost. Awful Condition of Vatnsdale*

In the spring Thorhall procured servants and built a house on his lands. As the days lengthened out the apparitions became less, until at midsummer a ship sailed up the Hunavatn in which was a man named Thorgaut. He was a foreigner, very tall and powerful; he had the strength of two men. He was travelling on his own account, unattached, and being without money was looking out for employment. Thorhall rode to the ship, saw him and asked if he would take service with him. Thorgaut said he would indeed, and that there would be no difficulties.

"You must be prepared," said Thorhall, "for work which would not be fitting for a weak-minded person, because of the apparitions which have been there lately. I will not deceive you about it."

"I shall not give myself up as lost for the ghostlings," he said.

"Before I am scared some others will not be easy. I shall not change my quarters on that account."

The terms were easily arranged and Thorgaut was engaged for the sheep during the winter. When the summer had passed away he took over charge of them, and was on good terms with everybody. Glam continued his rides on the roofs. Thorgaut thought it very amusing and said the thrall must come nearer if he wished to frighten him. Thorhall advised him not to say too much, and said it would be better if they did not come into conflict.

Thorgaut said: "Surely all the spirit has gone out of you. I shall not fall dead in the twilight for stories of that sort."

Yule was approaching. On the eve the shepherd went out with his sheep. The mistress said: "Now I hope that our former experiences will not be repeated."

"Have no fear for that, mistress," he said. "There will be something worth telling of if I come not back."

Then he went out to his sheep. The weather was rather cold and there was a heavy snowstorm. Thorgaut usually returned when it was getting dark, but this time he did not come. The people went to church as usual, but they thought matters looked very much as they did on the last occasion. The bondi wanted them to go out and search for the shepherd, but the churchgoers cried off, and said they were not going to trust themselves into the power of trolls in the night; the bondi would not venture out and there was no search. On Yule day after their meal they went out to look for the shepherd, and first went to Glam's cairn, feeling sure that the shepherd's disappearance must be due to him. On approaching the cairn they saw an awful sight; there was the shepherd, his neck broken, and every bone in his body torn from its place. They carried him to the church and no one was molested by Thorgaut.

Glam became more rampageous than ever. He was so riotous that at last everybody fled from Thorhallsstad, excepting the bondi and his wife.

Thorhall's cowherd had been a long time in his service and he had become attached to him; for this reason and because he was a careful herdsman he did not want to part with him. The man was very old and thought it would be very troublesome to have to leave; he saw, too, that everything the bondi possessed would be ruined if he did not stay to look after them. One morning after midwinter the mistress went to the cow-house to milk the cows as usual. It was then full day, for no one would venture out of doors till then, except the cowherd, who went directly it was light. She heard a great crash in the cow-house and tremendous bellowing. She rushed in, shouting that something awful, she knew not what, was going on in the cow-house. The bondi went out and found the cattle all goring each other. It seemed not canny there, so he went into the shed and there saw the cowherd lying on his back with his head in one stall and his feet in the other.

He went up and felt him, but saw at once that he was dead with his back broken. It had been broken over the flat stone which separated the two stalls. Evidently it was not safe to remain any longer on his estate, so he fled with everything that he could carry away. All the live-stock which he left behind was killed by Glam. After that Glam went right up the valley and raided every farm as far as Tunga, while Thorhall stayed with his friends during the rest of the winter. No one could venture up the valley with a horse or a dog, for it was killed at once. As the spring went on and the sun rose higher in the sky the spook diminished somewhat, and Thorhall wanted to return to his land, but found it not easy to get servants. Nevertheless, he went and took up his abode at Thorhallsstad. Directly the autumn set in, everything began again, and the disturbances increased. The person most attacked was the bondi's daughter, who at last died of it. Many things were tried but without success. It seemed likely that the whole of Vatnsdal would be devastated unless help could be found.

Chapter 34 – Grettir Visits his Uncle Jokull

We have now to return to Grettir, who was at home in Bjarg during the autumn which followed his meeting with Warrior-Bardi at Thoreyjargnup. When the winter was approaching, he rode North across the neck to Vididal and stayed at Audunarstad. He and Audun made friends again; Grettir gave him a valuable battle-axe and they agreed to hold together in friendship. Audun had long lived there, and had many connections. He had a son named Egill, who married Ulfheid the daughter of Eyjolf, the son of Gudmund; their son Eyjolf, who was killed at the All-Thing, was the father of Orin the chaplain of Bishop Thorlak.

Grettir rode to the North to Vatnsdal and went on a visit to Tunga, where dwelt his mother's brother, Jokull the son of Bard, a big strong man and exceedingly haughty. He was a mariner, very cantankerous, but a person of much consideration. He welcomed Grettir, who stayed three nights with him. Nothing was talked about but Glam's walking, and Grettir inquired minutely about all the particulars. Jokull told him that no more was said than had really happened.

"Why, do you want to go there?" he asked.

Grettir said that it was so. Jokull told him not to do it.

"It would be a most hazardous undertaking," he said. "Your kinsmen incur a great risk with you as you are. There does not seem to be one of the younger men who is your equal. It is ill dealing with such a one as Glam. Much better fight with human men than with goblins of that sort."

Grettir said he had a mind to go to Thorhallsstad and see how things were. Jokull said: "I see there is no use in dissuading you. The saying is true that Luck is one thing, brave deeds another."

"Woe stands before the door of one but enters that of another," answered Grettir. "I am thinking how it may fare with you yourself before all is done."

"It may be," said Jokull, "that we both see what is before us, and yet we may not alter it."

Then they parted, neither of them well pleased with the other's prophetic saying.

Chapter 35 – *Fight with Glam's Ghost*

Grettir rode to Thorhallsstad where he was welcomed by the bondi.

He asked Grettir whither he was bound, and Grettir said he wished to spend the night there if the bondi permitted. Thorhall said he would indeed be thankful to him for staying there.

"Few," he said, "think it a gain to stay here for any time. You must have heard tell of the trouble that is here, and I do not want you to be inconvenienced on my account. Even if you escape unhurt yourself, I know for certain that you will lose your horse, for no one can keep his beast in safety who comes here."

Grettir said there were plenty more horses to be had if anything happened to this one.

Thorhall was delighted at Grettir's wishing to remain, and received him with both hands. Grettir's horse was placed securely under lock and key and they both went to bed. The night passed without Glam showing himself.

"Your being here has already done some good," said Thorhall. "Glam has always been in the habit of riding on the roof or breaking open the doors every night, as you can see from the marks."

"Then," Grettir said, "either he will not keep quiet much longer, or he will remain so more than one night. I will stay another night and see what happens."

Then they went to Grettir's horse and found it had not been touched. The bondi thought that all pointed to the same thing. Grettir stayed a second night and again the thrall did not appear. The bondi became hopeful and went to see the horse. There he found the stable broken open, the horse dragged outside and every bone in his body broken. Thorhall told Grettir what had occurred and advised him to look to himself, for he was a dead man if he waited for Glam.

Grettir answered: "I must not have less for my horse than a sight of the thrall."

The bondi said there was no pleasure to be had from seeing him: "He is not like any man. I count every hour a gain that you are here."

The day passed, and when the hour came for going to bed Grettir said he would not take off his clothes, and lay down on a seat opposite to Thorkell's sleeping apartment. He had a shaggy cloak covering him with one end of it fastened under his feet and the other drawn over his head so that he could see through the neck-hole. He set his feet against a strong bench which was in front of him. The frame-work of the outer door had been all broken away and some bits of wood had been rigged up roughly in its place. The partition which had once divided the hall from the entrance passage was all broken, both above the cross-beam and below, and all the bedding had been upset. The place looked rather desolate. There was a light burning in the hall by night.

When about a third part of the night had passed Grettir heard a loud noise. Something was going up on to the building, riding above the hall and kicking with its heels until the timbers cracked again. This went on for some time, and then it came down towards the door. The door opened and Grettir saw the thrall stretch-ing in an enormously big and ugly head. Glam moved slowly in, and on passing the door stood upright, reaching to the roof. He turned to the hall, resting his arms on the cross-beam and peering along the hall. The bondi uttered no sound, having heard quite enough of what had gone on outside. Grettir lay quite still and did not move. Glam saw a heap of something in the seat, came farther into the hall and seized the cloak tightly with his hand. Grettir pressed his foot against the plank and the cloak held firm. Glam tugged at it again still more violently, but it did not give way. A third time be pulled, this time with both hands and with such force that he pulled Grettir up out of the seat, and between them the cloak was torn in two. Glam looked at the bit which he held in his hand and wondered much who could pull like that against him. Suddenly Grettir sprang under his arms, seized him round the waist and squeezed his back with all his might, intending in that way to bring him down, but the thrall wrenched his arms till he staggered from the violence. Then Grettir fell back to another bench. The benches flew about and everything was shattered around them. Glam wanted to get out, but Grettir tried to prevent him by stemming his foot against anything he could find. Nevertheless Glam succeeded in getting him outside the hall. Then a terrific struggle began, the thrall trying to drag him out of the house, and Grettir saw that however hard he was to deal with in the house, he would be worse outside, so he strove with all his might to keep him from getting out. Then Glam made a desperate effort and gripped Grettir tightly towards him, forcing him to the porch. Grettir saw that he could not put up any resistance, and with a sudden movement he dashed into the thrall's arms and set both his feet against a stone which was fastened in the ground at the door. For that Glam was not prepared, since he had been tugging to drag Grettir towards him; he reeled backwards and tumbled hind-foremost out of the door, tearing away the lintel with his shoulder and shattering the roof, the rafters and the frozen thatch. Head over heels he fell out of the house and Grettir fell on top of him. The moon was shining very brightly outside, with light clouds passing over it and hiding it now and again.

At the moment when Glam fell the moon shone forth, and Glam turned his eyes up towards it. Grettir himself has related that that sight was the only one which ever made him tremble. What with fatigue and all else that he had endured, when he saw the horrible rolling of Glam's eyes his heart sank so utterly that he had not strength to draw his sword, but lay there well-nigh betwixt life and death. Glam possessed more malignant power than most fiends, for he now spoke in this wise:

"You have expended much energy, Grettir, in your search for me. Nor is that to be wondered at, if you should have little joy thereof. And now I tell you that you shall possess only half the strength and firmness of heart that were decreed to you if you had not striven with me. The might which was yours till now I am not able to take away, but it is in my power to ordain that never shall you grow stronger than you are now. Nevertheless your might is sufficient, as many shall find to their cost. Hitherto you have earned fame through your deeds, but henceforward there shall fall upon you exile and battle; your deeds shall turn to evil and your guardian-spirit shall forsake you. You will be outlawed and your lot shall be to dwell ever alone. And this I lay upon you, that these eyes of mine shall be ever before your vision. You will find it hard to live alone, and at last it shall drag you to death."

When the thrall had spoken the faintness which had come over Grettir left him. He drew his short sword, cut off Glam's head and laid it between his thighs. Then the bondi came out, having put on his clothes while Glam was speaking, but he did not venture to come near until he was dead. Thorhall praised God and thanked Grettir warmly for having laid this unclean spirit. Then they set to work and burned Glam to cold cinders, bound the ashes in a skin and buried them in a place far away from the haunts of man or beast. Then they went home, the day having nearly broken.

Grettir was very stiff and lay down to rest. Thorhall sent for some men from the next farms and let them know how things had fared. They all realised the importance of Grettir's deed when they heard of it; all agreed that in the whole country side for strength and courage and enterprise there was not the equal of Grettir the son of Asmund.

Thorhall bade a kindly farewell to Grettir and dismissed him with a present of a fine horse and proper clothes, for all that he had been wearing were torn to pieces. They parted in friendship. Grettir rode to Ass in Vatnsdal and was welcomed by Thorvald, who asked him all about his encounter with Glam. Grettir told him everything and said that never had his strength been put to trial as it had been in their long struggle. Thorvald told him to conduct himself discreetly; if he did so he might prosper, but otherwise he would surely come to disaster. Grettir said that his temper had not improved, that he had even less discretion than before, and was more impatient of being crossed. In one thing a great change had come over him; he had become so frightened of the dark that he dared not go anywhere alone at night. Apparitions of every kind came before him. It has since passed into an expression, and men speak of "Glam's eyes" or "Glam visions" when things appear otherwise than as they are.

Having accomplished his undertaking Grettir rode back to Bjarg and spent the winter at home.

Eyrbyggja Saga, trans. Paul Schach and Lee M. Hollander
(University of Nebraska Press, 1959), ch. 33–4, and 50–5,
pp. 67–71 and 105–17.

Chapter 33 – Thorolf's Death and Burial

Snorri Godi now had Krakuness Forest worked and had much wood cut. It seemed to Thorolf Lamefoot that the forest was being ruined, so he rode to Helgafell and asked Snorri to return the forest to him. He said he had merely lent but had not given it to him. Snorri said this matter would be cleared up when the witnesses to the transaction testified. He said he would not give up the forest unless they testified against him. Thorolf left in a very ugly mood. He rode to Bolstead to see Arnkel. Arnkel received his father cordially and asked what his errand was.

Thorolf answered, "This is my reason for coming here: I see that things are not as they should be, what with this hostility between us. I wish now that we put an end to it and live on good terms as kinsmen should, for it is unseemly that we should be at odds. It seems to me that we could become powerful here in the district with your hardihood and my planning."

"I would like nothing better," said Arnkel, "than that our relations should improve."

"What I want," said Thorolf, "is that we begin our agreement and friendship by taking back Krakuness Forest from Snorri godi, for what irks me most is that he should withhold our property from us. But now he will not release the forest to me and insists that I gave it to him, but that is a lie."

Arnkel replied, "It was not out of friendship for me that you handed the forest over to Snorri, and I am not going to fight with him about the forest just on account of your malice. I know well enough that he is not legally entitled to the forest, but I don't care to reward you for your malice by the spectacle of Snorri and me litigating about it."

"I am thinking," said Thorolf, "that cowardice is the reason for your refusal rather than your not wanting me to enjoy the fight between you two."

"Have it your own way," said Arnkel, "but I am not going to begin litigation with Snorri about the forest as things stand."

With that father and son parted. Thorolf Lamefoot went home and felt exceedingly dejected about the turn matters had taken and about being thwarted in everything. He arrived home in the evening and spoke with no one. He sat down in the high seat and did not eat anything all evening. He remained sitting there after all the others had gone to bed. And in the morning when they got up, Thorolf was still sitting there and was dead. Then the mistress of the house sent a man to Arnkel to inform him of the passing of Thorolf. Arnkel rode up to Hvamm with several of his men servants. And when they came there, Arnkel learned for certain that his father was dead, sitting in the seat of honor; but all the people in the house were terrified because they all thought there was something uncanny about his death.

Arnkel now went into the kitchen and from there along the dais behind Thorolf. He warned all not to approach him from the front until the last service to the dead had been performed. Arnkel took Thorolf by the shoulders, and he had to exert all his strength to get him down from the high seat. Then he wrapped a cloth around Thorolf's head and prepared the body according to the custom of that time. After that he had the wall broken through behind him and had him pulled out through this opening. Then oxen were harnessed to a sled, Thorolf was laid in it, and they brought him up into Thorsardale. And it was not without a struggle before they reached the place where he was to be buried. They buried Thorolf securely and heaped stones over him. After that Arnkel rode home to Hvamm and took possession of all the property there which his father had owned. Arnkel stayed there for three days, and nothing of particular moment happened during this time. Then he went home.

Chapter 34 – Thorolf Haunts the Neighborhood. His Ghost is Laid by Arnkel

After the death of Thorolf Lamefoot, it seemed to many that there was something uncanny out of doors as soon as the sun got low. Add to this that as the summer wore on, people became aware that Thorolf was not lying quietly. They could never be out of doors in peace after the sun set. And besides that the oxen which had drawn Thorolf became troll-ridden, and all the cattle which came near the grave of Thorolf went mad and bellowed until they died. The shepherd at Hvamm was often chased home by Thorolf.

It happened one evening during autumn at Hvamm that neither the shepherd nor the sheep came home. In the morning a search was made, and the shepherd was found dead a short distance from the grave of Thorolf. He was black and blue all over, and every bone in him was broken. He was buried near Thorolf. But of all the sheep which had been in the valley, some were found dead, and the rest ran up into the mountains and were never found again. And if birds settled on the grave of Thorolf, they fell down dead.

Matters became so bad that no man dared graze his livestock up in the valley. Often during the night people at Hvamm heard loud noises outside. They also often heard how the house was being ridden. And when winter came, Thorolf often appeared inside the house at the farm; and he molested the mistress of the house most of all. Many a person took harm from this, and she herself almost went mad; and it ended with the mistress of the house dying from these apparitions. She was also taken up to Thorsardale and buried near Thorolf. After that people fled from the farm. Thorolf now began to haunt the valley to such an extent that all the farms there were deserted. And his haunting increased so greatly in violence that he killed some men and put others to flight. And all who had died were seen with him when he haunted places. People made a great outcry about this trouble. It seemed to them that it was up to Arnkel to deal with it. Arnkel invited all those to stay with him who liked it better there than elsewhere. For wherever Arnkel was present, there never was any injury from Thorolf and his company. So fearful were people of the hauntings of Thorolf that no one dared travel about during winter even on business. But when winter passed there came a fine spring. And when the frost was out of the ground, Arnkel sent a man to Karsstead to the sons of Thorbrand and asked them to go along with him to take Thorolf away out of Thorsardale and to find him a burial place elsewhere. All men were then equally obligated by law to participate in the burial of the dead (as they are now) if they were summoned. But when the sons of Thorbrand heard that, they said it was no concern of theirs to help Arnkel or any of his followers out of their difficulties.

Then old Thorbrand spoke. "It is necessary," he said, "to go on all those errands to which people are obligated by law, and you have now been requested to do something which you ought not to refuse."

Then Thorodd said to the messenger, "Go and tell Arnkel that I shall come for my brothers. I shall be at Ulfarsfell and meet him there."

Now the messenger went and told Arnkel this. He made ready, and there were twelve men in all. They had with them a sledge and oxen and tools for digging. They first went to Ulfarsfell and met Thorodd there. He had two other men with him. They crossed the ridge over to Thorsardale to the mound of Thorolf. They opened it and found the body of Thorolf there undecomposed and most hideous to look at. They lifted him out of the grave and laid him on the sledge and harnessed two strong oxen to it. They dragged him up to Ulfarsfell Ridge, and by then the oxen were spent. Others were hitched up, and they dragged him up on the ridge. Arnkel intended to move him to the Vadilshofdi Promontory and bury him there. But when they came in to the edge of the hill, the oxen went mad. They broke away, ran down off the ridge, and headed out along the mountain side above the fence at Ulfarsfell and headed toward the sea, and by that time they were completely spent. And Thorolf was so heavy by then that they were scarcely able to move him at all. So they took him to a little headland nearby and buried him there, and that place has since been called Bægifotshofdi ('Lamefoot's Headland'). Later Arnkel had a wall built across the headland above the burial mound so high that nothing could get over it except a bird in flight. Traces of it can still be seen. There Thorolf lay quietly as long as Arnkel was alive.

Chapter 50 – Thorgunna's Arrival in Iceland

During the summer in which Christianity was made the law in Iceland, a ship came off the high seas and landed at Snæfellsness. It was a ship from Dublin. There were Irishmen and men from the Hebrides on it, also a few Norwegians. They lay under the lee of the ledge called Rif for a long time during the summer, waiting for a breeze to sail across the fjord to Dogurdarness, and many came from around the peninsula to trade with them.

On board was a Hebridean woman named Thorgunna. Members of the crew said that she had brought some valuable things along such as were not easily obtained in Iceland. And when Thurid, the housewife at Froda, heard that, she was very curious to see these costly things; for she was quite fond of finery and much given to vain display. So she went to the ship to see Thorgunna and asked her if she had any women's attire of unusual quality. Thorgunna said her things were not for sale, but admitted that she possessed such clothing as she need not be ashamed to be seen in at festivals or other gatherings. Thurid asked to see these things and was permitted to do so. They pleased her very much, for they were excellently made, yet not costly. Thurid asked Thorgunna to sell them to her, but she refused. Then Thurid invited her to take lodging at her place, for she knew that Thorgunna liked to dress up, and she thought she would be able to get the lovely things away from her by and by.

Thorgunna replied, "I accept your offer of lodging with pleasure, but I want you to know that I do not care to pay much for it since I am quite able to work. I don't mind working, but I will not do any hard labor. And I will determine myself how much of my money I will pay out for my lodging."

Even though Thorgunna spoke rather harshly, Thurid insisted that she come along home with her. So her belongings were brought from the ship. She had a large locked chest and a smaller portable one. These things were transported to Froda. And when Thorgunna arrived there, she asked to be shown her bed. A bed was assigned to her in the sleeping-hall at some distance from the door. She unlocked the chest and took out her bedclothes, which were all elaborately worked. Over her bed she spread a fine English sheet and a silk counterpane. She also took from the chest bed curtains and the trimmings that belonged to them. They were such fine bed furnishings that the people thought they had never seen anything like them before.

Then mistress Thurid said, "Make me a price on the bed furnishings."

Thorgunna replied, "I will not sleep on straw for your sake even though you are elegant and put on airs."

That angered Thurid, and she did not again insist that she sell her the things.

Thorgunna worked at making cloth every day when there was no haying. But when there was good drying weather, she worked at drying the hay in the home-field. She had a rake made which she did not want anyone else to use.

Thorgunna was a large woman. She was tall and stout and well fleshed. Her eyebrows were dark and her eyes close-set. Her hair was brown and thick. She was generally of a good disposition and went to church every day before going to her work, but she was not easy-tempered or talkative for the most part. It was the opinion of the people that Thorgunna was probably in her fifties; yet she was still a most vigorous woman. At that time Thorir Woodenleg had come to Froda for maintenance, and also his wife Thorgrima Galdrakin. They and Thorgunna could not get along with each other. Kjartan, the farmer's son, was the one person with whom Thorgunna most wished to deal; and she loved him very much. But he was rather cool toward her, and for that reason she was often irritable. Kjartan was then thirteen or fourteen years old, and he was both large and personable.

Chapter 51 – The Froda Marvels

The summer was rather wet, but during the autumn there came some good days for drying. The haymaking at Froda had progressed to the extent that the entire home-field had been cut and almost half of the hay completely dried. Then there came a good drying day with calm, bright weather, so that there was not a single cloud to be seen in the sky. Farmer Thorodd got up early in the morning and assigned the work for the day. Some began bringing in the hay and others stacked it, but the women were assigned to dry the hay, and it was so arranged that Thorgunna was to toss and dry the cattle fodder. And the work progressed well during the day.

But early in the afternoon a small black cloud appeared in the sky to the north above Skor. It moved quickly across the sky straight for the farm. The people thought it would bring rain. Thorodd asked his hands to rake the hay together, but Thorgunna continued turning the hay most vigorously. She did not begin to rake it up even though she had been told to. The small cloud approached rapidly. And when it reached the farm at Froda, it was accompanied by such great darkness that the people could not see beyond the homefield and could scarcely make out their hands before their eyes. From this could came such a heavy rain that all the hay which was still lying flat was drenched. The cloud quickly passed over and the weather cleared up. Then people saw that it had rained blood. During the evening the weather again became good for drying the hay, and the blood quickly dried on all the hay except where Thorgunna had been working. There the blood did not dry, nor did it ever dry on the rake she had been using.

Thorodd asked Thorgunna what she thought this strange occurrence might signify. She said she did not know – "but it seems most likely to me," she replied, "that it forebodes the death of someone here."

Thorgunna went home in the evening. She went to her bed, took off her bloody clothing, and lay down. She sighed heavily. And people then saw that she had taken sick. This shower had come nowhere except to Froda. Thorgunna would not take any food that evening. And in the morning farmer Thorodd came to her and asked about her sickness and how she thought it would end. She replied that she thought this would be her last sickness.

Then she said, "I consider you the wisest person here on the farm. That is why I want to tell you my wishes regarding the disposition of my property and of my body. Because things will happen just as I say," she went on. "Even though you think there is nothing unusual about me, I assure you that evil will result if you disregard my wishes. Things have happened in such a way that I fear much harm will result in the end unless strong measures are taken."

Thorodd replied, "I do not doubt that you are pretty close to the truth in that. And for that reason I promise not to disregard your instructions."

Thorgunna said, "This is what I want you to do. If I die from this sickness, I want to have my body taken to Skalholt, for I have a feeling that that will sometime become the most celebrated place in this country. I am sure also," she said, "that there are now priests there to sing a mass for me. For this reason I want you to have my body taken there. In return you are to have as much of my property as will reimburse you for your expense. Of my undivided possessions Thurid is to have my scarlet cloak. I do this so that she will not take it amiss if I dispose of my other things as I wish. I want you to take as much of the property which I leave behind for my food and lodging as you or Thurid want. I have a gold ring which I want to wear when I am taken to the church. But my bedding and the bed furnishings are to be burned because they will bring no good to anyone, and I say this not because I begrudge anyone the enjoyment of these fine things. I would not do so if I knew they would be of use to someone. But I am so insistent about this because I would hate to have people suffer such great harm from me and my things as I know will come to them if they do not follow my instructions."

Thorodd promised to do as she had requested. After that Thorgunna's illness became worse. She was sick for only a few days before she died. The body was first taken to the church, and Thorodd had a coffin made for it. On the following day Thorodd had the bed furnishings brought outside and then fetched wood and made a large bonfire. Just then mistress Thurid came up and asked Thorodd what he intended to do with the bedclothes. He said he was going to burn them all up as Thorgunna had stipulated.

"I don't want such splendid things burned," she said.

Thorodd replied, "She laid great stress on it that much harm would come of it if we did not follow her instructions."

Thurid said, "That was nothing but envy. She begrudges other people the enjoyment of her things, and that's why she talked that way. No harm will come of it, whatever we do about this."

"I'm not sure," he said, "that things will not happen just as she predicted."

Then she put her arms around his neck and asked him not to burn the bed furnishings. She urged him so strongly that he finally changed his mind. The end of the matter was that Thorodd burned the feather beds and pillows and Thurid got the quilts, the covers, and all the curtains and hangings. And yet neither one was completely satisfied with this outcome.

After this they made ready to transport the body; and reliable men and good horses, which belonged to Thorodd, were chosen to make this journey. The body was wrapped in linen cloth, but not sewed in it, and then placed in the coffin. They then set out, following the roadways which lead southward across the moors. Nothing unusual happened until they came south across the Valbjarnar Flats. Here they got into very soft quagmires, and the body often slipped off the horse. They proceeded southward to the Nordra River and across the river at the Eyjarvad Ford. The river was very high. There were both strong gusts of wind and very heavy rain. They finally came to the farm called Lower Ness on the Stafholts tongue of land. They asked for food and lodging there, but the farmer refused to grant them hospitality. Since it had grown late, they felt they could not continue any farther, for they thought the Hvita River would be dangerous to cross at night. They unsaddled their horses and carried the body into a provision house near the housedoor. They went into the sitting room and took off their clothes, assuming that they would have to spend the night there without food. The members of the household went to bed while it was still daylight. But when all had got into their beds, they heard a loud noise in the provision house. They went to see whether thieves might have broken in; and when they got there, they saw a large woman. She was completely naked, without a stitch of clothing on her, and she was busying herself at the cooking fire. Those who saw her were so frightened that they did not dare come near her. And when the men who had brought the body learned of this, they went there and saw how things stood. It was indeed Thorgunna, and it seemed advisable to all of them not to interfere with her. And when she had finished what she was doing, she carried the food into the room. Next she set the table and placed the food upon it.

Then the men who had brought the body said to the farmer, "It may well turn out, before we leave, that you will pay dearly for having refused us accommodations."

Then both the farmer and his wife said, "We will certainly give you food and grant you whatever other accommodations you need."

And as soon as the farmer had offered them hospitality, Thorgunna went out of the room and out of the house and did not appear again. Then a light was made in the room. The wet clothing was taken off the guests, and they were given dry things to put on. After that they sat down at the table and blessed the food, and the farmer had holy water sprinkled throughout the house. The guests ate their food, and no one suffered any harm even though Thorgunna had prepared it. They slept all that night, enjoying full hospitality.

In the morning they made ready to continue their journey, and they had no further difficulty. But wherever people heard of these events, most of them deemed it advisable to grant them whatever food and lodging they needed. The rest of the journey was uneventful. And when they came to Skalholt, the treasures which Thorgunna had intended for the church were delivered there, and the priests were glad to receive them all. Thorgunna was buried there, and the men who had brought her body returned home. They had a good journey and arrived home safe and sound.

Chapter 52 – The Moon of Weird

At Froda there was a large kitchen, at the rear of which was a locked bed-closet, as was the custom at that time. In front, between the kitchen and the outer door, were two storerooms, one on either side of the passage. Dried fish was stored in one and flour in the other. Every evening it was customary to make cooking fires in the kitchen. People used to sit a long time by the fires before the evening meal was served. The evening the burial party returned, as the people were sitting at the fires there, they saw a half moon appear on the wainscoting. It was plain to see for all in the house. It went around the house from right to left, withershins, and it did not go away as long as the men sat by the fire. Thorodd asked Thorir Woodenleg what that might portend. Thorir replied that that was 'the moon of weird' – "and someone here is fated to die." And this moon of ill fortune appeared every evening that entire week.

Chapter 53 – The Spooks at Froda

It happened next that a shepherd came home greatly depressed. He spoke little, and what he did say was disagreeable. The people thought he must be bewitched, for he went about quite distracted and talking to himself. This went on for some time. When two weeks of winter had passed, the shepherd came home one evening, went to his bed, and lay down there. And next morning, when people came to his bed, he was dead. He was buried there at the church.

Very soon after that great hauntings began. One night Thorir Woodenleg went outside for a call of nature. And when he wanted to go back in, he saw the shepherd standing in front of the door. Thorir tried to enter, but the shepherd would not let him. Then Thorir tried to get away, but the shepherd ran after him, grabbed him, and threw him down against the door. He was badly hurt from this so that he was black and blue all over, but he managed to drag himself to his bed. He took sick from this and died. He was also buried at the church. Now both men, the shepherd and Thorir Woodenleg, haunted the place together. And because of this the people became greatly terrified, as was to be expected. After the death of Thorir a serving man of Thorodd took sick. He laid abed for three days before he died. Then one man after another died until six were dead.

By that time the Yule fast was approaching, though in those days the fasts were not observed in Iceland. The one storeroom was stacked so full of dried fish that the door could not be opened. The fish was piled all the way up to the crossbeam, and one had to use a ladder to get at the pile from the top. Now it happened, several nights, while people were sitting by the kitchen fires, that they heard a noise in the storage room as though something was tearing the dried fish. But when they looked, they found nothing alive there.

One time that winter, shortly before Yule, farmer Thorodd went out to Ness for some of his dried fish. There were six of them in all, in a ten-oared boat, and they were gone all night. That same evening, after Thorodd had left and when the kitchen fires were lit and people had come to sit by them, they saw a seal's head come up out of the fire pit. A serving woman, who was the first one to get there and to see this marvel, took up a cudgel which was lying in the doorway and struck the seal on the head with it. It only grew larger from the blow and glared up at the bed-furnishings of Thorgunna. Then a serving man went up and struck the seal, but it continued to come forth with every blow until the flippers could be seen. Then the serving man fell down in a faint. All who were there were struck with terror. Then the youth Kjartan and seized a large sledge hammer and struck the seal on the head with it. It was a powerful blow, and the seal shook his head and looked around. Kjartan let blow after blow rain upon him, and the seal sank down like a peg being driven into the ground. He kept on striking until the seal had sunk down so far that he could pound the floor together over his head. And thus it always happened throughout the winter that all spectors feared Kjartan most.

Chapter 54 – Thorodd Drowns and Haunts Froda

On the next morning, when Thorodd and his men rowed back from Ness with the dried fish, they all perished off the Enni Headland. The boat and the dried fish were washed up at the foot of Enni, but the bodies were not found. And when this news was learned at Froda, Kjartan and Thurid invited their neighbors to celebrate the funeral feast there. The ale intended for the Yule feast was now taken and used for the funeral feast. But the first evening of the funeral feast, when the guests had taken their seats, farmer Thorodd and his shipmates walked into the hall, dripping wet. All welcomed Thorodd cordially since they considered that a good omen. It was believed in those days that men who had perished at sea and then came to attend their funeral feast had been well received by Ran. For at that time a great deal of heathendom still prevailed even though all the people had been baptized and were nominally Christians. Thorodd and his men walked the length of the sitting room and sleeping room, which had two doors, and out into the kitchen, where they sat down at the fire without returning anyone's greeting. The members of the household fled from the kitchen, but Thorodd and his men remained sitting there until the fires had burned down to white ashes. Then they vanished. This happened every evening as long as the funeral feast lasted. There was much talk about this matter. Some were of the opinion that the visits would stop when the funeral feast was over.

When the people who had been invited to the feast returned home, the house was rather lonely. The first evening after they had left, the cooking fires were made as usual. And when the fires were burning, Thorodd came in with his company, and they were dripping wet. They sat down by the fires and began to wring out their clothing. And after they had sat down, Thorir Woodenleg and his six followers came in. They were all covered with earth. They shook out their clothing and scattered the earth on Thorodd and his men. The people of the household fled from the kitchen, as was to be expected; and on that evening they had neither light nor warm stones nor any other benefit from the fire. On the following evening the cooking fire was made in another room. It was thought that they would be less likely to come there. But things did not turn out that way, for everything happened in the same manner as on the previous evening. Both parties came to the fires. On the third evening Kjartan suggested that they make one large fire in the kitchen and the cooking fire in another room. This was done. The result was that Thorodd and the others sat by the large fire, while the members of the household sat by the small fire, and this continued throughout the Yule season.

The disturbance in the pile of dried fish also increased more and more. Day and night it sounded as though someone were tearing the stacked fish. There came the time when it was necessary to get some of the dried fish. The man who climbed up saw a tail which looked like a signed oxtail come up out of the pile. It was short and covered with seal hair. The man who had climbed up to the top of the pile took hold of the tail and pulled and asked the other people to come and help him. They climbed up, both men and women, and pulled at the tail, but they accomplished nothing. To all appearances the tail was that of a dead animal. But while they were pulling the hardest, the tail suddenly slipped through their hands and tore off the skin from the palms of those who had taken the firmest grip. The tail was never seen again. Then the dried fish was taken out, and it was seen that all the fish had been torn from their skins so that only the skins remained. And when the searched the pile to the bottom, they found not one living thing. Soon after these events Thorgrima Galdrakin, the wife of Thorir Woodenleg, took sick. She lay abed only a short while before she died; and on the very evening of the day she was buried, she appeared in the train of her husband Thorir. After the tail had disappeared, the visitation was renewed; and now more women died than men. Six persons perished in a row, and some fled from the hauntings and apparitions. In the autumn there had been thirty servants in the household. Of these, eighteen had died, five had fled, and only seven remained by the middle of February.

Chapter 55 – Snorri Helps Banish the Spooks

But when these marvels had reached this stage, Kjartan went to Helgafell to see his uncle Snorri godi to ask his advice as to what was to be done to deal with the visitations which had come upon them. By that time the priest whom Gizur the White had sent to Snorri had arrived there. Snorri sent the priest to Froda with Kjartan and his son Thord Cat and six additional men. He advised them to burn the bed furnishings of Thorgunna and to summon all the revenants to a court to be held at the door of the house. He asked the priest to conduct divine services there, to consecrate water, and to hear the people's confessions. So they rode to Froda and summoned men from the nearest farms to accompany them.

They arrived at Froda on the evening before Candlemas just as the kitchen fires were being lit. By that time mistress Thurid had been taken ill in the same manner as those who had died. Kjartan went in at once and saw that Thorodd and his followers were sitting by the fire as was their custom. Kjartan took down the bed furnishings of Thorgunna. Then he went to the kitchen and fetched glowing embers from the fire; and going outside, he burned all the bed furnishings which had belonged to Thorgunna.

Thereupon Kjartan summoned Thorir Woodenleg, and Thord Cat cited farmer Thorodd for haunting the house without permission and depriving people of health and life. All who were sitting by the fire were summoned. Then the door court was set up, the charges were stated, and the procedure was exactly as at an assembly court. The testimony of the witnesses was heard, the cases were summed up, and the verdicts given. When sentence was pronounced against Thorir Woodenleg, he got up and said, "Sat I have while the sitting was good." Thereupon he left by way of the door before which the court was not being held.

Then sentence was pronounced against the shepherd. And when he heard it, he stood up and said, "Go I shall now, though I think I should have gone before."

And when Thorgrima Galdrakin heard sentence being pronounced over her, "she arose and said, "Stayed I have while the staying was good."

Then each one in turn, as his sentence was pronounced, got up, said something, and left. It was obvious from these comments that they were all reluctant to leave.

Finally sentence was pronounced against farmer Thorodd. And when he heard it, he rose and said, "There's no welcome here; let's away all." Then he departed.

After that Kjartan and the others went in. The priest carried holy water and holy relics throughout the entire house. On the following day the priest conducted divine services and sang a solemn mass, after which all apparitions and hauntings at Froda ceased. Thurid recovered completely from her illness. In the spring following these marvels, Kjartan obtained servants and lived at Froda for a long time afterward and became a most outstanding man.

Bibliography

Baier, Katharina and Werner Schäfke. "When the Dead No Longer Rest: The Religious Significance of Revenants in Sagas Set in Viking Age Settlements Around the Time of the Conversion." In *Death in the Middle Ages and Early Modern Times: The Material and Spiritual Conditions of the Culture of Death*. Ed. Albrecht Classen. De Gruyter, 2016.131–54.

Blair, John. "The Dangerous Dead in Early Medieval England." In *Early Medieval Studies in Memory of Patrick Wormald*. Eds. Stephen Baxter, Catherine Karkov, Janet Nelson, and David Pelteret. Ashgate, 2009.539–60.

Caciola, Nancy. "Wraiths, Revenants and Ritual in Medieval Culture." *Past and Present* 152 (1996): 3–45.

Caciola, Nancy. "Revenants, Resurrection, and Burnt Sacrifice." In *Afterlives: The Return of the Dead in the Middle Ages*. Cornell University Press, 2016.113–56.

Caciola, Nancy. " 'Night is Conceded to the Dead': Revenant Congregations in the Middle Ages." In *Contesting Orthodoxy in Medieval and Early Modern Europe: Heresy, Magic and Witchcraft*. Eds. Louise Nyholm Kallestrup and Raisa Maria Toivo. Palgrave Macmillan, 2017.17–33.

Chadwick, Nora. "Norse Ghosts: A Study in the *Draugr* and the *Haugbui*." *Folklore* 57/2 (1946a): 50–65.

Chadwick, Nora. "Norse Ghosts II: A Study in the *Draugr* and the *Haugbui*." *Folklore* 57/3 (1946b): 106–27.

Gordon, Stephen. "Disease, Sin, and the Walking Dead in Medieval England, c. 1100–1350: A Note on the Documentary and Archaeological Evidence." In *Medicine, Healing and Performance*. Ed. Stephan Gordon. Oxbow, 2014.55–70.

Gordon, Stephen. "Monstrous Words, Monstrous Bodies: Irony and the Walking Dead in Walter Map's *De Nugis Curialium*." *English Studies* 96 (2015a): 379–402.

Gordon, Stephen. "Social Monsters and the Walking Dead in William of Newburgh's *Historia rerum Anglicarum*." *Journal of Medieval History* 41/4 (2015b): 446–65.

Jakobsson, Ármann. "The Fearless Vampire Killers: A Note about the Icelandic *Draugr* and Demonic Contamination in *Grettis Saga*." *Folklore* 120/3 (2009): 307–16.

Jakobsson, Ármann. "Vampires and Watchmen: Categorizing the Medieval Icelandic Undead." *Journal of English and Germanic Philology* 110/3 (2011): 281–300.

Jakobsson, Ármann. "Traversing the Uncanny Valley: Glámr in Narratological Space." In *Paranormal Encounters in Iceland 1150–1400*. Eds. Ármann Jakobsson and Miriam Mayburd. Medieval Institute Publications, 2020.89–108.

Kanerva, Kirsi. "The Role of the Dead in Medieval Iceland: A Case Study of *Eyrbyggja Saga*." *Collegium Medievale* 24 (2011): 23–49.

Kanerva, Kirsi. "Rituals for the Restless Dead: The Authority of the Deceased in Medieval Iceland." In *Authorities in the Middle Ages*. Eds. Sini Kangas, Mia Korpiola, and Tuija Ainonen. De Gruyter, 2013.205–28.

Kanerva, Kirsi. "From Powerful Agents to Subordinate Objects? The Restless Dead in 13th and 14th-Century Iceland." In *Death in Medieval Europe: Death Scripted and Death Choreographed*. Ed. Joelle Rollo-Koster. Taylor and Francis, 2017.40–70.

Keyworth, David. "The Aetiology of Vampires and Revenants: Theological Debate and Popular Belief." *Journal of Religious History* 34/2 (2010): 158–73.

Martin, John. "Law and the (Un-)dead: Medieval Models for Understanding the Hauntings in *Eyrbyggja Saga*." *Saga-Book* 29 (2005): 67–82.

Merkelbach, Rebecca. "The Monster in Me: Social Corruption and the Perception of Monstrosity in the Sagas of the Icelanders." *Quaestio Insularis* 15 (2014): 22–37.

Rooney, Kenneth. *Mortality and Imagination: The Life of the Dead in Medieval English Literature*. Brepols, 2011.

Sayers, William. "The Alien and Alienated as Unquiet Dead in the Sagas of the Icelanders." In *Monster Theory: Reading Culture*. Ed. Jeffrey Jerome Cohen. University of Minnesota Press, 1996.242–63.

Schmitt, Jean-Claude. *Ghosts in the Middle Ages: The Living and the Dead in Medieval Society*. Trans. Teresa Fagan. Chicago University Press, 1994.

Simpson, Jacqueline. "Repentant Soul or Walking Corpse? Debatable Apparitions in Medieval England." *Folklore* 114/3 (December 2003): 389–402.

Tulinus, Torfi. "Revenants in Medieval Icelandic Literature." *Caeitele Echinox* 21 (2011): 58–74.

Urbanski, Charity. "The Wiley Lecture: Monsters in Anglo-Norman Historiography; Two Notes on William of Newburgh's Revenants." *Haskins Society Journal* 32 (2020): 133–48.

5   Werewolves

Just as medieval revenants differed from their closest modern analogues, vampires and zombies, medieval werewolves were also very different from their modern cousins. During the twentieth and early twenty-first centuries, most werewolves were depicted as humans who had been infected by the bite of a werewolf and then became werewolves themselves, changing involuntarily into feral, blood-thirsty creatures during the full moon. The humans who suffer from this affliction generally lose their ability to reason while in their wolf state, as well as any memory of what they did while in wolf form. Werewolves were regarded as fearsome creatures in the Middle Ages too, as were wolves in general, but medieval werewolf beliefs differed substantially from our modern werewolf tropes. First, the means by which humans were believed to transform into werewolves was not the full moon, but some magical token or act, such as removing one's clothing, a magical ring, the branch of a magical sapling, or even a curse. Second, werewolves were not believed to be created through infection. In many cases, we simply do not know why a person possesses this token or is able to transform into a wolf, and in others their transformation is clearly the result of a curse laid upon them. Third, the type of person often represented as a werewolf in the medieval sources is a noble warrior, a knight, baron, or king. Finally, and perhaps most importantly, it was believed that those who transformed into wolves did not lose their human reason, but emphatically retained it. In fact, this ability to reason and its association with the humanity of the subject even while they are in their wolf form are the focus of many medieval werewolf stories.

This chapter begins with a foundational shape-shifting tale that was widely read in Europe during the Middle Ages, Ovid's story of Lycaon from *The Metamorphoses*. It then moves on to several northern European tales of werewolves from the twelfth, thirteenth, and fourteenth centuries. These include a trio of Breton *lais* (short tales in verse): Marie de France's *Bisclavret* written in the 1160s or 1170s; the anonymous *Melion*, most likely composed in the final decade of the twelfth century; and the anonymous *Biclarel*, a reworking of Marie de France's *Bisclavret* that was completed about 1342. The *lais* are followed by the fourteenth-century Latin romance *Arthur and Gorlagon*, the tale of Sigmund and Sinfjotli from the late-thirteenth-century *Saga of the Volsungs*, and an account of a wolf couple from Gerald of Wales's *History and Topography of Ireland*, dated to around 1188.

DOI: 10.4324/9780429243004-6

We begin with Ovid's Lycaon due to its wide circulation in Europe during the High Middle Ages and the influence it exerted on medieval authors and tales about shape-shifting more generally. According to Ovid, Jupiter decided to visit Earth and see for himself if the rumors about the criminal state of humanity were true. When Jupiter visited Lycaon, the tyrant of Arcadia, and revealed himself as a god, Lycaon proved to be one of the worst of humanity's criminal offenders. He decided to test Jupiter's omniscience by serving him boiled and roasted human flesh. To make matters worse, Lycaon intended to murder Jupiter that night while the god slept as a guest in his home. These acts transgressed two of the strictest taboos in Roman society, those against cannibalism and betraying the trust of a guest. Irate, Jupiter called together a council of the gods to determine what to do about humanity's wickedness. During the council, he told the gods of Lycaon's evil deeds and the fate he suffered for them. Jupiter recounts how, just as Lycaon set the table for his ghoulish banquet, he brought Lycaon's house down around him and destroyed his household gods, causing the tyrant to flee in fear. As Lycaon reached the countryside, he transformed into a howling wolf, his outer form now matching his inner wickedness. Lycaon was still the blood-thirsty creature he had been in human form, but now his violence was directed at livestock rather than people.

Ovid's account of Lycaon focuses on his wickedness and impiety, as well as the poetic justice of his transformation into a wolf – a form that reflects his feral and violent interior state. Ovid does not explicitly state that Lycaon's transformation is due to Jupiter's curse, but, in other versions of the tale, Jupiter's curse is clearly identified as the cause. While Lycaon loses his ability to speak and is trapped in his wolf state in Ovid's account, Ovid also mentions that the wolf retains some of Lycaon's former traits: his gleaming eyes, violent face, and grey hair. Unfortunately, Ovid does not mention whether Lycaon retains his human reason. This element is important to us because it features so prominently in the high medieval werewolf tales from northern Europe.

The first of the medieval tales examined here is Marie de France's *Bisclavret*. This *lai* tells the story of a noble baron, who periodically transforms into a fearsome werewolf by removing his clothing and spends a few days living in the forest every week (and presumably roaming around the countryside doing harm and eating people – at least, this is what Marie tells us that werewolves do in the first several lines of the *lai*). Confused by her husband's absences, Bisclavret's wife persuades him to tell her the truth about his weekly trips into the forest. Horrified to hear that her husband regularly transforms into a beast, she sends another knight into the forest to steal his clothing, trapping him in his wolf form. She then marries the second knight and pretends her first husband simply vanished.

After a year in the forest, Bisclavret encounters the king while he is out hunting. After being pursued almost to death by the king's hunting dogs, he ingratiates himself with the monarch by licking his foot. Most importantly, Bisclavret reveals that he is rational through his actions. The king considers this rational wolf a marvel and takes him back to court where Bisclavret proves his loyalty to the king and everyone remarks how noble and well-behaved he is. However, when Bisclavret finally sees the knight who married his wife, he attacks him. The king is thrown by Bisclavret's uncharacteristic behavior, but protects him. When they eventually encounter Bisclavret's wife, Bisclavret attacks her so ferociously that he tears the nose from her face. Instead of destroying Bisclavret, however, the king and his councilors decide to torture the wife to find out what she knows. The wife reveals that she was responsible for stealing Bisclavret's clothing and trapping him in his wolf form, and the king forces her to send for Bisclavret's clothing in the hope of restoring him to his human form. At first Bisclavret refuses to even acknowledge the clothing until they allow him privacy in a closed room. When the king and some knights return to the room, they find him transformed back into a human. Bisclavret is joyfully welcomed back to court, but his wife and her second husband are exiled, and Marie notes that several of the woman's daughters were born without noses.

The later tales of *Melion* and *Biclarel* repeat Marie's basic narrative of a nobleman who is trapped in his wolf state by his wife but finds favor with the king and is finally restored to his human state, with some variations. In *Melion*, one of King Arthur's knights marries an Irish princess and reveals his secret to her when she begs him to kill a stag for her. In this case, Melion's wife assists in her husband's transformation, using his magical ring to turn her husband into a wolf before absconding with the ring and her husband's clothes, and running back to Ireland with Melion's squire. Melion himself takes a ship to Ireland to search for his wife and eventually joins a pack of ten other wolves who are explicitly killing both livestock and people. In response to the locals' complaints, the king of Ireland kills the ten other wolves, but spares Melion. Then King Arthur arrives in Ireland and Melion ingratiates himself, causing Arthur to keep Melion with him and everyone to remark on his courtliness. When Melion finally encounters his former squire, he attacks him. The squire confesses, and the king of Ireland summons his daughter who brings the magical ring to restore Melion to his human form. Melion briefly considers transforming his wife into a wolf to punish her, but decides to leave her instead and return to Britain with Arthur.

The story of *Biclarel* is more explicitly misogynist reworking of *Bisclavret*. Unlike the *lais* of *Bisclavret* and *Melion*, it is not a free-standing narrative, but a story embedded in a larger narrative, *Renart le Contrefait* (Renart the Counterfeit). It is one of the stories told by the narrator, Renart the fox, in answer to a young man's question about whether he should marry. Like our other Breton werewolves, Biclarel is a noble knight (in this case of King Arthur's court) who spends several days a month as a wolf in the forest, and whose only fault according to the author was believing his wife. In order to discover his secret, Biclarel's wife lectures him on the importance of honesty in marriage and accuses him of having a lover. When he finally admits that he goes off into the forest, removes his clothes, and changes into a wolf, his wife views it as the perfect opportunity to get rid of him by stealing his clothing and trapping him in his wolf form so she can run off with her lover.

One day, Biclarel is cornered in the forest by King Arthur and his hunting dogs and kneels in supplication before Arthur who takes pity on him. Like Bisclavret and Melion, Biclarel is considered a marvel. He is a courtly and rational wolf who behaves nobly, until he sees his wife and attacks her. Believing that Biclarel must have had a reason to attack the woman, Arthur allows him to wander through the court to see if he will attack anyone else. He does not. Instead, he looks for his wife who has decided to leave and attacks her again. The wife is rescued by townspeople, put in fetters, made to confess, and sends for Biclarel's clothing. As soon as the clothes are presented to Biclarel, he scrambles into them and regains his human form. As for his wife, Biclarel requests that she be sentenced to death, and Arthur orders her to be walled up alive. The story ends with a warning that anyone who wishes to keep a secret should never tell his wife.

The fourteenth-century story of *Arthur and Gorlagon* reprises the same basic werewolf narrative with some new twists. In this case, King Arthur offends Queen Guinevere by kissing her in public. Guinevere tells the king that he does not understand the heart and nature of women, and Arthur vows to spare no pains and to fast until he has gained this information. Arthur sets off on a quest to discover the heart, nature, and ways of women that takes him to the court of three kings: Gargol, Torleil, and Gorlagon. When Arthur arrives at the court of Gargol, he tells him of his quest but is immediately persuaded to break his vow of fasting and eats with him. Gargol then sends Arthur to his brother Torleil to seek the answer to his question. At Torleil's court, Arthur is again persuaded to break his vow of fasting and eats with Torleil, who in turn sends him to their third brother, Gorlagon. When Arthur arrives at Gorlagon's court, he is entreated to dismount and eat on numerous occasions, but this time he steadfastly refuses to do so until he receives his answer. Gorlagon promises to answer his question by telling him a story about a certain king, but warns him that he will be little the wiser once he has heard the tale.

Gorlagon narrates a story about a king who was connected to a magical sapling that had sprouted from the ground the moment the king was born. The fates had decreed that whoever cut down this sapling and touched it to his head, saying "be a wolf and have the understanding of a wolf," would be made a wolf. Recognizing the potential danger of the magical sapling falling into the wrong hands, the king guarded it closely and visited it often. Unfortunately, the king had a beautiful wife who loved the son of another king and was determined to get rid of her husband to be with her lover. Like Biclarel's wife, the king's wife pesters her husband to reveal why he visits the garden with this sapling so many times a day, pledging that she will not eat and feigning illness until he finally reveals his secret. Fearing that his beloved wife might die, the king finally tells her the truth. Thrilled to finally have the means to dispose of her husband, the wife cuts down the sapling and touches the king's head with it, but she fumbles the incantation. Instead of saying "be a wolf and have the understanding of a wolf," she says "be a wolf and have the understanding of a man." Her husband immediately transforms into a wolf and flees into the woods pursued by hounds, but retains his human reason.

The wife married her lover and transferred the rule of the kingdom to him. Meanwhile, the king spent two years in the forest in wolf form before finding a female wolf and having two cubs with her. Bent on revenge, the wolf-king killed the children of his former wife and her new husband with the help of his wolf family. Not satisfied with killing her children, the wolf-king considered how else he might harm his former wife and killed two of her brothers. This time, his cubs were caught and hanged. Driven mad with grief, the wolf-king began killing the local animals and eventually the local people as well. This destruction was reported to a kindly, neighboring king who vowed to hunt down the wolf and end its rampage. The wolf-king overheard the plans being made to kill him and decided to run to this king and behave as a supplicant. As in the lais, the wolf-king overcomes the apprehension of the king and his nobles with his humble and devoted behavior toward them and is taken back to court where he behaves impeccably.

When this king has to leave on business that will take him away for several days, he leaves the wolf in the care of his queen, who hates the wolf and keeps him chained up in their bedchamber. When the queen then arranges to meet her lover, the wolf cannot contain his fury at the betrayal of his master. He breaks his chain and mauls the lover, but leaves the queen unharmed. The queen lies to the servants who rush in, telling them that the wolf has eaten her son and attacked the man they find lying half-dead, and that he would have killed her as well if they had not come to her aid. To deceive the king, she hides their son and his nurse, bloodies her clothes, cuts her hair in mourning, and tells her husband that the wolf has devoured their son and attacked his servant. The wolf, however, leaps into his master's arms and acts delighted to see him. Confused, the king questions whether the wolf who has always been so tame and loyal could be responsible for such a crime. In the end, the wolf leads the king to the room where his son is hidden and they find him alive with his nurse. He then takes the king to back to the servant he attacked earlier and attacks him again. After questioning by the king, the servant finally confesses to his crimes and those of the queen. The servant is flayed alive and hanged for his crimes, while the queen is torn limb from limb by horses and then fed to the flames.

The king then ponders the wolf's intelligence and actions and concludes that he must be a man transformed into a wolf by some magical art. The wolf demonstrates that he agrees with the king, and the king decides to let the wolf lead him and some of his men back to his own country in the hope that they can return him to his human form. The wolf leads them across the sea to his own kingdom where the locals are lamenting the fate of their king, who was turned into a wolf with a magical sapling by his queen and replaced by a tyrant, so the king conquers the country and captures its king and queen. Under torture and starvation, the queen finally confesses and produces the sapling, which the king uses to restore the wolf-king to his human state. The newly restored king sentences his rival to death, but merely divorces his wife out of clemency, and regains the rule of his kingdom. Gorlagon tells Arthur that he has now learned the heart, nature, and ways of women. The tale appears to be over at this point, but Arthur asks the king who the woman sitting opposite him is, why she has a bloody head on a plate in front her, and weeps whenever the king smiles, and kisses the bloody head whenever he kisses his wife. Gorlagon reveals that she is his former wife who transformed him into a wolf and that her punishment is to suffer perpetual infamy by having to kiss the decapitated head of her former lover whenever the king kisses his new queen. At this, Arthur finally accepts Gorlagon's offer to dismount and eat.

Like modern werewolf tales, these stories broadly treat the theme of the beast within the man. However, their resemblance to modern werewolf stories largely ends there. These high and late medieval northern European werewolf tales reflect cultural concerns much different than their modern cousins. All of them cast the werewolf as a noble warrior, a knight, or a king. All of them, except Gorlagon, voluntarily transform into werewolves on a regular basis and go into the forest to live a feral existence centered on hunting animals and humans, all retain their human ability to reason, all ingratiate themselves with a king by demonstrating intelligence and courtly behavior, and all are trapped in their wolf state by unfaithful, deceptive wives. First and foremost, these werewolf tales reflect the fact that noblemen in the high and late Middle Ages were expected to live two very different lives: a life of refined behavior and manners at court, and a life devoted to warfare and bloodshed in the service of their king. The transformation from a handsome and courtly knight or king into a bloodthirsty wolf mimics the transformation from courtier to warrior that nobles routinely undertook, and the association between warriors and wolves goes back much further. Germanic and Scandinavian cultures share a warrior wolf tradition that pre-dates their conversions to Christianity, with some warriors wearing the skins of wolves into battle and imitating the wolf's ferocity by going into a battle frenzy.

We also see this association between wolves and warriors in the late fourteenth-century *Saga of the Volsungs*, where Sigmund and Sinfjotli don enchanted wolf skins, transform into wolves, and roam the countryside being hunted and killing men. In this case, the heroes voluntarily put on the magical skins after taking them from two kings they find sleeping in a house. Once they put on the skins, however, they find they cannot take them off. They are forced to remain in their wolf forms for ten days while being hunted. They also retain their human reason, as we see when the two communicate in their wolf howls and when Sigmund heals Sinfjotli. Once they are able to take off the wolf skins, they burn them so they can do no further harm. Sigmund and Sinfjotli's donning the wolf skins reverses the practice of taking off one's clothes to transform into a wolf that we see with Bisclavret and Biclarel, but it achieves the same outcome. The men voluntarily change into wolves, but are unable to change back when they want to.

The ancient association between wolves and warriors informs medieval werewolf tales, as does the idea that the warrior voluntarily becomes a wolf when going into battle; however, these tales are not really concerned with trance-like battle frenzies. The crux of the werewolf tales examined in this chapter is the fact the that the man remains trapped in his wolf state and cannot regain his human form at will and reintegrate into society. Most of the werewolves in this chapter require assistance to transform back into humans, and it is their rationality and ability to control their behavior, even while in their animal state, that enable them to win that assistance. The tales of *Bisclavret, Melion, Biclarel*, and *Arthur and Gorlagon* all emphasize the werewolf's intelligence, his noble behavior, his good manners, his loyalty and tameness toward the king, and the fact that he only displays violence toward those who have wronged him. Modern werewolf stories largely dwell on the horror of involuntarily becoming a wolf and being unable to remember one's actions while a wolf, but in these medieval tales, the true horror is being trapped in a wolf's body, unable to speak, while fully retaining one's humanity.

Although the werewolves are fearsome, shape-shifting creatures, it is not their bloodthirsty, feral nature that is emphasized in the stories. In fact, the werewolf is not portrayed so much as a monster as a hero and an object of sympathy. The wives in *Bisclavret, Melion, Biclarel*, and *Arthur and Gorlagon* are the real monsters for betraying their husbands and trapping them in their wolf form. All of these women are punished in some fashion, while their werewolf husband is welcomed back into noble society after having proven himself loyal to the king. In the case of Bisclavret's wife, the punishment is extended to the next generation as her missing nose becomes a hereditary trait that she passes on to her daughters.

Noble women in medieval Europe were, of course, expected to be faithful to their husbands and accept that they would routinely engage in battle and brutally kill other men. In these tales, the wife fails to live up to either of these expectations. Bisclavret's wife is absolutely horrified when she learns about her husband's wolf adventures and decides to return the love of a knight who has been wooing if he will help her get rid of her husband. Although we are not told precisely why Melion's wife decides to leave him after witnessing his transformation, she certainly takes the opportunity to race back to Ireland as quickly as she can. In the cases of Biclarel and Gorlagon, we are explicitly told that their wives had been searching for an opportunity to get rid of them in order to be with other men. The villain in these tales is not the werewolf, it is his wife.

The final werewolf tale in this chapter is something of a departure from the others and demonstrates different concerns. In his *History and Topography of Ireland*, the twelfth-century Cambro-Norman cleric, Gerald of Wales, includes a tale about a man and a woman who have both been transformed into wolves. In this case, their transformation is the result of a curse put on a whole town by a saint, the Abbot Natalis. Due to Natalis' curse, every seven years a man and a woman from the town of Ossory are forced to go into exile as wolves. When the seven years are up, if they have survived, they can return to the town and regain their human form, and another man and woman must take their place. These wolves retain not only their human reason, but their ability to speak as well. In fact, speech is central to Gerald's story as it is only through speech that the man/wolf is able to persuade a priest to accompany him back to his partner who is dying. The wolves beg the priest to perform last rites for the woman/wolf, which the very confused priest does, but he hesitates to give her the viaticum (the consecrated communion host) until the man/wolf pulls back the woman/wolf's skin to reveal her human form. The priest then gives the woman the sacrament, and the man/wolf guards him through the night and leads him back on his journey the next day.

Gerald's wolf story appears within a larger account of Ireland in which he portrays the Irish as barbaric people who need to be civilized and Ireland as teeming with wonderous and fearsome creatures (including the Irish). Although Gerald was writing for an audience that would have included the same nobles who might have read Marie de France's *Bisclavret* or the other *lais*, the tenor of his story is strikingly different from the *lais*, as are his concerns. Gerald's wolves are ordinary people, not noble warriors, they are involuntarily exiled and made into wolves as the result of a saint's curse, and they not only retain their human reason, but they can speak as well. Unlike the other werewolves we have examined, these wolves are also able to reveal their human forms, at least briefly, to gain human assistance. Although they are cursed to a seven-year exile in the fearsome form of wolves, and Gerald points out that they might not survive this exile, they are not trapped in the same way as the other werewolves we have seen, unable to communicate with humans. The werewolf couple are exiled, cut off from humanity and civilization, and forced to live in the forest as animals. And not just any animal. They take on the form of one of the most feared creatures in medieval Europe.

Gerald certainly demonstrates the power of Saint Natalis with this story about saintly curses and miraculous shape-shifting, but he is more concerned with the priest's actions than the werewolves. For example, Gerald does not tell us what the werewolves do in the forest, only that they have been exiled. For Gerald, what the werewolves do during their exile is not the central question. Instead, he is concerned with whether the priest should have given last rites to a wolf, and whether these were really wolves or humans after all. Sacraments were and still are reserved for humanity; they transmit God's grace to humans, and so giving last rites, and especially communion, to an animal would have been a serious breach of the priest's duties.

In the final paragraphs of the story, Gerald tells us that the priest revealed this story in confession and that a synod or council was called to investigate the matter. Gerald provided written testimony about the story he had heard, and the priest was sent to the pope, presumably to seek absolution. He follows this with a discussion of whether beings with the appearance of brutes who retain their human reason should be classified as animals, in apparent support of the priest's decision to give communion to the woman/wolf. Gerald gives several examples of magical transformations but argues that these are only illusory and that magical arts cannot actually transform one thing into another. The thing only appears to be transformed. However, he states that true transformations can occur if they are effected by God. Drawing upon Augustine's discussion of *monstra* (monsters) in the *City of God*, Gerald concludes that such transformations are proof of God's power. In this case, Saint Natalis' ability to transform the couple from Ossory into wolves is a demonstration of God's power working through the saint.

The tales in this chapter explore the boundary between human and animal, the opposition of civilization and barbarity, the connection between violence and the bestial, and the central role of rationality in defining humanity. Whether the transformation of human into wolf is the result of a curse or a magical token, the transformation is only partial and external as long as the subject maintains their human ability to reason, and one of the main themes in these stories is the wolf's struggle to regain his humanity. Medieval tales of lycanthropy offer us a window onto debates about the violence of warriors, the duties of noble wives, and even the proper uses of the sacraments. They also assure us that humanity ultimately resides in the behavior and intellect of the subject, not their external appearance.

PRIMARY SOURCES

Ovid, *The Metamorphoses of Ovid*, trans. Henry T. Riley (George Bell and Sons, 1889), pp. 16–17.

FABLE VII.

> *Lycaon, king of Arcadia, in order to discover if it is Jupiter himself who has come to lodge in his palace, orders the body of an hostage, who had been sent to him, to be dressed and served up at a feast. The God, as a punishment, changes him into a wolf.*

I had *now* passed Maenalus, to be dreaded for its dens of beasts of prey, and the pine-groves of cold Lycaeus, together with Cyllene. After this, I entered the realms and the inhospitable abode of the Arcadian tyrant, just as the late twilight was bringing on the night. I gave a signal that a God had come, and the people commenced to pay their adorations. In the first place, Lycaon derided their pious supplications. Afterwards, he said, I will make trial, by a plain proof, whether this is a God, or whether he is a mortal; nor shall the truth remain a matter of doubt. He then makes preparations to destroy me, when sunk in sleep, by an unexpected death; this mode of testing the truth pleases him. And not content with that, with the sword he cuts the throat of an hostage that had been sent from the nation of the Molossians, and then softens part of the quivering limbs in boiling water, and part he roasts with fire placed beneath. As soon as he had placed these on the table, I, with avenging flames, overthrew the house upon the household Gods, worthy of their master. Alarmed, he himself takes to flight, and having reached the solitude of the country, he howls aloud, and in vain attempts to speak; his mouth gathers rage from himself, and through its *usual* desire for slaughter, it is directed against the sheep, and even still delights in blood. His garments are changed into hair, his arms into legs; he becomes a wolf, and he still retains vestiges of his ancient form. His hoariness is still the same, the same violence *appears* in his features; his eyes are bright as before; *he is still* the same image of ferocity.

"Thus fell one house; but one house alone did not deserve to perish; wherever the earth extends, the savage Erinnys reigns. You would suppose that men had conspired to be wicked; let all men speedily feel that vengeance which they deserve to endure, for such is my determination."

Marie de France, "Bisclaveret," in *Guingamor, Lanval, Tyolet, le Bisclaveret*, trans. Jessie L. Weston (D. Nutt, 1900), pp. 83–94.

In the days of King Arthur there lived in Brittany a valiant knight of noble birth and fair to look upon; in high favour with his lord and much loved by all his fellows. This knight was wedded to a fair and gracious lady whom he loved tenderly, and she too loved her lord, but one thing vexed her sorely – three days in every week would her husband leave her, and none knew whither he went, or what he did while thus absent.

And every time the lady vexed herself more and more, till at last she could no longer keep silence, and when her husband came back, joyful and glad at heart after one of these journeys, she said to him: "My dear lord, there is something I would fain ask thee, and yet I scarce dare, for fear lest thou be angry with me."

Then her lord drew her to him, and kissed her tenderly. "Lady," he said, "fear not to ask me, there is nothing I would not gladly tell thee, if it be in my power."

"In faith," she said, "now is my heart at rest. My lord, didst thou but know how terrified I am in the days I am left alone; I rise in the morning affrighted, and lie down at night in such dread of losing thee that if I be not soon reassured I think me I should die of it. Tell me, I pray thee, where thou goest, and on what errand, that I who love thee may be at rest during thine absence."

"Lady," he answered, "for the love of God ask me no more, for indeed if I told thee evile would surely come of it; thou would'st cease to love me, and I should be lost."

When the lady heard this she was but ill-pleased, nor would she let her lord be at peace, but day by day she besought him with prayers and caresses, till at length he yielded and told her all the truth. "Lady," he said, "there is a spell cast upon me: three days in the week am I forced to become a were-wolf; and when I feel the change coming upon me I hide me in the thickest part of the forest, and there I live on prey and roots till the time has expired."

When he had told her this his wife asked him what of his garments? Did he still wear them in his wolf's shape?

"Nay," he said, "I must needs lay them aside."

"And what dost though do with them?"

"Ah, that I may not tell thee, for if I were to lose them, or they should be stolen from me, then must I needs be a wolf all my days, nothing could aid me save that the garments be brought to me again. So for my own safety I must needs keep the matter secret."

"Ah, my dear lord, why hide it from me? Surely thou hast no fear of me who love thee above all else in the world? Little love canst thou have for me! What have I done? What sin have I committed that thou should'st withdraw thy confidence? Thou wilt do well to tell me."

Thus she wept and entreated till at length the knight yielded, and told her all.

Wife," he said, "without the forest on the highway, at a cross road, is an old chapel wherein I have often found help and succour. Close to it, under a thick shrub, is a large stone with a hollow beneath it; under that stone I hide my garments till the enchantment hath lost its power and I may turn me homewards."

Now when the lady had heard this story fell out even her husband had it fell out even as her husband had foretold, for her love was changed to loathing and she was seized with great a dread and fear of him. She was terrified to be in his presence, yet he was her lord, and she knew not how she might escape from him.

Then she bethought her of a certain knight of that country, who had loved her long, and wooed her in vain ere she wedded her lord; and one time when her husband went forth, she sent for him in secret, and bade him come and give her counsel on a matter that troubled her much. When he came she bade him swear an oath to keep secret what she might tell him, and when he had sworn she told him all the story, and prayed him for the sake of the love he once bore her to free her from one who was neither beast nor man, and yet was both.

The knight, who loved her still, was ready to do all she might desire, and she said, "Tis but to steal his clothes, for then he can no more become a man, but must dwell in the forest as a wolf all his days, and someone will assuredly slay him." So he went forth, and did after her bidding, and brought her the garments, and she hid them away saying, "Now am I safe, and that monster can return no more to terrify me."

When the time went and on and her husband came not, the lady feigned to be anxious for his welfare, and she sent his men forth to seek him; they went through all the country but could find no trace of their lord, so at length they gave up the search, and all deemed had been slain on one of his mysterious journeys And when year had passed and the lady thought the wolf had surely been killed, she wedded the knight who had aided her and thought no more of the husband she had betrayed.

But the poor were-wolf roamed the forest in suffering and sorrow, for though a beast outwardly yet he had the heart and brain of a man, and knew well what had happened, and he grieved bitterly, for he had loved his wife truly and well.

Now chanced one day that the king it that land rode a-hunting in that very forest and the hounds came the track of the were-wolf and roused him from his lair and gave chase to him. All day he fled before them through the woodland, and at last when they were close upon him and he was in sore peril of being overtaken and torn in pieces the king came riding after the hounds, and the wolf swerved aside and fled to him, seizing him by the stirrup, and licking his foot in sign of submission.

The king was much astonished and, called to his companions to come swiftly. "See here, my lords," he said, "what think ye of this marvel? See how this beast entreats mercy of me; he hath the sense of a man! Drive off the dogs, for I will not have him injured. Turn we homewards, I take this beast in my peace and will hunt no more in this forest lest by chance he be slain."

With that they turned their bridles and rode homewards; but the wolf followed behind, and would not be driven back, even when they came to the royal castle. The king was greatly pleased, for he thought the matter strange and marvellous; no such tale had he ever heard before; and since he had taken a great liking for the beast he bade his knights not merely to do the wolf no harm, but to treat him with all care and kindness, on pain of losing the royal favour. So all day the wolf roamed the court, free among the knights, and at night he slept in the king's own chamber. Wherever the king went, there he would have his wolf go too, and all the courtiers made much of the beast, seeing that it pleased their lord, and finding that he did no harm to any man among them.

Now when long time had passed the king had occasion hold solemn court; he summoned all his barons from far and near, and among them came the knight who had betrayed the were-wolf, and wedded his lady; he had little thought that his rival was yet in life, still less that he was so near at hand. But as soon as the wolf beheld him he sprang upon him savagely, tearing him with his teeth, and would have slain him if the king had not called him off, and even then twice again he would have seized him.

Every one in the castle was astonished at the rage shown by the beast, which had always been so take and gentle, and a whisper went round that surely there must be something which no one knew against the knight, for the wolf would scarce have attacked him without cause. All the time the court lasted the wolf had to be kept in close guard. When at length it broke up the knight who had been attacked was one of the first to leave – and small marvel it were. But when the knight had gone the wolf was once more as tame and friendly as he had been from the first, and all the courtiers made a pet of him as they a had done aforetime, and forgot as time went on, that he had ever shown himself so savage.

At length the king bethought him that he would make progress through his kingdom, and the same time hunt for a while the forest where he had found the wolf. As his custom was he took the beast with him.

Now the lady, the were -wolf's treacherous wife, hearing that the king would abide some time in that part of country, prayed for an audience that she might win the royal favour by presenting rich gifts, for she knew well that the king loved not her second husband as he had loved the first.

The king appointed a day and hour for the audience, but when the lady entered the presence chamber suddenly the wolf flew upon her, and before any could hinder had bitten the nose from off her face. The courtiers drew out their weapons and would have slain the beast, when a wise man, one of the king's councillors, stayed them. "Sire," he said, "hearken to me – this wolf has been long with us, there is not one of us here who has not been near to him, and caressed him, over and over again; yet not a man of us has he ever touched, or even shown ill-will to any. But two has he ever attacked, this lady here and the lord, her husband. Now, sire, bethink thee well – this lady was the wife of the knight thou didst hold dear aforetime, and who was lost long since, no man knowing what came to him. Take my counsel, put this lady in guard and question her closely as to whether she can give any reason why the wolf should hate her. Many a marvel hath come to pass in Brittany, and methinks there is something stranger than we wot of here."

The king thought the old lord's counsel good; he caused the lady and her husband to be put in prison apart, and questioned separately with threats if they kept silence; till at length the lady, terrified, confessed, how she had betrayed her first husband by causing his garments to be stolen from him when he was in a wolf's shape Since that time he had disappeared; she knew not whether he were alive dead, but she thought that perchance this wolf was he. When the king heard this he commanded them to fetch the garments belonging to the lost knight, whether it were pleasing to the lady or no; and when they were brought he laid them before the wolf and waited to see what would chance.

But the wolf made as if he saw them not, and the wise councillor said, "Sire, if this beast be indeed a were-wolf he will not change shapes while there are any to behold him; since it is only with great pain and difficulty he can do so. Bid them take wolf and garments into thine own chamber, and fasten the doors upon him; then leave him for a while, and we shall see if he become man."

The king thought this counsel good, and he himself took the beast into his chamber and made the doors fast.

Then they waited space that seemed long enough to the king and when the old lord told him might well do so, he took two nobles with him and unlocked the doors, and entered, and lo, on the king's couch lay the long lost knight in a deep slumber.

The king ran to him and embraced him warmly; and when the first wonder had somewhat passed, he bade him take back all the lands of which he had been robbed, and over and above he bestowed upon him many rich gifts.

The treacherous wife and her second husband were banished from the country; many years they lived in a strange land and had children and grand-children – but all their descendants might be known by this, that the maidens were born without noses, so that they won the surname of *énasées* (noseless).

And the old books say that this adventure was verily true, and that it was in order that the memory of it should be preserved to all time that the Bretons put it in verse, and called it "The Lai of the Were-Wolf."

"Melion," in *Tales from the Old French*, trans. Isabel Butler (Constable, 1910), pp. 73–92.

In the days when Arthur reigned, he who conquered lands and dealt out rich gifts to knights and barons, there was with him a young lord whose name, I have heard, was Melion. Full brave and courteous was he, and made himself beloved of all; and he was of right great chivalry and goodly fellowship.

The king had a full rich following, and throughout all the world he was famed for courtesy and prowess, and bounty and largess. Now on that day when all the knights made their vows – and know ye that well they held to them – this same Melion pledged him to one that thereafter brought him sore mischance. For he said he would never love any maid, howsoever noble and fair, who had ever loved any other man, or had been talked of by any. For a long time matters went on in this wise: those who had heard the vow spread it abroad in many places, and told it to the damsels, and all maids who heard had great hatred of Melion. And they who were in the royal chambers and served the queen, and of such there were above a hundred, held council concerning the a matter, and swore they would never love him, or hold speech with him. No lady desired to look on him, or any maid to talk with him.

Now when Melion heard this he was right heavy thereof; no more did he desire to seek adventure, and no will had he to bear arms. Full heavy he was and sorrowful, and he lost somewhat of his fame. Now the king had news of the matter and had great grief thereof, and he called the knight to him, and spoke with him. "Melion," saith King Arthur, "what hath befallen thy wisdom and thy worth and thy chivalry? Tell me what aileth thee and conceal not. If thou would have I land or manor, or any other thing – so that it be in my realm – it shall be thine according to thy desire; for gladly would I lighten thy sorrow," so saith the king to him, "if that I might. Now upon the sea shore I have castle, in all the world is not such another; fair it is with wood and river and forest which are full dear to thee, and this castle will I give thee for thy cheer; good delight may ye find therein."

So the king gave it to him in fee; and Melion gave him thanks thereof, and went away to his castle, taking with him an hundred knights. Right pleasant was that country to him, and so was the forest that he held full dear; and when he had lived there a year through, he grew greatly to love the land, for he sought no disport but he found it in the forest.

Now on a day, Melion and his foresters rode to the chase; with him he took his huntsmen, who loved him with true love, inasmuch as he was their liege lord, and all honour was found in him. Soon they came upon a great stag, and forth- right let loose the dogs upon him. There- after it fell that Melion drew rein amid a heath that he might the better listen for his pack. With him was a squire, and in his leash he held two greyhounds; and anon, across the heath, the which was green and fair, he saw come a damsel on a fair palfrey, and right rich was her array. For she was clothed in scarlet samite, laced full seemly, and about her neck hung a mantle of ermine, never did queen wear better. Well fashioned was she of body, and comely of shoulder; her hair was yellow, her mouth small and shapely, and red as any rose; gray-blue were her eyes, and clear and laughing; right fair was all her seeming, full winsome and gracious; and all alone without fellows came she.

Melion rideth to meet her, and courteously he greeted her: "Sweet, I salute you in the name of the Glorious One, of Jesus the King; tell me of what house you are, and what bringeth you hither." And the damsel maketh answer: "Even that will I tell you in all truth: I am of good parentry and born of noble lineage, and from Ireland have I come to you. Know ye that I am much your lover. Never have I loved any man save you only, and never will love any; so great praise have I heard of you that no other save you alone have I ever desired to love, and never shall I feel love for any other."

Now when Melion heard that his vows were fulfilled, he clipped her about the middle, and kissed her thirty times over. Then he called together his folk, and told them the adventure; and they looked upon the damsel, and in all the realm was none so fair. So Melion took her to his castle, and the people rejoiced greatly. He married her with great splendor, and made great cheer thereof, that for fifteen whole days the tourneys lasted.

For three years he dearly cherished her, and during those three years they had two sons, whereof he was right glad and joyful. And on a day he rode into the for- est, taking with him his much loved wife, and a squire to carry his bow and arrows. He soon came upon a stag, and they pursued it, but fled away with lowered head. Thereafter they came into heath, and in a thicket the knight saw standing a right great stag; laughing, he looked down at his wife.

"Dame," saith he, "if I would, I could show you right great stag. Look ye, he is yonder in that thicket." "By my faith, Melion," said she, "know ye that if I have not the flesh of that stag never more will I eat morsel." Therewith she falleth in a swoon from her palfrey. Melion raised her up, but might not comfort her, and bitterly she began to weep. "Dame," saith he, "mercy in God's name. Weep no more, I beg of thee. Here in my hand I have a ring; see it now on my finger. Two gems it hath in its setting, one white and one red, never were any seen of like fashion. Now hear ye a great marvel of them: if ye touch me with the white, and lay it upon my head when I am stripped naked, I shall become a great wolf, big of body; and for your love I will take the stag, and bring you of its flesh. But I pray you, in God's name, that ye await me here, and keep for me my garments. With you I leave my life and my death; for I shall have no comfort if I be not touched with the other gem, for never again shall I become man." There- with he called his squire to take off his shoes; the youth stepped forward and unshod him, and Melion went into the wood and laid aside his garments, and remained wholly naked, save that he wrapped his cloak about him. Now when his wife saw him stripped of all his raiment, she touched him with the ring, and he became a great wolf, big of body. So fell he into sore mischance.

The wolf set off running full swiftly to the place where he saw the stag lie; forthwith he set himself upon the track, – now great will be the strife before he hath it, taken and caught and had its flesh. Meantime the lady saith to the squire: "Now let us leave him to take his fill of the chase." Therewith she got her to horseback; no whit did she tarry, but she took with her the squire, and straightway turned her towards Ireland, her own land. She came to the haven, where she found a ship; forthwith she addressed her to the sailors, and they carried her to Dublin, a city upon the seashore, that held of her father, the king of Ireland, Now hath she all that she asks. And so soon as she came to the port, she was received with great joy: with this let us leave her, and speak we again of Melion.

Melion, as he pursued the stag, pressed wondrous hard, and at length he drove it into a heath where he soon brought it down. Then he took a great collop of it, and carried it away in his mouth. Swiftly he returned again to the place where he had left his wife, but did not find her, for she had taken her way towards Ireland. Right sorry was he, and knoweth not what to do when he findeth her not in that spot. But none the less, though he was a wolf, yet had he the sense and memory of a man. So he lurked and waited until evening fell; and he saw men loading a ship that was to set sail that night and go straightway to Ireland. Thither he went, and waited till it grew quite dark, when he entered into it at adventure, for he recked little of his life. There he crouched down under a wattle, and hid and concealed himself. Meantime, the sailors bestirred themselves, for the wind was fair, and so they set forth towards Ireland, and each had that he desired. They spread aloft their sails, and steered by the sky and stars; and the next day, at dawn, they saw the shore of Ireland. And when they were come into port Mellon tarried no longer, but issued out of his hiding-place, and sprang from the ship to the sand. The sailors cried out upon him, and threw their gear at him, and one struck him with a staff, so that well nigh had they captured him. Glad was he when he escaped them; and he went up into a mountain, and looked long over the land where he knew his enemies dwelt. Still had he the collop he had brought from his own do- main, but now, in that his hunger was great, he ate it; sorely had the sea wearied him.

And then he went away into a forest, where he found cows and oxen, and of these he killed and destroyed many. So began his war, and in this first onset he slew more than a hundred. The folk that dwelt in the greenwood saw the damage he wrought to the beasts, and ran flocking into the city, and told and recounted to the king that there was a wolf in the forest that wasted all the land, and had slain many of their horned beasts. And for all this they blamed the king.

So Melion ran through the forests and waste places, and over the mountains, until he joined company with ten other wolves; and he so cajoled and blandished them that they followed after him, and did all his desire. Far and wide they wandered through the land, and sore mis- handled both men and women. So lived they a year long, and wasted all that region, harrying the land and slaying the folk. Well knew they how to guard them- selves, and by no means could the king entrap them.

One night they had wandered far, and wearied and spent, they lay in a wood near Dublin, on a little hill by the sea shore. Beyond the wood was a meadow, and all round about was plain country. There they entered to rest, but there they will be ensnared and betrayed. They had been seen of a countryman, who ran forthright to the king: "Lord," saith he, "in the wood yonder lie the eleven wolves." And when the king heard him he was right glad, and spoke to his men of the matter.

Now the king called together his men: "Barons," saith he, "hearken to this: know ye of a sooth this man hath seen all eleven wolves in my forest." Then round about the wood they let spread the snares with which they were wont to take the wild boar. And when the snares were spread, the king went thither without tarrying, and his daughter said she would come with him to see the chase of the wolves. Straightway they went into the forest in all quiet and secretness, and surrounded the whole wood, for they had folk in plenty, who bore axes and staves, and some their naked swords. Then they cheered on their dogs to the number of a thousand, and these soon found the wolves. Melion saw that he was betrayed, well knew he that sore mischance had befallen him. The wolves were hard pressed by the dogs, and in their flight they came upon the snares, and all were torn to pieces and slain, save only Melion. He sprang over the traps, and fled into a great wood; so by his wit he escaped them. Meantime the folk went back to the town, and the king made great joy. Greatly he rejoiced that he had ten of the eleven wolves; well was he revenged on them, in that one only had escaped. But his daughter said: "That one was the biggest. And yet will he work you woe."

When Melion had stolen away he went up into a mountain; full heavy and sorrowful was he because of the wolves he had lost. Great travail had been his, but anon he shall have help. Now at this time Arthur came into Ireland to make peace, for there was war in the land, and he was fain to bring the foes into accord, in that it was his desire to subdue the Romans, and he wished to lead these men with him to battle. The king came privately, bringing with him no great host; some twenty knights only had he in his train. Sweet was the weather, and fair the wind, and the ship was full rich and great; trusty was her helmsman, and full well was she dight, and plenteously garnished with men and arms. Their shields were hung along the side, – right well Melion knew them. First he spied the shield of Gawain, then saw he that of Twain, and then the shield of Idel the king; and all this was dear and pleasant to him. Then saw and knew he the shield of Arthur, and wit ye well, he had great joy thereof; glad and blithe was he, for he hoped yet to have mercy. So came they sailing towards the land; but now the wind was contrary to them, and they might not make the port, whereof they were right sorry. turned they towards another haven some two leagues from the city, where, of old, had been a great castle which was now ruined; and when they were come thither, darkness fell, and it was night.

So the king is come into port; sore wearied and spent is he, for the ship had much discomforted him. And he called his seneschal: "Go forth," saith he, "and see where I may lie this night." The seneschal turned back into the ship, and called the chamberlain, saying: "Come forth with me, and let us make ready the king's lodging." So they issued out of the ship, and came to the castle; and they had two candles brought thither, and forthwith had them lighted; and they let bring carpets and coverlets, and speedily was the chamber well garnished. Then the king issued forth, and went straight to his lodging, and when he came therein right glad was he to find it so fair.

Now Melion had not tarried, but straightway went to meet the ship. Near the moat he halted; right well he knew them all, and well he knoweth that if he hath not comfort of the king, he shall come to his death in Ireland. Yet he knoweth not what to do, for he is a wolf, and so hath no power of speech; yet none the less will he go thither, and set him- self at adventure. When he came to the king's door, right well knew he all the barons; for nought staid he, but hath passed straight in to the king, though it be at the hazard of death. At the king's feet he cast himself down,- nor would he rise; whereof, lo you, Arthur hath great wonder, and he saith: "A marvel see I; this wolf hath come hither to seek me. Now see ye well that he is of my household, and woe to the man who shall lay hands on or hurt him."

When supper was made ready and the barons had washed, the king likewise washed and seated himself. Napkins were spread before them; and the king called to Idel and made him sit at his side. And Melion lay at the king's feet, – well knew he all the barons. Oftentimes the king looked down at him, and anon gave him a piece of bread the which he took and began to eat. Then greatly the king marvelleth, and saith to King Idel: "Look now, know ye of a sooth this wolf knoweth our ways." Then the king gave him a piece of roast meat, and gladly the wolf ate it; whereat Gawain saith: "Lords, look you, this wolf is out of all nature." And the barons all say one to another that never saw they so courteous a wolf. Thereupon the king let wine be set before the wolf in a basin, and so soon as he seeth it, he drinketh it, and certes, he was full fain of it; good plenty he drank of that wine, as the king well saw.

Now when they arose from meat and the barons had washed, they issued out upon the sands. And always the wolf followed after the king, and might not be kept from him, wheresoever he went. And when the king desired to go to rest, he commanded that his bed be made ready. So he withdrew him to sleep, for he was sore wearied; but with him went the wolf, and he lay at the king's feet, nor might any man dispart them.

Passing glad was the king of Ireland in that Arthur had come to him; great joy had he thereof. Early at dawn, he rose, and went to the haven together with his barons. Straight to the haven they came riding, and each company gave fair welcome to other. Arthur showed the king much love, and did him much honour. When he saw him come before him, he would not be proud, but raised him up and kissed him. And anon the horses were made ready, and without any tarrying they mounted and rode towards the city.

The king mounteth upon his palfrey, and good convoy he hath of his wolf, who would not be disparted from him, but kept always at his stirrup. Passing glad was the king of Ireland because of Arthur, and the company was rich and mighty. So came they to Dublin, and lighted down from their horses before the high palace. And when Arthur went up into the donjon tower, the wolf held him by the lap of his garment; and when King Arthur was seated, the wolf lay at his feet.

The king hath looked down at his wolf, and hath called him up close to the dais. Side by side sit the two kings, and right rich is their following; right well are the barons served, for throughout all the household great plenty is dealt out. But Melion looketh about him, and midway- down the hall he saw him who had brought thither his wife; well knew he that she had crossed the sea and was come into Ireland. Forthwith he seized the youth by the shoulder – no stand can he make against the wolf – but Melion brought him to the ground amid the hall. And he would have straightway killed and destroyed him, had it not been for the king's sergeants, who ran thither in sore disorder; and from out all the palace they brought rods and staves, and anon they would have slain the wolf had not Arthur cried out: "By my faith, ill befall whoso layeth hands on him, for know ye, the wolf is my own."

Then saith Idel, the son of Irien: "Lords, ye misdo herein; the wolf would not have set upon the youth, and if he had not sore hated him." "Thou sayest well, Idel," quoth the king; and therewith he left the dais, and passed down the hall to the wolf, and saith to the youth: "Thou shalt tell us why he set upon thee, or else thou shalt die." Melion looked up at the king, and gripped the youth so hard he cried out, and prayed the king's mercy, and said he would make known the truth. So now he telleth the king how the lady had brought him thither, and how she had touched Melion with the ring, and how she had borne it away with her into Ireland; so hath he spoken and told all, even as it befell.

Then Arthur bespoke the king: "Now know I well this is sooth, and right glad am I of my baron; let the ring be given over to me, and likewise thy daughter who stole it away; evilly hath she be- trayed her lord." So the king went thence, and entered into his daughter's chamber, and with him went King Idel, and he so coaxed and cajoled her that she gave him the ring, and he brought it to King Arthur. Now so soon as Melion saw the ring right well he knew it; and he came to the king, and knelt down and kissed his two feet. King Arthur would fain have touched him with the ring, but Gawain would not so have it: "Fair uncle," saith he, "do not so, but rather lead him into a chamber apart where ye twain may be alone together, that he have not shame ofthe folk."

Then the king called to him Gawain, and Idel likewise he took with him: so led he the wolf into a privy chamber, and when they had come within, shut the door fast. Then he laid the ring upon the wolf's head, and all his visage changed, and his face became human. So turned he to man again, and he spoke, and fell down at the king's feet. They covered him over with a mantle; and when they saw him very man, they made great joy. But the king fell a-weeping for pity, and weeping asked him how it fell that by sin he had lost him. And then he let summon his chamberlain, and bade him bring rich raiment. Fairly they clothed and arrayed him, and so led him into the hall; and all they of the household greatly marvelled when they saw Melion come in amongst them.

Then the king of Ireland led forth his daughter, and gave her over to Arthur that he might do as he would with her, whether it were to slay or to burn her. Saith Melion: "I will touch her with the ring, nor will I forbear." But Arthur said to him: "Do not so, rather let her be, for the sake of thy fair children." All the barons likewise besought him, and Melion accorded it.

Now King Arthur abode in Ireland until he had assuaged the war; then he went again into his own land, and with him took Melion; full glad and blithe was he thereof. But his wife he left in Ireland, and commanded her to the devil; never again would he love her for that she had done him such wrong; never would he take her unto him again, rather would he have let burn or hang her. And he said: "Whoso believeth his wife in all things cannot help but come into mischance at the end, for it is not meet to set your trust in all her sayings."

True is the lay of Melion, so all good barons declare.

"Biclarel," in *Melion and Biclarel: Two Old French Werwolf Lays*, ed. and trans. Amanda Hopkins (Liverpool Online Series Critical Editions of French Texts, 2005), pp. 84–105.

He is very foolish who marries
A fickle wench:
It is just not worth it for him to suffer
[4] And to expose himself to all that shame
With great risk to soul and body,
From which he will never be free;
And he who understood women's hearts well
[8] Would never be in such peril.
But, on account of this, no-one ever understands them,
For I'll tell you one thing, and you'll do another.
You can know it through Biclarel,
[12] Who will tell you the truth of it very well.
Biclarel was a knight –
Strong and brave and fierce,
Full of nobility and virtue –
[16] Of the household of King Arthur.
But he could be greatly blamed for this:
That he believed what his wife said;
There are still a great many such men.
[20] Love attacked Biclarel greatly.

He gave his heart to a lady,
And she made him love her so violently
That he trusted in her so greatly
[24] That he committed himself to marrying her.
Madness has taken hold of a man completely
When he loses his good freedom
And binds himself to spend his life
[28] Doing what he should have refused.
Biclarel married the lady,
And whatever she said he praised;
He loved her very much and esteemed her highly
[32] And she him, so she used to say.
As it pleased God, Biclarel
Had a trait that he hid
And that no-one but he would have known,
[36] Had it not been for his foolishness.
It is rare that someone hears of such a trait,
Because every month he became a beast;
Two or three whole days
[40] He would live as a beast in the forest;
He would dwell amongst other beasts
And eat the raw flesh of beasts,
And in the form of a big, strong wolf,
[44] With a sturdy hide and bony limbs;
He did not lose his wits because of this,
Nor his memory or his intelligence.
I am telling you the truth, complete
[48] And certain, according to authority.
It is set down in the book of the Grail;
You will hear it there, if you read all of it.
He had stayed in the forest for three days
[52] When he returned to the lodging.
When Biclarel came back from the forest,
He kept near him his wife
Who had given her heart entirely
[56] To a knight whom she loved.
Then she approached him with guile,
And tackled him through deception
With great humility, and both tears and laughter.
[60] Piteously, she began to speak to him:
'My lord, when God, who created everything,
Granted our marriage
And willed that between us we should be
[64] One body and have one heart,
One blood and one will,

The one should thus be grafted in the other,
Without concealment and without deception.
[68] Thus we two must honour each other.
If it is not like this, we shall be doing wrong
And transgressing greatly against God.
As for me, I am not transgressing in this:
[72] In heart and body I am your friend
Without concealing action or desire;
Never was my heart tempted
To hide from you anything that I feel.
[76] Do not suppose that I am lying to you:
If I were to hide one of my thoughts from you,
I believe that I should die in that same hour.
God did not wish to join us
[80] So that we could conceal our thoughts from each other,
Nor be sly or secretive,
But to be open with one another,
For if you hide anything from me,
[84] You will have the worst of it in the end.
When wife and husband are joined
And one takes his possessions away from the other,
And each keeps his private purse,
[88] They cannot hold the true path,
Nor can they come to a good end;
And, like two companions, each one
Wishes to keep his own moneybox;
[92] They cannot remain without grief for very long.
Companionship must be uniform,
It must not be concealment or mastery,
Because when one hides or conceals
[96] Good companionship dissolves,
Nor will it leave until such time
As one of them takes to deception
Out of contempt or malice.
[100] Companionship breaks down through such fault,
And God himself will abandon them
Just as soon as each of them goes his own way.
As for me, I will do nothing of the sort;
[104] I have and know nothing that I do not tell you,
But you know something and behave like this,
Whereby you let companionship down,
In that you hide your whole heart from me;
[108] God will hate you for it, I fear.
I shall pay for your sin
And yet I am not in any way tarnished by it.'

'Why', said Biclarel, 'did you
[112] Lie about this if you have no knowledge of it?
If I have done anything wrong, say so,
And my answer will be enough to absolve me.'
'By my faith', she said, 'let it be said!
[116] You have some hideaway or other
And some hidden and secret path,
Where no one sees you
Except those whom you wish,
[120] And you hide this matter from me.
I do not know if you go there to good purpose,
But, as for me, I think it is for wickedness,
And I wish to say this to you:
[124] From me, who am your friend,
How can you ever hide
Your comings and goings?
You are on the lookout for another beloved instead of me.
[128] Certainly, my lord, it grieves me;
I have very great suffering in my heart through it,
If it is true that I ever knew you.
For I am well separated from you,
[132] When you side against me
And take your hidden paths
Which should be open to me.
Truly, henceforth I wish to live no longer
[136] Since you do not want to accord with me in love.'
Then the lady began to weep
And thereupon to beg him urgently for death,
Saying: 'I am very ill-fated.
[140] It would have profited me more to have my heart removed
Than to have taken a husband who hates me,
And who knows no reason for it.'
Biclarel was greatly astonished
[144] When he heard his wife speak in this way.
'Lady', he said, 'never think
That I have any beloved except you;
I would rather be cut to pieces
[148] Than ever be defiled thus.
But I have a secret of my own
That no one knows or guesses –
I would not speak of it except to God –
[152] For I should nevermore have honour,
Nor should I be esteemed in any court
If everyone ever knew of it.
You should not take offence about it

[156] If you do not know about this matter,
Because I am not wronging you in anything
Nor against anyone else, as far as I know.'
When his words had been spoken,
[160] He had not been forgiven by the lady
Who began to cry intently
As she took in his speech.
'My lord', she said, 'now things are worse:
[164] Now you take me for a person of little worth,
An idiot and a gossip,
A wicked and quarrelsome woman,
Evil, weak, full of anger,
[168] When you dare not tell me your secrets.
Now we must each consider ourselves to be living alone:
You will take your bed and lodgings by yourself
And will run your own affairs,
[172] And put your trust in someone else.
Since I am not worthy
To know, you must have someone else.
I am deceived above all women,
[176] And am both shamed and dishonoured
When I have lost both soul and body;
Now death is very slow in coming to me.'
When Biclarel saw what was happening,
[180] And realized that he could not hold out,
'Lady', he said, 'you shall know it,
But you will have it on this condition,
And you will swear it to me from your heart,
[184] That you will speak of it to no one.'
'My lord', she said, 'you will not lose by it:
May you cleave my neck if I speak of it.
How can you think I will speak about it?
[188] You are my heart and my life,
My hope and my expectation;
I should have lost God's faith
And be hell's gatekeeper
[192] If I were to reveal your confidences.
My honour lies in your confidences:
Everyone, great and lesser, knows this.
Your secret is my livelihood,
[196] It is the thing that honours and nurtures me;
Your secret is the basis of my life;
It is the thing that entirely sustains me;
I should fall into a very bad state
[200] If I were to reveal your secret.

I should now rightly be a wife,
But at present I am not:
In this case I am not a wife at all;
[204] I should prefer to lose my life
Than to reveal your secret
Or ever cause you shame.
You have never yet seen
[208] That my neighbours knew
Anything of your wrath nor your anger,
Because I only have to tell them,
And surely I deserve praise
[212] For remaining silent about that which never occurred,
Because many women confirm and swear
Things that they never knew.
I am not of such a character
[216] Because I do not care to fabricate.
You have led a wicked life
When something is being hidden from me.'
Then Biclarel revealed to her
[220] What he had always hidden.
'Lady', he said, 'I have such a destiny,
Without suffering or fear,
For each month I become a beast.
[224] I remain in the woods and the forest;
I go and hide in a secluded place
And I take off all my clothes,
And then, for two or three days, I am
[228] A wild beast in the woods;
And as long as I am there, I eat
Raw flesh, like other beasts.
When I have been there, I come back
[232] And come out from that same secret spot.
But anyone who took my clothes away from me
Would cause me very great hardship,
For I should remain a beast
[236] Until I regained them
Or until I had to die,
Since no one would be able to save me.
And for that reason I set out secretly,
[240] So that no-one steals my clothes from me.
Now I have told you my secret;
Now may you willingly accept
That no-one should learn of my trait,
[244] Nor ever know about my condition.'
When the lady heard this,

She feared and suspected him the less because of it,
And she thought: 'Now I have achieved
[248] What I have sought for a long time.'
And she said: 'I've got what I want.
May you be my beloved and I yours:
I believe everything you tell me.
[252] May you be free from all ill wishes.
My heart is so kind and bountiful
That I know nothing other than how to make peace.'
With that she fell silent and said no more;
[256] She kept what she heard in her heart.
When the time came that he had to go,
Biclarel left for the woods.
His wife paid very little heed,
[260] But as she noticed him leave,
She followed him carefully
Until she saw him at his secret place.
She saw clearly where he put his clothes;
[264] She saw clearly his method and his manner.
She took his clothes and carried them away with her
And was very happy and cheerful.
She said: 'I am rid of my husband,
[268] In order to be with my beloved.'
Then she let her beloved know
That he could now take his pleasure
And that her husband was dead,
[272] And he need never fear him.
The knight whose beloved she was
Made no delay as soon as he heard;
His beloved whom he loved so much
[276] He married very willingly,
And he lived with her for a long time.
Biclarel returned to his clothing;
When he did not find it, he was dismayed.
[280] At once he saw that he had been deceived
By his wife who had betrayed him;
And then he withdrew into the woods,
And lived like a beast
[284] As best he could.
I shall cease telling you of him,
And you will hear more about him later.
I wish to tell you again about King Arthur,
[288] Who was accustomed to hold a feast on all holy days,
Pentecost, All Saints, Christmas,
For which he was praised by everyone;

He would gather together all the barons
[292] Whom he remembered in his heart.
Ladies and squires would come there
And all those who held lands from him,
Such was his commandment.
[296] One Pentecost it happened
That the king wished to go hunting
To amuse himself on his great feast day.
Three or four days before that day,
[300] As much for the hunting as for his enjoyment,
And to catch venison
To make up his ample provisions,
He made a great effort to hunt
[304] And took plenty of hounds there.
They rushed into the woods without hesitation.
Biclarel was in the forest
In the form of a terrifying wild beast.
[308] The dogs that were in the thicket
And making a great commotion
Pursued this beast;
They followed it strenuously.
[312] Biclarel, who was fierce and strong,
Definitely did not wait for the hounds,
But did his utmost to escape.
He was not stripped of his wits,
[316] Even though he had changed into a beast.
He came running towards the king,
The dogs following after him.
He went straight to Arthur's stirrup
[320] And there he remained completely still.
He put on a humble mien towards him.
He aroused very great pity in the king
When he saw the beast appearing
[324] That came to him for safety,
And said: 'Beast, rely on me
And I shall protect you from the dogs.'
Then he drove the dogs from him,
[328] And immediately Biclarel prostrated himself.
Pity took hold of King Arthur;
He began to call his knights.
The beast was on its knees,
[332] For it was submitting itself humbly.
Everyone marvelled greatly at it;
Each made the sign of the cross many times,
And all said openly

[336] That this was of great significance:
'This beast has intelligence.
King, take pity on it now;
Do not let it be killed
[340] By the hunters nor overcome by the dogs.'
And the king granted them this:
Thereupon, it was under the king's protection;
He went back to his city.
[344] The beast stayed beside him all the time:
It placed itself at his stirrup.
All the time it displayed humility,
Down every track, down every path.
[348] The king looked at it gladly
And did not despise it at all.
It lay at the door of his bedchamber.
The feast-day arrived, the knights arrived
[352] And conducted themselves very nobly.
There were ladies and knights,
More than two thousand two hundred.
Biclarel's wife was there,
[356] Who was newly married;
She was both noble and honoured
In silk and gilded brocade.
She conducted herself very nobly,
[360] As befits the high estate she held.
There were many people of all kinds.
Tables were set out in the hall;
Each knight seated himself
[364] And had his wife next to him.
The beast followed the king constantly
And pleased him very much.
Then the beast entered the palace
[368] With outstretched neck, at a single bound;
It saw at the table its wife,
Who sat amongst many other people,
Well adorned and seated highly.
[372] It grasped her in its teeth by the hair,
And gave her a great blow in the middle of her face:
And nearly mutilated her face.
And pushed her right down to the ground;
[376] It would soon have killed her
When the knights ran to her,
Who were absolutely astounded by this.
They would have used great violence against it,
[380] If it had not been for the king's love.

When the king learned of this deed,
He was extremely surprised
And said: 'Never without reason
[384] Would the beast have attacked her.
Now let us see what will happen
And what the beast will do next,
That behaves so humbly towards everyone
[388] Except towards this woman alone.'
That evening everyone came back to sup;
They took their places at the tables and on the dais;
But the lady was not there
[392] Because she was too afraid,
For she knew about the beast,
Who it was and what was in its heart.
She realized her crime against it;
[396] For this reason she would not agree to come.
The king commanded that the beast
Should roam around amidst the feast,
To find out if it distressed anyone
[400] Or if it would do harm to anyone.
It was done as the king said;
The beast gave no sign to anyone:
It lay down and humbled itself before everyone,
[404] As it never wished anything but good to all.
But when it did not find its wife,
Who had stripped it of all honour,
It began to make loud lamentation;
[408] Then it began to leave the palace
And went down the steps;
It went into the town.
The lady, who was wounded,
[412] Knew perfectly well why it was,
So she had sought and asked leave to depart
For fear that she might fare worse.
Down the steps went the beast
[416] That had not yet achieved its goal.
It searched until it found her;
She had mounted a horse
Because she wished to leave.
[420] As soon as the beast saw her,
It threw itself at her chest, grasping her with its teeth;
It knocked her from the horse down to the ground
And very quickly leapt on her.
[424] It would soon have killed and devoured her,
When the people rescued her,

And she cried: 'Ah!'
The beast backed away
[428] And began to make great lamentation,
And cried and howled loudly,
So that there was no one from the palace
Who did not marvel at it.
[432] Even the king crossed himself
And swore that he must know
The truth of the situation.
At once he ordered the lady to be seized
[436] And had her put in cruel fetters,
And he swore that he would put her to death
Or she would tell him the truth.
When she heard the king,
[440] She complied in order to save her life.
She confessed the whole truth,
Both how she had betrayed her lord,
Through her lies and through her trickery,
[444] And even where she hid his clothing.
Everyone was most astounded
When they heard her words.
They brought Biclarel there,
[448] Who was so afflicted by his wife.
The king had the clothes brought:
Biclarel scrambled into them and became a man.
Then he recounted all his misfortune,
[452] How his wife had overcome him.
He petitioned that she be killed,
And consequently she was placed between walls
From which she could never come out.
[456] This adventure happened at that time.
Thus you see how stupidly he behaves
Who reveals to his wife
Secrets that should be hidden,
[460] If he does not wish them revealed to everyone.

F.A. Milne and A. Nutt, "Arthur and Gorlagon," *Folklore* 15:1 (March 25, 1904), pp. 40–67.

Arthur and Gorlagon

(1) At the City of the Legions King Arthur was keeping the renowned festival of Pentecost, to which he invited the great men and nobles of the whole of his kingdom, and when the solemn rites had been duly performed he bade them to a banquet, furnished with everything thereto pertaining. And as they were joyfully

partaking of the feast of rich abundance, Arthur, in his excessive joy, threw his arms around the Queen, who was sitting beside him, and embracing her, kissed her very affectionately in the sight of all. But she was dumbfounded at his conduct, and, blushing deeply, looked up at him and asked why he had kissed her thus at such an unusual place and hour.

Arthur: Because amidst all my riches I have nothing so pleasing and amidst all my delights nothing so sweet, as thou art.

The Queen: Well, if, as you say, you love me so much, you evidently think that you know my heart and my affection.

Arthur: I doubt not that your heart is well disposed towards me, and I certainly think that your affection is absolutely known to me.

The Queen: You are undoubtedly mistaken, Arthur, for you acknowledge that you have never yet fathomed either the nature or the heart of a woman.

Arthur: I call heaven to witness that if up to now they have lain hid from me, I will exert myself, and sparing no pains, I will never taste food until by good hap I fathom them.

So when the banquet was ended Arthur called to him Caius, his sewer, and said, "Caius, do you and Walwain my nephew mount your horses and accompany me on the business to which I am hastening. But let the rest remain and entertain my guests in my stead until I return." Caius and Walwain at once mounted their horses as they were bidden, and hastened with Arthur to a certain king famed for his wisdom, named Gargol, who reigned over the neighbouring country; and on the third day they reached a certain valley, quite worn out, for since leaving home they had not tasted food nor slept, but had ever ridden on uninterruptedly night and day. Now immediately on the further side of that valley there was a lofty mountain, surrounded by a pleasant wood, in whose recesses was visible a very strong fortress built of polished stone. And Arthur, when he saw it at a distance, commanded Caius to hasten on before him with all speed, and bring back word to him to whom the town belonged. So Caius, urging on his steed, hastened forward and entered the fortress, and on his return met Arthur just as he was entering the outer trench, and told him that the town belonged to King Gargol, to whom they were making their way. Now it so happened that King Gargol had just sat down at table to dine; and Arthur, entering his presence on horseback, courteously saluted him and those who were feasting with him. And King Gargol said to him, "Who art thou? and from whence? And wherefore hast thou entered into our presence with such haste?"

Arthur: "I am Arthur," he replied, "the King of Britain: and I wish to learn from you what are the *heart, the nature, and the ways of women*, for I have very often heard that you are well skilled in matters of this kind."

Gargol: Yours is a weighty question, Arthur, and there are very few who know how to answer it. But take my advice now, dismount and eat with me, and rest to-day, for I see that you are overwrought with your toilsome journey; and to-morrow I will tell you what I know of the matter.

Arthur denied that he was overwrought, pledging himself withal that he would never eat until he had learnt what he was in search of. At last, however, pressed by the King and by the company who were feasting with him, he assented, and, having dismounted, he sat at table on the seat which had been placed for him opposite the King. But as soon as it was dawn, Arthur, remembering the promise which had been made to him, went to King Gargol and said, "O my dear King, make known to me, I beg, that which you promised yesterday you would tell me to-day."

Gargol:	You are displaying your folly, Arthur. Until now I thought you were a wise man: as to the heart, the nature, and the ways of woman, no one ever had a conception of what they are, and I do not know that I can give you any information on the subject. But I have a brother. King Torleil by name, whose kingdom borders on my own. He is older and wiser than I am: and indeed, if there is any one skilled in this matter, about which you are so anxious to know, I do not think it has escaped him. Seek him out, and desire him on my account to tell you what he knows of it.

So having bidden Gargol farewell, Arthur departed, and instantly continuing his journey arrived after a four days' march at King Torleil's, and as it chanced found the King at dinner. And when the King had exchanged greetings with him and asked him who he was, Arthur replied that he was King of Britain, and had been sent to the King by his brother King Gargol, in order that the King might explain to him a matter, his ignorance of which had obliged him to approach the royal presence.

Torleil:	What is it?
Arthur:	I have applied my mind to investigate the heart, the nature, and the ways of women, and have been unable to find anyone to tell me what they are. Do you therefore, to whom I have been sent, instruct me in these matters, and if they are known to you, do not keep them back from me.
Torleil:	Yours is a weighty question, Arthur, and there are few who know how to answer it. Wherefore, as this is not the time to discuss such matters, dismount and eat, and rest to-day, and to-morrow I will tell you what I know about them.

Arthur replied, "I shall be able to eat enough by-and-by. By my faith, I will never eat until I have learned that which I am in search of." Pressed, however, by the King and by those who were sitting at table with him, he at length reluctantly consented to dismount, and sat down at the table opposite the King. But in the morning he came to King Torleil and began to ask him to tell what he had promised. Torleil confessed that he knew absolutely nothing about the matter, and directed Arthur to his third brother. King Gorlagon, who was older than himself, telling him that he had no doubt that Gorlagon was mighty in the knowledge of the things he was inquiring into, if indeed it was certain that anyone had any knowledge of them. So Arthur hastened without delay to his destined goal, and after two days reached the city where King Gorlagon dwelt, and, as it chanced, found him at dinner, as he had found the others.

After greetings had been exchanged Arthur made known who he was and why he had come, and as he kept on asking for information on the matters about which he had come, King Gorlagon answered, "Yours is a weighty question. Dismount and eat: and to-morrow I will tell you what you wish to know."

But Arthur said he would by no means do that, and when again requested to dismount, he swore by an oath that he would yield to no entreaties until he had learned what he was in search of. So when King Gorlagon saw that he could not by any means prevail upon him to dismount, he said, "Arthur, since you persist in your resolve to take no food until you know what you ask of me, although the labour of telling you the tale be great, and there is little use in telling it, yet I will relate to you what happened to a certain king, and thereby you will be able to test the heart, the nature, and the ways of women. Yet, Arthur, I beg you, dismount and eat, for yours is a weighty question and few there are who know how to answer it, and when I have told you my tale you will be but little the wiser.

Arthur: Tell on as you have proposed, and speak no more of my eating.
Gorlagon: Well, let your companions dismount and eat.
Arthur: Very well, let them do so.

So when they had seated themselves at table, King Gorlagon said, "Arthur, since you are so eager to hear this business, give ear, and keep in mind what I am about to tell you."

(*Here begins about the wolf.*)

There was a king well known to me, noble, accomplished, rich, and far-famed for justice and for truth. He had provided for himself a delightful garden which had no equal, and in it he had caused to be sown and planted all kinds of trees and fruits, and spices of different sorts: and among the other shrubs which grew in the garden there was a beautiful slender sapling of exactly the same height as the King himself, which broke forth from the ground and began to grow on the same night and at the same hour as the King was born. Now concerning this sapling, it had been decreed by fate that whoever should cut it down, and striking his head with the slenderer part of it, should say, "Be a wolf and have the understanding of a wolf," he would at once become a wolf, and have the understanding of a wolf. And for this reason the King watched the sapling with great care and with great diligence, for he had no doubt that his safety depended upon it. So he surrounded the garden with a strong and steep wall, and allowed no one but the guardian, who was a trusted friend of his own, to be admitted into it; and it was his custom to visit that sapling three or four times a day, and to partake of no food until he had visited it, even though he should fast until the evening. So it was that he alone understood this matter thoroughly.

Now this king had a very beautiful wife, but though fair to look upon she did not prove chaste, and her beauty was the cause of her undoing. For she loved a youth, the son of a certain pagan king; and preferring his love to that of her lord, she had taken great pains to involve her husband in some danger so that the youth might be able lawfully to enjoy the embraces for which he longed. And observing that the King entered the garden so many times a day, and desiring to know the reason, she often purposed to question him on the subject, but never dared to do so. But at last one day, when the King had returned from hunting later than usual, and according to his wont had entered the plantation alone, the Queen, in her thirst for information, and unable to endure that the thing should be concealed from her any longer (as it is customary for a woman to wish to know everything), when her husband had returned and was seated at table, asked him with a treacherous smile why he went to the garden so many times a day, and had been there even then late in the evening before taking food. The King answered that that was a matter which did not concern her, and that he was under no obligation to divulge it to her; whereupon she became furious, and improperly suspecting that he was in the habit of consorting with an adulteress in the garden, cried out, "I call all the gods of heaven to witness that I will never eat with you henceforth until you tell me the reason." And rising suddenly from the table she went to her bedchamber, cunningly feigning sickness, and lay in bed for three days without taking any food.

On the third day, the King, perceiving her obstinacy and fearing that her life might be endangered in consequence, began to beg and exhort her with gentle words to rise and eat, telling her that the thing she wished to know was a secret which he would never dare to tell anyone. To which she replied, "You ought to have no secrets from your wife, and you must know for certain that I would rather die than live, so long as I feel that I am so little loved by you," and he could not by any means persuade her to take refreshment. Then the King, in too changeable and irresolute a mood and too devoted in his affection for his wife, explained to her how the matter stood, having first exacted an oath from her that she would never betray the secret to anyone, and would keep the sapling as sacred as her own life.

The Queen, however, having got from him that which she had so dearly wished and prayed for, began to promise him greater devotion and love, although she had already conceived in her mind a device by which she might bring about the crime she had been so long deliberating. So on the following day, when the King had gone to the woods to hunt, she seized an axe, and secretly entering the garden, cut down the sapling to the ground, and carried it away with her. When, however, she found that the King was returning, she concealed the sapling under her sleeve, which hung down long and loose, and went to the threshold of the door to meet him, and throwing her arms around him she embraced him as though she would have kissed him, and then suddenly thrust the sapling out from her sleeve and struck him on the head with it once and again, crying, "Be a wolf, be a wolf," meaning to add "and have the understanding of a wolf," but she added instead the words "have the understanding of a man." Nor was there any delay, but it came about as she had said; and he fled quickly to the woods with the hounds she set on him in pursuit, but his human understanding remained unimpaired. Arthur, see, you have now learned in part the heart, the nature, and the ways of woman. Dismount now and eat, and afterwards I will relate at greater length what remains. For yours is a weighty question, and there are few who know how to answer it, and when I have told you all you will be but little the wiser.

Arthur: The matter goes very well and pleases me much. Follow up, follow up what you have begun.

Gorlagon: You are pleased then to hear what follows. Be attentive and I will proceed. Then the Queen, having put to flight her lawful husband, at once summoned the young man of whom I have spoken, and having handed over to him the reins of government became his wife. But the wolf, after roaming for a space of two years in the recesses of the woods to which he had fled, allied himself with a wild she-wolf, and begot two cubs by her. And remembering the wrong done him by his wife (as he was still possessed of his human understanding), he anxiously considered if he could in any way take his revenge upon her. Now near that wood there was a fortress at which the Queen was very often wont to sojourn with the King. And so this human wolf, looking out for his opportunity, took his shewolf with her cubs one evening, and rushed unexpectedly into the town, and finding the two little boys of whom the aforesaid youth had become the father by his wife, playing by chance under the tower without anyone to guard them, he attacked and slew them, tearing them cruelly limb from limb. When the bystanders saw too late what had happened they pursued the wolves with shouts. The wolves, when what they had done was made known, fled swiftly away and escaped in safety. The Queen, however, overwhelmed with sorrow at the calamity, gave orders to her retainers to keep a careful watch for the return of the wolves. No long time had elapsed when the wolf, thinking that he was not yet satisfied, again visited the town with his companions, and meeting with two noble counts, brothers of the Queen, playing at the very gates of the palace, he attacked them, and tearing out their bowels gave them over to a frightful death. Hearing the noise, the servants assembled, and shutting the doors caught the cubs and hanged them. But the wolf, more cunning than the rest, slipped out of the hands of those who were holding him and escaped unhurt.

Arthur, dismount and eat, for yours is a weighty question and there are few who know how to answer it. And when I have told you all, you will be but little the wiser.

Gorlagon:
: The wolf, overwhelmed with very great grief for the loss of his cubs and maddened by the greatness of his sorrow, made nightly forays against the flocks and herds of that province, and attacked them with such great slaughter that all the inhabitants, placing in ambush a large pack of hounds, met together to hunt and catch him; and the wolf, unable to endure these daily vexations, made for a neighbouring country and there began to carry on his usual ravages. However, he was at once chased from thence by the inhabitants, and compelled to go to a third country: and now he began to vent his rage with implacable fury, not only against the beasts but also against human beings. Now it chanced that a king was reigning over that country, young in years, of a mild disposition, and far-famed for his wisdom and industry: and when the countless destruction both of men and beasts wrought by the wolf was reported to him, he appointed a day on which he would set about to track and hunt the brute with a strong force of huntsmen and hounds. For so greatly was the wolf held in dread that no one dared to go to rest anywhere around, but everyone kept watch the whole night long against his inroads.

So one night when the wolf had gone to a neighbouring village, greedy for bloodshed, and was standing under the eaves of a certain house listening intently to a conversation that was going on within, it happened that he heard the man nearest him tell how the King had proposed to seek and track him down on the following day, much being added as to the clemency and kindness of the King. When the wolf heard this he returned trembling to the recesses of the woods, deliberating what would be the best course for him to pursue. In the morning the huntsmen and the King's retinue with an immense pack of hounds entered the woods, making the welkin ring with the blast of horns and with shouting; and the King, accompanied by two of his intimate friends, followed at a more moderate pace. The wolf concealed himself near the road where the King was to pass, and when all had gone by and he saw the King approaching (for he judged from his countenance that it was the King) he dropped his head and ran close after him, and encircling the King's right foot with his paws he would have licked him affectionately like a suppliant asking for pardon, with such groanings as he was capable of. Then two noblemen who were guarding the King's person, seeing this enormous wolf (for they had never seen any of so vast a size), cried out, "Master, see here is the wolf we seek! see, here is the wolf we seek! strike him, slay him, do not let the hateful beast attack us!" The wolf, utterly fearless of their cries, followed close after the King, and kept licking him gently. The King was wonderfully moved, and after looking at the wolf for some time and perceiving that there was no fierceness in him, but that he was rather like one who craved for pardon, was much astonished, and commanded that none of his men should dare to inflict any harm on him, declaring- that he had detected some signs of human understanding in him; so putting down his right hand to caress the wolf he gently stroked his head and scratched his ears. Then the King seized the wolf and endeavoured to lift him up to him. But the wolf, perceiving that the King was desirous of lifting him up, leapt up, and joyfully sat upon the neck of the charger in front of the King.

The King recalled his followers, and returned home. He had not gone far when lo! a stag of vast size met him in the forest pasture with antlers erect. Then the King said "I will try if there is any worth or strength in my wolf, and whether he can accustom himself to obey my commands." And crying out he set the wolf upon the stag and thrust him from him with his hand. The wolf, well knowing how to capture this kind of prey, sprang up and pursued the stag, and getting in front of it attacked it, and catching it by the throat laid it dead in sight of the King. Then the King called him back and said, "Of a truth you must be kept alive and not killed, seeing that you know how to show such service to us." And taking the wolf with him he returned home.

Arthur, dismount and eat. For yours is a weighty question, and there are few who know how to answer it; and when I have told you all my tale you will be but little the wiser.

Arthur: If all the gods were to cry from heaven "Arthur, dismount and eat," I would neither dismount nor eat until I had learnt the rest.

Gorlagon: So the wolf remained with the King, and was held in very great affection by him. Whatever the King commanded him he performed, and he never showed any fierceness towards or inflicted any hurt upon any one. He daily stood at table before the King at dinner time with his forepaws erect, eating of his bread and drinking from the same cup. Wherever the King went he accompanied him, so that even at night he would not go to rest anywhere save beside his master's couch.

Now it happened that the King had to go on a long journey outside his kingdom to confer with another king, and to go at once, as it would be impossible for him to return in less than ten days. So he called his Queen, and said, "As I must go on this journey at once, I commend this wolf to your protection, and I command you to keep him in my stead, if he will stay, and to minister to his wants." But the Queen already hated the wolf because of the great sagacity which she had detected in him (and as it so often happens that the wife hates whom the husband loves), and she said, "My lord, I am afraid that when you are gone he will attack me in the night if he lies in his accustomed place and will leave me mangled." The King replied, "Have no fear of that, for I have detected no such symptom in him all the long time he has been with me. However, if you have any doubt of it, I will have a chain made and will have him fastened up to my bed-ladder." So the King gave orders that a chain of gold should be made, and when the wolf had been fastened up by it to the steps, he hastened away to the business he had on hand.

	Arthur, dismount and eat. For yours is a weighty question, there are few who know how to answer it; and when I have told you all my tale you will be but little the wiser.
Arthur:	I have no wish to eat; and I beg you not to invite me to eat any more.
Gorlagon:	So the King set out, and the wolf remained with the Queen. But she

did not show the care for him which she ought to have done. For he always lay chained up though the King had commanded that he should be chained up at night only. Now the Queen loved the King's sewer with an unlawful love, and went to visit him whenever the King was absent. So on the eighth day after the King had started, they met in the bedchamber at midday and mounted the bed together, little heeding the presence of the wolf. And when the wolf saw them rushing into each other's impious embraces he blazed forth with fury, his eyes reddening, and the hair on his neck standing up, and he began to make as though he would attack them, but was held back by the chain by which he was fastened. And when he saw they had no intention of desisting from the iniquity on which they had embarked, he gnashed his teeth, and dug up the ground with his paws, and venting his rage over all his body, with awful howls he stretched the chain with such violence that it snapped in two. When loose he rushed with fury upon the sewer and threw him from the bed, and tore him so savagely that he left him half-dead. But to the Queen he did no harm at all, but only gazed upon her with venom in his eye. Hearing the mournful groans of the sewer, the servants tore the door from its hinges and rushed in. When asked the cause of all the tumult, that cunning Queen concocted a lying story, and told the servants that the wolf had devoured her son, and had torn the sewer as they saw while he was attempting to rescue the little one from death, and that he would have treated her in the same way had they not arrived in time to succour her. So the sewer was brought half dead to the guest-chamber. But the Queen fearing that the King might somehow discover the truth of the matter, and considering how she might take her revenge on the wolf, shut up the child, whom she had represented as having been devoured by the wolf, along with his nurse in an underground room far removed from any access; every one being under the impression that he had in fact been devoured.

Arthur, dismount and eat. For yours is a weighty question, and few there are who know how to answer it: and when I have told my tale you will be but little the wiser.

Arthur: I pray you, order the table to be removed, as the service of so many dishes interrupts our conversation.

Gorlagon: After these events news was brought to the Queen that the King was returning sooner than had been expected. So the deceitful woman, full of cunning, went forth to meet him with her hair cut close, and cheeks torn, and garments splashed with blood, and when she met him cried, "Alas! Alas! Alas! my lord, wretched that I am, what a loss have I sustained during your absence!" At this the King was dumbfounded, and asked what was the matter, and she replied, "That wretched beast of yours, of yours I say, which I have but too truly suspected all this time, has devoured your son in my lap; and when your sewer was struggling to come to the rescue the beast mangled and almost killed him, and would have treated me in the same way had not the servants broken in; see here the blood of the little one splashed upon my garments is witness of the thing." Hardly had she finished speaking, when lo! the wolf hearing the King approach, sprang forth from the bedchamber, and rushed into the King's embraces as though he well deserved them, jumping about joyfully, and gambolling with greater delight than he had ever done before. At this the King, distracted by contending emotions, was in doubt what he should do, on the one hand reflecting that his wife would not tell him an untruth, on the other that if the wolf had been guilty of so great a crime against him he would undoubtedly not have dared to meet him with such joyful bounds.

So while his mind was driven hither and thither on these matters and he refused food, the wolf sitting close by him touched his foot gently with his paw, and took the border of his cloak into his mouth, and by a movement of the head invited him to follow him. The King, who understood the wolf's customary signals, got up and followed him through the different bedchambers to the underground room where the boy was hidden away. And finding the door bolted the wolf knocked three or four times with his paw, as much as to ask that it might be opened to him. But as there was some delay in searching for the key – for the Queen had hidden it away – the wolf, unable to endure the delay, drew back a little, and spreading out the claws of his four paws he rushed headlong at the door, and driving it in, threw it down upon the middle of the floor broken and shattered. Then running forward he took the infant from its cradle in his shaggy arms, and gently held it up to the King's face for a kiss. The King marvelled and said, "There is something beyond this which is not clear to my comprehension." Then he went out after the wolf, who led the way, and was conducted by him to the dying sewer; and when the wolf saw the sewer, the King could scarcely restrain him from rushing upon him. Then the King sitting down in front of the sewer's couch, questioned him as to the cause of his sickness, and as to the accident which had occasioned his wounds. The only confession, however, he would make was that in rescuing the boy from the wolf, the wolf had attacked him; and he called the Queen to witness to the truth of what he said. The King in answer said, "You are evidently lying: my son lives: he was not dead at all, and now that I have found him and have convicted both you and the Queen of treachery to me, and of forging lying tales, I am afraid that something else may be false also. I know the reason why the wolf, unable to bear his master's disgrace, attacked you so savagely, contrary to his wont. Therefore confess to me at once the truth of the matter, else I swear by the Majesty of highest Heaven that I will deliver thee to the flames to burn." Then the wolf making an attack upon him pressed him close, and would have mangled him again had he not been held back by the bystanders.

What need of many words? When the King insisted, sometimes with threats, sometimes with coaxing, the sewer confessed the crime of which he had been guilty, and humbly prayed to be forgiven. But the King, blazing out in an excess of fury, delivered the sewer up to be kept in prison, and immediately summoned the chief men from the whole of his kingdom to meet, and through them he held an investigation into the circumstances of this great crime, Sentence was given. The sewer was flayed alive and hanged. The Queen was torn limb from limb by horses and thrown into balls of flame.

Arthur, dismount and eat. For yours is a mighty question, and there are few who know how to answer it: and when I have told my tale you will be but little the wiser.

Arthur: If you are not tired of eating, you need not mind my fasting a little longer.

Gorlagon: After these events the King pondered over the extraordinary sagacity and industry of the wolf with close attention and great persistence, and afterwards discussed the subject more fully with his wise men, asserting that a being who was clearly endued with such great intelligence must have the understanding of a man, "for no beast," he argued, "was ever found to possess such great wisdom, or to show such great devotion to any one as this wolf has shown to me. For he understands perfectly whatever we say to him: he does what he is ordered: he always stands by me, wherever I may be: he rejoices when I rejoice, and when I am in sorrow, he sorrows too. And you must know that one who has avenged with such severity the wrong which has been done me must undoubtedly have been a man of great sagacity and ability, and must have assumed the form of a wolf under some spell or incantation." At these words the wolf, who was standing by the King, showed great joy, and licking his hands and feet and pressing close to his knees, showed by the expression of his countenance and the gesture of his whole body that the King had spoken the truth.

Then the King said, "See with what gladness he agrees with what I say, and shows by unmistakable signs that I have spoken the truth. There can now be no further doubt about the matter, and would that power might be granted me to discover whether by some act or device I might be able to restore him to his former state, even at the cost of my worldly substance; nay, even at the risk of my life." So, after long deliberation, the King at length determined that the wolf should be sent off to go before him, and to take whatever direction he pleased whether by land or by sea. "For perhaps," said he, "if we could reach his country we might get to know what has happened and find some remedy for him."

So the wolf was allowed to go where he would, and they all followed after him. And he at once made for the sea, and impetuously dashed into the waves as though he wished to cross. Now his own country adjoined that region, being, however, separated from it on one side by the sea, though in another direction it was accessible by land, but by a longer route. The King, seeing that he wished to cross over, at once gave orders that the fleet should be launched and that the army should assemble.

Arthur, dismount and eat. For yours is a weighty question: and few there are who know how to answer it: and when I have told my tale you will be but little the wiser.

Arthur: The wolf being desirous of crossing the sea, is standing on the beach. I am afraid that if he is left alone he will be drowned in his anxiety to get over.

Gorlagon: So the King, having ordered his ship, and duly equipped his army, approached the sea with a great force of soldiers, and on the third day he landed safely at the wolf's country; and when they reached the shore the wolf was the first to leap from the ship, and clearly signified to them by his customary nod and gesture that this was his country. Then the King, taking some of his men with him, hastened secretly to a certain neighbouring city, commanding his army to remain on shipboard until he had looked into the affair and returned to them. However, he had scarcely entered the city when the whole course of events became clear to him. For all the men of that province, both of high and low degree, were groaning under the intolerable tyranny of the king who had succeeded to the wolf, and were with one voice lamenting their master, who by the craft and subtilty of his wife had been changed into a wolf, remembering what a kind and gentle master he was.

So having discovered what he wanted to know, and having ascertained where the king of that province was then living, the King returned with all speed to his ships, marched out his troops, and attacking his adversary suddenly and unexpectedly, slew or put to flight all his defenders, and captured both him and his Queen and made them subject to his dominion.

Arthur, dismount and eat. For yours is a mighty question: and there are few who know how to answer it: and when I have finished my tale you will be but little the wiser for it.

Arthur: You are like a harper who almost before he has finished playing the music of a song, keeps on repeatedly interposing the concluding passages without anyone singing to his accompaniment.

Gorlagon: So the King, relying on his victory, assembled a council of the chief men of the kingdom, and setting the Queen in the sight of them all, said, "O most perfidious and wicked of women, what madness induced you to plot such great treachery against your lord! But I will not any longer bandy words with one who has been judged unworthy of intercourse with anyone; so answer the question I put to you at once, for I will certainly cause you to die of hunger and thirst and exquisite tortures, unless you show me where the sapling lies hidden with which you transformed your husband into a wolf. Perhaps the human shape which he has lost may thereby be recovered." Whereupon she swore that she did not know where the sapling was, saying that it was well known that it had been broken up and burnt in the fire. However, as she would not confess, the King handed her over to the tormentors, to be daily tortured and daily exhausted with punishments, and allowed her neither food nor drink. So at last, compelled by the severity of her punishment, she produced the sapling and handed it to the King. And the King took it from her, and with glad heart brought the wolf forward into the midst, and striking his head with the thicker part of the sapling, added these words, "Be a man and have the understanding of a man." And no sooner were the words spoken than the effect followed. The wolf became a man as he had been before, though far more beautiful and comely, being now possessed of such grace that one could at once detect that he was a man of great nobility. The King seeing a man of such great beauty metamorphosed from a wolf standing before him, and pitying the wrongs the man had suffered, ran forward with great joy and embraced him, kissing and lamenting him and shedding tears. And as they embraced each other they drew such long protracted sighs and shed so many tears that all the multitude standing around were constrained to weep. The one returned thanks for all the many kindnesses which had been shown him: the other lamented that he had behaved with less consideration than he ought. What more? Extraordinary joy is shown by all, and the King, having received the submission of the principal men, according to ancient custom, retook possession of his sovereignty. Then the adulterer and adulteress were brought into his presence, and he was consulted as to what he judged ought to be done with them. And he condemned the pagan king to death. The Queen he only divorced, but of his inborn clemency spared her life, though she well deserved to lose it. The other King, having been honoured and enriched with costly presents, as was befitting, returned to his own kingdom.

Now, Arthur, you have learned what the heart, the nature, and the ways of women are. Have a care for yourself and see if you are any the wiser for it. Dismount now and eat, for we have both well deserved our meal, I for the tale I have told, and you for listening to it.

Arthur: I will by no means dismount until you have answered the question I am about to ask you.

Gorlagon: What is that?

Arthur: Who is that woman sitting opposite you of a sad countenance, and holding before her in a dish a human head bespattered with blood, who has wept whenever you have smiled, and who has kissed the bloodstained head whenever you have kissed your wife during the telling of your tale?

Gorlagon: If this thing were known to me alone, Arthur (he replied), I would by no means tell it you; but as it is well known to all who are sitting at table with me, I am not ashamed that you also should be made acquainted with it. That woman who is sitting opposite me, she it was who, as I have just told you, wrought so great a crime against her lord, that is to say against myself. In me you may recognise that wolf who, as you have heard, was transformed first from a man into a wolf, and then from a wolf into a man again. When I became a wolf it is evident that the kingdom to which I first went was that of my middle brother, King Gorleil. And the King who took such great pains to care for me you can have no doubt was my youngest brother, King Gargol, to whom you came in the first instance. And the bloodstained head which that woman sitting opposite me embraces in the dish she has in front of her is the head of that youth for love of whom she wrought so great a crime against me. For when I returned to my proper shape again, in sparing her life, I subjected her to this penalty only, namely, that she should always have the head of her paramour before her, and that when I kissed the wife I had married in her stead she should imprint kisses on him for whose sake she had committed that crime. And I had the head embalmed to keep it free from putrefaction. For I knew that no punishment could be more grievous to her than a perpetual exhibition of her great wickedness in the sight of all the world. Arthur, dismount now, if you so desire, for now that I have invited you, you will, so far as I am concerned, from henceforth remain where you are.

So Arthur dismounted and ate, and on the following day returned home a nine days' journey, marvelling greatly at what he had heard.

Völsunga Saga: The Story of the Volsungs and Niblungs, trans. Eiríkr Magnússon and William Morris (Walter Scott, 1888), VIII, pp. 76–8.

Chap. VIII. The Death of King Siggeir and of Signy

The tale tells that Sigmund thought Sinfjotli too young to help him get his revenge, and wanted first of all to harden him with manly deeds; so in summer they fared wide through the woods and slayed men for their wealth; Sigmund deemed him to take much after the kin of the Volsungs, though he thought that he was Siggeir's son, and deemed him to have the evil heart of his father, with the might and daring of the Volsungs; because of this, he thought him in nowise a kin-loving man, for very often he would bring Sigmund's wrongs to his memory, and prick him on to slay King Siggeir.

Now on a time as they fared abroad in the woods for the getting of wealth, they found a certain house, and two men with great gold rings asleep therein: now these twain were spell-bound skin-changers (werewolves), and wolf-skins were hanging up over them in the house; and every tenth day they were able to come out of those skins; and they were kings' sons: so Sigmund and Sinfjotli donne the wolf-skins on them, and then they were unable to come out of them, though forsooth the same nature went with them as heretofore (they werw still human and rational); they howled as wolves howl, but both knew the meaning of that howling; they lay out in the wild-wood, and each went his way; and they made a pact betwixt them, that they should risk the onset of seven men, but no more, and that he who was first to be set on should howl in wolfish wise: "Let us not depart from this," says Sigmund, "for thou art young and over-bold, and men will deem the quarry good, when they take thee."

Now each went his way, and when they were parted, Sigmund meets certain men, and gives forth a wolfs howl; and when Sinfjotli heard it, he went straightway thereto, and slew them all, and once more they parted. But before Sinfjotli had fared long through the woods, eleven men met him, and he wrought in such wise that he slew them all, and was wearied therewith, and crawls under an oak, and there takes his rest.

Then Sigmund came, and said "Why didst thou not call on me? "

Sinfjotli said, "I was loth to call for thy help for the slaying of eleven men."

Then Sigmund rushed at him so hard that he staggered and fell, and Sigmund bit him in the throat. Now that day they could not come out of their wolf-skins: but Sigmund lays the other on his back, and bears him home to the house, and cursed the wolf-gears and gave them to the trolls (Sigmund tells the trolls to take the wolf skins as a form of cursing them). Now on a day he saw where two weasels went, and how that one bit the other in the throat, and then ran straightway into the thicket, and took up a leaf and laid it on the wound, and thereon his fellow sprang up healed; so Sigmund went out and saw a raven flying with a blade of that same herb to him; so he took it and drew it over Sinfjotli's wound, and he straightway sprang up as whole as though he had never been hurt. Thereafter they went home to their earth-house, and abode there till the time came for them to put off the wolf-shapes; then they burnt them up with fire, and prayed that no more hurt might come to any one from them; but in that uncouth guise they wrought many famous deeds in the kingdom and lordship of King Siggeir.

Now when Sinfjotli was come to man's estate, Sigmund deemed he had tried him fully, and . . . turns his mind to the avenging of his father. . . .

Gerald of Wales, *The Historical Works of Giraldus Cambrensis, Containing the Topography of Ireland and the History of the Conquest of Ireland*, trans. Thomas Forester (Bell, 1887), II.xix, pp. 79–84.

Of the Prodigies of Our Times, and First of a Wolf Which Conversed with a Priest

I now proceed to relate some wonderful occurrences which have happened within our times. About three years before the arrival of earl John in Ireland, it chanced that a priest, who was journeying from Ulster towards Meath, was benighted in a certain wood on the borders of Meath. While, in company with only a young lad, he was watching by a fire which he had kindled under the branches of a spreading tree, lo! a wolf came up to them, and immediately addressed them to this effect: "Rest secure, and be not afraid, for there is no reason you should fear, where no fear is!" The travellers being struck with astonishment and alarm, the wolf added some orthodox words referring to God. The priest then implored him, and adjured him by Almighty God and faith in the Trinity, not to hurt them, but to inform them what creature it was that in the shape of a beast uttered human words. The wolf, after giving catholic replies to all questions, added at last: "There are two of us, a man and a woman, natives of Ossory, who, through the curse of one Natalis, saint and abbot, are compelled every seven years to put off the human form, and depart from the dwellings of men. Quitting entirely the human form, we assume that of wolves. At the end of the seven years, if they chance to survive, two others being substituted in their places, they return to their country and their former shape. And now, she who is my partner in this visitation lies dangerously sick not far from hence, and, as she is at the point of death, I beseech you, inspired by divine charity, to give her the consolations of your priestly office."

At this word the priest followed the wolf trembling, as he led the way to a tree at no great distance, in the hollow of which he beheld a she-wolf, who under that shape was pouring forth human sighs and groans. On seeing the priest, having saluted him with human courtesy, she gave thanks to God, who in this extremity had vouchsafed to visit her with such consolation. She then received from the priest all the rites of the church duly performed, as far as the last communion. This also she importunately demanded, earnestly supplicating him to complete his good offices by giving her the viaticum. The priest stoutly asserting that he was not provided with it, the he-wolf, who had withdrawn to a short distance, came back and pointed out a small missal-book, containing some consecrated wafers, which the priest carried on his journey, suspended from his neck, under his garment, after the fashion of the country. He then intreated him not to deny them the gift of God, and the aid destined for them by Divine Providence; and, to remove all doubt, using his claw for a hand, he tore off the skin of the she-wolf, from the head down to the navel, folding it back. Thus she immediately presented the form of an old woman. The priest, seeing this, and compelled by his fear more than his reason, gave the communion; the recipient having earnestly implored it, and devoutly partaking of it. Immediately afterwards, the he-wolf rolled back the skin, and fitted it to its original form.

These rites having been duly, rather than rightly, performed, the he-wolf gave them his company during the whole night at their little fire, behaving more like a man than a beast. "When morning came, he led them out of the wood, and, leaving the priest to pursue his journey, pointed out to him the direct road for a long distance. At his departure, he also gave him many thanks for the benefit he had conferred, promising him still greater returns of gratitude, if the Lord should call him back from his present exile, two parts of which he had already completed. At the close of their conversation, the priest inquired of the wolf whether the hostile race which had now landed in the island would continue there for the time to come, and be long established in it. To which the wolf replied: "For the sins of our nation, and their enormous vices, the anger of the Lord, falling on an evil generation, hath given them into the hands of their enemies. Therefore, as long as this foreign race shall keep the commandments of the Lord, and walk in his ways, it will be secure and invincible but if, as the downward path to illicit pleasures is easy, and nature is prone to follow vicious examples, this people shall chance, from living among us, to adopt our depraved habits, doubtless they will provoke the divine vengeance on themselves also."

The like judgment is recorded in Leviticus: "All these abominations have the inhabitants of the land done, which were before you, and the land is defiled. Beware, therefore, that the land spue not you out also, when ye defile it, as it spued out the nation which was before you." All this was afterwards brought to pass, first by the Chaldeans, and then by the Eomans. Likewise it is written in Ecclesiasticus: "The kingdom is made over from one nation to another, by reason of their unjust and injurious deeds, their proud words, and divers deceits."

It chanced, about two years afterwards, that I was passing through Meath, at the time when the bishop of that land had convoked a synod, having also invited the assistance of the neighbouring bishops and abbots, in order to have their joint counsels on what was to be done in the affair which had come to his knowledge by the priest's confession. The bishop, hearing that 1 was passing through those parts, sent me a message by two of his clerks, requesting me, if possible, to be personally present when a matter of so much importance was under consideration; but if I could not attend, he begged me at least to signify my opinion in writing. The clerks detailed to me all the circumstances, which indeed I had heard before from other persons; and, as I was prevented by urgent business from being present at the synod, I made up for my absence by giving them the benefit of my advice in a letter. The bishop and synod, yielding to it, ordered the priest to appear before the pope with letters from them, setting forth what had occurred, with the priest's confession, to which instrument the bishops and abbots who were present at the synod affixed their seals.

It cannot be disputed, but must be believed with the most assured faith, that the divine nature assumed human nature for the salvation of the world; while in the present case, by no less a miracle, we find that at God's bidding, to exhibit his power and righteous judgment, human nature assumed that of a wolf. But is such an animal to be called a brute or a man? A rational animal appears to be far above the level of a brute; but who will venture to assign a quadruped, which inclines to the earth, and is not a laughing animal, to the species of man? Again, if any one should slay this animal, would he be called a homicide? We reply, that divine miracles are not to be made the subjects of disputation by human reason, but to be admired. However, Augustine, in the 16th book of his *Civit. Dei*, chapter 8, in speaking of some monsters of the human race, born in the East, some of which had the heads of dogs, others had no heads at all, their eyes being placed in their breasts, and others had various deformities, raises the question whether these were really men, descended from the first parents of mankind. At last, he concludes, "We must think the same of them as we do of those monstrous births in the human species of which we often hear; and true reason declares that whatever answers to the definition of man, as a rational and mortal animal, whatever be its form, is to be considered a man." The same author, in the 18th book of the *Civit, Dei*, chapter 18, refers to the Arcadians, who, chosen by lot, swam across a lake and were there changed into wolves, living with wild beasts of the same species in the deserts of that country. If, however, they did not devour human flesh, after nine years they swam back across the lake, and re-assumed the human form. Having thus further treated of various transformations of man into the shape of wolves, he at length adds, "I myself, at the time I was in Italy, heard it said of some district in those parts, that there the stable-women, who had learnt magical arts, were wont to give something to travellers in their cheese which transformed them into beasts of burthen, so that they carried all sorts of burdens, and after they had performed their tasks resumed their own forms." Meanwhile, their minds did not become bestial, but remained human and rational." So in the Book which Apuleius wrote, with the title of the *Golden Ass*, he tells us that it happened to himself, on taking some potion, to be changed into an ass, retaining his human mind.

In our own time, also, we have seen persons who, by magical arts, turned any substance about them into fat pigs, as they appeared (but they were always red), and sold them in the markets. However, they disappeared as soon as they crossed any water, returning to their real nature; and with whatever care they were kept, their assumed form did not last beyond three days. It has also been a frequent complaint, from old times as well as in the present, that certain hags in Wales, as well as in Ireland and Scotland, changed themselves into the shape of hares, that, sucking teats under this counterfeit form, they might stealthily rob other people's milk. We agree, then, with Augustine, that neither demons nor wicked men can either create or really change their natures; but those whom God has created can, to outward appearance, by his permission, become transformed, so that they appear to be what they are not; the senses of men being deceived and laid asleep by a strange illusion, so that things are not seen as they actually exist, but are strangely drawn by the power of some phantom or magical incantation to rest their eyes on unreal and fictitious forms.

It is, however, believed as an undoubted truth, that the Almighty God, who is the Creator of natures, can, when he pleases, change one into another, either for vindicating his judgments, or exhibiting his divine power; as in the case of Lot's wife, who, looking back contrary to her lord's command, was turned into a pillar of salt; and as the water was changed into wine; or that, the nature within remaining the same, he can transform the exterior only, as is plain from the examples before given.

Of that apparent change of the bread into the body of Christ (which I ought not to call apparent only, but with more truth transubstantial, because, while the outward appearance remains the same, the substance only is changed), I have thought it safest not to treat; its comprehension being far beyond the powers of the human intellect.

Bibliography

Boyd, Matthieu. "Melion and the Wolves of Ireland." *Neophilologus* 93/4 (2009): 555–70.

Brady, Lindy. "Feminine Desire and Conditional Misogyny in *Arthur and Gorlagon*." *Arthuriana* 24/3 (2014): 23–44.

Bynum, Caroline Walker. "Metamorphosis, or Gerald and the Werewolf." *Speculum* 73/4 (1998): 987–1013.

Campbell, Emma. "Political Animals: Human/Animal Life in *Bisclavret* and *Yonec*." *Exemplaria* 25/2 (2013): 95–109.

Carey, John. "Werewolves in Ireland." *Cambrian Medieval Celtic Studies* 44 (2002): 37–72.

Cartlidge, Neil. "The Werewolf of Wicklow: Shapeshifting and Colonial Identity in the *Lai de Melion*." In *Medieval Romance and Material Culture*. Ed. Nicholas Perkins. D.S. Brewer, 2015.75–89.

Cheilik, Michael. "The Werewolf." In *Mythical and Fabulous Creatures: A Source Book and Research Guide*. Ed. Malcolm South. Greenwood Press, 1987.265–93.

Cohen, Jeffrey J. "Gowther Among the Dogs: Becoming Inhuman c. 1400." In *Becoming Male in the Middle Ages*. Eds. Jeffrey Jerome Cohen and Bonnie Wheeler. Garland, 1997.219–44.

Cohen, Jeffrey J. "The Werewolf's Indifference." *Studies in the Age of Chaucer* 34 (2012): 351–6.

Crane, Susan. "How to Translate a Werewolf." In *The Medieval Translator 10/Traduire au Moyen Age 10*. Eds. Jacqueline Jenkins and Olivier Bertrand. Brepols, 2007.365–74.

Davidson, H.R. Ellis. "Shape-Changing in the Old Norse Sagas." In *A Lycanthropy Reader: Werewolves in Western Culture*. Ed. Charlotte Otten. Syracuse University Press, 1986.142–66.

Diamond, Arlyn. "Loving Beasts: The Romance of *William of Palerne*." In *The Spirit of Medieval English Popular Romance*. Eds. Ad Putter and Jane Gilbert. Longman, 2000.142–56.

Dillinger, Johannes. "'Species', 'Phantasia', 'Raison': Werewolves and Shape-shifters in Demonological Literature." In *Werewolf Histories*. Ed. Willem de Blécourt. Palgrave Macmillan, 2015.142–58.

Friedman, John. "Werewolf Transformation in the Manuscript Era." *The Journal of the Early Book Society* 17 (2015): 36–95.

Gerstein, Mary Roche. "Germanic Warg: The Outlaw as Werewolf." In *Myth in Indo-European Antiquity*. Ed. Gerald Larson. University of California Press, 1974.131–57.

Gilmore, Gloria. "Marie de France's *Bisclavret*: What the Werewolf Will and Will Not Wear." In *Encountering Medieval Textiles and Dress: Objects, Texts, Images*. Eds. Désirée Koslin and Janet Snyder. Palgrave, 2002.67–84.

Guðmundsdóttir, Aðalheiður. "The Werewolf in Medieval Icelandic Literature." *Journal of English and Germanic Philology* 106/3 (2007): 277–303.

Guynn, Noah. "Hybridity, Ethics, and Gender in two Old French Werewolf Tales." In *From Beasts to Souls: Gender and Embodiment in Medieval Europe*. Eds. Jane Burns and Peggy McCracken. University of Notre Dame Press, 2013.157–84.

Hinton, Norman. "The Werewolf as *Eiron*: Freedom and Comedy in *William of Palerne*." In *Animals in the Middle Ages: A Book of Essays*. Ed. Nona Flores. Garland, 1996.133–46.

Hopkins, Amanda. "*Bisclavret* to *Biclarel* via *Melion* and *Bisclaret*: The Development of a Misogynous *Lai*." In *The Court Reconvenes: Courtly Literature Across the Disciplines*. Eds. Barbara Altman and Carleton Carroll. Boydell & Brewer, 2003.317–23.

Jakobsson, Ármann. "Beast and Man: Realism and the Occult in *Egils Saga*." *Scandinavian Studies* 83/1 (2011): 29–44.

Karkov, Catherine. "Tales of the Ancients: Colonial Werewolves and the Mapping of Post-Colonial Ireland." In *Postcolonial Moves: Medieval Through Modern*. Eds. Patricia Ingham and Michelle Warren. Palgrave Macmillan, 2003.95–9.

Leshock, David. "The Knight of the Werewolf: *Bisclavret* and the Shape-Shifting Metaphor." *Romance Quarterly* 46/3 (1999): 155–65.

Panxhi, Lindsey. "Rewriting the Werewolf and Rehabilitating the Irish in the *Topographia Hibernica* of Gerald of Wales." *Viator* 46/3 (2015): 21–40.

Pluskowski, Aleksander. *Wolves and the Wilderness in the Middle Ages*. Boydell, 2006.

Pluskowski, Aleksander. "Before the Werewolf Trials: Contextualising Shape-changers and Animal Identities in Medieval North-Western Europe." In *Werewolf Histories*. Ed. Willem de Blécourt. Palgrave Macmillan, 2015.82–118.

Salisbury, Joyce. *The Beast Within: Animals in the Middle Ages*. Routledge, 1994.

Schiff, Randy. "Cross-Channel Becomings-Animal: Primal Courtliness in *Guillame de Palerne* and *William of Palerne*." *Exemplaria* 21/4 (2009): 418–38.

Sconduto, Leslie. *Metamorphoses of the Werewolf: A Literary Study from Antiquity through the Renaissance*. McFarland & Company, 2008.

Small, Susan. "The Medieval Werewolf Model of Reading Skin." In *Reading Skin in Medieval Literature and Culture*. Ed. Katie Walter. Palgrave Macmillan, 2013.81–97.

Speidel, Michael. *Ancient Germanic Warriors: Warrior Styles from Trajan's Column to Icelandic Sagas*. Routledge, 2004.

Tuczay, Christa. "Into the Wild – Old Norse Stories of Animal Men." In *Werewolf Histories*. Ed. Willem de Blécourt. Palgrave Macmillan, 2015.61–81.

Warner, Lawrence. "Langland and the Problem of *William of Palerne*." *Viator* 37 (2006): 397–415.

Whitacre, Andrea. "The Body that is Not One: Overclothing as Bodily Transformation in the *Topographia Hibernica*." *Essays in Medieval Studies* 34/1 (2018): 99–112.

White, David Gordon. *Myths of the Dog-Man*. University of Chicago Press, 1991.

Wood, Lucas. "The Werewolf as Möbius Strip, or Becoming Bisclavret." *Romanic Review* 102/1–2 (2011): 3–25.

Wood, Lucas. "Of Werewolves and Wicked Women: *Melion*'s Misogyny Reconsidered." *Medium Ævum* 84/1 (2015): 60–88.

6 Dragons

The dragon is often portrayed as the archetypal medieval monster in modern popular culture, so it may be surprising to discover that there are remarkably few dragons in medieval literary texts. Judging by modern television shows, movies, and books, we would expect that the noble heroes of every medieval epic, poem, or romance battled with a dragon, but that is just not the case. While a few of the heroes of medieval literature faced a dragon, dragons appeared much more frequently in medieval art, heraldry, folklore, and hagiography (writings about the lives of the saints). However, dragons were not a product of the Middle Ages, nor were the creatures in any way exclusive to western Europe; they are found in a wide variety of cultures across the globe. In western Europe, the belief in dragons pre-dates Christianity. Dragons featured in ancient Greek and Roman mythology, as well as in Germanic and Norse mythology, and dragons were frequently depicted in the art of all of these cultures. For instance, depictions of dragons (*draco* in Latin) were used in late-Roman military standards (the *draco* was the symbol of the cavalry cohort and was carried by a *draconarius*), and dragons were used across pre-Christian northern Europe as both decorative and apotropaic devices. Intricate dragon or serpentine interlace was a common feature in Anglo-Saxon, Germanic, and Scandinavian art, and these same groups often displayed dragons on the prows of their ships to ward off evil.

These ancient European dragons and their medieval descendants took many forms. While we typically think of dragons as flying, fire-breathing monsters with four legs, the first known depiction of a dragon in this canonical form did not occur until around 1236 (BL MS Harley 3244 fol. 59r). Ancient and medieval dragons came in a wide variety of shapes and sizes, and with a range of deadly attributes. They could be massive or relatively small; they could live on the land or in the sea; they could be overgrown snakes lacking limbs or wings (*serpens, lindworm*, or *wyrm*); they could be multiheaded, horned, lizard-like beasts; they could be scaley or smooth; guard a treasure hoard or not; and they could potentially kill you with their venom, their blood, or by breathing fire or venom. The basic ancient and medieval dragon template was essentially a large snake or lizard, but every author and artist who depicted them could mix and match the other features and choose their own dragon adventure.

DOI: 10.4324/9780429243004-7

In the pre-Christian sources examined in this chapter, dragons most often represent evil, as well as embodying anti-social or negative characteristics associated with humans. With the conversion of western Europe to Christianity, dragons began to carry overtly Christian connotations. In the medieval Christian iconographic tradition, dragons were frequently understood as representations of the devil or disguised demons, but they could also symbolize temptation or sin itself. Dragons were often depicted facing off against saints and being bested by them in some way, either by being tamed, banished, or killed. A multitude of images exist portraying saints like George, Michael, and Margaret slaying dragons, and encounters with dragons appear frequently in saints' lives. Secular heroes may have rarely encountered dragons, but saints battled them with amazing regularity.

The dragons examined in this chapter are drawn from both Christian and pre-Christian sources. They are all from western Europe and include some found in medieval secular texts and some from medieval saints' lives. Because the meaning of the dragon shifts with the conversion to Christianity, the sources are not presented in a strictly chronological order, but are divided into pre-Christian and Christian, regardless of their date of production. Even dividing the sources in this way raises issues, as the two portrayals of dragons that are designated as pre-Christian, Beowulf's battle with a dragon and Sigurd's battle with Fafnir from the *Saga of the Volsungs*, come from sources that were written down by Christian authors who were narrating events situated in a distant, pre-Christian past. Even so, we will see that these pre-Christian dragons carried different meanings than their overtly Christian counterparts and spoke to very different cultural concerns.

Our first dragon appears at the end of the Old English poem, *Beowulf*. The poem treats events in Scandinavia during the early sixth century and was likely circulated orally for a long time before it was finally committed to writing around the year 1000 by an anonymous Christian cleric whose main interest in the story appears to have been its monsters. The sole surviving manuscript containing the work, BL Cotton MS Vitellius A XV, also features a *Life of Saint Christopher*, *The Wonders of the East*, a *Letter of Alexander to Aristotle*, and the poem *Judith* (a retelling of the biblical Book of Judith) that all feature monsters or treat monstrous behavior in some form. Beowulf encounters the dragon at the end of a long and illustrious career. As a young warrior, Beowulf had defeated the monster Grendel and Grendel's mother; he had then risen to become king of the Geats (a group of people living in a region of southern Sweden known as Geatland) and had ruled them for 50 years. At the end of his life, Beowulf's people are being terrorized by a dragon who was awakened from its slumber by the theft of a cup from its treasure hoard. The dragon is described as inhabiting a barrow near the sea, emerging at night to fly over the settlements of the Geats and burning their houses with his fiery breath. This dragon had lain dormant for over 300 years until its treasure was disturbed, and now it was bent on destroying the Geats. Although he was now elderly, Beowulf was still duty bound to protect his people. He chose 11 warriors to accompany him in his battle with the dragon and also brought along the slave who had caused the trouble in the first place by stealing the cup from the dragon's hoard.

The scene of Beowulf's battle with the dragon is full of foreshadowing of the hero's death. We are never in any doubt that this will be Beowulf's final battle and that he will lose his life. Beowulf initially faces the dragon alone, as a true hero, urging his men to stay out of harm's way until he needs them. When Beowulf does need his warriors, all but one have disappeared into the forest. Even though most of his men abandoned him during the fight, Beowulf kills the fiery dragon with the help of the faithful Wiglaf, but only after breaking his sword and sustaining a mortal wound. As the poison from the dragon makes its way through his body, Beowulf asks to be brought to the treasure hoard so he can see the riches he has won with his death.

Beowulf's death is both heroic and tragic. He dies saving his people from the dragon, but knows that they will soon perish without his protection. The dragon that Beowulf faces is in many ways the perfect foil for the king of the Geats. A hero like Beowulf could hardly die of old age, and this giant, fire-breathing, flying dragon is an appropriately terrifying and formidable foe for Beowulf to face in his last battle. Beowulf does not overcome the dragon easily, but requires the help of Wiglaf, and, even with this help, he receives a deadly wound in the battle. Beowulf destroys the dragon and protects his people in the short run, but he dies from his wound and leaves the Geats without a defender in the longer term. Beowulf's death and the bleak pessimism of the poem's conclusion stand in stark contrast to the other stories about dragons featured in this chapter, as we will see.

One of the most interesting things about Beowulf's dragon is that it is so clearly contrasted with Beowulf himself. Beowulf is repeatedly described in the poem as the ruler of men and the people's protector, while the dragon is described as an implacable enemy of men, bent on destruction and fueled by greed. Beowulf, the good king, is also repeatedly described as a ring-giver, meaning that he distributes gold to his men. Distributing the gold, armor, and weapons won through warfare was a necessary part of good kingship that maintained the bonds of loyalty between a king and his warriors, but the dragon does precisely the opposite; he hoards gold and prevents it from circulating and fulfilling its social purpose. Unlike the anti-social dragon that hoards gold, Beowulf's final act is giving his own gold necklace to Wiglaf in a last gesture of generosity, affection, and good lordship. Finally, Beowulf's response to the dragon is measured and calculated. He assesses the situation, finds the culprit responsible for awakening the dragon, and calmly prepares to meet his death, while the dragon is portrayed as acting in a frenzy of rage.

Our next dragon comes from another "pre-Christian" source, *The Saga of the Volsungs*, written by a Christian author in Old Norse in the late thirteenth century about events in a semi-legendary past. While the dragon Fafnir from *The Saga of the Volsungs* is also portrayed as terrifying, he differs considerably from the one in *Beowulf*. Beowulf's dragon can fly, breathes fire, appears enveloped in flames and smoke, and is ruthless and indiscriminate in his killing. Fafnir, on the other hand, is more of a massive, limbless snake who began life as a dwarf and was only transformed into a dragon after murdering his own father to acquire a cursed treasure hoard known as the Otter's Ransom. Fafnir is described as giant and fearsome, but there is no indication that he kills men indiscriminately. Instead, he breathes poison into the air to keep men away from him. Fafnir seems to be quietly tending his treasure hoard until Sigurd comes along. Unlike Beowulf, the hero Sigurd does not set out to battle the dragon to protect his people; Sigurd is persuaded to kill Fafnir by his foster-father, Regin, who tells him of the fabulous wealth he will gain by killing the dragon and taking its treasure. Regin also happens to be Fafnir's own brother and nurses a grudge against Fafnir for killing their father and keeping the Otter's Ransom for himself. Unlike Beowulf, Sigurd does not die in his battle with the dragon. He emerges from the battle unscathed and with the ability to understand the speech of birds.

Bent on wreaking his revenge on Fafnir, Regin convinces Sigurd to dig a hole in the track that Fafnir has made in the earth and conceal himself there with a sword in order to pierce the dragon's heart when it passes. Sigurd agrees to kill the dragon, if Regin will make him a sword. After two failed attempts, Regin forges a sword worthy of Sigurd, and Sigurd goes to hide himself and wait for Fafnir. When Fafnir comes along the track to get a drink of water from a local stream, Sigurd only manages to plunge his sword into Fafnir's shoulder, missing his heart, but the wound still proves to be mortal. As Fafnir lays dying, he asks Sigurd who he is, and who sent him. Sigurd at first refuses to tell Fafnir his name, presumably so Fafnir could not curse him by name with his dying breath, but Sigurd soon reveals his identity. Fafnir then figures out that Regin has sent Sigurd to kill him and tells him that the treasure he has come to claim is cursed and will mean his death. Sigurd responds by saying that everyone must die someday and that at least he will be wealthy until then. Once Fafnir is dead, Regin returns and asks Sigurd to roast the dragon's heart so he can eat it. Sigurd tests the heart to see if it is done and tastes the dragon's blood, which gives him the ability to understand the speech of birds. Sigurd then hears the nearby nuthatches discussing the fact that Regin intends to betray and murder him and keep the treasure for himself and decides to kill Regin by decapitating him. He then eats half of Fafnir's heart and keeps the other half which he later gives to his wife, Gudrun. Finally, Sigurd follows Fafnir's track back to his lair and takes the cursed treasure hoard.

Compared to Beowulf's battle with a dragon, Sigurd's encounter with Fafnir seems more like an ambush than a battle in which the stakes are life and death. Sigurd conceals himself and mortally wounds Fafnir fairly easily with a single stroke of his sword. The nature of the dragon is also dramatically different from what we saw in *Beowulf*. Fafnir is rational; he may have been transformed into a dragon by his evil deeds, but he still retains his ability to reason and to speak. And, instead of murdering people in a raging fury, Fafnir seems to have mostly kept to himself. Although we are assured by the author of the saga that Fafnir is evil and quite capable of killing, he is almost a sympathetic figure: someone whose own greed has caused his transformation into a terrible beast. The function that the dragon fulfils in this story is also different than in *Beowulf*. Beowulf's encounter with the dragon comes at the end of his life, when he is no longer a young warrior but an aged king who has ruled for 50 years. Sigurd's adventure with Fafnir occurs near the beginning of his story, when he is still proving his valor. In fact, the plan to kill Fafnir is interrupted by Sigurd running off to avenge the death of his father in another act of heroism. Slaying Fafnir establishes Sigurd's reputation as a hero and provides him with wealth and wisdom, along with the ability to understand birds; it also paves the way for his later adventures with Brynhild and Gudrun, as the curse hanging over Fafnir's treasure ultimately proves to be Sigurd's undoing.

The "pre-Christian" dragons included here function as symbols of evil. Beowulf's dragon represents the irrational and destructive forces of nature as well as providing a model of bad lordship in which people are destroyed and gold is hoarded. Fafnir's evil is of a more personal nature in that his own greed has caused him to murder his father and transform into a dragon, but his avarice and treasure hoarding also signify bad lordship, even if they are not as clearly contrasted with Sigurd's actions as is the case in *Beowulf*. Dragons remain symbols of evil in the Christian sources examined below, but that evil is now explicitly situated within a Christian context and connected to Satan, the demonic, temptation, and sin. We see this very clearly in medieval bestiaries, books which explain the allegorical meanings of various real and mythological creatures. For example, a section of the moralized commentary on the dragon in a twelfth-century English bestiary (BL Harley MS 4751 fol. 59r) reads:

> To this dragon the devil is likened, who is a most enormous serpent. As it often rushes forth from its cavern into the air and the air glows around it, so does the devil, raising himself from the depths (of hell), transform himself into an angel of light and delude stupid people with the false hope of glory and human joy. As it (the dragon) is said to be crested, so is he himself (Satan) the king of pride. It (the dragon) has its power not in its teeth but in its tail, and so his power being lost, he deceives with a lie those whom he attracts to himself. It lies hid about the paths by which the elephants go, and so the devil always pursues men who are fond of display. It binds their legs with coils and if it is able entangles them, and so he entangles their road to heaven with the knots of sins; and it kills them by suffocation, and so if any one dies entangled in the chain of sins, without doubt he is condemned to hell.
>
> (Translation by George C. Druce, "The Elephant in
> Medieval Legend and Art," *Journal of the Royal
> Archaeological Institute* 76 (1919): 1–73)

Because the dragon was regarded as symbolizing the devil and sin itself within the Christian tradition, it featured in numerous saints' lives and provided a perfect foil for a few pious High and Late Medieval knights. As we will see, both saints and Christian knights defeated dragons with the aid of Christ.

Our next few dragons come from accounts of saints' lives compiled by the friar Jacobus de Voragine around 1260 into a hugely popular book known as *The Golden Legend*. This collection of saints' lives draws together a variety of existing stories, some of which were already many centuries old, and contains accounts of several saints who were believed to have battled dragons: Saints Michael, George, Margaret of Antioch, and Martha, the sister of Mary and friend of Christ. The saint perhaps most associated with the dragon is the archangel Michael, who leads the army of heaven against the forces of evil. Jacobus tells us that Michael drove the dragon (Lucifer) and his followers out of heaven, but is frustratingly vague about the dragon's appearance or even the battle. Since Michael represents the forces of God, his triumph over the dragon is assured. Although Jacobus does not mention it, Revelation 12 describes a second encounter between Michael and Lucifer in the form of a dragon at the end of the world. In this case, we are given more information about the dragon, which is an enormous red beast with seven heads, ten horns, and seven crowns on its heads. It is so massive that it sweeps a third of the stars out of the sky with its tail as it attempts to devour an infant, generally understood to be Christ. Again, the dragon/Lucifer and his angels battle with Michael and the heavenly host, and, again, Lucifer loses and is hurled to Earth with his angels.

Although he has other functions, like weighing the souls of the dead to determine whether they will ascend to heaven or be condemned to hell, Michael is frequently represented as a winged warrior slaying a dragon that represents Satan in Christian artwork. The dragon that Michael vanquishes can take a variety of forms, from the relatively lizard-like dragon found in an alabaster relief panel at the Victoria and Albert Museum, to the more demonic figure that features a black, furry, humanoid body with a reptilian frill seen in the *Hours of Marguerite d'Orleans*. In whatever configuration the dragon appears, he represents Satan, the embodiment of evil and the enemy of humanity. In most cases, Michael appears to be barely exerting himself to conquer the dragon, reflecting the medieval Christian assumption that God and His forces will always triumph over evil. We see something very similar in the stories and images of other saints.

The second saint most associated with the dragon is George, the patron saint of England. Like Michael, George is a warrior. Jacobus de Voragine tells us that George held the rank of tribune in the Roman army and that his very name means "holy fighter, because he fought against the dragon." George encountered this dragon in Libya, where it lived in a lake, killing everyone who came within reach of its poisonous breath. Unable to vanquish the dragon, the townspeople were forced to appease it first by feeding it sheep and then, when the sheep were depleted, a sheep and a young person every day. Eventually, the town was running low on young people as well as sheep. To make matters worse, the young people sacrificed to the dragon were chosen by lot, and it happened that the king's own daughter was selected as tribute. Dismayed, the king resigned himself to sacrificing his daughter for the sake of the town. He decked her out in royal array and sent her toward the lake, just as George was passing by. George saw her distress and promised to help her in the name of Christ. As the dragon emerged from the lake, George made the sign of the cross, commended himself to God, and brought the dragon to its knees with a mighty blow; he then ordered the princess to throw her girdle over its neck, and she led the dragon away like a little dog on a leash. George told the people that Christ had sent him to save them and demanded that everyone in the town convert to Christianity and accept baptism if they wanted him to kill the dragon. When this was done, George drew his sword and killed the dragon. The immense size of the dragon required four yoke of oxen to haul it outside the city walls. The king then built a church to honor the Virgin Mary and George that featured a spring in its altar whose water cured diseases. Jacobus adds that another version of the story says that upon seeing the girl about to be swallowed by the dragon, George merely made the sign of the cross, rode up to the dragon, and killed him.

In both versions of George's story, the Christian warrior is pitted against an embodiment of evil who devastates the local livestock and people. The dragon in this story is often interpreted as representing the pagan beliefs of the town's inhabitants, which required both animal and human sacrifice (paganism is a general term for polytheistic religions, and it was generally applied by Christians to all other religions except Judaism). Paganism was also associated with idolatry. Christians viewed paganism as a form of devil worship and believed that pagan gods were demons. These associations are made quite clear in Jacobus' story about George's martyrdom that follows his encounter with the dragon. During a confrontation between George and the prefect Dacian over Dacian's persecution of Christians, the saint explicitly yells at the prefect, "All your gods are demons, and our God alone is the Creator of the heavens!" The story goes on to implicitly compare the human and animal sacrifices the pagans make with the self-sacrifice that George makes as a Christian – George refuses to sacrifice to the pagan gods in order to save himself and chooses to die for his faith. George brings an end both to the dragon's reign of terror and the barbarity of the local pagans, as he kills the dragon and converts the townspeople to Christianity.

As for George's battle with the dragon, we are never in any doubt about whether the saint will triumph over this incarnation of evil, sin, and paganism. In both versions of the story offered by Jacobus de Voragine, George calls upon the power of Christ by making the sign of the cross before rushing toward the dragon, and this is the key to the saint's success. We are told in no uncertain terms that George does not defeat the dragon on his own, but with Christ's aid. Christ's aid is also a prominent feature in the story of George's martyrdom that follows his encounter with the dragon. Christ appears to George and comforts him during his captivity, and when George prays to the Lord to destroy the pagan temple, it is immediately consumed by a fire sent from heaven. Although George was still executed, we are told that just after the execution, a fire fell from heaven that killed Dacian and his attendants. George's martyrdom, like his victory over the dragon, magnifies the glory of Christ.

In the story of Saint Margaret of Antioch, Jacobus emphasizes her chastity and triumph over the devil in the form of a dragon. In this case, the Christian virgin Margaret refuses to marry the pagan prefect Olybrius and denigrates his gods. Olybrius' lust for Margaret then turns to rage, and he has her tortured and imprisoned. During her imprisonment, Margaret prays to God to allow her to see the enemy she is fighting, and a hideous dragon appears. Jacobus notes that in one version of the story, Margaret makes the sign of the cross and the dragon immediately disappears, while an alternate version says that the dragon swallowed her in one gulp, but she made the sign of the cross while in the beast's stomach, causing the dragon to split open and allowing her to emerge unscathed. Jacobus then dismisses the alternate version as apocryphal and not to be taken seriously. In either case, once the dragon disappears, the devil returns in the form of a man. Margaret prays for assistance and physically beats the devil, capturing his head under her foot and taunting him that he is under the foot of a woman. The devil is extremely annoyed at being beaten by a girl, especially since her pagan parents were friends of his. Margaret then forces the devil to confess that he has come to compel her to obey the prefect and that he tempts Christians in particular because he hates virtuous people and wants to lead them astray. She then lifts her foot and tells him to leave, and the devil disappears. Having defeated the devil, Margaret was confident that she could withstand whatever tortures the prefect prepared for her. While Margaret was bravely enduring various tortures, a miraculous earthquake struck that interrupted them, causing many onlookers to convert to Christianity and be sentenced to death as a consequence. Fearing that prolonging Margaret's torture would only lead to more people converting to Christianity, Olybrius ordered her to be beheaded.

While we are not told much about Margaret's dragon, other than that it is large and hideous, we are explicitly told that it is the devil in disguise. Whether Margaret was swallowed by the dragon, or merely threatened by it, she was able to defeat it easily by making the sign of the cross and invoking the aid of Christ. Margaret's ability to defeat the dragon is portrayed to be more remarkable than was the case in George's story. Jacobus dwells on Margaret's youth, gender, and assumed feminine weakness, whereas George is described as a soldier whose ability to fight is never in question. Although both George and Margaret require Christ's help to defeat their dragons, and both stories emphasize the strength of the saint's faith rather than their physical prowess, Margaret's physical weakness, gender, and youth make her triumph over the dragon/Satan more exceptional and hence redounds even more to the glory of Christ. The lesson for readers is that Christ is so powerful that *even a girl* can defeat a dragon if her faith is strong. We see an echo of this play on assumed feminine weakness in the fact that the princess in George's story is able to lead the dragon around with her girdle like a little dog on a leash once George has subdued it using the power of Christ.

The final saint associated with a dragon included in *The Golden Legend* is Saint Martha, the sister of Mary and hostess of Christ. Jacobus tells us that after Christ's Ascension, Martha, her brother Lazarus, Mary Magdalene, and Maximus were put adrift on the sea by pagans and landed in southern France. After converting many of the locals, they encountered an amphibian dragon who was part fish and part beast and lived in the Rhone killing sailors. Remarkably, this dragon receives a very detailed description. This dragon was larger than an ox, longer than a horse and had sharp teeth and had a pair of bucklers (shields) on either side of its body. It had come from Galatia in Asia and was the hybrid offspring of the water-serpent Leviathan and a Galatian animal known as Onachus, which Jacobus tells us was known for shooting burning feces that could cover long distances at anyone who pursued it. Sadly, the Rhone dragon does not seem to have inherited this defense; at least, we are not told that it shot flaming dung at its pursuers, only that it ate people in a fairly conventional manner. This is a shame and a real missed opportunity as a dragon that shot burning feces would potentially be the greatest dragon ever! Martha happened upon this dragon while it was eating a man in the forest one day.

She sprinkled the dragon with holy water and had a cross held in front of it, and the beast was immediately as tame as a sheep. Martha then tied her girdle around it and held it still while others killed it with stones and lances. Jacobus then recounts that the dragon was called Tarasconus and the place is still called Tarascon after him, although it was previously called Nerluc or black place because of the darkness of the forest there. Martha then established a convent in Tarascon and built a church dedicated to the Virgin Mary there.

By now, the saints' ability to defeat dragons by invoking the power of Christ should be very familiar. Martha's dragon is exceptional because we are given such a detailed description of it, but her ability to tame it with Christ's help is not. Again, the saint's faith is what enables Martha to channel Christ's power and overcome the evil dragon. As we saw with Saint George, Martha's dragon can also be interpreted as an embodiment of the paganism and hence the relatively sinful and uncivilized state of the locals, at least from the perspective of the Christian author. Martha and her Christian companions have been converting the local population from their paganism, effectively civilizing them and offering them salvation in place of their accustomed sinfulness. And the place where Martha encounters the dragon was once known as Nerluc (the black place) due to the dark and shadowy nature of the forest. In addition to harboring an evil dragon, this dark, shadowy forest was also a perfect location for other evil, pagan spirits. Martha's defeat of the dragon coincides with the Christianization of the area and the conversion of this "dark place" from the error of paganism, and it is followed by the establishment of a community of nuns and a church dedicated to the Virgin. With Martha's defeat of the dragon, the light of Christianity replaces the darkness of paganism.

Our two final dragons come from a very different type of source – high medieval romance. While hagiography focuses on the strength of the saint's faith and the power of Christ, romances are more concerned with individual glory and knightly quests. The first dragon comes from the twelfth-century Old French romance known as *Yvain, the Knight of the Lion* (Le Chevalier au Lion). Written by the Christian cleric and poet Chrétien de Troyes around 1180, Yvain is a knight of King Arthur's court who is rejected by his wife, Laudine, for being so focused on chivalrous exploits that he fails to come home. After going mad with grief and being cured, Yvain sets out to regain Laudine's love by embarking on a series of chivalrous exploits, precisely the activity that had caused Laudine to reject him in the first place. At the beginning of his quest to regain Laudine's love, Yvain is riding through the woods deep in thought when he encounters a dragon holding a lion by its tail and burning it with its fiery breath. Yvain decides to help the lion and slay the dragon, reasoning that he should kill the dragon because it is a venomous and wicked creature. Chrétien emphasizes the dragon's evil nature by repeating that fire emanates from its mouth because it is so wicked and comparing the evil dragon to the noble and honorable lion. Unlike the saints who protected themselves with the sign of the cross, Yvain protects himself with his shield to avoid the flames pouring from the dragon's cauldron-sized mouth. Protected from the flames, Yvain cleaves the dragon in two and then hacks the dragon into tiny pieces. Grateful at being rescued from the horrible dragon, the noble lion humbles himself before Yvain and submits to him. Yvain wipes the dragon gore from his sword and sets off again, only to find that the lion comes with him. The lion stays by Yvain's side for the rest of the romance, serving and protecting him.

We are given few details about the dragon's appearance. We are told that it is venomous, wicked, and that it breathes fire from its huge mouth. This fiery breath is its most important attribute, and Yvain easily dispatches the dragon by using his shield to protect himself from the fire. Yvain's battle with the dragon is very short, and the most notable aspect of the story is the moral contrast set up between the wickedness of the dragon and the nobility of the lion. Yvain chooses to help the noble lion and kill the dragon, thus choosing the path of good and rejecting evil. While Yvain does not invoke the power of Christ in any explicit way, he is still faced with a choice between good and evil here, and he chooses good. Yvain's encounter with the dragon can also be read as a Christian allegory. Faced with a choice between Satan in the form of a wicked dragon, and Christ in the form of a noble lion, Yvain chooses to fight for Christ. While lions were frequently associated with earthly kings, they were also associated with Christ, the king of heaven. Medieval bestiaries explain that lion cubs are born dead and are only brought to life on the third day when their father breathes on them, echoing the Crucifixion and Resurrection of Christ. Chrétien probably meant for his readers to associate the lion both with King Arthur, Yvain's earthly lord, and Christ, the knight's heavenly lord. Yvain's choice in this battle sets the tone for the rest of his story as he and the lion defeat other incarnations of evil: a giant, three knights, and two demons. Yvain, who has proven himself to be a virtuous knight and triumphed over several forms of evil, finally regains the love of Laudine and returns home accompanied by the lion, a symbol of Christ and of knightly virtue.

Our final dragon appears in *The Romance of Fulk Fitzwarin*, which was likely written in verse in the later thirteenth century, but only survives in a prose version from the early fourteenth century. While Yvain was a fictional knight, the historical Fulk Fitzwarin was a powerful marcher lord who was outlawed by King John around 1200 due to a dispute over ancestral rights to Whittington Castle in Shropshire; he spent a few years in exile before being reconciled with the king and died around 1258. The romance commemorating Fulk's life was likely commissioned by a family member to rehabilitate his reputation and glorify his memory. The romance is a mix of legendary material, historical narrative, and fabulous accounts of Fulk's exploits during his exile.

After King John outlaws and exiles our hero, Fulk sets off on a series of overseas adventures, including a stop in Cartagena, where he finds a beautiful castle, but a land that is empty of human or animal inhabitants. Fulk and his companions finally find someone who can tell them why the land is uninhabited. According to this informant, the Duke of Cartagena holds the castle, and his daughter was carried off by a flying dragon who took the maiden to his lair in a mountain by the sea and ate her. The dragon had also devastated the land and killed everyone around, which was why there were no inhabitants. Even the duke no longer dared to live in his castle. Fulk and his companions return to their ship and find the mountain where the dragon lives. Fulk reminds his friend, Mador, who is nervous about encountering such a terrifying beast, that they have already faced many dragons and other dangers and that God has always delivered them. Fulk and another companion, Sir Audulf, then climb to the dragon's lair. Fulk crosses himself in the name of the Father, the Son, and the Holy Ghost before entering the lair, and inside they find the duke of Cartagena's daughter weeping and traumatized, but physically unharmed. The dragon's lair is surrounded by human bones, remnants of all the other knights the dragon has eaten, and the maiden warns them to leave quickly if they do not want to become the dragon's next meal. Fulk refuses to leave, and the maiden explains that the dragon has not harmed her, but he has held her captive and forces her to clean the blood of his human victims from his face and beard after he eats. She also explains that this dragon sleeps on a couch made of gold, which he uses to cool himself as he is excessively hot. Finally, we learn that this dragon has human senses and fears that the maiden will kill him while he sleeps.

Fulk determines to face the dragon and rescue the maiden (this is one of the very few stories in which a knight actually rescues a damsel from a dragon). They are all leaving the cave when the dragon appears flying toward them, belching flames and smoke into the air. The dragon is described as ugly, with a large head, square teeth, cruel claws, and a long tail. It swoops toward Fulk, tearing his shield in two with its claws. Fulk tries to strike the dragon with his sword, but the dragon's hard outer shell prevents Fulk from doing any damage. The dragon flies a little further off to launch a new attack, which Fulk dodges by hiding behind a tree. Realizing that he cannot harm the dragon by attacking it frontally, Fulk waits for it to turn so he can attack its side. Fulk then succeeds in cutting the dragon in two near its tail. Wounded, the dragon tries to seize the damsel, but grabs Sir Audulf instead, forcing Fulk to cut off the dragon's claw to release his friend from its grip. Audulf is saved, but his hauberk was ripped by the dragon's talons, and he later requires medical assistance. Finally, Fulk stabs the dragon in the mouth and kills it. After resting to catch his breath, Fulk takes the gold out of the dragon's lair and brings it back to his ship. They then return the damsel to the duke of Cartagena. The grateful duke offers Fulk his daughter's hand in marriage along with all of Cartagena, but Fulk refuses as he is already married, so the duke and Fulk exchange gifts and Fulk sets sail again for other adventures.

Fulk's dragon and his battle with it are remarkable for being so detailed. Here, we have a very specific account of the dragon's appearance, habits, and motives and a battle in which there is at least some suspense. The dragon manages to break Fulk's shield and wound Sir Audulf before Fulk discovers how to defeat it. Of course, we are not really in much suspense about who will eventually emerge victorious, and we are given quite a few clues leading up to the battle that Fulk will triumph as his piety and faith in God are noted on several occasions. We are also explicitly told that Fulk crossed himself before entering the dragon's lair, thus calling upon the protective power of Christ. Like the saints whose faith allowed them to channel God's power and defeat their dragons, Fulk's piety enables him to do the same.

Fulk's encounter with the dragon comprises a very small part of the account of his life and is only one of many fantastic adventures attributed to Fulk. In the larger context of Fulk's story, this brief detour to Cartagena serves to burnish his reputation as a heroic and pious knight and to draw a distinct contrast between the good and noble Fulk and his nemesis, the evil King John of England. Fulk spends his entire exile having similar adventures in which he battles various monsters, rescues maidens, and proves his chivalry, unlike the lecherous King John who had a reputation for defiling the wives and daughters of his vassals and whose numerous poor decisions and military losses resulted in him acquiring the unflattering nickname Softsword. In fact, John has been compared to the dragon at Cartagena. Like the dragon, King John devastated the land; consuming his people's wealth in the form of taxes and fines; mistreating his people by imprisoning, torturing, and occasionally executing them; and generally acting as a scourge upon the land. Fulk, on the other hand, is portrayed as a virtuous and pious Christian knight, someone who aids the oppressed, leads his men wisely, and ultimately returns to England as a hero and regains the ancestral land that John wrongfully took from him.

The dragons in these texts invariably symbolize evil in some form, whether it is bad lordship, personal greed, sin, temptation, or Satan himself. In the pre-Christian sources, the dragon proves to be a truly formidable foe, capable of killing a hero like Beowulf, even as he is slain by him. In the Christian sources, however, the dragon is almost always overcome by the saint or the hero through the power of Christ. Even in the case of Yvain, where the hero does not explicitly call upon Christ's aid, his meeting with the dragon and the lion presents him with a choice between good and evil, and he chooses to defeat the wicked dragon. The dragon in the Christian stories is still portrayed as formidable, but the lack of any real doubt as to the outcome of the saint's or hero's battle with the dragon deprives the monster of much of his terror. The Christian dragon may embody sin, vice, and the demonic, but it primarily serves to reinforce Christian beliefs in God's omnipotence, the power of faith, and the ultimate triumph of good over evil.

PRIMARY SOURCES

Beowulf, trans. Lesslie Hall (D.C. Heath & Co, 1892), pp. 75–97.

XXXII.
THE HOARD AND THE DRAGON.

He sought of himself who sorely did harm him,
But, for need very pressing, the servant of one of
The sons of the heroes hate-blows evaded,
Seeking for shelter and the sin-driven warrior
Took refuse within there. He early looked in it,
***** when the onset surprised him,
He a gem-vessel saw there: many of suchlike
Ancient ornaments in the earth-cave were lying,
As in days of yore some one of men of
Illustrious lineage, as a legacy monstrous,
There had secreted them, careful and thoughtful,

Dear-valued jewels. Death had offsnatched them,
In the days of the past, and the one man moreover
Of the flower of the folk who fared there the longest,
Was fain to defer it, friend-mourning warder,
A little longer to be left in enjoyment
Of long-lasting treasure. A barrow all-ready
Stood on the plain the stream-currents nigh to,
New by the ness-edge, unnethe of approaching:
The keeper of rings carried within a
Ponderous deal of the treasure of nobles,
Of gold that was beaten, briefly he spake then:
"Hold thou, Oh Earth, now heroes no more may,
The earnings of earlmen. Lo! erst in thy bosom
Worthy men won them; war-death hath ravished,
Perilous life-bale, all my warriors,
Liegemen belovèd, who this life have forsaken,
Who hall-pleasures saw. No sword-bearer have I,
And no one to burnish the gold-plated vessel,
The high-valued beaker: my heroes are vanished.
The hardy helmet behung with gilding
Shall be reaved of its riches: the ring-cleansers slumber
Who were charged to have ready visors-for-battle,
And the burnie that bided in battle-encounter
O'er breaking of war-shields the bite of the edges
Moulds with the hero. The ring-twisted armor,
Its lord being lifeless, no longer may journey
Hanging by heroes; harp-joy is vanished,
The rapture of glee-wood, no excellent falcon
Swoops through the building, no swift-footed charger
Grindeth the gravel. A grievous destruction
No few of the world-folk widely hath scattered!"
So, woeful of spirit one after all
Lamented mournfully, moaning in sadness
By day and by night, till death with its billows
Dashed on his spirit. Then the ancient dusk-scather
Found the great treasure standing all open,
He who flaming and fiery flies to the barrows,
Naked war-dragon, nightly escapeth
Encompassed with fire; men under heaven
Widely beheld him. 'Tis said that he looks for
The hoard in the earth, where old he is guarding
The heathenish treasure; he'll be nowise the better.
So three-hundred winters the waster of peoples
Held upon earth that excellent hoard-hall,
Till the forementioned earlman angered him bitterly:

The beat-plated beaker he bare to his chieftan
And fullest remission for all his remissness
Begged of his liegelord. Then the hoard was discovered,
The treasure was taken, his petition was granted
The lorn-mooded liegeman. His lord regarded
The old-work of earth-folk – 'twas the earliest occasion.
When the dragon awoke, the strife was renewed there:
He snuffed 'long the stone then, stout-hearted found he
The footprint of foeman; too far had he gone
With cunning craftiness close to the head of
The fire-spewing dragon. So undoomed he may 'scape from
Anguish and exile with ease who possesseth
The favor of Heaven. The hoard-warden eagerly
Searched o'er the ground then, would meet with the person
That caused him sorrow while in slumber reclining:
Gleaming and wild he oft went round the cavern,
All of it outward; not any of earthmen
Was seen in that desert. Yet he joyed in the battle,
Rejoiced in the conflict: of the turned to the barrow,
Sought for the gem-cup; this he soon perceived then
That some man or other had discovered the gold,
The famous folk-treasure. Not fain did the hoard-ward
Wait until evening; then the ward of the barrow
Was angry in spirit, the loathèd one wished to
Pay for the dear-valued drink-cup with fire.
Then the day was done as the dragon would have it,
He no longer would wait on the wall, but departed
Fire-impelled, flaming. Fearful the start was
To earls in the land, as it early thereafter
To their giver-of-gold was grievously ended.

XXXIII.
BRAVE THOUGH AGED. – REMINISCENES.

The stranger began then to vomit forth fire,
To burn the great manor; the blaze then glimmered
For anguish to earlmen, not anything living
Was the hateful air-goer willing to leave there.
The war of the worm widely was noticed,
The feud of the foeman afar and anear,
How the enemy injured the earls of the Geatmen,
Harried with hatred: back he hied to the treasure,
To the well-hidden cavern ere the coming of daylight.
He had circled with fire the folk of those regions,
With brand and burning; in the barrow he trusted,

In the wall and his war-might: the weening deceived him.
Then straight was the horror to Beowulf published,
Early forsooth, that his own native homestead,
The best of buildings, was burning and melting,
Gift-seat of Geatmen. 'Twas a grief to the spirit
Of the good-mooded hero, the greatest of sorrows:
The wise one weened then that wielding his kingdom
'Gainst the ancient commandments, he had bitterly angered
The Lord everlasting: with lorn meditations
His bosom welled inward, as was nowise his custom.
The fire-spewing dragon fully had wasted
The fastness of warriors, the water-land outward,
The manor with fire. The folk-ruling hero,
Prince of the Weders, was planning to wreak him.
The warmen's defender bade them to make him,
Earlmen's atheling, an excellent war-shield
Wholly of iron: fully he knew then
That wood from the forest was helpless to aid him,
Shield against fire. The long-worthy ruler
Must live the last of his limited earth-days,
Of life in the world and the worm along with him,
Though he long had been holding hoard-wealth in plenty.
Then the ring-prince disdained to seek with a war-band,
With army extensive, the air-going ranger;
He felt no fear of the foeman's assaults and
He counted for little the might of the dragon,
His power and prowess: for previously dared he
A heap of hostility, hazarded dangers,
War-thane, when Hrothgar's palace he cleansèd,
Conquering combatant, clutched in the battle
The kinsmen of Grendel, of kindred detested.
'Twas of hand-fights not least where Higelac was slaughtered,
When the king of the Geatmen with clashings of battle,
Friend-lord of folks in Frisian dominions,
Offspring of Hrethrel perished through sword-drink,
With battle-swords beaten; thence Beowulf came then
On self-help relying, swam through the waters;
He bare on his arm, lone-going, thirty
Outfits of armor, when the ocean he mounted.
The Hetwars by no means had need to be boastful
Of their fighting afoot, who forward to meet him
Carried their war-shields: not many returned from
The brave-mooded battle-knight back to their homesteads.
Ecgtheow's bairn o'er the bight-courses swam then,
Lone-goer lorn to his land-folk returning,

Where Hygd to him tendered treasure and kingdom,
Rings and dominion: her son she not trusted,
To be able to keep the kingdom devised him
'Gainst alien races, on the death of King Higelac.
Yet the sad ones succeeded not in persuading the atheling
In any way ever, to act as a suzerain
To Heardred, or promise to govern the kingdom;
Yet with friendly counsel in the folk he sustained him,
Gracious, with honor, till he grew to be older,
Wielded the Weders. Wide-fleeing outlaws,
Ohthere's sons, sought him o'er the waters:
They had stirred a revolt 'gainst the helm of the Scylfings,
The best of the sea-kings, who in Swedish dominions
Distributed treasure, distinguished folk-leader.
'Twas the end of his earth-days; injury fatal
By swing of the sword he received as a greeting,
Offspring of Higelac; Ongentheow's bairn
Later departed to visit his homestead,
When Heardred was dead; let Beowulf rule them,
Govern the Geatmen: good was that folk-king.

XXXIV.
BEOWULF SEEKS THE DRAGON. – BEOWULF'S REMINISCENES.

He planned requital for the folk-leader's ruin
In days thereafter, to Eadgils the wretched
Becoming an enemy. Ohthere's son then
Went with a war-troop o'er the wide-stretching currents
With warriors and weapons: with woe-journeys cold he
After avenged him, the king's life he took.
So he came off uninjured from all of his battles,
Perilous fights, offspring of Ecgtheow,
From his deeds of daring, till that day most momentous
When he fate-driven fared to fight with the dragon.
With eleven companions the prince of the Geatmen
Went lowering with fury to look at the fire-drake:
Inquiring he'd found how the feud had arisen,
Hate to his heroes; the highly-famed gem-vessel
Was brought to his keeping through the hand of th' informer.
That in the throng was thirteenth of heroes,
That caused the beginning of conflict so bitter,
Captive and wretched, must sad-mooded thenceward
Point out the place: he passed then unwillingly
To the spot where he knew of the notable cavern,
The cave under earth, not far from the ocean,

The anger of eddies, which inward was full of
Jewels and wires: a warden uncanny,
Warrior weaponed, warded the treasure,
Old under earth, no easy possession
For any of earth-folk access to get to.
Then the battle-brave atheling sat on the naze-edge,
While the gold-friend of Geatmen gracious saluted
His fireside-companions: woe was his spirit,
Death-boding, wav'ring; Weird very near him,
Who must seize the old hero, his soul-treasure look for,
Dragging aloof his life from his body:
Not flesh-hidden long was the folk-leader's spirit.
Beowulf spake, Ecgtheow's son:
"I survived in my youth-days many a conflict,
Hours of onset: that all I remember.
I was seven-winters old when the jewel-prince took me,
High-lord of heroes, at the hands of my father,
Hrethel the hero-king had me in keeping,
Gave me treasure and feasting, our kinship remembered;
Not ever was I *any* less dear to him
Knight in the boroughs, then the bairns of his household,
Herebald and Hæthcyn and Higelac mine.
To the eldest unjustly by acts of a kinsman
Was murder-bed strewn, since him Hæthcyn from horn-bow
His sheltering chieftain shot with an arrow,
Erred in his aim and injured his kinsman,
One brother the other, with blood-sprinkled spear:
'Twas a feeless fight, finished in malice,
Sad to his spirit; the folk-prince however
Had to part from existence with vengeance untaken.
So to hoar-headed hero 'tis heavily crushing
To live to see his son as he rideth
Young on the gallows: then measures he chanteth,
A song of sorrow, when his son is hanging
For the raven's delight, and aged and hoary
He is unable to offer any assistance.
Every morning his offspring's departure
Is constant recalled: he cares not to wait for
The birth of an heir in his borough-enclosures,
Since that one through death-pain the deeds hath experienced.
He heart-grieved beholds in the house of his son the
Wine-building wasted, the wind-lodging places
Reaved of their roaring; the riders are sleeping,
The knights in the grave; there's no sound of the harp-wood,
Joy in the yards, as of yore were familiar.

XXXV.
REMINISCENES (continued). BEOWULF'S LAST BATTLE.

"He seeks then his chamber, singeth a woe-song
One for the other; all too extensive
Seemed homesteads and plains. So the helm of the Weders
Mindful of Herebald heart-sorrow carried,
Stirred with emotion, nowise was able
To wreak his ruin on the ruthless destroyer:
He was unable to follow the warrior with hatred,
With deeds that were direful, though dear he not held him.
Then pressed by the pang this pain occasioned him,
He gave up glee, God-light elected;
He left to his sons, as the man that is rich does,
His land and fortress, when from life he departed.
Then was crime and hostility 'twixt Swedes and Geatmen,
O'er wide stretching water warring was mutual,
Burdensome hatred, when Hrethel had perished,
And Ongentheow's offspring were active and valiant,
Wished not to hold to peace oversea, but
Round Hreosna-beorh often accomplished
Cruelest massacre. This my kinsman avenged,
The feud and fury, as 'tis found on inquiry,
Though one of them paid it with forfeit of life-joys,
With price that was hard: the struggle became then
Fatal to Hæthcyn, lord of the Geatmen.
Then I heard that at morning one brother the other
With edges of irons egged on to murder,
Where Ongentheow maketh onset on Eofor:
The helmet crashed, the hoary-haired Scylfing
Sword-smitten fell, his hand then remembered
Feud-hate sufficient, refused not the death-blow.
The gems that he gave me, with jewel-bright sword I
'Quited in contest, as occasion was offered:
Land he allowed me, life-joy at homestead,
Manor to live on. Little he needed
From Gepids or Danes or in Sweden to look for
Trooper less true, with treasure to buy him;
'Mong foot-soldiers ever in front I would hie me,
Alone in the vanguard, and evermore gladly
Warfare shall wage, while this weapon endureth
That late and early often did serve me
When I proved before heroes the slayer of Dæghrefn,
Knight of the Hugmen: he by no means was suffered
To the king of the Frisians to carry the jewels,

The breast-decoration; but the banner possessor
Bowed in the battle, brave-mooded atheling.
No weapon was slayer, but war-grapple broke then
The surge of his spirit, his body destroying.
Now shall weapon's edge make war for the treasure,
And hand and firm-sword." Beowulf spake then,
Boast-words uttered – the latest occasion:
"I braved in my youth-days battles unnumbered;
Still I am willing the struggle to look for,
Fame-deeds perform, folk-warden prudent,
If the hateful despoiler forth from his cavern
Seeketh me out!" Each of the heroes,
Helm-bearers sturdy, he thereupon greeted
Belovèd co-liegemen – his last salutation:
"No brand would I bear, no blade for the dragon,"
Wist I a way my word-boast to 'complish
Else with the monster, as with Grendel I did it;
But fire in the battle hot I expect there,
Furious flame-burning: so I fixed on my body
Target and war-mail. The ward of the barrow
I'll not flee from a foot-length, the foeman uncanny.
At the wall 'twill befall us as Fate decreeth,
Each one's Creator. I am eager in spirit,
With the winged war-hero to away with all boasting.
Bide on the barrow with burnies protected,
Earls in armor, which of *us* two may better
Bear his disaster, when the battle is over.
'Tis no matter of yours, and man cannot do it,
But me and me only, to measure his strength with
The monster of malice, might-deeds to 'complish.
I with prowess shall gain the gold, or the battle,
Direful death-woe will drag off your ruler!"
The mighty champion rose by his shield then,
Brave under helmet, in battle-mail went he,
'Neath steep-rising stone-cliffs, the strength he relied on
Of one man alone: no work for a coward.
Then he saw by the wall who a great many battles
Had lived through, most worthy, when foot-troops collided,
Stone-arches standing, stout-hearted champion,
Saw a brook from the barrow bubbling out thenceward:
The flood of the fountain was fuming with war-flame:
Not nigh to the hoard, for season the briefest
Could he brave, without burning, the abyss that was yawning,
The drake was so fiery. The prince of the Weders

Caused then that words came from his bosom,
So fierce was his fury; the firm-hearted shouted:
His battle-clear voice came in resounding
'Neath the gray-colored stone. Stirred was his hatred,
The hoard-ward distinguished the speech of a man;
Time was no longer to look out for friendship.
The breath of the monster issued forth first,
Vapory war-sweat, out of the stone-cave:
The earth re-echoed. The earl 'neath the barrow
Lifted his shield, lord of the Geatmen,
Tow'rd the terrible stranger: the ring-twisted creature's
Heart was then ready to seek for a struggle.
The excellent battle-king first brandished his weapon,
The ancient heirloom, of edges unblunted,
To the death-planners twain was terror from other.
The lord of the troopers intrepidly stood then
'Gainst his high-rising shield, when the dragon coiled him
Quickly together: in corslet he bided.
He went then in blazes, bended and striding,
Hasting him forward. His life and body
The targe well protected, for time-period shorter
Than wish demanded for the well-renowned leader,
Where he then for the first day was forced to be victor,
Famous in battle, as Fate had not willed it.
The lord of the Geatmen uplifted his hand then,
Smiting the fire-drake with sword that was precious,
That bright on the bone the blade-edge did weaken,
Bit more feebly than his folk-leader needed,
Burdened with bale-griefs. Then the barrow-protector,
When the sword-blow had fallen, was fierce in his spirit,
Flinging his fires, flamings of battle
Gleamed then afar: the gold-friend of Weders
Boasted no conquests, his battle-sword failed him
Naked in conflict, as by no means it ought to,
Long-trusty weapon. 'Twas no slight undertaking
That Ecgtheow's famous offspring would leave
The drake-cavern's bottom; he must live in some region
Other than this, by the will of the dragon,
As each one of earthmen existence must forfeit.
'Twas early thereafter the excellent warriors
Met with each other. Anew and afresh
The hoard-ward took heart (gasps heaved then his bosom):
Sorrow he suffered encircled with fire
Who the people erst governed. His companions by no means
Were banded about him, bairns of the princes,

With valorous spirit, but they sped to the forest,
Seeking for safety. The soul-deeps of one were
Ruffled by care: kin-love can never
Aught in him waver who well doth consider.

XXXVI.
WIGLAF THE TRUSTY. – BEOWULF IS DESERTED BY FRIENDS AND BY SWORD.

The son of Weohstan was Wiglaf entitled,
Shield-warrior precious, prince of the Scylfings,
Ælfhere's kinsman: he saw his dear liegelord
Enduring the heat 'neath helmet and visor.
Then he minded the holding that erst he had given him,
The Wægmunding warriors' wealth-blessèd homestead,
Each of the folk-rights his father had wielded;
He was hot for the battle, his hand seized the target,
The yellow-bark shield, he unsheathed his old weapon,
Which was known among earthmen as the relic of Eanmund,
Ohthere's offspring, whom, exiled and friendless,
Weohstan did slay with sword-edge in battle,
And carried his kinsman the clear-shining helmet,
The ring-made burnie, the old giant-weapon
That Onela gave him, his boon-fellow's armor,
Ready war-trappings: he the feud did not mention,
Though he'd fatally smitten the son of his brother.
Many a half-year held he the treasures,
The bill and the burnie, till his bairn became able,
Like his father before him, fame-deeds to 'complish;
Then he gave him 'mong Geatmen a goodly array of
Weeds for his warfare; he went from life then
Old on his journey. 'Twas the earliest time then
That the youthful champion might charge in the battle
Aiding his liegelord; his spirit was dauntless.
Nor did kinsman's bequest quail at the battle:
This the dragon discovered on their coming together.
Wiglaf uttered many a right-saying,
Said to his fellows, sad was his spirit:
"I remember the time when, tasting the mead-cup,
We promised in the hall the lord of us all
Who gave us these ring-treasures, that this battle-equipment,
Swords and helmets, we'd certainly quite him,
Should need of such aid ever befall him:
In the war-band he chose us for this journey spontaneously,
Stirred us to glory and gave me these jewels,

Since he held and esteemed us trust-worthy spearmen,
Hardy helm-bearers, though this hero-achievement
Our lord intended alone to accomplish,
Ward of his people, for most of achievements,
Doings audacious, he did among earth-folk.
The day is now come when the ruler of earthmen
Needeth the vigor of valiant heroes:
Let us wend us towàrds him, the war-prince to succor,
While the heat yet rageth, horrible fire-fight.
God wot in me, 'tis mickle the liefer
The blaze should embrace my body and eat it
With my treasure-bestower. Meseemeth not proper
To bear our battle-shields back to our country,
'Less first we are able to fell and destroy the
Long-hating foeman, to defend the life of
The prince of the Weders. Well do I know 'tisn't
Earned by his exploits, he only of Geatmen
Sorrow should suffer, sink in the battle:
Brand and helmet to us both shall be common,
Shield-cover, burnie." Through the bale-smoke he stalked
then,
Went under helmet to the help of his chieftan,
Briefly discoursing: "Beowulf dear,
Perform thou all fully, as thou formerly saidst,
In thy youthful years, that while yet thou livedst
Thou wouldst let thine honor not ever be lessened.
Thy life thou shalt save, mighty in actions,
Atheling undaunted, with all of thy glory;
I'll give thee assistance." The dragon came raging,
Wild-mooded stranger, when these words had been uttered
(Twas the second occasion), seeking his enemies,
Men that were hated, with hot-gleaming fire-waves;
With blaze-billows burned the board to its edges:
The fight-armor failed then to furnish assistance
To the youthful spear-hero: but the young-agèd stripling
Quickly advanced 'neath his kinsman's war-target,
Since his own had been ground in the grip of the fire.
Then the warrior-king was careful of glory,
He soundly smote with sword-for-the-battle,
That it stood in the head by hatred ydriven;
Nægling was shivered, the old and iron-made
Brand of Beowulf in battle deceived him.
'Twas denied him that edges of iron were able
To help in the battle; the hand was too mighty
Which every weapon, as I heard on inquiry,

Outstruck in its stroke, when to struggle he carried
The wonderful war-sword: it waxed him no better.
Then the people-despoiler – third of his onsets –
Fierce-raging fire-drake, of feud-hate was mindful,
Charged on the strong one, when chance was afforded,
Heated and war-grim, seized on his neck
With teeth that were bitter; he bloody did wax with
Soul-gore seething; sword-blood in waves boiled.

XXXVII.
THE FATAL STRUGGLE. – BEOWULF'S LAST MOMENTS.

Then I heard that at need of the king of the people
The upstanding earlman exhibited prowess,
Vigor and courage, as suited his nature;
He his head did not guard, but the high-minded liegeman's
Hand was consumed, when he succored his kinsman,
So he struck the strife-bringing strange-comer lower,
Earl-thane in armor, that *in* went the weapon
Gleaming and plated, that 'gan then the fire
Later to lesson. The liegelord himself then
Retained his consciousness, brandished his war-knife,
Battle-sharp, bitter, that he bare on his armor:
The Weder-lord cut the worm in the middle.
They had felled the enemy (life drove out then
Puissant prowess), the pair had destroyed him,
Land-chief's related: so a liegeman should prove him,
A thaneman when needed. To the prince 'twas the last of
His era of conquest by his own great achievements,
The latest of world-deeds. The wound then began
Which the earth-dwelling dragon erstwhile had wrought him
To burn and to swell. He soon then discovered
That bitterest bale-woe in his bosom was raging,
Poison within. The atheling advanced then,
That along by the wall, he prudent of spirit
Might sit on a settle; he saw the giant-work,
How arches of stone strengthened with pillars
The earth-hall eternal inward supported.
Then the long-worthy liegeman laved with his hand the
Far-famed chieftain, gory from sword-edge,
Refreshing the face of his friend-lord and ruler,
Sated with battle, unbinding his helmet.
Beowulf answered, of his injury spake he,
His wound that was fatal (he was fully aware
He had lived his allotted life-days enjoying

The pleasures of earth; then past was entirely
His measure of days, death very near):
"My son I would give now my battle-equipments,
Had any of heirs been after me granted,
Along of my body. This people I governed
Fifty of winters: no king 'mong my neighbors
Dared to encounter me with comrades-in-battle,
Try me with terror. The time to me ordered
I bided at home, mine own kept fitly,
Sought me no snares, swore me not many
Oaths in injustice. Joy over all this
I'm able to have, though ill with my death-wounds;
Hence the Ruler of Earthmen need not charge me
With the killing of kinsmen, when cometh my life out
Forth from my body. Fare thou with haste now
To behold the hoard 'neath the hoar-grayish stone,
Well-lovèd Wiglaf, now the worm is a-lying,
Sore-wounded sleepeth, disseized of his treasure.
Go thou in haste that treasures of old I,
Gold-wealth may gaze on, together see lying
The ether-bright jewels, be easier able,
Having the heap of hoard-gems, to yield my
Life and the land-folk whom long I have governed."

XXXVIII.
WIGLAF PLUNDERS THE DRAGON'S DEN. – BEOWULF'S DEATH.

Then heard I that Wihstan's son very quickly,
These words being uttered, heeded his liegelord
Wounded and war-sick, went in his armor,
His well-woven ring-mail, 'neath the roof of the barrow.
Then the trusty retainer treasure-gems many
Victorious saw, when the seat he came near to,
Gold-treasure sparkling spread on the bottom,
Wonder on the wall, and the worm-creature's cavern,
The ancient dawn-flier's, vessels a-standing,
Cups of the ancients of cleansers bereavèd,
Robbed of their ornaments: there were helmets in numbers,
Old and rust-eaten, arm-bracelets many,
Artfully woven. Wealth can easily,
Gold on the sea-bottom, turn into vanity
Each one of earthmen, arm him who pleaseth!
And he saw there lying an all-golden banner
High o'er the hoard, of hand-wonders greatest,
Linkèd with lacets: a light from it sparkled,
That the floor of the cavern he was able to look on,

To examine the jewels. Sight of the dragon
Not any was offered, but edge offcarried him.
Then I heard that the hero the hoard-treasure plundered,
The giant-work ancient reaved in the cavern,
Bare on his bosom the beakers and platters,
As himself would fain have it, and took off the standard,
The brightest of beacons; the bill had erst injured
(Its edge was of iron), the old-ruler's weapon,
Him who long had watched as ward of the jewels,
Who fire-terror carried hot for the treasure,
Rolling in battle, in middlemost darkness,
Till murdered he perished. The messenger hastened,
Not loth to return, hurried by jewels:
Curiosity urged him if, excellent-mooded,
Alive he should find the lord of the Weders
Mortally wounded, at the place where he left him.
'Mid the jewels he found then the famous old chieftain,
His liegelord belovèd, at his life's-end gory:
He thereupon 'gan to lave him with water,
Till the point of his word piercèd his breast-hoard.
Beowulf spake (he gold-gems he noticed),
The old one in sorrow: "For the jewels I look on
Thanks do I utter for all to the Ruler,
Wielder of Worship, with words of devotion,
The Lord everlasting, that He let me such treasures
Gain for my people ere death overtook me.
Since I've bartered the agèd life to me granted
For treasures of jewels, attend ye henceforward
The wants of the war-thanes; I can wait here no longer.
The battle-famed bid ye to build them a grave-hill,
Bright when I'm burned, at the brim-current's limit;
As a memory-mark to the men I have governed,
Aloft it shall tower on Whale-Ness's uprising,
The earls of the ocean hereafter may call it
Beowulf's barrow, those who barks ever-dashing
From a distance shall drive o'er the darkness of waters."
The bold-mooded troop-lord took from his neck then
The ring that was golden, gave to his liegeman,
The youthful war-hero, his gold-flashing helmet,
His collar and war-mail, bade him well to enjoy them:
"Thou art latest left of the line of our kindred,
Of Wægmunding people: Weird hath offcarried
All of my kinsmen to the Creator's glory,
Earls in their vigor: I shall after them fare."
'Twas the agèd liegelord's last-spoken word in
His musings of spirit, ere he mounted the fire,

The battle-waves burning: from his bosom departed
His soul to seek the sainted ones' glory.

XXXIX.
THE DEAD FOES. – WIGLAF'S BITTER TAUNTS.

It had woefully chanced then the youthful retainer
To behold on earth the most ardent beloved
At his life-days' limit, lying there helpless.
The slayer too lay there, of life all bereavèd,
Horrible earth-drake, harassed with sorrow:
The round-twisted monster was permitted no longer
To govern the ring-hoards, but edges of war-swords
Mightily seized him, battle-sharp, sturdy
Leavings of hammers, that still from his wounds
The flier-from-farland fell to the earth
Hard by his hoard-house, hopped he at midnight
Not e'er through the air, nor exulting in jewels
Suffered them to see him: but he sank then to earthward
Through the hero-chief's handwork. I heard sure it throve
then
But few in the land of liegemen of valor,
Though of every achievement bold he had proved him,
To run 'gainst the breath of the venomous scather,
Or the hall of the treasure to trouble with hand-blows,
If he watching had found the ward of the hoard-hall
On the barrow abiding. Beowulf's part of
The treasure of jewels was paid for with death;
Each of the twain had attained to the end of
Life so unlasting. Not long was the time till
The tardy-at-battle returned from the thicket,
The timid truce-breakers ten all together,
Who durst not before play with the lances
In the prince of the people's pressing emergency;
But blushing with shame, with shields they betook them,
With arms and armor where the old one was lying:
They gazed upon Wiglaf. He was sitting exhausted,
Foot-going fighter, not far from the shoulders
Of the lord of the people, would rouse him with water;
No whit did it help him; though he hoped for it keenly,
He was able on earth not at all in the leader
Life to retain, and nowise to alter
The will of the Wielder; the World-Ruler's power
Would govern the actions of each of the heroes,
As yet He is doing. From the young one forthwith then

Could grim-worded greeting be got for him quickly
Whose courage had failed him. Wiglaf discoursed then,
Weohstan his son, sad-mooded hero,
Looked on the hated: "He who soothness will utter
Can say that the liegelord who gave you the jewels,
The ornament-armor wherein ye are standing,
When on ale-bench often he offered to hall-men
Helmet and burnie, the prince to his liegemen,
As best upon earth he was able to find him, –
That he wildly wasted his war-gear undoubtedly
When battle o'ertook him. The troop-king no need had
To glory in comrades; yet God permitted him,
Victory-Wielder, with weapon unaided
Himself to avenge, when vigor was needed.
I life-protection but little was able
To give him in battle, and I 'gan, notwithstanding,
Helping my kinsman (my strength overtaxing):
He waxed the weaker when with weapon I smote on
My mortal opponent, the fire less strongly
Flamed from his bosom. Too few of protectors
Came round the king at the critical moment.
Now must ornament-taking and weapon-bestowing,
Home-joyance all, cease for your kindred,
Food for the people; each of your warriors
Must needs be bereavèd of rights that he holdeth
In landed possessions, when faraway nobles
Shall learn of your leaving your lord so basely,
The dastardly deed. Death is more pleasant
To every earlman than infamous life is!"

Völsunga Saga: The Story of the Volsungs and Niblungs, **trans.**
Eiríkr Magnússon and William Morris (Walter Scott, 1888), XIII,
pp. 44–67

Chap. XIII. Of the Birth and Waxing of Sigurd Fafnir's-bane

. . . Now yet again Regin spoke to Sigurd, and said "Not enough is thy wealth,
and I grieve right sore that thou must needs run here and there like a churl's son;
but I can tell thee where there is much wealth for the winning, and great name and
honour to be won in the getting of it."

Sigurd asked where that might be, and who had watch and ward over it.

Regin answered, "Fafnir is his name, and but a little way hence he lies, on the
waste of Gnita-heath; and when thou comest there thou may well say that thou hast
never seen more gold heaped together in one place, and that none might desire
more treasure, though he were the most ancient and famed of all kings."

"Young am I," says Sigurd, "yet I know the fashion of this worm, and how none dare to go against him, so huge and evil is he."

Regin said, "Nay it is not so, the fashion and the growth of him is like other lingworms (longworm or dragon) and an over great tale men make of it; and your forefathers would have deemed the same; but thou, though thou be of the kin of the Volsungs, shall scarce have the heart and mind of those, who are told of as the first in all deeds of fame."

Sigurd said, "Yea, perhaps I have little of their hardihood and prowess, but thou hast naught to do, to lay a coward's name upon me, when I am scarce out of my childish years. Why dost thou egg me on to this so busily?"

Regin said, "Therein lies a tale which I must tell thee."

"Let me hear the same," said Sigurd.

Chap. XIV. Regin's Tale of His Brothers and of the Gold Called Andvari's Hoard

"Thus the tale begins," said Regin. "Hreidmar was my father's name, a mighty man and wealthy: and his first son was named Fafnir, his second Otter, and I was the third, and the least of them all both for prowess and good conditions, but I was cunning to work in iron, and silver, and gold, whereof I could make things that availed somewhat. Other skill my brother Otter followed, and he had another nature, for he was a great fisher, and above other men in this; he had the likeness of an otter by day, and dwelt always in the river, and took fish to the bank in his mouth, and his prey would he always bring to our father, and that availed him much: for the most part he stayed in his otter-gear, and then he would come home, and eat alone, and slumber, for on the dry land he might see naught. But Fafnir was by far the greatest and grimmest, and would have all things about called his.

"Now," says Regin, "there was a dwarf called Andvari, who ever abode in that waterfall, which was called Andvari's force, in the likeness of a pike, and got meat for himself, for there were many fish in the force; now Otter, my brother, was ever wont to enter into the force, and bring fish to land, and lay them one by one on the bank. And so it befell that Odin, Loki, and Hoenir, as they went their way, came to Andvari's force, and Otter had taken a salmon, and ate it slumbering upon the river bank; then Loki took a stone and cast it at Otter, so that he killed him; the gods were well content with their prey, and fell to flaying off the otter's skin; and in the evening they came to Hreidmar's house, and showed him what they had taken: thereon he laid hands on them, and doomed them to such ransom, as that they should fill the otter skin with gold, and cover it over without with red gold; so they sent Loki to gather gold together for them; he came to Ran (goddess of the sea), and got her net, and went therewith to Andvari's force, and cast the net before the pike, and the pike ran into the net and was taken. Then said Loki

"'What fish of all fishes,
Swims strong in the flood,

But hath learnt little wit to beware?
Thine head must thou buy.
From abiding in hell,
And find me the wan waters flame.'
He answered
"'Andvari folk call me,
Call Oinn my father,
Over many a force have I fared;
For a Norn of ill-luck,
This life on me lay
Through wet ways ever to wade.'

"So Loki beheld the gold of Andvari, and when he had given up the gold, he had but one ring left, and that also Loki took from him; then the dwarf went into a hollow of the rocks, and cried out, that that gold-ring, and all the other gold, should be the bane of every man who should own it thereafter." (Andvari lays a curse on all of the gold.)

Now the gods rode with the treasure to Hreidmar, and filled the otter-skin with it, and set it on its feet, and they must cover it over utterly with gold: but when this was done then Hreidmar came forth, and beheld yet one of the muzzle hairs, and bade them cover that as well; then Odin drew the ring, Andvari's loom, from his hand, and covered up the hair with it; then sang Loki

"Gold enough, gold enough,
A great weregild[1], thou hast,
That my head in good hap I may hold;
But thou and thy son
Are not fated to thrive,
The bane shall it be of you both."

"Thereafter," says Regin, "Fafnir slew his father and murdered him, nor did I get any of the treasure, and so evil he grew, that he fell to lying abroad, and begrudged any share in the wealth to any man, and so became the worst of all worms, and now lies always brooding upon that treasure: but for me, I went to the king and became his master-smith; and thus is the tale told of how I lost the heritage of my father, and the weregild for my brother."

So spoke Regin; but since that time gold is called Ottergild (Otter's gold), and for no other cause than this.

But Sigurd answered, "Much hast thou lost, and exceeding evil have thy kinsmen been! but now, make a sword by thy craft, such a sword as that no other can be made like it; so that I may do great deeds with it, if my heart avail thereto, and thou wouldst have me slay this mighty dragon."

Regin says, "Trust me well in this; and with that same sword shalt thou slay Fafnir."

Chap. XV. Of the Welding Together of the Shards of the Sword Gram

So Regin made a sword, and gave it into Sigurd's hands. He took the sword, and said

"Behold thy smithying, Regin!" and therewith smote it into the anvil, and the sword broke; so he cast it down, and bade him forge a better one.

Then Regin forged another sword, and brought it to Sigurd, who looked at it.

Then said Regin, "Perhaps thou art well content with this, hard master though thou be in smithying."

So Sigurd tested the sword, and it broke just as the first one; then he said to Regin

"Ah, art thou, perhaps, a traitor and a liar like those former kin of thine?"

Then he went to his mother, and she welcomed him kindly, and they talked and drank together.

Then spake Sigurd, "Have I heard right, that King Sigmund gave thee the good sword Gram in two pieces?"

"True enough," she said.

So Sigurd said, "Deliver them into my hands, for I would have them." She said he looked likely to win great fame, and gave him the sword.

Then Sigurd went to Regin, and bade him make a good sword with the pieces as he best could; Regin grew angry, but went into the smithy with the pieces of the sword, thinking meanwhile that Sigurd had pushed his head far enough into the matter of smithying. So he made a sword, and as he bore it forth from the forge, it seemed to the smiths as though fire burned along its edges. Now he bade Sigurd take the sword, and said he knew not how to make a sword if this one failed. Then Sigurd smote it into the anvil, and cleft the anvil down to its stock, and neither burst the sword nor broke it. Then he praised the sword much, and thereafter went to the river with a lock of wool, and threw it up against the stream, and the wool was cut in two when it met the sword. Then Sigurd was glad, and he went home.

But Regin said, "Now whereas I have made the sword for thee, will you hold to your word and will you go meet Fafnir?"

"Surely will I hold thereto," said Sigurd, "yet first must I avenge my father."

Now Sigurd the older he grew, the more he grew in the love of all men, so that every child loved him well.

Chap. XVI. The Prophecy of Grifir

There was a man called Grifir, who was Sigurd's mother's brother, and a little after the forging of the sword Sigurd went to Grifir, because he was a man who knew things to come, and what was fated to men: Sigurd asked him diligently how his life should go; but Grifir took a long time to reply, yet at last, because of Sigurd's exceedingly great prayers, he told him all his life and the fate thereof, even as it afterwards came to pass. So when Grifir had told him all even as he would, he went back home; and a little after he and Regin met.

Then said Regin, "Go and slay Fafnir, even as thou hast given thy word."

Sigurd said, "That work shall be wrought; but another is first to be done, the avenging of Sigmund the king and the other of my kinsmen who fell in that their last fight."

(*Chapter XVII Sigurd avenges his father, Sigmund, and returns to his foster-father Regin, who reminds him of his promise to kill Fafnir.*)

Chap. XVIII. Of the Slaying of the Worm Fafnir

Now Sigurd and Regin rode up the heath along the path where Fafnir was wont to creep when he went to the water; and folk say that thirty fathoms was the height of that cliff along which he lay when he drank from the water below. Then Sigurd spake:

"How sayedst thou, Regin, that this drake (dragon) was no greater than other lingworms; I think his track is marvellous great?"

Then said Regin, "Make a hole, and sit down in it, and when the worm comes to the water, smite him into the heart, and so do him to death, and win for thee great fame thereby."

But Sigurd said, "What will happen to me if I am in the way of the blood of the worm?"

Says Regin, "Of what use is it to counsel thee if thou art still afraid of everything? Little art thou like thy kin in stoutness of heart."

Then Sigurd rode right over the heath; but Regin left, sore afraid.

Sigurd fell to digging himself a pit, and while he was at that work, there came to him an old man with a long beard, and asked what he was doing there, and he told him.

Then the old man answered and said, "Thou doest after sorry counsel: rather dig thee many pits, and let the blood run into them; but sit thee down in one of the pits, and so thrust the worm's heart through."

And then he vanished away; but Sigurd made the pits even as it was shown to him.

Now crept the worm down to his place of watering, and the earth shook all around him, and he snorted forth venom on everything before him as he went; but Sigurd neither trembled nor was afraid at his roaring. So when the worm crept over the pits, Sigurd thrust his sword under his left shoulder, so that it sank in up to the hilt; then Sigurd leapt up from the pit and drew the sword back again, and his arm was all bloody, up to the very shoulder.

Now when that mighty worm was aware that he had his death-wound, then he lashed out head and tail, so that all things in front of him were broken to pieces.

So when Fafnir had his death-wound, he asked "Who art thou? and who is thy father? and what thy kin, that thou wert so hardy as to bear weapons against me?"

Sigurd answered, "Unknown to men is my kin. I am called a noble beast: neither father have I nor mother, and all alone have I come here."

Said Fafnir, "If you have neither father nor mother, of what wonder were you born then? But now, though you do not tell me your name on this my death-day, yet you know truly that you are lying to me."

He answered, "Sigurd am I called, and my father was Sigmund."

Says Fafnir, "Who egged you on to this deed, and why would you be driven to it? Have you never heard how all folk are afraid of me, and of the awe of my countenance? But an eager father thou hadst, O bright-eyed swain!"

Sigurd answered, "A hardy heart urged me on; and a strong hand and this sharp sword, which you now well know, stood me in stead in the doing of the deed; *Seldom hath hardy eld a faint-heart youth.*"

Fafnir said, "Well, I know that had you grown up amongst your kin, you might have good skill to slay folk in your anger; but more of a marvel is it, that you, a bondsman (slave) taken in war, should have the heart to set on me, for few among bondsmen have heart for the fight."

Said Sigurd, "Will you then cast it in my teeth that I am far away from my kin? I may have been a bondsman, but I was never shackled. God knows you have found me free enough."

Fafnir answered, "In angry wise dost thou take my speech (you think I speak in anger); but hearken, for that same gold which I have owned shall be your curse too."

Said Sigurd, "We would all like to keep our wealth till that day of days; yet each man shall die once and for all."

Said Fafnir, "Few things will you do according to my counsel; but take heed that you will be drowned if you fare unwarily over the sea; so remain rather on the dry land, for the coming of the calm tide."

Then said Sigurd, "Speak, Fafnir, and say, if thou art so exceedingly wise, who are the Norns who rule the lot of all mothers' sons."

Fafnir answers, "Many there be and wide apart; for some are of the kin of the Æsir, and some are of Elfin kin, and some there are who are daughters of Dvalin."

Said Sigurd, "What do you call the island where Surt (a fire giant who will destroy the world at the Ragnarok, or destruction of all things) and the Æsir mix and mingle the water of the sword?"

"Unshapen is that island called," said Fafnir.

And yet again he said, "Regin, my brother, has brought about my end, and it gladdens my heart that he will bring about yours too; for thus will things be according to his will."

And once again he spoke, "A countenance of terror I bore before all folk, after I began brooding over the heritage of my brother, and on every side did I spout out poison, so that none dared come near me, and of no weapon was I afraid, and never had I so many men before me that I did not deem myself stronger than all of them; for all men were sore afraid of me."

Sigurd answered and said, "Few may have victory by means of that same countenance of terror, for whoever comes amongst many shall one day find that no one man is by so far the mightiest of all."

Then says Fafnir, "Such counsel I give thee, that thou take thy horse and ride away at thy speediest, for often it happens, that he who gets a death-wound still avenges himself nonetheless."

Sigurd answered, "Such as thy counsels are I will nowise follow them; nay, I will ride now to thy lair and take for myself that great treasure of thy kin."

"Ride there then," said Fafnir, "and thou shalt find gold enough to suffice thee for all thy life-days; yet shall that gold be thy bane, and the bane of anyone who owns it"

Then up stood Sigurd, and said, "Home would I ride and lose all that wealth, if I thought that by losing it I should never die; but every brave and true man would like to have his hand on wealth till that last day; but thou, Fafnir, wallow in the death-pain till Death and Hell have thee."

And therewithal Fafnir died.

Chap. XIX. Of the Slaying of Regin, Son of Hreidmar

Thereafter Regin came to Sigurd, and said, "Hail, lord and master, a noble victory hast thou won in the slaying of Fafnir, whereas none before dared to stand in the path of him; and now shall this deed of fame be of renown while the world stands fast."

Then stood Regin staring on the earth a long while, and presently thereafter spoke from a heavy mood: "Mine own brother hast thou slain, and scarce may I be called blameless of the deed."

Then Sigurd took his sword Gram and dried it on the earth, and spoke to Regin "You ran off when I wrought this deed and tried this sharp sword with my hand and might; with all the might and main of a dragon must I strive, while thou wert laying in the heather-bush, knowing not if it were earth or heaven."

Said Regin, "Long might this worm have lain in his lair, if the sharp sword I forged with my hand had not been good when you needed it; had that not been, neither you nor any man would have prevailed against him as at this time."

Sigurd answered, "When men meet foes in fight, a stout heart is better than sharp sword."

Then said Regin, exceedingly heavily, "You have slain my brother, and scarce may I be blameless of the deed."

Then Sigurd cut out the heart of the worm with the sword called Ridil; but Regin drank of Fafnir's blood, and spoke, "Grant me a boon, and do a small thing. Take the heart to the fire, and roast it, and give it to me to eat."

Then Sigurd went his way and roasted it on a rod; and when the blood bubbled out he laid his finger on it to try it, if it were fully done; and then he set his finger in his mouth, and lo, when the heart-blood of the worm touched his tongue, straightway he knew the voice of all fowls, and heard how the wood-peckers chattered in the brush beside him.

"There sittest thou, Sigurd, roasting Fafnir's heart for another, that thou shouldest eat thine ownself, and then thou shouldest become the wisest of all men."

And another spoke: "There lies Regin, minded to betray the man who trusts in him."

But yet again said the third, "Let him smite the head from off him then, and be the only lord of all that gold."

And once more the fourth spoke and said, "Ah, the wiser were he if he followed after that good counsel, and rode thereafter to Fafnir's lair, and took that mighty treasure that lieth there, and then rode over Hindfell, where sleeps Brynhild; for there would he get great wisdom. Ah, wise he were, if he followed your advice, and thought of his own well-being; *for where wolf's ears are, wolf's teeth are near"*

Then cried the fifth: "Yea, yea, he is not so wise as I deem him, if he spares him, whose brother he hath slain already."

At last spoke the sixth: "Handy and good advice to slay him, and be lord of the treasure!"

Then said Sigurd, "The time is unborn when Regin shall be my bane; nay, rather one road shall both these brothers fare." And therewith he drew his sword Gram and struck off Regin's head. Then Sigurd heard the wood-peckers singing, even as the song says.

For the first sang:

Bind thou, Sigurd,
The bright red rings!
Not meet it is
Many things to fear.
A fair may know I,
Fair of all the fairest
Girt about with gold,
Good for thy getting.

And the second:

Green go the ways
Toward the hall of Giuki
That the fates show forth
To those who fare thither;
There the rich king
Reareth a daughter;
Thou shalt deal, Sigurd,
With gold for thy sweetling.

And the third:

A high hall is there
Reared upon Hindfell,
Without all around it
Sweeps the red flame aloft
Wise men wrought
That wonder of halls
With the unhidden gleam
Of the glory of gold.

Then the fourth sang:

> Soft on the fell
> A shield-maiden sleepeth
> The lime-trees' red plague
> Playing about her:
> The sleep-thorn set Odin
> Into that maiden
> For her choosing in war
> The one he willed not.
> Go, son, behold
> That may under helm
> Whom from battle
> Vinskornir bore,
> From her may not turn
> The torment of sleep.
> Dear offspring of kings
> In the dread Norns' despite.

Then Sigurd ate some of Fafnir's heart, and he kept the rest. Then he leapt on his horse and rode along the trail of the worm Fafnir, and so right unto his lair; and he found it open, and beheld all the doors and the gear of them that they were wrought of iron: yea, and all the beams of the house; and it was dug down deep into the earth: there found Sigurd gold exceedingly plenteous, and the sword Rotti; and thence he took the Helm of Awe, and the Gold Byrny (coat of chain mail), and many things fair and good. So much gold he found there, that he scarce thought two horses, or even three, might bear it thence. So he took all the gold and laid it in two great chests, and set them on the horse Grani, and took the reins, but he would not stir, neither would he abide whipping. Then Sigurd knew the mind of the horse, and leapt on the back of him, and whipped and spurred into him, and off the horse went as if he were unladen.

Jacobus de Voragine, *The Golden Legend*, trans. William Granger Ryan (Princeton University Press, 2012), ch. 145, 58, 93, and 105, pp. 591, 238–40, 368–70, and 409–10.

145. Saint Michael, Archangel

... The second victory was won by the archangel Michael when he drove the dragon, i.e., Lucifer, and all his followers out of heaven, a battle about which the Book of Revelation tells us: "There was a great battle in heaven. Michael and his angels fought with the dragon, and the dragon fought with his angels, and they prevailed not."

58. Saint George

. . . George, a native of Cappadocia, held the military rank of tribune. It happened that he once traveled to the city of Silena in the province of Lybia. Near this town there was a pond as large as a lake where a plague-bearing dragon lurked, and many times the dragon had put the populace to flight when they came out armed against him, for he used to come up to the city walls and poison everyone who came within reach of his breath. To appease the fury of this monster the townspeople fed him two sheep every day; otherwise he would invade their city and a great many would perish. But in time they were running out of sheep and could not get any more, so, having held a council, they paid him tribute of one sheep and one man or woman. The name of a youth or a maiden was drawn by lot, and no one was exempt from the draft; but soon almost all the young people had been eaten up. Then one day the lot fell upon the only daughter of the king, and she was seized and set aside for the dragon. The king, beside himself with grief said: "Take my gold and silver and the half of my kingdom, but release my daughter and spare her such a death." But the people were furious and shouted: "You yourself issued this decree, O king, and now that all our children are dead, you want to save your own daughter! Carry out for your daughter what you ordained for the rest, or we will burn you alive with your whole household!" Hearing this, the king began to weep and said to his daughter: "My dearest child, what have I done to you? Or what shall I say? Am I never to see your wedding?" And turning to the people he said: "I pray you, leave me my daughter for one week, so that we may weep together." This was granted, but at the end of the week back they came in a rage, crying: "Why are you letting your people perish to save your daughter? Don't you see that we are all dying from the breath of the dragon?" So the king, seeing that he could not set his daughter free, arrayed her in regal garments, embraced her tearfully, and said: "Woe is me, my darling child, I thought I would see sons nursing at your royal breast, and now you must be devoured by the dragon! Alas, my sweetest child, I hoped to invite princes to your wedding, to adorn the palace with pearls, to hear the music of timbrel and harp, and now you must go and be swallowed up by the beast." He kissed her and sent her off, saying: "O, my daughter, would that I had died before you, rather than lose you this way!" Then she threw herself at his feet and begged his blessing, and when, weeping, he had blessed her, she started toward the lake.

At this moment blessed George happened to be passing by and, seeing the maiden in tears, asked her why she wept. She answered: "Good youth, mount your horse quickly and flee, or you will die as I am to die." George responded: "Lady, fear not; but tell me, what are all these people waiting to see?" The damsel: "I see, good youth, that you have a great heart, but do you want to die with me? Get away speedily!" George: "I will not leave here until you tell me the reason for this." When she had told him all, he said: "Don't be afraid, child! I am going to help you in the name of Christ!" She spoke: "Brave knight, make haste to save yourself; if not, you will die with me. It is enough that I die alone, for you cannot set me free and you would perish with me."

While they were talking, the dragon reared his head out of the lake. Trembling, the maiden cried: "Away, sweet lord, away with all speed!" But George, mounting his horse and arming himself with the sign of the cross, set bravely upon the approaching dragon and, commending himself to God, brandished his lance, dealt the beast a grievous wound, and forced him to the ground. Then he called to the maiden: "Have no fear, child! Throw your girdle around the dragon's neck! Don't hesitate!" When she had done this, the dragon rose and followed her like a little dog on a leash. She led him toward the city; but the people, seeing this, ran for the mountains and the hills, crying out: "Now we will all be eaten alive!" But blessed George waved them back and said to them: "You have nothing to fear! The Lord has sent me to deliver you from the trouble this dragon has caused you. Believe in Christ and be baptized, every one of you, and I shall slay the dragon!" Then the king and all the people were baptized, and George, drawing his sword, put an end to the beast and ordered him to be moved out of the city, whereupon four yoke of oxen hauled him into a broad field outside the walls. On that day twenty thousand were baptized, not counting the women and children. The king built a magnificent church there in honor of Blessed Mary and Saint George, and from the altar flowed a spring whose waters cure all diseases. He also offered a huge sum of money to blessed George, who refused to accept it and ordered it to be distributed to the poor. Then he gave the king four brief instructions: to have good care for the church of God, to honor the priests, to assist with devotion at the divine office, and to have the poor always in mind. Finally, he embraced the king and took his leave. Some books, however, tell us that at the very moment when the dragon was about to swallow the girl alive, George, making the sign of the cross, rode upon and killed him.

93. Saint Margaret

. . . Margaret, a native of Antioch, was the daughter of Theodosius, a patriarch among the pagans. She was entrusted to the care of a nurse and, when she reached the age of reason, was baptized, for which reason her father hated her. One day, when she had grown to the age of fifteen and was guarding her nurse's sheep with other young girls, the prefect Olybrius was passing by and caught sight of this very beautiful girl. He burned with desire for her immediately and sent his men after her, saying: "Go and seize her! If she's freeborn, I'll make her my wife: if she's a slave, she'll be my concubine!"

Margaret was therefore presented for his inspection, and he questioned her about her parentage, her name, and her religion. She answered that she was a Christian. Said the prefect: "The first two titles fit you perfectly, because you are known to be noble and you are as lovely as a pearl; but the third does not suit you at all! No beautiful and noble girl like you should have a crucified God!" "How do you know," Margaret asked, "that Christ was crucified?" "From the Christians' books," he replied. Margaret: "Since you read in them both of Christ's suffering and of his glory, you should be ashamed to believe the one and yet deny the other!" She went on to declare that Christ had of his own will been crucified for our redemption but now lived immortal in eternity. This angered the prefect, and he ordered her to jail.

The next day he had her hauled before him and said: "Vain girl, pity your beauty and adore our gods, and all will go well for you!" Margaret: "I adore the God before whom the earth trembles, the sea storms, and all creatures are fearful!" The prefect: "Unless you yield to me, I'll have your body torn to shreds!" Margaret: "Christ gave himself up to death for me, and therefore I want to die for Christ!"

By the prefect's order she now was hung upon a rack and was beaten with rods and then lacerated with iron rakes, so cruelly that her bones were laid bare and the blood poured from her body as from a pure spring. The people standing by wept and said: "O Margaret, truly we grieve for you, because we see how cruelly your body is torn! Oh, what beauty you have lost by not believing in the gods! Now, then, believe, so as at least to remain alive!" Margaret: "O bad counselors, go away! Begone! This torture of the flesh is the salvation of the soul!" To the prefect she said: "Shameless dog! Ravenous lion! You have power over the flesh, but Christ keeps the soul to himself!" Meanwhile, the prefect, unable to bear the sight of such bloodletting, drew his hood over his eyes.

Margaret was taken down and put back in jail, where a marvelous light shone around her. There she prayed the Lord to let her see the enemy who was fighting her, and a hideous dragon appeared, but when the beast came at her to devour her, she made the sign of the cross and it vanished. Or, as we read elsewhere, the dragon opened its maw over her head, put out its tongue under her feet, and swallowed her in one gulp. But when it was trying to digest her, she shielded herself with the sign of the cross, and by the power of the cross the dragon burst open and the virgin emerged unscathed. What is said here, however, about the beast swallowing the maiden and bursting asunder is considered apocryphal and not to be taken seriously.

Again the devil, still trying to deceive Margaret, changed himself to look like a man. She saw him and resorted to prayer, and when she rose, the devil approached, took her hand, and said: "Let all you've done be enough for you, and just let me be!" But she grabbed him by the head, pushed him to the ground, planted her right foot on his head, and said: "Lie still at last, proud demon, under the foot of a woman!" The demon cried out: "O blessed Margaret, I'm beaten! If I'd been beaten by a young man I wouldn't mind, but by a tender girl . . . !" And I feel even worse because your father and mother were friends of mine!"

Margaret then forced him to tell her why he had come. He said it was to press her to obey the prefect's orders. She also made him say why he tempted Christians in so many ways. He answered that it was his nature to hate virtuous people, and that though he was often repulsed by them, he was plagued by desire to mislead them. He begrudged men the happiness that he had lost and could not retrieve for himself, so he strove to take it away from others. He added that Solomon had confined an infinite multitude of demons in a vase, and after his death the demons has caused fire to issue from the vase. This made men think that it contained a huge treasure. They therefore smashed the vase, and the demons escaped and filled the air. Then, after all this had been said, the virgin lifted her foot and said: "Begone, wretch!" and the demon promptly vanished.

Margaret therefore was reassured: she had defeated the chief, she would certainly outdo his hireling. The following day she was presented to the judge before a large gathering of people. Refusing again to sacrifice to the gods, she was stripped of her clothes and her body was burned with torches; and all wondered how so delicate a girl could withstand such torture. Then the judge had her bound and put in a tub full of water, in order to increase the suffering by varying the pain; but suddenly the earth shook and the virgin came out unharmed. At that five thousand men accepted the faith and were sentenced to death for the name of Christ. The prefect, fearing that still others would be converted, quickly gave order to behead blessed Margaret. She asked for time to pray, and prayed devoutly for herself and her persecutors and for all who would honor her memory and invoke her, adding a prayer that any woman who invoked her aid when faced with a difficult labor would give birth to a healthy child. A voice from heaven announced that her petitions had been heard, and she rose from her prayer and said to the headsman: "Brother, take your sword and strike me!" He did so and took off her head with a single stroke, and so she received the crown of martyrdom. Margaret suffered on the twentieth day of July, or, as we read elsewhere, on the twelfth of that month. . . .

105. Saint Martha

. . . After the Lord's ascension, when the dispersion of the disciples occurred, Martha, with her brother Lazarus, her sister Mary Magdalene, blessed Maximinus, who had baptized the sisters and to whom the Holy Spirit had entrusted them, and many others, were put on rafts by the infidels without oars, sails, rudders, or food; but with the Lord as pilot they made port at Marseilles. Then they went to the region around Aix and converted the local populace to the faith. Martha spoke eloquently and was gracious to all.

At that time, in the forest along the Rhone between Arles and Avignon, there was a dragon that was half animal and half fish, larger than an ox, longer than a horse, with teeth as sharp as horns and a pair of bucklers on either side of his body. This beast lurked in the river, killing all those who tried to sail by and sinking their vessels. The dragon had come from Galatia in Asia, begotten of Leviathan, an extremely ferocious water-serpent, and Onachus, an animal bred in the region of Galatia, which shoots its dung like darts at pursuers within the space of an acre: whatever this touches is burned up as by fire. She found him in the forest in the act of devouring a man, sprinkled him with blessed water, and had a cross held up in front of him. The brute was subdued at once and stood still like a sheep while Martha tied him up with her girdle, and the people killed him then and there with stones and lances. The inhabitants called the dragon *Tarasconus* and in memory of this event the place is still called Tarascon, though previously it had been called Nerluc, i.e., black place, because the forest thereabouts was dark and shadowy.

With the permission of Saint Maximinus and her sister, Martha stayed there and devoted herself continually to prayer and fasting. Eventually a large congregation of sisters formed around her, and a great basilica dedicated to Blessed Mary ever Virgin was built. . . .

"Yvain," in *The Complete Romances of Chrétien de Troyes*, trans. David Staines (Indiana University Press, 1990), pp. 296–7.

Absorbed in his thoughts, Sir Yvain was riding through a deep forest when he heard a loud cry of pain from the trees. He turned in the direction of the cry. When he reached a clearing, he saw a lion and a serpent, which was holding the lion by the tail and scorching his haunches with burning fire. Sir Yvain spent little time looking at this strange sight. When he considered which of the two he would help, he decided to go to aid the lion, because a serpent with its venom and treachery deserved nothing but harm. The serpent was venomous, and fire was darting from its mouth, so full of evil was the creature.

Intending first to kill the serpent, Sir Yvain drew his sword and advanced. He held his shield before his face as a protection against the flames gushing from the serpent's throat, which was more gaping than a pot. If the lion attacked him later, there would be a fight; yet whatever happened after, he still wished to aid the lion. Pity urged him and pleaded that he help and support the noble and honorable beast.

With his keen-cutting sword he attacked the evil serpent, pinning it to the ground and slicing it in two. He then struck it again and again until he had cut and hacked it to pieces. But he had to sever a piece of the lion's tail because the head of the wretched serpent still gripped the tail. He cut off as little as necessary; in fact, he could not have removed less. When he had freed the lion, he expected that the lion would spring at him and he would have to fight, but to the lion such an idea never occurred. Hear what the lion did. In a manner befitting the worthy and nobly born, he began to show that he was surrendering. He stood on his hind legs, stretched out his forepaws together to the knight, and bowed his head to the ground. Then he knelt down, his whole face wet with tears of humility. For certain Sir Yvain realized that the lion was thanking him and humbling himself before him, since he had delivered him from death by killing the serpent. This adventure delighted Yvain. He cleaned the serpent's venomous filth from his sword, which he then placed back in its scabbard. Then he resumed his journey. The lion walked close beside him, never to leave him, but to accompany him always to serve and to protect him.

"Fouke fitz Waryn," in *Medieval Outlaws: Twelve Tales in Modern English Translation*, ed. Thomas Ohlgren and trans. Thomas E. Kelley (Parlor Press, 2005), pp. 223–6.

Fouke Lands at the Castle of Cartagena

Fouke went ashore to discover a very beautiful castle; and, noticing that the gate was open, he ventured in. Once inside the castle, he found no one living there, neither humans nor animals. He was astonished to find such a beautiful place uninhabited. The whole surrounding countryside, moreover, was similarly deserted. Upon his return to the ship he told his followers what he had seen. At that Mador advised that they all go ashore. "Let's leave the ship here with a few men to guard our provisions, and we will perhaps soon find someone to tell us what's going on in this place." Once ashore, they met a peasant. Mador asked him what land this was, its name, and why it was not inhabited. The peasant told them that it was the kingdom of Iberia and the name of the land was Cartagena, held in fief by the King of Iberia. The castle here belonged to the Duke of Cartagena, who had a daughter, the fairest maiden in the realm of Iberia. One day this damsel unfortunately climbed to the top of the castle's main tower, from which she was carried off by a flying dragon. The beast took the damsel to a high mountain in the sea, and there ate her. This same dragon had devastated the land, killing everyone in sight, with the result that no one dared inhabit the place. Because the dragon was so horrifying the duke himself didn't dare enter the castle.

Fouke and the others returned to the ship and again set sail. As they approached a high mountain in the sea Mador exclaimed: "It's the mountain where the dragon lives; now we're all in real danger." "Hold your tongue, Sir Mador," said Fouke, "So far you haven't spotted anything to cause us harm here. Do you wish to die of fright? We have already seen many dragons, and God has delivered us from frequent dangers. Never yet have we been in any peril from which, thank God for it, we were unable to escape safely. Your cold comfort would put a coward to death."

Fouke Discovers the Damsel

Fouke took Audulf de Bracy, and the two of them climbed the steps leading up the high mountain. When they reached the mountain top they saw many hauberks, helmets, swords and other arms lying there. Scattered near the arms they observed human bones alongside a large and beautiful tree. There was also a fountain below, running with clear, placid water. Looking around further, Fouke noticed a cave carved inside a hollow rock. He drew his sword, and very boldly went inside, like one who entrusts himself entirely to God. Before doing so, however, he first raised his right hand and signed himself in the name of the Father, the Son, and the Holy Ghost. Inside the cave he found a very beautiful damsel weeping and wailing. In answer to Fouke's question as to her homeland she replied: "Sir, I am the daughter of the Duke of Cartagena, and I have been here for seven years. The only Christians I have ever seen here all come unwillingly. If it's in your power, for God's sake, leave here at once, for if the dragon returns you will never escape." In reply Fouke exclaimed: "I will not leave this place before I hear and see more. Damsel, how does the dragon treat you? Has he caused you any harm?" "Sir, the dragon is wild and powerful, and he can easily carry and armed knight into these mountains after he catches him in his talons. As you can judge by all the bones outside the cave, he has already carried and eaten many knights. He prefers human flesh to any other kind. In the process of killing he smears his hideous face and his beard with the blood of his victims. He then comes to me and makes me wash his face, beard and breast with clear water. When he wishes to sleep he goes to his couch made of fine gold; for his nature is such that he is excessively hot. In contrast, gold is very cool by nature; so in order to cool himself he sleeps on gold. Before going to bed, however, he takes a large stone, such as the one you see over there, and blocks the door with it. Because he possesses the senses of a human being he fears me greatly, and he is especially worried that I will kill him while he is asleep. I, for my part, am convinced that he will end up killing me first." "God forbid," said Fouke, "I promise you he shall not do so."

Fouke Fights the Dragon

Fouke took the damsel by the hand and entrusted her to Sir Audulf for her protection as they left the rock cave. They had scarcely come out into the open air when they saw the dragon flying in the sky above and heading straight towards them. From its hot mouth the beast belched forth smoke and horrible flames. It was a very ugly creature, with a large head, square teeth, cruel claws, and a long tail. As soon as the dragon spotted Fouke, it swooped down and struck at him with its claws, delivering such a blow on the shield that it tore it in two. Fouke raised his sword and, with all his strength, struck at the dragon's head. Given the hardness of the creature's outer shell and the horny matter on the front side of its body, the sword blow did no harm whatever to the beast, nor did it even cause it to waver in its flight. The dragon began his flight from afar in order to strike harder. Fouke, who could not stand the blow, dodged behind the tree beyond the fountain. He saw that he could not harm the dragon from the front side, so he waited until it made a turn. Then Fouke struck a convincing blow to the body near the tail, thereby cutting the beast in two. The dragon began to scream and yell. It rushed for the damsel with the intention of seizing her and carrying her away, but Sir Audulf defended her, The dragon clasped Sir Audulf so tightly in its claws, that he would have been crushed if Fouke had not come more quickly. After cutting off the beast's paw, Fouke was able to free Sir Audulf with great difficulty. Its sharp talons had already cut through the hauberk. Fouke struck the dragon squarely in the mouth with his sword, and in this way he finally killed it. Fouke was very weary, and rested a while before going to the dragon's lair. He took all of the gold he found there, and carried it to his galley. John de Rampaigne examined Sir Audulph's wound and dressed it, for he knew a lot about medicine.

Fouke and the Damsel Return to Cartagena

Mador turned his ship towards Cartagena; and they arrived in the country, and surrendered to the duke his daughter, who was overjoyed to see her again. The damsel told her lord what kind of life she had led, and how Fouke killed the dragon. The duke fell at the feet of Fouke, thanked him for saving his daughter; and begged him, if such were his pleasure, to stay here. He offered to give him all Cartagena along with his daughter in marriage. Fouke tanked him from the heart for his fine offer. He told the duke that he would take his daughter willingly, if only his Christianity would permit it. Unfortunately, he was a married man. Having said this, Fouke tarried there only until Sir Audulf's wounds were healed. To each of Fouke's men the duke gave rich gifts. He gave them many fine and beautiful jewels, as well as fair and fiery warhorses. At last Fouke took leave of the duke, who was very sorrowful at his departure.

Note

1 Weregild was money paid in compensation for a crime to the victim of the crime or their family. Odin, Loki, and Hoenir are paying Hreidmar a weregild for killing his son, Otter.

Bibliography

Acker, Paul. "Death by Dragons." *Viking and Medieval Scandinavia* 8 (2012): 1–21.
Bauschatz, Paul. *The Well and the Tree: World and Time in Early Germanic Culture*. University of Massachusetts Press, 1982.
Brown, Patricia. *The Role and Symbolism of the Dragon in Vernacular Saints' Legends, 1200–1500*. University of Birmingham Press, 1998.
Bruckner, Matilda. "The Lady and the Dragon in Chrétien's *Chevalier au lion*." In *From Beasts to Souls: Gender and Embodiment in Medieval Europe*. Eds. Jane Burns and Peggy McCracken. University of Notre Dame Press, 2013.65–86.
Byock, Jesse. "Sigurðr Fáfnisbani: An Eddic Hero Carved on Norwegian Stave Churches." In *Poetry in the Scandinavian Middle Ages. Proceedings of the Seventh International Saga Conference*. Ed. Teresa Pàroli. Presso la Sede del Centro Studi, 1990.619–28.
Cesario, Marilina. "*Fyrenne Dracan* in the *Anglo-Saxon Chronicle*." In *Textiles, Text, Intertext: Essays in Honour of Gale R. Owen-Crocker*. Eds. Maren Clegg-Hyer and Jill Frederick. Boydell Press, 2016.153–70.
Chadwick, Nora. "The Monsters and Beowulf." In *The Anglo-Saxons: Studies in Some Aspects of Their History and Culture Presented to Bruce Dickens*. Ed. Peter Clemoes. Bowes and Bowes, 1959.171–203.
De Vries, Jan. *Heroic Song and Heroic Legend*. Trans. B.J. Timmer. Oxford University Press, 1963.
Evans, Jonathan. "Semiotics and Traditional Lore: The Medieval Dragon Tradition." *Journal of Folklore Research* 22 (1985): 85–112.
Evans, Jonathan. "The *Heynesbók* Dragon: An Old Icelandic Maxim in its Legal-Historical Context." *Journal of English and Germanic Philology* 99/4 (2000): 461–91.
Forsyth, Neil. *The Old Enemy: Satan and the Combat Myth*. Princeton University Press, 1987.
Gardner, John. "Guilt and the World's Complexity: The Murder of Ongentheow and the Slaying of the Dragon." In *Anglo-Saxon Poetry: Essays in Appreciation for John C. McGalliard*. Eds. Lewis Nicholson and Dolores Frese. University of Notre Dame Press, 1975.14–22.
Hamblin, Vicki. "From Many Lives a Single Play: The Case of Saint Margaret and the Dragon." *Comparative Drama* 50/1 (2016): 33–61.
Hume, Kathryn. "From Saga to Romance: The Use of Monsters in Old Norse Literature." *Studies in Philology* 77 (1980): 1–25.
Kjesrud, Karoline. "A Dragon Fight in Order to Free a Lion." In *Riddarasǫgur: The Translation of European Court Culture in Medieval Scandinavia*. Eds. Karl G. Johansson and Else Mundal. Novus, 2014.225–44.
LeGoff, Jacques. "Ecclesiastical Culture and Folklore in the Middle Ages: Saint Marcellus of Paris and the Dragon." In *Time, Work, and Culture in the Middle Ages*. Trans. Arthur Goldhammer. University of Chicago Press, 1980.159–88.
Lionarons, Joyce. "The Sign of a Hero: Dragon-Slaying in *Þiðreks Saga af Bern*." *Proceedings of the Medieval Association of the Midwest* 2 (1993): 47–57.
Lionarons, Joyce. "*Beowulf*: Myth and Monsters." *English Studies* 77 (1996): 1–14.
Lionarons, Joyce. *The Medieval Dragon: The Nature of the Beast in Germanic Literature*. Hisarlik Press, 1998.

Lionarons, Joyce. "'Sometimes the Dragon Wins': Unsuccessful Dragon Fighters in Medieval Literature." In *Essays on Old, Middle: Modern English and Old Icelandic. In Honor of Raymond P. Tripp, Jr.* Ed. Loren Gruber. Edwin Mellen Press, 2000.301–16.

Momma, Haruko. "*Worm*: A Lexical Approach to the *Beowulf* Manuscript." In *Old English Philology: Studies in Honour of R.D. Fulk.* Eds. Leonard Neidorf, Rafael Pascual, and Tom Shippey. D.S. Brewer, 2016.200–14.

Mueller, Alex. "The Historiography of the Dragon: Heraldic Violence in the Alliterative *Morte Arthure.*" *Studies in the Age of Chaucer* 32 (2010): 295–324.

Orchard, Andy. *Pride and Prodigies: Studies in the Monsters of the Beowulf Manuscript.* D.S. Brewer, 1995.

Parker, Eleanor. "Siward the Dragon-Slayer: Mythmaking in Anglo-Scandinavian England." *Neophilologus* 98/3 (2014): 481–93.

Petroff, Elizabeth. "Transforming the World: The Serpent Dragon and the Virgin Saint." In *Body and Soul: Essays on Medieval Women and Mysticism.* Oxford University Press, 1994.97–109.

Réthelyi, Orsolya. "The Lion, the Dragon, and the Knight: An Interdisciplinary Investigation of a Medieval Motif." *Annual of Medieval Studies at CEU* 7 (2001): 9–37.

Riches, Samantha. "Encountering the Monstrous: Saints and Dragons in Medieval Thought." In *The Monstrous Middle Ages.* Eds. Bettina Bildhauer and Robert Mills. University of Wales Press, 2003.196–218.

Sävborg, Daniel. "Búi the Dragon: Some Intertexts of *Jómsvíkinga Saga.*" *Scripta Islandica* 65 (2014): 101–24.

Smith, Karen. "Serpent-Damsels and Dragon-Slayers: Overlapping Divinities in a Medieval Tradition." In *Christian Demonology and Popular Mythology.* Eds. Gábor Klaniczay and Éva Pócs. Central European University Press, 2006.121–38.

Symons, Victoria. "'Wreoþenhilt ond wyrmfah': Confronting Serpents in *Beowulf* and Beyond." In *Representing Beasts in Early Medieval England and Scandinavia.* Eds. Michael Bintley and Thomas Williams. Boydell Press, 2015.73–93.

Tarzia, Wade. "The Hoarding Ritual in Germanic Epic Tradition." *Journal of Folklore Research* 26 (1989): 99–121.

Tolkien, J.R.R. "*Beowulf*: The Monsters and the Critics." *Proceedings of the British Academy* 22 (1936): 245–95.

Turville-Petre, E.O.G. *Myth and Religion of the North: The Religion of Ancient Scandinavia.* Weidenfeld and Nicolson, 1964.

Wanner, Kevin. "Warriors, *Wyrms*, and *Wyrd*: The Paradoxical Fate of the Germanic Hero/King in *Beowulf.*" *Essays in Medieval Studies* 16 (1999): 1–15.

Index

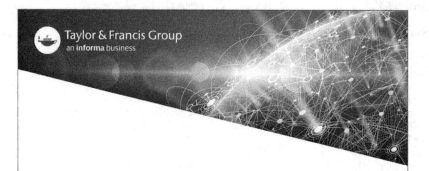

9 780367 197421